Boston
Sites and
Insights

Boston, Massachusetts

Numbers correspond to chapters.

Historic Trails: One good starting point for maps and information on the Freedom Trail (10), the Black Heritage Trail (35), and the Women's Heritage Trail (36), is the National Park Service Visitor Center, across from the Old State House (1).

Ⓣ indicates stop on the MBTA, Boston's Mass transit system.

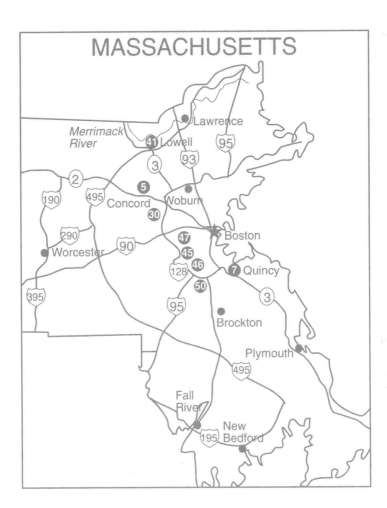

Numbers correspond to chapters.

Boston
Sites and
Insights

SUSAN WILSON

BEACON PRESS

Boston

Beacon Press
25 Beacon Street
Boston, Massachusetts 02108-2892

Beacon Press books
are published under the auspices of
the Unitarian Universalist Association of Congregations.

Printed in the United States of America

99   98   97   96   95   94   8   7   6   5   4   3   2

Earlier versions of the essays collected here appeared in the *Boston Globe*.

Photographs © by Susan Wilson
Text design by Irving Perkins Associates

Library of Congress Cataloging-in-Publication Data

Wilson, Susan (Susan Carolyn)
Boston sites and insights / Susan Wilson.
p.   cm.
Includes index.
ISBN 0-8070-7119-6
1. Boston (Mass.)—Guidebooks.   2. Historic sites—
Massachusetts—Boston—Guidebooks.   I. Title.
F73.18.W55   1994
917.44′610443—dc20   93-31514

This book is dedicated to my late parents,
Wilmer Douglas Relyea and Frances Louise Cornelli Relyea,
who taught me a love for the past
and a hope for the future.

Contents

PART ONE
POLITICS AS USUAL:
THE FREEDOM TRAIL AND BEYOND

PART TWO
FROM HERE TO ETERNITY:
HOUSES OF WORSHIP AND HOMES
FOR THE DEAD

PART THREE
THE ATHENS OF AMERICA:
ARTS AND ENTERTAINMENT IN BOSTON

PART FOUR
ATHENS TWO:
LITERARY BOSTON

PART FIVE
THE MANY FACES OF BOSTON:
MINORITIES, IMMIGRANTS,
AND UNSUNG HEROES

PART SIX

THE GREEN, GREEN GRASS OF HOME:
PARKS, PLAYGROUNDS, AND OPEN SPACES

Foreword

"THE CHIEF means of moral education," Alisdair MacIntyre wrote, "is the telling of stories." *Boston Sites and Insights* is a book of stories about the city of Boston. Though it poses at the most obvious level as the commentary of a wise, witty, and well-informed tour guide, Susan Wilson's book is implicitly a reflection on the moral education of America's founding city, and therefore, in some way, of the nation itself.

Americans, unlike citizens of other countries, are bound together as a people by the future, not the past. An immigrant can arrive here with the hope that she can become an American, with the full expectation that her children will. No such thing is possible for newcomers to Germany, say, or France or China. That is true not primarily because other countries are by definition xenophobic, but because their national ethos is tied more to the past than the future. The refrain of President Clinton's campaign anthem, "Can't stop thinking about tomorrow," expressed a deep strain in the American psyche, one of the elements that makes us an open people, and a hopeful one.

But you can't know where you're going if you don't know where you come from. For more than three centuries, newly arrived Americans have needed to fold into their own personal histories—histories of persecution often, of pogroms, of famine, of slavery, of flight—the history of the people who preceded them here. First, of course, the native peoples; then the English, Dutch, French, and Spanish, the kidnapped Africans, then the rest of us.

The chief means of the moral education of Americans *as* Americans has been the telling of stories—from the Pilgrim encounters with the Massachusett Indians to Paul Revere's ride to the Underground Railroad to the wagon trains moving west. As befits a vast country and a diverse people, the reach of this narrative seems almost endless, but, in fact, there is a soul to the American story, and it resides in Boston.

When John Winthrop pointed to what we now know as Bunker Hill in Charlestown, and invoked the biblical image of the "City on a Hill", he was hoping that the settlement itself would exemplify what made the New World different from the Old. Boston, with its bookish air, narrow streets, tidy rowhouses, and lively ethnic neighborhoods is often described as a European-like city, but it is the place, more than any other, in which

America invented itself. That heritage, of course, has put a special burden on subsequent generations of Bostonians to be part of the constant reinvention that history requires of this country. It is a burden we have not always carried gracefully.

Visitors to Boston, to its shrines and markers, its monuments and waterfront, gas lights and brick sidewalks, marvel that its charm is real, the creation not of theme park entrepreneurs, but of humans who have lived here. We live here still, of course, and we still create according to who we are. Now a bit more than half of us are white, a quarter are black, 10 percent are Hispanic, and nearly another 10 are Asian. Other divisions by class, culture, and turf are, as always, palpable in Boston. But, to use a local image, such differences are like spokes coming out of a hub, the right we all have to call this city ours.

Boston takes such rights very seriously. Revolutionary Boston—the Old State House, Faneuil Hall, the Freedom Trail—is a wonder, especially, for the way it still enables Irish or Italians or European Jews or Asians or Haitians to identify with that original band of Anglo-Saxons who created America's first character-ideal. Yet in the nineteenth and early twentieth centuries the image of those first English heroes was revered in ways that seemed to disqualify such newcomers from ever joining them as equals.

The stones of this city tell the African-American version of this story too, from the nation's first black slaves imported by the pious Winthrop to the Revolution's first martyr, Crispus Attucks, to Beacon Hill's African Meeting House where the overthrow of slavery was plotted. The descendants of slaves who came to Boston during the great twentieth century migration met the resistance of the remnant Puritan culture as all immigrants had, but blacks also met resistance from the immigrants themselves, a story that shadows Boston still. But the democratic meaning of that initial revolutionary impulse remains the measure of the city's soul. Now the story of numerous once-despised groups is as central to the city's story as their present and former neighborhoods are to its geography. And the "moral" of such education is crystal clear: the city founded by outcasts, and built by other outcasts, must welcome outcasts now.

Among Boston's citizens, from whatever outcast cadre they descend, a rank individualism has been a common note. Individualism looked like courage when it prompted the first settlers to come here; like treason when it stirred the colonial merchant class to rebel; like nobility when it was preached as abolition; like Yankee thrift when the Boston oligarchy opted out of public investment. In our own time, that individualism has tested the limits of our city's social cohesion as class conflict and racism have seemed to dominate politics and news. That is part of the story too, as is evident, say, when we look again at the hill in Charlestown that first inspired Winthrop; then inspired the Minutemen who held their fire until they saw the whites of British eyes; then inspired the fiercest opponents of busing for integration. Now the obelisk on Bunker Hill stands as a monument to many things, not the least of which is the city's new hope of racial reconciliation.

Boston's most familiar places reward such close examination. Its theaters, cemeteries, art museums, parks, libraries, ballparks, universities, and churches—all have stories relating aspects of the one story which, in its triumph and also defeat, makes us a people. The story makes us Boston.

As you will shortly find, Susan Wilson is the master of that story. She has collected here not just fresh retellings of the old yarns—Mrs. Gardner's strange house, the confusion between Breed's Hill and Bunker's, the Brahmin at Friday Symphony—but an offering of closely researched new versions of Boston sagas that even life-long residents will find illuminating. This is a book for visitors, certainly—the best introduction to the "sites" I know of. But its "insights" add up to a kind of biography of the city, an account of a life still being lived.

This is a collection, as we began by saying, of Boston's best stories; a summary of all that this city has taught us, for better and for worse; a precis of the many reasons we—and our whole nation—have for treasuring Boston; a justification, one could even say, for the fact that we love it so.

JAMES CARROLL
Boston, Massachusetts
October 1993

Acknowledgments

FIRST AND foremost, I want to thank Jan Shepherd, editor of the *Boston Globe Calendar,* without whom "Sites and Insights" would never have existed. In the spring of 1987, Jan helped me develop the idea of a feature column on Boston's historic landmarks, and continued to support, encourage, and publish me as the series grew into a book. Thanks also to the staff of the *Boston Globe* library, who helped me sift through antiquated clips, locate obscure files, and track down details for the original *Globe* stories. Among the librarians who aided my research efforts on a regular basis were Marc Shechtman, Richard Pennington, Lisa Tuite, Nancy Alban, Bill Boles, Donna Buonopane, Jim Cawley, Wanda Joseph-Rollins, Barbara Potts, and Colneth Smiley.

I am grateful to all the personnel and friends at the fifty sites included in this book who generously offered their time, tales, opinions, and expertise in the research process. Since I interviewed an average of six people per site, there are at least three hundred individuals included in this thank you. A few are mentioned or quoted in the stories herein; many more simply gave their knowledge to the general fact pool of each story. Without their cooperation and enthusiasm, none of this could have happened.

There were certain individuals in particular to whom I turned time and again—both as sources of original information on historic sites and as willing editors of portions of my manuscript. They proved to be expert resources whose judgment and advice I came to count on. I am indebted to them all: Henry Lee, Richard Heath, Ken Heidelberg, Marilyn Richardson, John Manson, Philip Bergen, Blanche Linden-Ward, Bill Stokinger, Byron Rushing, Ann Wadsworth, and Elliot Norton. The material resources of the Boston Public Library, the library of the Bostonian Society, and the Boston Athenaeum were an essential tool in my process of discovery. We are fortunate to have such exceptional research libraries in our midst.

When I first began writing "Sites and Insights," I took the intensive spring training course offered by the nonprofit educational tour group Boston By Foot. Director Polly Flansburgh and her colleagues were then, and remain now, an enlightened and inspirational group, with whom I have maintained communication over the years—sharing facts, ideas, and mutual admiration. Inspiration and enlightenment also came from my history teachers in the public schools of Madison, New Jersey, and from my undergraduate and graduate-school history professors at Tufts University, Medford, Massachusetts.

The photographs in this volume were made possible by the generosity of Eastman Kodak, which provided film, paper, and chemicals. Thanks to Flo Scott, of Crimson Tech in Cambridge, for facilitating that connection and contribution.

The heartiest accolades for my editor at Beacon Press, Susan Worst, for believing in this project and sticking it out through the hard times; for Judith Rosen, my literary agent; for Robert Smyth of Yellow Moon Press in Cambridge, my computer guru, occasional photo assistant, and late-night pizza provider; and for the soon-to-be-Reverend Jennifer Justice, who edited, advised, consoled, and encouraged me throughout.

Finally, thank you to the city of Boston—for being there, surprisingly intact, for such a long, long time.

Preface

IN APRIL of 1987, "Sites and Insights" made its debut as a monthly feature column in the *Boston Globe*. The idea behind the column was quite simple: to explore historic treasures in the Greater Boston area, from public buildings, museums, and parks to houses of worship and centers of the arts and entertainment.

The intent of the columns—and the intent of this book, which grew from them—was to observe Boston's rich past in a way that was both accessible to the general public and enlightening to serious students of history. Boston, after all, is the ultimate walking town, with many of its most illustrious sites surprisingly close to one another. I wanted to engage the reader's imagination, and to encourage both Bostonians and Boston visitors to discover—or rediscover—the history around them. Hence, one goal for "Sites and Insights" was to dig deeper than the Boston guidebooks then on the market. This meant not only spending time exploring each site, but also, in the process, unearthing long-lost facts, debunking tired legends, and finding interesting anecdotes and tales that brought each site to life.

The research process often began by observing secondary sources, then returning to their roots. I perused archives maintained by the sites or other historical repositories, sifted through nineteenth- and twentieth-century newspaper clippings, and, most importantly, interviewed the people who lived with, in, or around these sites—caretakers, archivists, interpreters, historians, curators, librarians, ministers, park rangers, publicists, volunteers, and other insightful observers who knew the sites intimately and in some cases had known them for decades.

When Beacon Press agreed to publish *Sites and Insights* as a book, the question of which columns or chapters to include naturally arose. *Globe* columns were selected, re-edited, updated, and rewritten for a book format. Other topics were then chosen for further research, to round out our collective notion of a well-balanced book. In both the columns and the book, a deliberate effort was made to be inclusive and to acknowledge that Boston's history was molded by women and men of all socio-economic classes and a multitude of races, religions, and national origins.

Once we decided to include fifty sites (we had to stop somewhere) we tried to be as appropriate and selective as possible. Most of the places included are in Boston and its immediate environs; when out-of-town sites were added, they involved stories that were vital to an understanding of the area's heritage. All of the sites had to be old—really, really old; an institution or area first developed in the 1930s, for instance, was much too new to deal with in this particular volume. The sites also had to exist in their original form, at least to the extent described by the late Dan Coolidge in his discussion of the Old South Meeting House: "There's been an awful lot of replacement of the fabric of the Old South," explained Coolidge, the Old South Association's "Architect of the Fabric," in 1990. "But the space is really just the same. It's what Buckminster Fuller called the 'Model T Syndrome.' You know, where over the auto's life you get a dent in the bumper and replace it. You put on new wheels . . . you replace and repair the parts bit by bit until many of them are not the original. But it's still very much a Model T!"

In a sense, this book is full of some of Boston's most precious Model Ts, and many of its most precious memories. Still, it's only one small segment—a starter package, if you will—of the many historic and cultural sites Boston has to offer those who are willing to read, wonder, and wander.

SUSAN WILSON
Cambridge, Massachusetts
August 1993

Note to the Reader

THANKS TO the cooperation of staff at each of the sites, we were able to make visitor information as up-to-date as possible before going to press. Please note, however, that hours, days, tours, access facilities, and even phone numbers do periodically change.

PART I

Politics as Usual: The Freedom Trail and Beyond

THOUGH THE history of Boston is close to four centuries long, one particular segment of that past is better known and more widely chronicled than any other. The last third of the eighteenth century and the opening of the nineteenth—often referred to as the American Revolutionary and Early National periods—are perennially linked with the town of Boston in the popular imagination.

Boston's political history actually began in 1630, when John Winthrop and the Puritans of the Massachusetts Bay Company first settled the Shawmut peninsula. They originally called it Trimountain, before settling on the name Boston. These English colonists were not the first people to live in the area. Native American tribes, including the Wampanoag, Nipmuck, and Massachusset, had inhabited various parts of eastern Massachusetts for thousands of years. A variety of European voyages of discovery had passed through the Boston area as well, perhaps as early as Leif Eriksson's in the eleventh century, but with great regularity throughout the sixteenth and early seventeenth centuries. In 1620, the people we now know as the Pilgrims—who, like the later Puritans, were seeking religious freedom—had established the first permanent English settlement in New England at Plymouth, to the south of Boston.

During the seventeenth century, the English colonists of Puritan Boston were concerned with survival and growth—with laying foundations for religious, political, and economic patterns of life. Throughout that century, arguments continually arose over religious issues. By the eighteenth century, new and different growing pains gradually became apparent. As the British colonies prospered and expanded far away from the "Mother Country," certain colonists grew to resent control by the British monarch and Parliament, particularly in the area of "taxation without representation." The result was the American War for Independence.

1

Many of the men and women who helped incite the Revolution lived, worked, and worshiped in Boston—in buildings, churches, and open lands that we can still observe and visit today. Patriot Paul Revere made his home in Boston's oldest neighborhood, the North End. That quaint structure is now the oldest wooden dwelling standing on its original site in the city. During the 1760s and 1770s, Sam Adams, Joseph Warren, James Otis, John Hancock, and their radical patriot colleagues delivered orations, rallied crowds, and fanned the flames of revolution in still-extant sites like the Town House (today's Old State House), Faneuil Hall, and the Old South Meeting House. When fighting finally broke out between Britain and the colonists in April of 1775, it happened in the suburban towns of Lexington and Concord—on lands now commemorated in Minute Man National Historical Park. From there, hostilities moved back to Charlestown, where the Battle of Bunker Hill erupted two months later.

As men like Sam Adams were intently severing connections with English rule, others, like his cousin John Adams, were working to create a new American nation and forge ties with amicable international neighbors. John Adams and his wife Abigail—now credited as one of America's first active and outspoken feminists—lived south of Boston, in the town of Quincy, in homes now preserved as part of Adams National Historic Site. Once the war was over and American independence was officially recognized by Great Britain, the Adams family provided the young nation with two of its early presidents, John and John Quincy Adams. In 1789, John Adams was the nation's first vice-president, alongside General George Washington. Washington, of course, had also spent considerable time in Boston, as commander-in-chief of the Continental Army.

When President Washington decided to build a U.S. Navy in the 1790s, that was partly accomplished in Boston—in the form of USS *Constitution*, which remains the oldest fully commissioned warship afloat in the world. Meanwhile, the rapid growth of the Commonwealth of Massachusetts and its government necessitated a move from the Old State House to a new one, built atop the venerable slope known as Beacon Hill. In other cities, older buildings were often demolished to make way for the new. In Boston, however, an unusual number of original structures—from the Old State House and the Old South Meeting House to Old City Hall—were preserved for posterity after their replacements were built.

The first ten chapters of this book describe many of these Revolutionary-era sites and their stories. Included as well is the tale of how these landmarks were eventually linked to form the most famous historic walking tour in the world—Boston's Freedom Trail. You'll find three other Freedom Trail sites—the Old North Church, King's Chapel, and the Granary Burying Ground—in Part 2, since we thought it appropriate to include churches having active modern congregations with other houses of worship and cemeteries.

The Old State House

PEOPLE HAVE called the antique structure a variety of names over the past three centuries—from the New Town House, the Province House, and the Court House to City Hall, the State House, and even the Temple of Liberty. But Philip Bergen, librarian of the Bostonian Society, has an even more interesting epithet for one of Boston's most eclectic buildings: "I like to call it the oldest historic subway kiosk in the United States!"

It's true. Boston's oldest public building has housed the State Street "T" (subway) stop in its sub-basement since 1903—a downtown station where the Orange and Blue lines still meet. But the "kiosk" above, popularly known today as the Old State House, is not your ordinary public transportation entranceway. Within its walls, colonial patriot and lawyer James Otis argued against the Writs of Assistance and helped pave the road for the Revolution. Just outside those same walls, the 1770 Boston Massacre set the revolutionary spirit ablaze. And from the building's second-floor balcony, the Declaration of Independence was first read aloud to the town of Boston.

Located at the intersection of State and Washington streets, the Old State House alternately served Boston as a court house, a primeval stock exchange, a city hall, the seat of British royal governors, and, as the name implies, as the seat of the Massachusetts state government. Though the structure houses a fascinating museum of Boston and American Revolutionary-era history today, it's still called the Old State House to differentiate it from the "new" Massachusetts State House on Beacon Hill, which itself is almost two centuries old (see Chapter 8). But that's getting a bit ahead of our story.

As with most public buildings of the period, the edifice built on the corner of Cornhill and King streets (now Washington and State) in 1713 was specifically designed to be a multipurpose structure. The previous building, the wooden Town House built through the bequest of Puritan trader Robert Keayne in 1657, had housed merchants downstairs and governing bodies above—housed them, that is, until it was destroyed in the Great Fire of 1711. Hence, when the New Town House was built on the old one's ashes, everyone assumed it too would serve a variety of community needs.

The New Town House was wisely constructed with red brick, rather than flammable wood, and financed by the royal province, Suffolk County, and the town of Boston—all of whom planned to use its several chambers. William Payne was credited as the builder; the designer, if there was one, remains unknown.

During the renovations of the early 1990s, the Bostonian Society added new exhibit areas and displays to the Old State House.

Like the original Town House, the new one had a "merchants' exchange" on the first floor. A precursor of today's stock exchange, it was a place where traders talked shop, swapped information, and received up-to-date news on prices and commodities. The building's location was ideal for such endeavors: the waterfront and Long Wharf, where most ships' captains first stopped in Boston, was close by at the time. Over the next hundred and fifty years, Long Wharf all but disappeared, as periodic landfill projects extended the mainland and State Street into Boston Harbor. Today's financial district, incidentally, grew up around that old merchants' exchange.

Other early users of the first floor, where a museum and gift shop stand today, were provincial and county records offices, and a post office. Meanwhile, the third floor attic—now a curatorial office—housed the Boston board of health, for which Paul Revere worked during 1799 and 1800. The building's basement served variously as a warehouse, a wine cellar, and, possibly, a fire station. John Hancock rented space there in 1766, probably to store his imported merchandise.

The balcony, which opened out from the second floor, had many functions as well. Beneath it lay a granite platform and steps where at least one colonial forger was forced to stand with a large paper on his chest that read, "CHEAT." From the balcony itself, news items were read, often to the accompaniment of trumpet and drum. New laws, new wars, new governors, new monarchs, and recently deceased monarchs were all heralded there.

The second floor—which now contains several museum galleries and a multipurpose hall—was an epicenter of thunderous argument and theatrical antics throughout the eighteenth century. The east end, from which the balcony opened, harbored the Council Chamber of the British royal governors. At the west end was a small Court Chamber. Between the two was the large Representatives Hall, where the Massachusetts Assembly met, steadily earning itself a reputation as the most independent and outspoken of the colonial legislatures.

Visitors to the second floor now see a room with changing exhibits on Boston history, plus several smaller chambers and a nineteenth-century spiral staircase. There's no trace today of the gallery built there in 1766, an interior balcony which was used to pack crowds of vociferous citizens into Massachusetts Assembly meetings—a vital element in building support for the eventual revolution.

In 1761, the second floor became the stage upon which one of the most dramatic events associated with the Old State House was acted out. It was then that lawyer James Otis, Jr., made a blazing eight-hour speech against the Writs of Assistance, which authorized royal authorities to enter private buildings and ships to search colonial property for smuggled goods.

"Otis was a flame of fire," recalled John Adams in reminiscences he penned half a century later. "With a promptitude of classical allusions, a depth of research, a rapid summary of historical events and dates . . . and a torrent of impetuous eloquence, he hurried away everything before him. . . . Then and there was the first scene of the first act of opposition to the arbitrary claims of Great Britain. Then and there the child Independence was born."

Otis, as it turned out, lost the battle but won the war. His case failed, and the Writs of Assistance continued to be implemented. But the revolutionary spirit was ignited, coming to fruition fifteen years later.

Like many historic figures, Otis had his idiosyncrasies. George Washington had malodorous, ill-fitting wooden dentures; Benjamin Franklin allegedly sired a large brood of illegitimate children. Otis, for his part, had a tendency toward mental instability. Although he had been known for erratic behavior, self-contradiction, nonsensical chatter, and periodic melancholia over the years, the final blow, quite literally, came in September 1769, when an angry British officer, John Robinson, cracked Otis on the head in a local tavern. From that point on, observed Adams, Otis rambled and wandered "like a ship without a helm." Fourteen years later the glorious old patriot died—as he himself had predicted—after being struck by lightning while watching a summer thunderstorm in Andover.

The other legendary event most closely associated with the Old State House—the Boston Massacre of 1770—took place below the building's historic balcony. The approximate site is marked by a small circle of stones on the traffic island facing that balcony. Historic accounts of the incident are as varied and contradictory as the people who wrote them; an abbreviated, eclectic version follows.

Tensions ran high between the red-coated British "regulars" stationed in Boston and the local residents. Some radicals—like Sam Adams, John's rabble-rousing cousin—fanned every flame they could, hoping to incite outright American rebellion. On Monday, March 5, 1770, a young wigmaker's apprentice kept pestering a British officer about an unpaid barber bill, although the bill was paid and the officer even had a receipt. A soldier (perhaps the same one) eventually butted the taunting kid with his musket.

Crowds began to assemble, and the situation grew to a standoff, as a few more soldiers arrived and the growing crowds got rowdy.

Church bells began ringing and someone yelled "Fire!" (Ringing bells were often used as fire alarms.) Why and exactly when the bells were rung, incidentally, are widely argued points. They may have been ringing to announce the impending danger, much like a modern siren; or they may not have started tolling until *after* the shout of "Fire!" Whatever the order of events, the British soldiers fired their guns, and five men eventually died from the wounds inflicted. Among the dead was an African-American former slave named Crispus Attucks.

Patriot activists milked the incident for all it was worth. Paul Revere made and distributed his famous engraving of the "massacre," closely based on Henry Pelham's original, featuring the Old State House in the background. The factually inaccurate image was used as propaganda to push the colonies closer to rebellion.

Once the rebellion was under way, the Old State House was host to another historic event—the first local reading of the Declaration of Independence. Though dated July 4, 1776, the text had taken considerable time arriving from Philadelphia. Finally, on July 18, the revolutionary document was read from the second-floor balcony. Later that evening, the carved figures of the royal lion and unicorn were torn down from the roof. Each year that reading is repeated on Independence Day, with the same Old State House balcony as its stage. Rooftop replicas of the lion and unicorn, however, are not pillaged following the modern-day ceremonies—but remain intact, as reminders of prerevolutionary days.

After the reading of the Declaration of Independence, the one-time town, province, and court house officially became the Massachusetts State House. Meanwhile, King Street was renamed State Street, symbolically making royalty give way to the new republic. Cornhill's name was eventually changed, too, in honor of the first U.S. president. George Washington proudly rode a white horse down the long highway from Boston Neck to the Old State House, as he made his first official entrance into Boston as president, in 1789.

A year before, on February 6, 1788, the Massachusetts Convention had ratified the United States Constitution in an official ceremony inside the Old State House. Two hundred years later to the day, the U.S. Postal Service issued a twenty-two-cent stamp commemorating the anniversary of that event. The image was a 1793 engraving of the Old State House, designed by Richard Sheaff of Needham.

It was not long before the Commonwealth of Massachusetts outgrew the cramped quarters of this old building. Architect Charles Bulfinch was commissioned to design a new state house on John Hancock's former Beacon Hill properties. In 1798, with great pomp and procession, the state government officially moved from the old to the new structure.

From 1798 until 1881—when the Old State House became a museum site operated by the Bostonian Society—the aging structure endured a variety of incarnations, facelifts, and fires, as well as structural and decorative changes. Boston bought the building from the state in 1803. Between 1830 and 1841 it served as Boston's city hall, and underwent a Greek Revival renovation still evident in its interior columns and curved doors. It was during that period, in 1835, that abolitionist William Lloyd Garrison was chased through Boston streets by an angry mob hoping to lynch him for his radical views; Garrison fled into the south entrance of the Old State House, finding shelter and support there from Mayor Theodore Lyman, Jr.

Save for that eleven-year stint as City Hall, the Old State House was primarily a commercial center for much of the nineteenth century, leased by the city to sundry shops and offices. By 1870, fifty of those tiny offices filled the small building; meanwhile, shopkeepers plastered the exterior with billboards, giving it a cheesy, carnival look.

The outside of the Old State House, by the way, was not always the natural red brick we see today. Though much of the brick dates from the original 1713 structure, it was painted a variety of stone, buff, and ochre colors for decades. Only in 1909 was the brick restored to its natural shade.

A fortuitous combination of good fate and good friends has been responsible for the endurance of the Old State House into the twentieth century. Fire, of course, was a major threat since the beginning. Not only did fire create the space where the Old State House was built, when flames engulfed the 1657 wooden Town House in 1711, but fire also caused major damage to the new brick-based building, especially in 1747 and 1921.

An even greater threat to the Old State House, however, was public apathy and antagonism. As the building became an eyesore toward the end of the nineteenth century, some citizens wanted to raze it altogether. They argued that removing the building would eliminate the horrendous downtown traffic jams which had been escalating even in the late 1800s. They reasoned further that the Old State House was no longer a "genuine relic" worth preserving, since it had been rebuilt and renovated so many times. At one point during the debate, the city of Chicago offered to buy the old building, and to move it brick by brick to the shores of Lake Michigan—giving it the honor it deserved. The threat apparently worked.

The historic structure's Boston saviors were noted antiquarian William Whitmore and a group that would later be known as the Bostonian Society. Though the building is still owned by the city of Boston, the Bostonian Society—the only organization solely committed to interpreting and preserving Boston history—has operated the Old State House as a museum since 1882. It was most recently reopened to the public in 1992, following a seven-million-dollar, eighteen-month structural renovation, funded through the National Park Service. Meanwhile, a Bostonian Society campaign raised money for sparkling new exhibits, programs, and collections management.

Today, the Old State House is a fascinating potpourri of many architectural styles and multiple incarnations. Walls, staircases, roofs, and artifacts have come and gone—as have objects closely associated with the building's history. Those models of the lion and unicorn, for example—the symbols of British royalty that were torn down by jubilant Bostonians when independence from Britain was declared—were replaced for a century by carved scrolls. When the structure opened as a museum in 1882, however, replicas of the old creatures were put back in place.

By contrast, the carved wooden Sacred Cod, first installed in the Old State House in 1784 as "a memorial of the importance of Cod Fishery to the welfare of the Commonwealth," left and never returned. In 1798, the wooden fish was ceremoniously moved to the new State House, where it hangs today in the assembly hall of the House of Representatives.

Plenty of other historical objects are found in the newly redesigned, accessible, and interactive Old State House museum today. Permanent exhibits on the first floor explore Boston during the Revolution and the history of the Old State House. In the second-floor galleries are changing exhibits featuring topics such as John Hancock and his family, early inns and taverns, Boston's West End, and the history of the Massachusetts Supreme Judicial Court. An introductory video, located in a small first-floor chamber near the gift shop, is the perfect way to begin your visit.

Over almost three hundred years of existence, the Old State House has played host to a variety of historic figures. One of the most unlikely, in a sense, was Britain's Queen Elizabeth II, who visited on July 11, 1976—thus becoming the first British sovereign to visit Boston. Participating in America's official Bicentennial celebration, Her Majesty noted that colonial patriots like Paul Revere and Samuel Adams would surely have been surprised at her honored presence there—the Queen is, after all, the great-great-great-great-granddaughter of King George III, who reigned over Britain and her colonies during the American War for Independence.

"But perhaps they would also have been pleased," she added with a royal grin.

THE ESSENTIALS

ADDRESS: Intersection of Washington and State streets, Boston. Bostonian Society research library, 15 State Street, Boston.

TELEPHONE: Museum, (617) 720-3290; Bostonian Society, (617) 720-1713; Bostonian Society Library, (617) 720-3285.

VISITOR INFORMATION: Open 9:30 A.M.–5:00 P.M. daily; closed Easter, Thanksgiving, Christmas, and New Year's Day. Small admission fee. Gallery tours by appointment. Interpreters for National Park Service Freedom Trail discuss Old State House from outside the front door. Wheelchair lift and doorbell on Washington Street entrance; inside, only the first floor is wheelchair accessible.

2 Faneuil Hall

YOU'D THINK the first question most visitors would ask when entering historic Faneuil Hall would be "Why is it called the Cradle of Liberty?" Actually, some do come with a sense of the great events that happened in this hallowed structure: "Is this the place where patriot Sam Adams made all those revolutionary speeches?" Indeed it is. And a statue of old Sam stands proudly in the building's backyard.

Still, one of the commonest single queries encountered there by National Park Service rangers is how to pronounce the dang thing (or, at least, how the building acquired such a curious name). Over the years, folks have come looking to find Filene Hall, Fenway Hall, Fawn Hall, Fanooly, and Finneal, not to mention a place called Nathaniel Mall.

As it turns out, Faneuil Hall was named for the man who paid for its construction in 1742, local merchant Peter Faneuil. According to Boston tradition, it's pronounced *Fan*-el or *Fan*-yuhl, though Faneuil's French Huguenot ancestors undoubtedly said Feh-*noy*. Young Peter Faneuil and his peers added to the confusion, since his anglicized name, "P. Funel," was originally engraved on his tombstone in the Granary Burying Ground.

The hard-to-pronounce hall that Faneuil built soon became a landmark of American history. It is the place where Samuel Adams regularly advocated overthrow of tyrannical British rule, where William Lloyd Garrison appealed for an end to slavery, where Susan B. Anthony denounced the second-class status of women, where Suzette LaFlesche, an Omaha, advocated Native American rights, and the place where John F. Kennedy gave his final preelection speech in 1960. Today Faneuil Hall can still be rented as a meeting place or political pulpit, but it's also regularly used for activities as diverse as concerts, commencements, spelling bees, debates, awards ceremonies, lectures, banquets, and naturalization ceremonies. In fact, one of the few things you specifically *can't* do in this building is plot to overthrow the government. Rules have obviously changed in Faneuil Hall since 1776.

Meanwhile, the lower level of the building remains true to its legacy as Boston's first major marketplace building—it's filled with a broad variety of shops. The structure's fourth floor has a historic use as well: the Ancient and Honorable Artillery Company, the first military company chartered in the Western Hemisphere, still maintains a headquarters and museum in a spot they've occupied since 1746.

The man responsible for Faneuil Hall, Peter Faneuil (1700–1743), was a scandalously wealthy man by the time he was forty—reputedly the richest

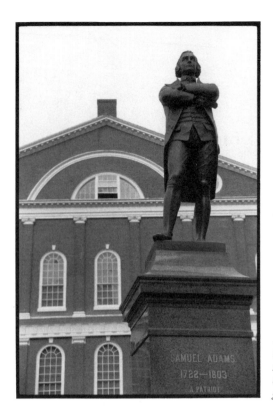

Sculptor Anne Whitney's statue of Revolutionary-era activist Sam Adams stands guard behind Faneuil Hall.

in all of Boston. He hadn't expected to gain his wealth by inheriting his uncle Andrew's fortune. Andrew Faneuil was a shipping magnate and landowner whose chosen heir was his nephew Benjamin, Peter's brother. But Andrew's will specifically forbade his heir to marry, and young Benjamin made the mistake of ignoring that instruction. As a result, Benjamin inherited just five shillings—essentially pocket change—from Uncle Andrew. Young Peter, who remained single all his life, got the lion's share instead.

Peter Faneuil proved as talented at spending his fortune as he was in abstaining from nuptials. He was not an attractive fellow, to be sure; a contemporary source describes him as "a fat, squat, lame man, hip-short with a high shoe." But he became Boston's "jolly bachelor," fond of the high life, prominent display, Madeira wines, and his Tremont Street mansion, with its seven acres of gardens.

He was also a bright merchant and a concerned public benefactor. One of his major concerns was the anarchistic method of food marketing in Boston. During the seventeenth and early eighteenth centuries, vendors would scatter throughout the town, selling at irregular sites with irregular hours; others would travel from house to house, peddling from carts. Peter Faneuil was among those who advocated a permanent downtown market where buyers could take care of all their needs at once—the precursor of modern, one-stop shopping.

So Faneuil made the town an offer it couldn't refuse: he would build an open marketplace structure in downtown Dock Square, and donate it to the city. Actually, the town could refuse the offer—and almost did. The final vote at the town meeting was 367 yeas to 360 nays. (Many merchants feared that the competitive nature of central markets would drive down their prices and profits; a group of them had already defeated another attempt at a Boston marketplace several years earlier.)

Almost as an afterthought, Faneuil also proposed that an auditorium, or meeting hall, be built on the second floor of his new marketplace. This would provide Boston with its own version of the English guildhall, in which official meetings of a town's voting citizens were held. Boston, one of the King of England's first and finest colonies, had the most democratic government of its time. Until 1822, local decisions were made in town meeting, where voters assembled, debated, and decided the issues. Before Faneuil Hall was built, such gatherings were often held in borrowed "meetinghouses," as Puritan churches were called, or in the small Town House (the precursor of the Old State House). Hence, the great second-floor chamber at Faneuil's new hall became Boston's first and only "town meeting hall."

The completed 1742 building, designed by artist John Smibert, was considered quite beautiful in its day. It was two stories high, with elegant side arches, a beautiful Georgian design, and open arcades on the ground-floor merchant level. Red Medford brick, imported English glass and metal trim, and a gilded grasshopper weather vane all added to its allure.

Six months after the hall's completion, Peter Faneuil died of "too much good living" at the age of forty-three. A public memorial was held for him in the hall. His brother Benjamin and Benjamin's wife, Mary, inherited the rest of Peter's wealth, while the city kept the building.

So much did the town love Faneuil Hall, in fact, that it rebuilt the building when it burned down in 1761, financing the project by public lottery. In 1805, Boston paid to double the hall's size—to today's heftier proportions—and hired celebrated architect Charles Bulfinch to oversee the restoration. The cost of $56,700 was covered partly by the sale of Fort Hill and partly by taxation. Not until 1898 did the Bulfinch Faneuil Hall of 1805–06 undergo major structural changes. At that time, the city appropriated $104,500 to update, fortify, and fireproof the aging building, and to provide it with new furniture.

The most recent renovation of the building was essentially completed in 1992. This six-million-dollar overhaul improved wheelchair access, added elevator service to all four floors, made the restrooms more accessible, repaired the roof, restored exterior brick and woodwork, reinforced the structure, plastered and repainted the interior, updated electrical and mechanical systems, rehabilitated and redesigned the ground floor, added new sound and light systems, and worked to conserve the hall's artwork.

Since its earliest days, Faneuil Hall was a space for all seasons and all reasons. Peter Faneuil, for example, was the first but not the only Bostonian to lie in state in the hall. The body of Crispus Attucks—an African-American killed in the 1770 Boston Massacre—was taken there on the way to the Granary Burying Ground. The bodies of Wendell Phillips, Daniel Webster, and other charismatic orators who once spoke at Faneuil Hall were also laid out there for crowds to mourn.

Despite its many and varied functions, it was certainly the hall's constant use by a cast of American Revolutionary–era characters that earned Faneuil Hall its everlasting nickname, the Cradle of Liberty. Beginning in 1763, patriot Sam Adams and his colleagues ushered in the greatest period of town meetings in Boston history—thereby making Faneuil Hall a focus of revolutionary activity. Adams, James Otis, Dr. Joseph Warren, and other "Sons of Liberty" could often be seen there, arguing against such British impositions as the 1763 Sugar Act, the 1765 Stamp Act, the 1767 Townshend Act, or the 1773 tax on tea. In 1772, a meeting within the hall created the first "committees of correspondence" in the colonies. When such meetings grew too large for the hall, incidentally, they were often hustled over to the larger space at the Old South Meeting House. Sometimes, however, more heated assemblages spilled into violent episodes in the streets.

Supervisory park ranger John Manson loves to point out the ironies in Faneuil Hall's history: Nineteenth-century abolitionists like William Lloyd Garrison and Frederick Douglass held forth there, but the Faneuil family fortune was partly earned from the slave trade. Susan B. Anthony, other suffragists, and modern-day women's rights advocates met there; on the other hand, so did a group called MALES, the Massachusetts Association to Limit the Extension of Suffrage, in 1915. Patriots assembled at Faneuil Hall to protest unfair British taxation, while Faneuil family boats were among those pillaged in the Tea Party affair; moreover, members of our own Internal Revenue Service have met there to honor their most efficient tax collectors! Colonial patriots partied and celebrated there; so, too, did British soldiers, who used Faneuil Hall as a barracks and a theater during their occupation of Boston.

Other than some Medford brick on the exterior back wall, and the weather vane, nothing of the original 1742 building remains today. That vane, however, is one of Faneuil Hall's most distinctive touches. Peter Faneuil copied the hall's grasshopper from vanes atop the London Royal Exchange and his uncle's mansion. Periodically refurbished over the years, the thirty-eight-pound, fifty-two-inch grasshopper is considered an original: it still has a copper interior, a gilded exterior, glass-doorknob eyes, and a copper vest, into which "time capsules" are periodically tucked.

Designed by Shem Drowne, the grasshopper has left its perch more than once over the centuries. It hopped off during a 1755 earthquake, was knocked off during an 1889 flag-lowering, and was removed several times for repairs. It was also stolen once, in 1974. After a week-long, citywide search—and the retrieval of twenty-eight other stolen weather vanes in the course of that search—the gilded grasshopper was located under a pile of flags in the Faneuil Hall cupola. (The reason for the grasshopper's flight has never been discovered.) The grasshopper's most recent excursion was out for regilding and over to the Boston Museum of Fine Arts, where it briefly sat on display during the 1990–92 renovation of Faneuil Hall. It was one of the rare opportunities Bostonians have had to meet the gilded insect almost eye-to-eye, since its normal perch is eighty feet above ground level.

Many of the other distinctive features of today's Faneuil Hall originated in the Bulfinch enlargement of 1805–06. During that renovation a third story was added, and floor space was doubled as the building was widened. Doric and Ionic columns were added inside—typical of the Federalist neoclassical style which Bulfinch preferred and which is so apparent in his architectural masterpiece, the Massachusetts State House on Beacon Hill.

Bulfinch also created the galleries that circle the Great Hall, providing a place where women could watch lectures, debates, and other goings-on down below. Women, of course, could not vote in town meetings, since eighteenth-century law specified that only white, male, property-owning, churchgoing citizens over the age of twenty-one could vote. Historical statistics show that these stipulations eliminated 90 percent of the population.

Most of the artwork that graces the interior of the Great Hall is from the nineteenth and twentieth centuries. Much of it was not created for Faneuil Hall and was first displayed elsewhere. The "artificial stone" eagle on the back gallery, for example—molded from a mixture of lime putty and pulverized marble—was made for a State Street bank in 1798, then moved to the Great Hall when the bank building was demolished in 1824. The large clock set below the eagle was the 1850 gift of Boston schoolchildren, purchased with their pennies. Two paintings that once hung in the Great Hall—images of British monarch George III and of Peter Faneuil—are gone, probably whisked away during the British evacuation of Boston in 1776. In their place are portraits of a host of men linked with Faneuil Hall's past.

While the nineteenth-century paintings and busts in Faneuil Hall are originals—including G. P. A. Healy's mammoth 1850 *Webster's Reply to Hayne*, immortalized in social studies textbooks across the nation—the eighteenth-century images are copies, mostly done in oils. During the centennial celebrations of 1876, the original oils—including portraits of George Washington, Samuel Adams, and John Quincy Adams—were moved to Boston's Museum of Fine Arts, where they remain to this day; part of the rationale was that the artworks were endangered in a firetrap like Faneuil Hall (unfireproofed, remember, until 1898.)

Some artistic enigmas to ponder: Why was Washington's horse painted with his backside facing the viewer in Gilbert Stuart's painting? Park ranger John Manson's theory is that the painter was unhappy with the fee offered him for his work. And why, in Dennis Malone Carter's 1857 *Retreat from Breed's Hill*, do all the soldiers have the same face? A commentary on brother fighting brother? Or perhaps on the family of man?

"The family of man" is an accurate phrase to use at Faneuil Hall, since of the multitude of historic busts and paintings displayed in the Great Hall only one depicts a woman—Mrs. James (Mercy Otis) Warren, sister to James Otis, and a famous poet and author who wrote a history of the American War for Independence. The original painting of Mrs. Warren hangs in the Museum of Fine Arts; the picture in Faneuil Hall is a giant Polaroid copy.

★   ★   ★

On the fourth floor, two stories above the Great Hall, is the home of the Ancient and Honorable Artillery Company of Massachusetts. The company was chartered in 1638 and began lodging at Faneuil Hall in 1746, just four years after the hall was built. Today the company maintains there a meeting hall, a library, and a museum of military history, which contains antique and modern firearms, flags, and other artifacts.

Meanwhile, down below, twentieth-century merchants carry on their business in the old marketplace as merchants did in 1742. The setting has changed: old arcade entrances have been replaced by doors and walls, while the many scattered stalls of yore are now divided into larger areas for a variety of new shops and services. An information desk, staffed by National Park Service rangers is also located on the market level, as is a new elevator with access to all floors. Unlike many Boston historic buildings, Faneuil Hall has never been in danger of demolition—perhaps because of these merchants, who have always provided a visible reminder of Peter Faneuil's wish and his legacy.

"Besides, the merchants here have always paid rent," observed one former tenant. "And that may make this the only self-supporting monument in America!"

THE ESSENTIALS

ADDRESS: In Faneuil Hall Marketplace, Dock Square, Boston.

TELEPHONE: National Park Service office, (617) 242-5675; City Superintendent, (617) 635-3105; Ancient and Honorable Artillery Company, (617) 227-1638; Boston National Historical Park Visitor Center, (617) 242-5642.

VISITOR INFORMATION: Great Hall and main floor information desk open 9:00 A.M.–5:00 P.M. daily, except Thanksgiving, Christmas, and New Year's Day, or during city-sponsored events. Free. Interpretive talks every half hour, 9:30 A.M.–4:30 P.M. Wheelchair access to all four floors via elevator on ground floor; restrooms accessible.

3   The Old South Meeting House

THOUGH IT'S lodged amidst the noisy bustle of Boston's Downtown Crossing shopping district, the Old South Meeting House retains the proud look and aura of a bygone era. As the second home to one of Boston's earliest Puritan congregations, the meetinghouse was first and foremost a church. Outside, you can still see its soaring white steeple, pointing toward the heavens. Inside are other vestiges of that sacred,

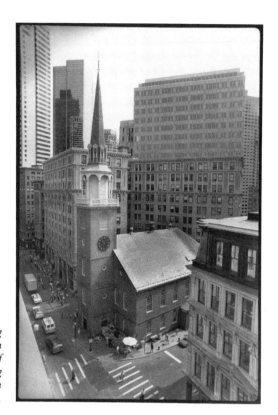

The Old South Meeting House survived British abuse, the Great Fire of 1872, and the wrecking ball of downtown developers.

historic past—numbered box pews, wraparound balconies, a chandelier, Doric columns, a lofty preaching pulpit, and multipaned window sashes.

But the building's importance to American history isn't merely religious. It was here, in December of 1773, that patriots gathered to protest the British tax on tea and Samuel Adams gave the secret signal to descend on Griffin's Wharf, where they threw the biggest Tea Party in history.

It was also on this site that black poet Phillis Wheatley worshiped, Ben Franklin was baptized, General George Washington bemoaned the British desecration of the town, Boston's "Mother Goose" sang hymns, Joseph Warren decried the horrors of the Boston Massacre, and twentieth-century free speech advocates held court. It was here, too, that the movement to preserve historic urban structures won its first victory, more than a century ago.

Despite its obvious importance—and despite ongoing lectures, concerts, educational programs, and special events at the Old South Meeting House today—an unsettling number of Bostonians and tourists know surprisingly little about the building and its history. Henry Lee, a longtime member of the Old South Association, suggests, "For long periods of time the Old South was a well-kept secret. Unlike the Paul Revere House, USS *Constitution*, and even the Old State House, it's one site on the Freedom Trail that doesn't have instant recognition."

One of the greatest misconceptions about the meetinghouse relates to the building's function. With a belfry and steeple outside, and pulpit and pews inside, it certainly *looks* like a church. But though it began its life as a Puritan house of worship, it hasn't served as a church since 1872.

The valuable downtown corner of Milk and Washington streets, where Old South has stood since 1729, was once Governor John Winthrop's garden. (Winthrop served as colonial governor of Massachusetts for four terms between 1630 and his death in 1649.) In 1669, the Reverend John Norton's wife, Mary, held title and donated the plot to a Puritan offshoot group who called their congregation the Third Church of Christ. On the site this dissident congregation of twenty-eight built a medieval-looking place of worship remembered as the Cedar Meeting House.

The group's split from Boston's original First Church arose from a complex theological argument over baptism and membership rights known as "the halfway covenant." Theological arguments were very much a part of daily life in seventeenth-century Boston. Staunch Puritans and even later Congregationalists, for example, banned Christmas celebrations as "pagan rituals" adopted by Roman Catholics. Moreover, the Puritans felt that musical instruments—including organs—defiled the pure word of God and had no place in church.

The Cedar Meeting House endured until 1729, when its growing congregation—popularly known as the Old South Church by then—tore it down, replacing it with a newer, larger, brick building. This simple, elegant Georgian structure opened for religious services on April 26, 1730—and is essentially the one we know today as the Old South Meeting House.

It's true that the authentic-looking pews were crafted in 1947, and the belfry is empty: Old South's original bell was discarded after it cracked tolling an 1815 fire alarm and its replacement was moved to a new Copley Square church in 1872. Still, a good deal of the building's fabric and furnishings—including the pulpit's sounding board, some gallery sections, an old gallery stairway, and much of the exterior work—has remained from the 1729 building. The original 1766 tower clock, for instance, is still in place. Its archaic mechanism of brass, wood and iron rods, gears, braces, and pendulum—installed by Gawen Brown in prerevolutionary times— still keeps excellent time.

Over the years, Old South has been an ever-evolving building, deco-rated and redecorated to fit changing tastes, styles, and uses. During the nineteenth century, for example, its red brick exterior was covered with white or gray paint, while the normally plain interior walls and ceilings were festooned with gaudy Victorian *trompe l'oeil* paintings. In the 1870s, the U.S. Post Office turned it into a wide-open mail-sorting and shuffling room, and even added two unsightly chambers off the sides of the slim front tower. Those bulky exterior chambers were removed after the postal service departed for more permanent quarters in 1876.

Thanks to historical research, today's Old South is much closer in sub-stance, style, color, and form to the eighteenth-century meetinghouse begun by master mason Joshua Blanchard in 1729. Blanchard and his colleagues—who may have included architect Robert Twelves—were influenced by other Boston church designs of the time, as well as by the London churches of Christopher Wren. The Old South's interior, however, was clearly based on that of the 1669 Cedar Meeting House which it was built to replace.

The Old South congregation wanted their meetinghouse to be as simple, unadorned, and pure as their services. Hence the building was constructed plain, long, and low, with simple red brick laid in an alternating pattern called Flemish Bond. The roof was slate—sturdy enough to survive the 1744 earthquake, albeit with major repairs. The windows were clear glass, not stained. The tower—topped by a belfry, steeple, bull's-eye windows, and a gilded weather vane—reached 183 feet toward heaven.

The Georgian exterior was matched by stark classical detail inside. Pews were built in both the slip and the box styles; the former were long, narrow seats, while the latter were private rectangular enclaves, each protected by a low wall and a latching half-door. Those box pews were rented to wealthier families, who decorated them to fit their individual tastes with, for example, special fabrics, varied seating arrangements, assorted shelves, and footwarmers. The two layers of upstairs galleries included seating for "less desirable" elements of Boston society: slaves, servants, the town poor, and teenage boys.

Up front, of course, was the pulpit. The version in place today was built in 1857 and buttressed by a "wineglass" front from the 1808 version. Ministers preached from the Old South pulpit for the building's first 143 years—though fiery orators of all types have held forth there over the centuries. From eighteenth-century radicals like Sam Adams and Joseph Warren to twentieth-century political hopefuls like John Silber and former Klansman David Duke, speakers have regularly used this meetinghouse to discuss, debate, and disseminate religious and secular issues and information.

Whereas eighteenth- and nineteenth-century speakers counted on good lungs and the fine old sounding board above the pulpit to make themselves heard, modern orators usually use the Old South's public address system. Today's lecturers have another advantage: they can keep track of the time using the replica of the 1805 Simon Willard clock that hangs on the south gallery's balustrade. In early days, however, ministers' sermons were timed by a large hourglass—which was flipped several times, incidentally, since Sunday services lasted up to six hours.

Faneuil Hall was often the venue of choice for Bostonians to gather and debate the topics of the day. But until that public hall was enlarged to its present size (in the Charles Bulfinch project of 1805–06) the Old South Meeting House was the town's largest and most accessible indoor space. Hence, both before and since 1806, the grand auditorium at Old South has remained Boston's prime space for public meetings and cultural events when Faneuil Hall is unavailable or under repair. This was the case just prior to the Revolution, and again when Faneuil Hall closed for major renovations from 1990 to 1992.

Multimedia exhibits at the meetinghouse today explain in detail how

Boston and the Old South became major centers for prerevolutionary debate. Three favorite stories in particular illustrate Old South's role.

The first tale concerns the gathering of a reported 5,000 men who crammed into the hall on December 16, 1773, shortly before embarking on the Boston Tea Party. Since the building's legal capacity is now just 650 people—plenty of space for the concerts, theatrical presentations, lectures, and even weddings that take place there today—historians can't quite account for that 5,000 figure. Some joke that Americans were smaller in the eighteenth century—a popular myth with virtually no historical basis; others say that colonial observers tended to vastly overestimate crowds. The galleries were also bigger at the time.

Colonials might also have been wedged in the windows, as they were when a second well-known Revolutionary event took place in 1775. Dr. Joseph Warren reportedly had to climb through the pulpit window to give Old South's annual Boston Massacre Oration, since the crowd had already completely filled the building. Warren was ready for one of the bravest speeches of his life and theatrically dressed for the occasion in a Ciceronian toga.

The third story is much less amusing for lovers of Boston's historic structures. In 1775, when British forces occupied the city, their troops took over Old South, ripped out most of its interior furnishings, chopped up the old pews and pulpit for firewood, and turned the hall into a riding school for General John Burgoyne and his horses. After the British had been forcibly evacuated from the city in 1776, General George Washington viewed and reviled the ruin. "My wife swears she can still smell the British horses in the stairwell!" insists Lowell Warren, president of the Old South Association and a collateral descendant of Dr. Warren.

Still, the Revolution was not the roughest period for the Old South. There was the Great Fire of 1872, a massive blaze that consumed sixty acres and 776 buildings between Washington Street and the harbor. Miraculously, the meetinghouse sustained only minor exterior damage. But even before the fire broke out, the Old South congregation had voted to build a new church in the Back Bay—the Copley Square structure now popularly known as the *New* Old South Church. With the congregation went many precious artifacts and furnishings—including the bell from the now empty belfry—as well as title to valuable real estate the church had acquired.

Once the Old South Meeting House was no longer occupied by a congregation, savvy developers began plotting to demolish the aging building and use its prime downtown acreage for commercial pursuits. In 1874, the land sitting under Old South was valued at $400,000 (a vast sum in today's dollars). But the public outcry over plans to level this historic building began one of the proudest moments in Boston and American history.

Creatively crafted sight-and-sound exhibits in the Old South Meeting House tell the tale of its salvation: Philanthropist Mary Hemenway, a supporter of the (then) innovative kindergarten movement, led the effort to save the Old South from the wrecker's ball. Hemenway not only donated substantial money and time to preserving the building, she also established Old South's earliest American history educational programs for both teachers and students, collectively called Old South Work, in 1883. Meanwhile, several of Boston's most preeminent citizens—such as Wendell Phillips, Julia Ward Howe, James Russell Lowell, and Ralph Waldo Emerson—climbed to the pulpit for public readings of their works and to plead for the building's preservation. Local citizens, especially women from Boston's "better" families, rallied and organized countless community fairs, balls, and fund-raisers. Finally, in 1877 the Old South Association was formed—a private, nonprofit organization that continues to operate the Old South Meeting House to this day.

The late historian Walter Muir Whitehill, former president of the Old South Association, best summarized America's first urban historic preservation success when he called the saving of Old South "the first instance in Boston where respect for the historical and architectural heritage of the city triumphed over considerations of profit, expediency, laziness, and vulgar convenience."

Since 1878 the Old South has been a museum. Until new, modern exhibits were installed in 1987, that museum remained a curious nineteenth-century-style "reliquary," containing a hodgepodge of interesting, sometimes strange, objects. Among those items—many of which are still stored in the basement safe or on display upstairs—are a note from George Washington to his dentist, describing repairs on his wooden dentures; buttons that belonged to John Hancock; a ring made from a chunk of Plymouth Rock; a vial of Tea Party tea; a tea set fused into a Daliesque whole by the 1872 fire; and an original volume of Phillis Wheatley's poetry.

Today Old South still faces challenges to its survival. Will its vibrant array of programs and publications, and its secure place on the Freedom Trail, ensure that the building is preserved for generations of history lovers to come? Bostonians should heed the words spoken by Wendell Phillips in his 1876 pleas to save the Old South: "I can only say we come here to save what our fathers consecrated to the memories of the most successful struggle the race has ever made for the liberties of man. You spend half a million for a school-house. What school so eloquent as these walls?

"The saving of this landmark is the best monument you can erect to the men of the Revolution."

THE ESSENTIALS

ADDRESS: 310 Washington Street, at Downtown Crossing, Boston.
TELEPHONE: (617) 482-6439.
VISITOR INFORMATION: Open 10:00 A.M.–4:00 P.M. weekdays, 10:00 A.M.–5:00 P.M. weekends, November 1–March 31; open 9:30 A.M.–5:00 P.M. daily, April 1–October 31; closed Thanksgiving, Christmas Eve, Christmas, and New Year's Day. Small admission fee. "Middays at the Meeting House" lecture and concert series Thursdays at 12:15 P.M., October through April, free with admission. The exterior of the building is a regular part of all Freedom Trail tours (see Chapter 10 for details). Special tours also available through the Old South itself; call for details. Building and exhibits are wheelchair accessible; restrooms are not.

4 The Paul Revere House

THE SMALL, dark, craggy clapboard house at 19 North Square is an odd sight amidst the taller brick buildings of the North End. And given the structure's almost medieval demeanor, it should come as no surprise that it's the only seventeenth-century wooden dwelling still standing on its original site in downtown Boston. The building's main claim to fame, however, is that the illustrious Revolutionary War hero Paul Revere owned and lived in the house from 1770 to 1800.

Today more than 200,000 guests annually visit Revere's former abode, now a beautifully maintained museum operated by the Paul Revere Memorial Association. Most visitors presumably come to learn more about the Boston patriot and his famous "midnight ride." In the process they learn about "the man behind the myth," about family and home life in colonial America, and about the War for Independence—while discovering the multicultural heritage of one of Boston's oldest neighborhoods.

Paul Revere was not born at 19 North Square, nor did he die there. He bought the home in 1770, at the age of thirty-five. By then he was an established silversmith—a trade learned from his French immigrant father, Apollos Rivoire. The house was sturdy if not terribly stylish (it was already ninety years old when he purchased it), and the neighborhood was perfect for Revere's needs.

North Square, also known as Clark's Square, was a long, narrow triangle just a block from the busy waterfront docks and taverns. In the late eighteenth century, the square had occasional markets, a town pump, a watchhouse, and a meetinghouse. Revere's neighbors included mastmakers, spinsters, a soap boiler, government officials, and merchants. Moreover, his own silversmith shop was at the head of Clark's Wharf, just a short walk away.

Only five months after his first wife, Sarah, died of childbirth complications in 1773, Revere married his second wife, Rachel Walker. Though his remarriage may seem hasty by contemporary standards, it was in keeping with the custom of the time; most eighteenth-century men and women remarried as soon as possible after the death of a spouse, to provide care and support for their large families.

The stocky, dark, hard-working Revere eventually fathered sixteen children, eight with each wife. It was a reasonable number, considering the high childhood mortality rate of the time and the fact that his oldest and youngest children were thirty years apart. Coincidentally, everything his offspring did seemed to happen in fives: Revere had five children living with him when he moved to North Square, five children died before their fifth birthdays, only five outlived him, and between five and eight lived with him in the North Square house at any given time. The last fact helps answer one common query of Revere House visitors: How did the whole family fit in these four rooms? The sixteen Revere children never simultaneously lived under the same roof. Moreover, Revere's home had a third-story addition at the front—an addition that was removed during the renovations of 1906–08. A wooden lean-to outside the Revere kitchen also added space, but that structure too is long gone.

Just as surprising to visitors as Revere's family life are the real facts about his role in the American War for Independence. Contrary to popular belief, Revere wasn't considered a hero in his own time. Furthermore, Henry Wadsworth Longfellow's legendary 1861 poem "Paul Revere's Ride"— which helped make both Revere and Longfellow household names—was inaccurate at best.

> Listen, my children, and you shall hear
> Of the midnight ride of Paul Revere,
> On the eighteenth of April, in Seventy-five;
> Hardly a man is now alive
> Who remembers that famous day and year. . . .
>
> One, if by land, and two, if by sea;
> And I on the opposite shore will be,
> Ready to ride and spread the alarm
> Through every Middlesex village and farm, . . .

Revere did ride into the countryside on the night of April 18, 1775, to warn colonists that the British were coming. But so did William Dawes, Samuel Prescott, and some three dozen other men, whose names just weren't as easy to rhyme as Revere. The message they were all delivering was that the redcoats, camped out on Boston Common, were traveling "by sea," that is, across the Charles River to Cambridge. From there they would march to Concord, to seize and destroy colonial stores of arms. Revere, as it turns out, boated to Charlestown, then borrowed a steed. He was captured on the way to Concord, however, so never finished his ride. Dr. Prescott did, and the colonists in the countryside were duly warned— and prepared—for the battles of Lexington and Concord, which ensued the following morning (see also chapters 5 and 13).

Visiting the Revere House today, one quickly realizes that Revere the political revolutionary was equally—if not more—important as an "industrial revolutionary." In a lighted display case are samples of what Revere did best—metalwork. He fashioned silver into spoons, bowls, tea sets, and dental wiring. He created copper plates to reproduce political cartoons and engravings. He cast bells large and small, including an enormous 1804 specimen on display in the courtyard outside the house. Nine hundred and fifty-nine bells in all, from cow bells to the church bell at King's Chapel, were made in his family's foundry between 1792 and 1828.

Though history books often call Paul Revere a silversmith, his contemporaries used the term *goldsmith*. During Revere's time, American goldsmiths like himself worked largely in silver, while their British counterparts still made much from gold; British clients apparently had lots more money to spend than their colonial cousins.

In his later years, Revere became a true industrialist, rolling sheet copper at his Canton mill—copper which covered, among other things, the bottom of "Old Ironsides" and the top of the new State House. By that time, the busy entrepreneur had moved from North Square into a larger house on Charter Street. But the story is there in Revere's old home. Incidentally, the Revere firm's descendant company, Revere Brass and Copper, Inc., is still in business.

Though most visitors come to 19 North Square to learn more about Paul Revere, the Revere House is much more than the colonial silversmith's one-time abode. Its history began in 1676, when one of Boston's many "Great Fires" consumed much of the North End, clearing the land it later occupied. (The house destroyed in that blaze was owned by Puritan minister Increase Mather, whose son, Cotton Mather, gained later notoriety for his vocal support of the Salem witchcraft trials and executions.)

Some four years after the fire, the structure that would become the Revere House was built. It was purchased by a wealthy merchant named Robert Howard in 1681. Though it looks downright primitive by con-

The "Best Chamber" at the Paul Revere House is decorated with furniture and furnishings typical of a successful late eighteenth-century middle-class artisan like Revere.

temporary standards, the house was considered spacious and modern in the late seventeenth century. The asymmetrical building had a steeply pitched roof, with a prominent front overhang above the second story. Light filtered in through the diamond-paned casement windows, while broad, open fireplaces heated the major chambers. Covering the house's heavy timber frame was clapboard siding. The foundation was fieldstone, the shingles wood. (Such wooden construction was soon to become obsolete, by the way, since several devastating fires eventually convinced Bostonians that brick and stone structures had better survival rates in a congested urban setting.)

At the Revere House today, visitors see an amalgam of Howard's early colonial period and Revere's Revolutionary-era occupancy, which began ninety years later. True to Howard's time is the house's current two-story construction; as noted above, when Revere was in residence, a third-story addition was attached at the front. While three of the house's chambers reflect Revere's decor and furnishings, the fourth—a large first-floor room called the Hall—is set up to simulate Howard's era.

The Hall's odd-looking furniture—which some visitors perceive as oriental or Spanish—is typical of the late seventeenth century, as are the bare floors and rug-covered tables. Several of the house's oldest items are also exhibited in the Hall, including a hand-colored 1635 Dutch map. (In early colonial times, maps were much more common as wall decorations than paintings or drawings.) On the other hand, the Hall also houses some historical incongruities. The beautiful, exposed post-and-beam house frame, for example, would have been boxed over in Howard's time. Moreover, the Hall's seventeenth-century kitchen fireplace doesn't belong there; the original survives in the fieldstone cellar, an area now closed to the public.

In the rest of the house, the furniture and furnishings are those of a successful middle-class artisan like Paul Revere. Six of the items on display, including a veneered bow-front dresser, an upholstered chair, and a sewing table in the upstairs "Best Chamber," are Revere family pieces.

The owner of the house two doors away was Nathaniel Hichborn, Revere's first cousin. "Whenever there are Hitchbourn [sic] names in Boston," wrote Revere biographer Esther Forbes, "there were sure to be Reveres nearby." So it is in the Granary Burying Ground in death, and so it was on the cobbled streets of North Square in life.

Boatbuilder Hichborn bought the handsome, three-story brick mansion two doors down from Revere's house a few years after his cousin Paul moved in. The English Renaissance structure, sometimes labeled early Georgian, was built for glazier Moses Pierce around 1711. Though the homes were but thirty years apart in construction (separated by a third house, where the Revere House courtyard and herb gardens sit today), they were worlds apart in style.

The Revere House's wood exterior and craggy angles stand in sharp contrast to the Hichborn's brick walls, low roof, shallow-arched window crests, and relative symmetry. The huge old fireplaces in Paul's place look archaic next to the smaller, heat-efficient, painted ones at Nathaniel's. (Neither house had any indoor amenities more convenient than a chamber pot.)

Operated by the Paul Revere Memorial Association since 1970, the Pierce-Hichborn House offers guests a fascinating architectural and cultural comparison to Revere's. It also provides office space for site staff and an education center for small classes. Unlike those at the Revere House, all Pierce-Hichborn House tours are guided and take place on a set schedule.

Between their eighteenth-century lives as patriot residences and their twentieth-century incorporation as museums, the Revere and Hichborn houses served other important social functions. During the nineteenth century, the center of Boston's upper- and middle-class life shifted from the North End to other sections of town. The North End, in turn, began playing host to new generations of immigrants (see Chapter 37). Irish, Jewish, Portuguese, and (finally) Italian newcomers crowded into the increasingly impoverished neighborhood. Houses like the Hichborn and Revere became tenements upstairs and shops downstairs. Had they not been adaptable to tenement life, the two homes might have met the wrecking ball long before the turn of the century.

The account of the Paul Revere House in the *Milton Record* of 1905 would hardly be recognized today: "It's a quaint, dirty, dilapidated wooden building with queer chimneys and overhanging upper story. . . . The lower floor is occupied by a Hebrew green grocery shop while the upper two floors are ordinary North End tenements." Among the retail stores that set up on the ground floor of the Revere House in the 1800s were a candy store, the Banca Italiana, F. A. Goduti Cigars, and a Jewish vegetable shop.

In order to ensure that the former Revere home would not be destroyed, John P. Reynolds, Jr., a Revere great-grandson, bought it in 1902. Over the next few years, the Paul Revere Memorial Association was organized, and architect Joseph Chandler was hired to restore the building. On April 18, 1908, the hundred and thirty-third anniversary of the overblown "midnight ride," the house officially opened its doors to the public as a museum.

Today, the Paul Revere Memorial Association sponsors historic research, publishes popular and scholarly works, oversees the house's furnishings, mounts rotating exhibits, creates afternoon activities for youngsters, and offers a variety of educational programs for children and adults. One popular school program, "Paul Revere: The Man Behind the Myth," encourages students to analyze old pictures, handle replicas of Revere's saddlebags and shirt, uncover the inaccuracies of Longfellow's poem, and wander through an intriguing slice of American life.

Revere House educational programs also focus on the North End's rich cultural history, examining its various immigrant groups. Director Nina Zannieri even admits that the thought of redecorating one of the rooms in the Revere House—presumably the "Children's Room"—as a nineteenth-century tenement space has a certain appeal. It would certainly fit into her underlying philosophy.

"In our presentations we try to talk about how the house was used during, before, and after Revere. Not to denigrate Paul Revere, an important person whose business career requires much more study, but these houses are dynamic, not static. Some people may prefer houses that deal with an isolated time frame. But ours really reflect change."

THE ESSENTIALS

ADDRESS: 19 North Square, Boston.

TELEPHONE: (617) 523-2338.

VISITOR INFORMATION: Open 9:30 A.M.–5:15 P.M. daily, April 14–October 31; 9:30 A.M.–4:15 P.M. daily for the rest of the year. Closed Thanksgiving, Christmas, and New Year's Day, and on Mondays in January, February, and March. Revere House is part of those Freedom Trail tours that include the North End (see Chapter 10 for details). Revere House tour is self-guided, with interpreters on duty. Only guided tours at Pierce-Hichborn House; call for information and times. Small admission fee for each house; combination tickets available. Both houses partly wheelchair accessible, with assistance; call for further information.

5 | Minute Man National Historical Park

ANYONE WHO'S ever attended an American grade school knows at least *something* about the historic towns of Lexington and Concord. Those two suburban towns—located less than twenty miles northwest of Boston—are generally associated with the opening battles of the American War for Independence, and with the famed "shot heard 'round the world." For some, the names elicit visions of colonial resistance to British aggression on Concord's North Bridge or the Lexington Green; others remember bands of minute men and British redcoats exchanging fire as the British regulars marched back toward Boston down the long Battle Road.

Aside from these basic facts, however, misconceptions about the battles at Lexington and Concord—and about what really happened on that fateful day of April 19, 1775—do abound. Fortunately, Minute Man National Historical Park exists to bring the true history of the early days of the Revolution to life—if, indeed, that can be done. The problem is, of course, that discrepancies abound between even the most astute chroniclers of American history. How many soldiers were involved in the skirmishes? What were their motives? Where was "the shot" fired, and by whom? On these points, and many others, accounts by Concord historians often disagree with those from Lexington, Massachusetts accounts conflict with

Each year on Patriots' Day, costumed re-enactors recreate the battles at Lexington and Concord that marked the beginning of the American War for Independence.

Virginian ones, and American records contradict those of the British. Keeping those limitations in mind, here is a brief outline of April 19, 1775.

Trouble had been brewing between England and its American colonies long before 1775—and long before the famous Boston Tea Party of 1773, the Boston Massacre of 1770, and earlier protests against "taxation without representation." In fact, the far-off colonists—more precisely, the white, wealthy, male colonists with voting privileges—had actually experienced a great deal of autonomy during Boston's one hundred and fifty-odd years of growth. When Britain tried to tighten royal control over the colonies—whether with words, regulations, or fairly insignificant taxes—many colonists balked. Radicals like Samuel Adams and John Hancock fanned the flames of revolution, milking every minor incident they could to incite the colonists to revolt. Until 1775, however, their efforts had little effect.

When British General Thomas Gage decided to send seven hundred "redcoats" into the Concord countryside on April 19, 1775, it wasn't an invasion or a battle he had in mind. The British knew that the colonists had been storing arms in that rural town, and marched out the eighteen miles from Boston Common to seize and destroy those stores. Without arms, there could be no revolution, no battle, no bloodshed.

Numerous in-town tip-offs led Paul Revere, William Dawes, and their colleagues to ride into the countryside, warning Lexington and Concord residents of the secret British mission. Although Revere alone received the popular credit, thanks to Henry Wadsworth Longfellow's beloved but inaccurate "Paul Revere's Ride," the man who actually got the word to Concord was twenty-nine-year-old Dr. Samuel Prescott—Dawes was forced to turn back, and Revere was captured (the site of that capture is marked in stone on Route 2A, between the park's Battle Road Visitor Center and Hanscom Drive).

It's probable that neither side intended to fight, draw blood, or kill "the enemy"; but they did so nonetheless. The first bloody encounter on April 19 was at Lexington Common, where Captain John Parker and his seventy-seven militiamen met the seven hundred British troops at dawn. A shot was fired by someone—perhaps British, perhaps a colonist. At the end of much confusion, British fire, and unheeded commands, eight Americans lay dead.

After moving on to Concord, the British began collecting and burning any colonial military supplies they could find. Colonial militiamen at Concord's North Bridge saw the fires and smoke, and erroneously assumed their homes were being destroyed. That assumption led to an encounter at the North Bridge—an encounter only a few minutes long—leaving two dead on each side. It was the first time Americans fired a volley at the British; Concord's Major John Buttrick gave the order.

The longest, most deadly part of the day was the running battle along the Battle Road, as minute men and militia from surrounding communities joined the attack on the British, who gradually retreated to Bunker Hill. Visitors can still explore these battle sites—beginning with Meriam's Corner and moving through Hardy's Hill, the Bloody Angles, the Bluff, Fiske Hill, and beyond—aided by detailed park maps, brochures, booklets, displays, and knowledgeable interpreters.

The British were surely surprised by the fighting abilities of their colonial counterparts; but they were also grossly outnumbered. By day's end, some 3,500 militiamen had battled some 1,700 redcoats (which included reinforcements). An estimated 94 colonials died, compared to 273 British troops.

Contrary to popular belief, the colonial militiamen were neither superior marksmen nor guerrilla fighters hiding behind a thick forest of trees as the British column marched down the road. One historian has estimated that the colonials hit their mark with maybe one out of every three hundred musket balls. Furthermore, historian Thomas Boylston Adams reminds us that the trees thickly lining park roads today were not there in 1775. "All the land was bare of trees by then," Adams explains. "The reason was simple: people needed firewood for fuel." When the militiamen fired at the British marching down the road, they were running through open pastures, meadows, fields, and home lots—interspersed with occasional orchards and woodlands—and darting behind homes, rocks, and bushes.

While popular histories often paint the colonial fighters who flocked to battle on April 19 as a bunch of untrained, ragtag farmers, that was hardly so. From earliest colonial times, Massachusetts settlements and towns had their own militias—a necessity since there was no standing army. In general, every able-bodied man between sixteen and sixty was a militia member. "They drilled once or twice a year," says park ranger Mark Nichopor, "whether they needed it or not."

Clearly, such minimal drilling was not enough to make a skilled army. Hence, in 1774, when the strain between Britain and the colonies was reaching a dangerous level, the Suffolk Resolves of 1774 asked each town to set aside one-quarter of their militia force as "minute men," a skilled group of soldiers who could muster at a moment's notice. Though in appearance the regular militia and the minute men were identical, the minute men were generally younger, better organized, and better trained. (All the Concord minute men and militia who turned out for the April 19 fight billed the town for their services, as was the custom for such work.)

In sum, these farmers were fighters, too, many of whom had honed their battle skills in the French and Indian War twenty years earlier. Though they lacked the sparkling uniforms of the British, large numbers of them came to the April 19 encounters cleanshaven and sporting their best clothes. "The Acton Minute Men Company stopped on the way to powder their hair white," reveals Nichopor, "and one guy from Danvers turned out for muster in his wedding clothes!"

Since 1963, costumed "minute men" have periodically visited Minute Man National Historical Park, recreating and commemorating historic events. They also make appearances around the country and the world, often for civic and charity purposes. Each group represents an area town, and membership is based on interest rather than direct lineage. Since participation in these groups peaked during the Bicentennial year, many members tend to be dedicated older men, though younger "patriots" are certainly represented.

Although the war contributions of minute- and militiamen are better documented, women played a role at Lexington and Concord as well. Women were not only the linchpin of the home economy but essential to the war effort; they helped enforce embargoes on British goods, protected military stores from the British, and actively supported military activities.

Furthermore, according to volunteer Gene Prowten, who helped organize the modern-day Boxborough Minute Men, "If there hadn't been women, there wouldn't have been a 19th of April!" It seems that Dr. Samuel Prescott was out courting one Lydia Mulliken the night Revere and Dawes began their ride from Boston. Miss Mulliken's father apparently threw paramour Prescott out—which resulted in his meeting the two alarm riders and then taking the warning on to Concord.

Three objects closely identified with the start of the Revolutionary War in Lexington and Concord are sources of patriotic pride—and occasional confusion.

The Minute Man statue that stands majestically by North Bridge was commissioned by the town of Concord for the 1875 centennial. The seven-foot bronze "embattled farmer" was the work of sculptor Daniel Chester French. French, who later gained worldwide fame for statues like the seated Lincoln in the (Washington, D.C.) Lincoln Memorial, was just twenty-four years old at the time. For the minute man, his first monument contract, he used the classic Roman statue known as the Apollo

Belvedere—a plaster cast of which was at the Boston Athenaeum—plus several living men as models. He was paid just $1,000 plus expenses for the work, though the exposure and experience were priceless.

Another minute man statue stands on Lexington's town green, where Massachusetts Avenue meets Bedford Street in the town center. Crafted by Henry Hudson Kitson in 1900, this spirited fighter represents Captain John Parker, who lined up his militiamen on Lexington Common for the first encounter with British troops on April 19. The statue's "minute man" designation is not quite accurate, however. Despite the 1774 Suffolk Resolves, Lexington had not yet organized or financed such a unit from its militia by April of 1775; unless the term is used loosely to mean "citizen-soldier," Parker, his seventy-seven courageous soldiers, and the statue are not technically minute men.

Then there's the North Bridge. It's not the "*Old*" North Bridge—though plenty of people call it that—and it isn't the bridge on which the battle was fought. The present North Bridge is a 1956 creation of the Massachusetts Department of Public Works, though it is constructed on the site of the original. It's higher than the 1760 bridge—which may help it survive the floods that have always plagued the slow-moving Concord River—but looks similar to its historic ancestor. The model for this incarnation was Amos Doolittle's engraving, a copy of which hangs in the newly renovated Concord Museum at the intersection of the Cambridge Turnpike and Lexington Road. The 1760 bridge was not destroyed by the British, though they did tear planks from it to stave off the minute men on April 19. It was, however, dismantled in 1793, when many roads in the area were realigned. The next bridge on the site was an elaborate Victorian version, built for the 1875 centennial. That and two subsequent commemorative bridges were damaged and removed before the current one was built.

Minute Man National Historical Park was established by an act of Congress and entrusted to the National Park Service in 1959, to commemorate the events of April 19, 1775, and the opening battle in the American War for Independence. Though best known for the small area near the North Bridge and the Minute Man statue, the sprawling 875-acre park has much, much more to offer visitors. The best way to begin discovering the park is from the Battle Road Visitor Center, on Route 2A in Lexington. There, a color film describes the mounting tensions between the British and the colonists, and exhibits set the tone for exploring the park. Park rangers can direct you to period buildings and to a number of lesser-known but equally engaging sites along the Battle Road. The North Bridge area, at the far western end of the park, is especially interesting if visitors hike up the winding dirt road to the nearby North Bridge Visitor Center and Park Headquarters, in the 1911 Buttrick Mansion.

Today the park is embarking on a variety of projects aimed at better protecting its significant cultural resources, improving opportunities for visitors to understand the events of the American Revolution and the colonial era, and developing new facilities. On the books for the mid-to-late-1990s are plans to recreate the feel of earlier times by restoring the historic landscape, with its varied patterns of tilled fields, pastures, meadows, orchards, gardens, and woodlots. Additional segments of the original Battle Road that diverge from the modern Route 2A will be closed to vehicular traffic and restored to their eighteenth-century appearance.

Planning for the 1990s also stresses major improvements in interpretation, educational outreach, and visitor access. Along the Battle Road, a network of foot and bicycle trails will make it possible for visitors to leave their cars behind and experience the New England landscape. The trail system, with appropriate signage, will follow segments of stone fences and other features used for cover by the American militia as it fired on the retreating column of redcoats. The trail network will also introduce broader themes, from changes in the landscape caused by glaciation to changes brought about by human use, all helping to put the events of April 19, 1775, in a more comprehensible context.

The Battle Road, the North Bridge Visitor Center, and the Wayside Barn are also scheduled for new exhibit design. The historic Meriam House, site of the start of the running battle after the North Bridge fight, will become a visitor contact station, and at key locations visitors will continue to meet costumed interpreters who will demonstrate Revolutionary-era militia activities and trades. A varied program of educational offerings will also be developed cooperatively with regional school systems.

Exploring the battle sites at Lexington and Concord need not end within the park itself. Although the park's collections include only a few artifacts related to April 19, 1775, other area museums, libraries, and collections contain a wealth of interesting items. Treasures at the Concord Museum, for example, include one of the two lanterns used at the Old North Church to signal British movements, while the Lexington Historical Society has pistols dropped by British major John Pitcairn when his horse bolted at a volley of musket fire. Battle exhibits focusing on Lexington are displayed at the Museum of Our National Heritage, and the pride of the Bedford Library is the flag that the Bedford minute men reportedly carried with them to the North Bridge in 1775.

THE ESSENTIALS

ADDRESS: Park runs along Route 2A through towns of Concord, Lincoln, and Lexington. Mailing address, Box 160, Concord, MA 01742.

TELEPHONE: North Bridge Visitor Center, (508) 369-6993 and (617) 484-6156; Battle Road Visitor Center, (617) 862-7753.

VISITOR INFORMATION: North Bridge Visitor Center open daily, year round; closed Christmas and New Year's Day. Battle Road Visitor Center generally open mid-April through October; call for exact dates and hours, which vary year to year. Free. Call for schedules of guided walks, talks, and audio-visual displays. Both visitor centers and their restrooms are wheelchair accessible; best wheelchair access to North Bridge is from Monument Street parking lot; paths and trails throughout park vary in accessibility, depending on surface, slope, and steps.

6 The Bunker Hill Monument

IT'S JUST about as strange a site as you could imagine: right in the middle of an old, working-class, largely Irish Boston neighborhood stands a 221-foot Egyptian obelisk memorializing a British military victory.

One of eight historic sites that make up Boston National Historical Park, and one of the Freedom Trail's most distinctive stops, the Bunker Hill Monument commemorates the Battle of Bunker Hill, fought on June 17, 1775. Though that bloody encounter is widely remembered as the first decisive battle of the American War for Independence, the fact is the American colonists actually *lost* to their British foes. So why build a spectacular monument to a seemingly sad defeat?

Two months after the running battle at Lexington and Concord (see Chapter 5), the colonists moved to occupy the hill on which the monument now stands. British troops made three assaults on the rebels, though their first and second efforts ended in British retreats. The third British assault knocked the colonists off the hill and out of Charlestown altogether.

As defeats go, however, the Battle of Bunker Hill was a glorious one. An army of provincial New England farmers had repelled two out of three British attacks, decimating the well-trained "redcoats' " ranks before their own final retreat. Colonial resentment of British oppression swiftly crystallized after this bloody encounter, unleashing the full-fledged Revolutionary War.

Britain's pyrrhic victory is only one of several curious or forgotten facts, misnomers, and misquotes associated with the Battle of Bunker Hill. The name, for example, is dead wrong. It should be *Bunker's* Hill, named for George Bunker, a rich landowner who moved to Massachusetts from England in 1634. That detail turns out to be irrelevant, however, since the battle was actually fought—and the monument stands—on Breed's Hill. Bunker's Hill is a half-mile to the northwest, where Saint Francis de Sales Church stands today.

Moreover, the most famous quotation to emerge from historical accounts of the battle—"Don't fire 'til you see the whites of their eyes"—is of dubious authenticity at best. While some historians attribute it to colonial Colonel William Prescott, others insist the words were General Israel Putnam's. No one knows who, if anyone, used the phrase that day. In any case it wasn't original; it had been an oft-quoted Prussian military order for three decades before the Revolutionary War broke out.

None of these minor historical questions seems to have fazed public interest in the site, nor dampened New England pride in the name Bunker

*Colonial Colonel William
Prescott wields his saber at
the base of the towering
Bunker Hill Monument.*

Hill. Attracting more than 140,000 visitors every year, the monument is also the center of celebrations every June 17. A longstanding Suffolk County holiday, the annual observance of Bunker Hill Day rounds out a gala Charlestown weekend filled with splashy parades, traditional flag-raisings, military salutes, and assorted festivities.

Long before the Battle of Bunker Hill, the Charlestown peninsula was known primarily as a pleasant place to pass through. The glaciers had passed through, for instance, leaving three distinctive drumlins, or hills, behind. The Pawtucket had passed through, naming the land Mishawum, or "great spring." John Winthrop's Puritan settlers also passed through, departing largely because the spring wasn't all that great (presumably, it was then unpotable). Since fresher water was available on the nearby Shawmut peninsula, Winthrop and others relocated there in 1630, eventually renaming it Boston (see Chapter 29).

In the century before the Revolution, however, Charlestown developed into a prosperous seaport, and a center of American economic independence. Paul Revere borrowed a horse in Charlestown to make his 1775 ride to the Lexington countryside. Charlestown was also the area that British troops—sequestered in Boston after Lexington and Concord—meant to fortify as a hedge against colonial aggression.

Placing troops on the three strategic hills overlooking Boston—Breed's and Bunker's in Charlestown, and Dorchester Heights—was what British general Thomas Gage should have done; generals William Howe and Henry Clinton pressed him to do so. When Gage didn't move, however, Colonel William Prescott did. On the night of June 16, 1775, the Pepperell farmer and his ill-trained provincial troops moved quietly through the night toward Breed's Hill. There they swiftly and silently built an earthen fort, called a redoubt, and prepared to defend their position when the sleeping British soldiers awoke.

No one knows why Prescott advanced and built on Breed's Hill rather than Bunker's. Perhaps he thought Breed's provided a better defensive position or closer firing range. Perhaps his fellow officers, including many not from Boston, didn't know one hill from the other; British maps interchanged the names of the two hills, or called all three of Charlestown's mounds "Bunker's Hill."

However it was, the bloody encounter that ensued the next day was forever known as the Battle of Bunker Hill. That encounter was the deadliest of the Revolutionary War. By the end of a siege that lasted less than two hours, Charlestown's grassy slopes were littered with some 1,500 bodies, and most of its 400 buildings were burned.

British casualties outnumbered colonial ones two to one. An estimated 500 colonials and 1,034 British soldiers died, despite the colonists' inferior weaponry—marginally accurate muskets, and no bayonets. According to legend, British troops had twice the manpower of their colonial foes; many popular accounts state that 1,000 colonists battled 2,200 British soldiers. New research, however, suggests that more than 2,000—and perhaps as many as 5,000—New Englanders came to fight that day.

Even if the colonists weren't outnumbered, their fight is still impressive. "The actual numbers probably don't matter," says Tom Brown, a professor emeritus in American History at the University of Massachusetts/Amherst. "The rule of thumb is that the attacking force should outnumber the defenders three to one. The British failed to do that."

No one will debate that Britain paid dearly for that victory on the hill. The British carried off their dead, interring many in the Boston Common burying ground. British major John Pitcairn, shot by a free black American named Peter Salem, fell into his own son's arms. Pitcairn was buried, ironically, in a crypt below the Old North Church on Salem Street—the same church from which, two months earlier, two lanterns had warned the colonists of the British attack "by sea."

Of all the colonial soldiers who died that day, the most prominent was Dr. Joseph Warren—a highly respected patriot, organizer, orator, doctor, and writer, known by many British as the most troublesome of all the rebellious colonists. So dearly was the patriot doctor missed that in 1794 fellow members of the local King Solomon's Lodge of Free and Accepted Masons erected an eighteen-foot wooden Tuscan pillar atop Breed's Hill in his memory. The monument, inscribed to honor "Major-General Joseph Warren and his Associates" was the first Bunker Hill monument on this site. A replica stands inside the base of the current granite obelisk.

★ ★ ★

The present Bunker Hill Monument began in a controversy and ended in a bake sale. The controversy erupted in 1818, when Major General Henry Dearborn published a pamphlet of his recollections of the Battle of Bunker Hill. Dearborn claimed that Colonel John Stark and his New Hampshire regiments were never given adequate credit for their major role; moreover, he insisted that revered Revolutionary hero General Israel Putnam was cowardly in that battle, and incapacitated by a gall bladder attack for most of the day. The full truth of who did what—when, where, and how—amidst all the confusion of the battle will never really be known.

The outcries that ensued over Dearborn's claims brought back fading memories of the colonists' valiant defense at Bunker Hill—an event whose fiftieth anniversary was seven years away. Meanwhile, acreage atop Russell's Pasture, as the old battleground was then called, had come up for sale. Dr. John Collins Warren, a distinguished surgeon and a nephew of the late Joseph Warren, bought the first three acres. Soon, with the formation of the Bunker Hill Memorial Association, some fifteen acres were in hand.

Realizing that the aging Marquis de Lafayette had planned a trip to the United States to celebrate the fiftieth anniversary of the Revolutionary War, the association arranged to have that venerable military ally participate in a ceremony to lay the cornerstone of a new, larger monument on Bunker Hill. The ceremony took place in 1825, and featured an oration by Daniel Webster. Forty elderly Bunker Hill veterans attended the event.

It wasn't until eighteen years later, on June 17, 1843, that the 221-foot, 6,700-ton granite monument was finally dedicated—with another oration by Daniel Webster, and thirteen *extremely* elderly Bunker Hill veterans in attendance. The lapse of time was due not so much to the difficulty of building the obelisk—though it was a major construction feat—as to finances.

The Bunker Hill Memorial Association had held a competition for an architectural plan. In the final selection for monument design, the Egyptian obelisk was chosen over the column form. The obelisk had been popular in Egyptian, Greek, and Roman cultures as a symbol of heroism, glory, and death. Most recently, it had reappeared in the West with nineteenth-century Egyptian and Greek revival styles.

A granite quarry was purchased in Quincy for a mere $325. Meanwhile, engineer Gridley Bryant developed the "first commercial railroad in America" to carry the huge twelve-foot blocks of dressed granite to a wharf on the Neponset River. From there the blocks were barged to Charlestown. Those early railroad cars were horse drawn, and the whole process fairly traumatic for the granite. Eventually, overland ox-carts were brought in to finish the hauling job.

Much to the dismay of supervising architect Solomon Willard, expenses mounted exponentially. Donations came in, large and small, and eleven of the original fifteen surrounding acres were sold to raise funds. Still the money wasn't enough. When, in 1840, it looked as though the half-completed obelisk was never going to be finished, the women took over.

Sarah Josepha Hale, "America's first woman editor," ran the Boston-based *Godey's Ladies Magazine*. Grandstanding from her journal, and inspiring newspapers to do the same, Hale and a small army of women organized "the Fair," a spectacular week-long cake and cookie sale held near Faneuil Hall. The women netted an unprecedented $30,035.53, which—along with two major contributions from individuals—enabled the monument to be completed soon thereafter. In all, the monument cost $156,218.14 to build, with all but $7,000.00 raised by public subscription.

In the century and a half since its dedication, the towering Bunker Hill Monument has changed hands several times. Bankrupted by the costs of their investment despite a longstanding ten-cent admission fee, the Bunker Hill Memorial Association turned the monument over to the city of Boston in 1919. The city also found the property too costly to maintain well, and finally, during the 1976 Bicentennial, transferred it to the National Park Service.

Physically, the site has had its ups and downs. A steam-propelled "elevator" that existed from 1842 to 1844—used first for hauling granite, then briefly adapted for people—is long gone. Now it's 294 huffing, puffing steps to the top. Statues of Prescott and Warren are displayed outside the monument base and inside the adjacent 1903 marble lodge, but many of the old firearms, paintings, and other artifacts once shown in the monument or lodge are now stored elsewhere.

On the other hand, paperwork from "the Fair," drawings from the monument design contest, and other Charlestown-related curios can be found at the free Bunker Hill Museum, run by the Charlestown Historical Society at 43 Monument Square, and open from May to September. A few blocks away, at 55 Constitution Road, is Raytheon's $1.4-million Bunker Hill Pavilion, with a thirty-minute multimedia, surround-sound show on the battle. Finally, at the monument itself, National Park Service rangers tell the story of the battle in hourly talks, using a series of dioramas in the monument lodge for illustration.

The monument's cultural and symbolic life has also changed. The Bunker Hill memorial was the first monument built through public donations, and the country's first publicized tourist attraction. Before 1885, it was the first and most prominent monument in the country—*the* American obelisk. In that year, however, the Washington Monument in Washington, D.C.—an obelisk grander and 335 feet taller than Bunker Hill's—was completed. Once the Washington Monument became the national symbol, only Bostonians kept the Charlestown obelisk first in their hearts.

But which Bostonians? That, too, has changed over the decades. Originally built by Federalist party members—wealthy, upper-class merchants, bankers, and manufacturers—the Bunker Hill Monument later came to be identified with the Whig party. When Charlestown became a working-class Irish area, the obelisk became a "democratic" symbol. "Even during the Boston busing crisis of the early 1970s," explains Professor Tom Brown, "Charlestown people opposed to busing invoked the Bunker Hill Monument. They said that they, just as in 1775, were resisting outside tyrannical authority. Since its inception, people have spoken about being or acting 'under the shadow of the Bunker Hill Monument.' So it's a living symbol, not a dead artifact. And it's the liveliest symbolic site in Boston."

THE ESSENTIALS

ADDRESS: Monument Square, Charlestown, Boston.
TELEPHONE: (617) 242-5641.
VISITOR INFORMATION: Monument open 9:00 A.M.–4:30 P.M. daily. Lodge/exhibit area open 9:00 A.M.–5:00 P.M. daily except Thanksgiving, Christmas, and New Year's Day. Free. Ranger-conducted battle talks given hourly, 10:00 A.M.–4:00 P.M., except at 1:00 P.M. Musket-firing demonstrations given on the half hour, 10:30 A.M.–3:30 P.M., Wednesday–Sunday during the summer months. Grounds wheelchair accessible via a fairly steep paved ramp from main entrance; lodge/exhibit area requires one step up; restrooms accessible; monument itself not wheelchair accessible.

7 Adams National Historic Site

IF YOU'RE looking for the history of the American Revolution, the city of Quincy is not the first place you might consider. Yet in downtown Quincy, only ten miles south of Boston via the Southeast Expressway, is a bucolic thirteen-acre spread of gardens, rolling lawns, and scattered structures known as the Adams National Historic Site. This beautiful old South Shore estate was once home to two eminent patriots, John and Abigail Adams. Moreover, two of the site's smaller, more rustic structures are the birthplaces of John and John Quincy Adams, the only father and son to become presidents of the United States. The Quincy site also harbors the stories of many more members of the Adams family—an illustrious political dynasty that lived and worked the land there from colonial times through 1927.

John Adams (1735–1826), known as the level-headed counterpart to his radical cousin Sam Adams, was a member of the First and Second Continental congresses, the first vice-president of the United States, and the second president of the new nation. Adams was the patriot lawyer who argued the Boston Massacre case in court and garnered European support for the American cause on numerous diplomatic missions abroad. Meanwhile he wrote the Constitution of the Commonwealth of Massachusetts, and helped Thomas Jefferson fine-tune the Declaration of Independence.

Equally revolutionary was John's wife, Abigail Smith Adams (1744–1818), one of America's earliest and most notable feminists. In marriage, Abigail and John were true partners and equals. Beginning with John's departure for the First Continental Congress in 1774, Abigail took sole charge of hearth and home, effectively balancing child-rearing with managing the family farm and business. When the American War for Independence began, Abigail opened her home as a sanctuary for soldiers and refugees from Boston. While her husband was serving the nation at home and abroad, she constantly wrote to him of personal and political matters—from the gory details of the Battle of Bunker Hill to tales of melting down her pewter spoons to mold bullets for patriot guns.

The most quoted of Abigail's letters to John was written in March 1776, when she advised her husband and his colleagues to think through the implications of their declarations of independence: "By the way, in the new code of laws which I suppose it will be necessary for you to make, I desire you would remember the ladies and be more generous and favorable to them than your ancestors! Do not put such unlimited power into the hands of the husbands. Remember all men would be tyrants if they could. If particular care and attention is not paid to the ladies, we are determined to foment a rebellion."

Tales of John and Abigail, of course, are only part of the allure of Adams National Historic Site. The most logical place to start a tour is at the

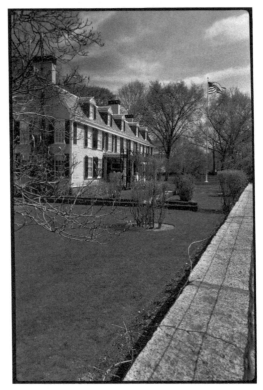

The "Old House" at Adams National Historic Site is famous for its beautifully landscaped grounds and gardens, and for honoring 150 years of Adams family history.

National Park Service Visitor Center, newly opened in 1993 and located at 1250 Hancock Street. Chronologically speaking, the next stop would be a small triangle of land at 133–141 Franklin Street. There sit the birthplaces of John Adams and John Quincy Adams, two modest wood-frame houses that later generations would describe as in the New England "saltbox" style. Though the rambling acres of farmland that once surrounded these homes are long gone, their significance and charm remain intact. They are the two oldest surviving presidential birthplaces in the United States—and the site where the Adams saga began.

The John Adams Birthplace had several owners before his father, Deacon John Adams, bought the house in 1720. William Needham had been granted the land in 1640, though the 1681 structure that sits there today was built by a subsequent owner, Joseph Penniman. While living in this home, Deacon John's wife, Susanna, bore three sons. The eldest became our second president. Though Deacon John died in 1761, both this and the neighboring house continued to be used by Adams family members into the early nineteenth century.

Seventy-five feet away stands the John Quincy Adams Birthplace, a structure built by Samuel Belcher in 1663 and sold to Deacon John in 1744. When Deacon John died, his son John inherited the tiny home. John and Abigail subsequently lived there through the births of five children and the period of colonial upheaval and war. The couple's second child was future president John Quincy Adams, born in 1767. It was in this home that Abigail raised her family, managed the Adams farm and business, molded pewter bullets, and wrote her voluminous war correspondence to her husband. Though John was frequently away on political missions, he too put the stamp of history on this site: he wrote the Massachusetts Constitution in his law office on the first floor.

Sparsely furnished with colonial period pieces and reproductions, these two modest houses offer visitors a telling glimpse of daily life in early New England. National Park Service rangers enjoy comparing modern conveniences to their colonial counterparts ("It's a spit or reflector oven, but we call it a colonial microwave"), and explaining to guests how twentieth-century phrases originated in seventeenth-century life. The colonial table was called a board, for example, because that's what it was—a big, long board; so the expression "room and board" meant a room to sleep in and a board to eat on. Generally, the family would sit on a long common bench along the side of the board, while the father would sit at the end in a chair; hence "chair-man of the board." The phrase "sleep tight" also came from a piece of early American furniture: mattresses were supported by criss-crossed ropes underneath, and sleeping simply wasn't comfortable unless the ropes were kept taut.

John and Abigail Adams did not live in this rustic simplicity forever. Though John was a farmer at heart, his fame and fortune were constantly growing. (His fortune, alas, never kept pace with his fame.) In 1785, John was appointed the first U.S. minister to Britain's Court of Saint James. Weary of long wartime separations, Abigail and the family decided to join John in Europe. Upon their return in 1788, the Adams family moved into a larger, more elegant home about two miles away—the mansion at 135 Adams Street, now known as the Old House. This house, along with its surrounding outbuildings, country gardens, and rolling greens, is the centerpiece of the Adams site today.

When visitors stop by the Old House, however, they are not seeing the Adams mansion as it looked in the days of John and Abigail. The home and its environs are more like an archaeological dig, reflecting layer upon layer of changes, renovations and additions.

When John and Abigail settled at the Old House, the land was known as the Vassall-Borland estate, a farm that once included more than forty acres. The seven-room home they found there had been built by Jamaican sugar planter Leonard Vassall in 1730–31. When the Adamses arrived in 1788, they envisioned it as a working farm, filled with orchards, gardens, and serenity. John named the place Peacefield, partly for that serenity and partly for the treaty of peace he had recently negotiated abroad. Abigail called it "a wren's house," in recognition of the fact that it was significantly smaller than the mansion they had left behind in England.

The couple furnished the Old House with secondhand furniture from John's missions abroad. Many of these pieces are still in the house today. Abigail also began adding chambers and halls to their small, low-ceilinged abode—a practice followed by Adams descendants. By 1927, the original seven-room house had grown into a twenty-one-room mansion.

John and Abigail were the only Adamses to live in the Old House year-round; later generations tended to simply spend the summer there. The second-generation owner, John Quincy Adams (1767–1848), was too involved in politics to give the house as much time and care as his parents did. Still, when not away fulfilling his duties as president, diplomat, or member of Congress, John Quincy loved to experiment with planting trees on the grounds. Like his father, he used the home as a "summer White House."

Charles Francis Adams (1807–1886) represented the third generation to run the Adams estate. Although this skilled U.S. congressman and diplomat initially considered demolishing the house and starting from scratch, Charles Francis settled for beautifying and altering the original site. Under his guidance, John and Abigail's working farm took on the demeanor of a Victorian gentleman's country estate. The old farm buildings on the east lawn were torn down, and a wooden fence was replaced with a stone wall. Charles Francis also built the magnificent Stone Library to house his family's overflowing book collection, and added the carriage house complex, providing quarters for the coachman and a stable for horses.

When the fourth generation of Adamses took charge, a few final alterations were made. While author Henry Adams visited and wrote there at times—he finished his nine-volume *History of the United States* at the Old House—it was brother Brooks Adams who acted as official caretaker and brought the estate into the twentieth century.

After the eccentric Brooks died in 1927, the clock stopped, as it were, on the Adams estate. The house, furnishings, gardens, outbuildings, and grounds that visitors see today are essentially the same as they were the day

Brooks passed on—a gloriously agreeable clutter of art, artifacts, porcelain, plantings, and chambers that reflect four generations of Adams family living and three different centuries of style.

Among the fascinating sights you'll see on a Park Service tour of the Old House:

- The Paneled Room, to the left of the front entrance, was part of the original house. Though later generations admired the rich mahogany walls, Abigail whitewashed them to make the room brighter for her guests.
- The Long Room was part of Abigail's east-wing expansion of the house. The nine Louis XV chairs were brought back by John from his service as minister to The Hague. Though some of the chairs look "normal," several have unusually puffy seats—designed to accommodate the overflow of ladies' hooped skirts. "The furnishings here are like global maps," explains Chief of Interpretation Caroline Keinath, referring to the wonderful hodgepodge of historic styles in the Long Room. "And the paintings of family and friends that line the walls are like today's photograph albums."
- John's Study, upstairs, includes his desk, where he wrote to his close friend Thomas Jefferson. Literate and lingering correspondence was an Adams family specialty. In 1813, John wrote to Jefferson, "You and I ought not to die, before we have explained ourselves to each other." Thirteen years later, on July 4, 1826—the fiftieth anniversary of the Declaration of Independence on which they'd worked together—both Jefferson and Adams died, unbeknownst to one another.
- Though modern Americans tend to be born and die in sterile hospitals, earlier ages had more humane views of life's passages. Abigail passed away in her Dutch bed in the President and First Lady's Bedroom, while John saw his last light of day in his study.
- The circle of several flatirons heating in the Laundry were used by the servants who worked under Brooks Adams. He required his staff to follow his example and change clothing three times daily— white attire in the morning, gray at midday, and black at night— which must have kept them ironing all day.
- The Kitchen is outfitted with eight bells, installed by Charles Francis Adams. Each bell was connected to a different chamber, and each had a different tone, enabling servants to know which room required attendance. The bells have sometimes inspired site staff to joke about the other Addams family of comic strip and movie fame, responding with, "You rang?"

When Brooks Adams died in 1927, the Old House came into the hands of the Adams Memorial Society, who opened it to visitors for nineteen years. In 1946, the society turned the property over to the National Park Service, which has operated the Adams estate ever since. In 1979, the two birthplaces were reunited with the Old House as part of the Adams National Historic Site, and restored to their colonial appearance.

Today, the Adams site maintenance staff takes gentle care of the historic structures and grounds. Regular duties can involve anything from identifying historic plant species and clipping the ancient box hedge, to grading the driveways or reshingling Brooks Adams's doghouse, the smallest of the site's eleven historic structures. Meanwhile, the administrative, management, cultural resource, and interpretive divisions are often at work on new projects. Most of the house's 30,000 historic objects, for example, have been catalogued on computer. Ideas for working with the Quincy community on special events and for linking the area's historic sites are already being implemented. New since 1993, for example, is the National Park Service Visitor Center on Hancock Street, and interpretation at the United First Parish Church at 1306 Hancock, which contains the crypt of the two Adams presidents and their wives. The visitor center also has the only public restrooms on the Adams site.

Meanwhile, the Adams National Historic Site remains "a beautiful landscape and a country setting," in the eyes of Caroline Keinath. "It chronicles a hundred and fifty years of Adams history, but unlike many other historic sites, it's not a museum or a public hall. It's a home."

And quite a revolutionary home, at that.

THE ESSENTIALS

ADDRESS: Adams National Historic Site (Adams Estate), 135 Adams Street, Quincy. John and John Quincy Adams birthplaces, 133 and 141 Franklin Street, Quincy. National Park Service Visitor Center, 1250 Hancock Street, Quincy.

TELEPHONE: (617) 770-1175.

VISITOR INFORMATION: Open 9:00 A.M.–5:00 P.M. daily, April 19 to November 10. Admission fee for adults. Guided tours only; last tour begins 4:00 P.M. Parking and accessible restrooms at Visitor Center. Limited wheelchair access to ground floors of homes via moveable ramps; no upstairs access.

8 The State House

TO SOME, the Massachusetts State House is just a lovely landmark—a glittering golden dome on Beacon Hill, overlooking Boston Common. But take one step inside this Freedom Trail attraction, and you'll find a wealth of history at hand. Over here, for example, the Marquis de Lafayette walked when he came to Boston to help lay the cornerstone for the Bunker Hill Monument. Over there is where legions of young Union soldiers

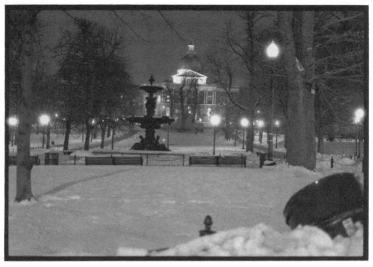

The distinctive golden-domed Massachusetts State House sits above Boston Common, at the crest of Beacon Hill.

stood, receiving arms, ammunition, and other equipment before embarking for the bloody American Civil War. And that's only the beginning. Protesters and presidents, abolitionists and antiabortionists, Native American chiefs and "Indian fighters," senators and suffragists have all been through these marbled halls and elegant chambers since the "new" State House doors first opened on January 11, 1798.

Some of the history inside these old walls is in the form of fascinating tales told by well-versed guides and informative guidebooks. But much of that history is in more tangible form—statues, models, plaques, paintings, furnishings, chambers, and artifacts that bring the past into the present day. Herewith our unorthodox guide:

It wasn't simply that the Old State House, built in 1713 on Cornhill and King streets (now Washington and State), was getting too small to house the expanding state government; after the American Revolution, state leaders wanted an official edifice that properly reflected the grandeur of our prosperous new republic.

Meanwhile, young Charles Bulfinch—Boston's first native-born professional architect—had been traveling in Europe from 1785 to 1787, thanks to an inheritance from a wealthy uncle. Architectural historians believe that Bulfinch's designs for the State House, first submitted when the architect was only twenty-four years of age, were derived from buildings he observed firsthand in London. Certainly he was influenced by English neoclassical style, as evidenced in the State House facade we see today.

Of course a site for the new State House had to be chosen as well. Many Boston locations, as well as spots in faraway towns like Watertown and

Worcester, had been considered. But John Hancock's family's cow pasture—with its overview of Boston from the summit of Beacon Hill—was the first choice, and was eventually purchased for the project. The cornerstone for the State House was laid near the top of the pasture on July 4, 1795, by colonial patriots Samuel Adams and Paul Revere. That symbolic stone was hauled in by fifteen white horses, representing the thirteen original states plus two new ones, Vermont and Kentucky. The new Massachusetts State House—featuring the distinctive dome, tall white columns and trim, and red-brick facade that we all recognize today—was officially completed on January 11, 1798. The cost was the wonderfully curious sum of $133,333.33—not so wonderful, of course, to those who thought the price tag exorbitant.

Though the Bulfinch State House was much larger and grander than its predecessor, it was not long before the government began outgrowing even these quarters. Throughout the nineteenth and early twentieth centuries, land purchases increased the building's original 1.6-acre lot to its current 6.7 acres. Each of the major new wings and renovation projects—completed in 1831, 1856, 1895, and 1917—was intended to be architecturally "subservient" to the original design. A small-scale model of the original 1798 Bulfinch facade, minus the subsequent additions, can be seen in the entryway just outside the State House's Doric Hall.

Many of the original columns, including those on the facade and in Doric Hall, were hewn from enormous pine trunks, carved on the State House lawn. As fireproofing of the building became a growing concern in the late nineteenth century, these wooden pillars were eventually replaced by steel and plaster facsimiles.

Other cosmetic and structural changes over the past two centuries have included both color and composition. The distinctive red-brick exterior, for example, was painted alternately white and yellow for many years, beginning in 1825; only in 1928 was the last coat of yellow sandblasted off, revealing the original red brick, which has been maintained ever since.

A gaggle of great writers, from Shakespeare and Chaucer to Alain de Lille and John Lydgate, have all noted in one way or another that "all that glitters is not gold." While none were discussing the Massachusetts State House in particular, they might as well have been.

Though internationally renowned for its distinctive gold dome, the State House has actually been gilded for only a bit more than half its life. The thirty-foot-high cupola, with a diameter of fifty feet, began as uncovered, lead-colored wood. When that surface began to deteriorate, Paul Revere & Sons covered it with copper in 1802. Not until 1874 was expensive twenty-three-carat gold leaf added over the copper-sheet base, though such a project had been debated for years. The cost in 1874 was $2,862.50. Almost a century later, in 1969, regilding ran up a significantly heftier bill of $36,443.00; gold was selling for $40 an ounce at the time.

The dome has not always been gold in the twentieth century, either. During the blackouts of World War II, for example, it was camouflaged with battleship-gray paint.

★   ★   ★

Visitors can go just about anywhere in the State House today, with or without the aid of a tour guide. The logical starting place—and the spot to pick up guides and guidebooks—is just inside the building's left front door. On the right is the main reception room, called Doric Hall for the ten not-quite-Doric columns scattered within. For the past two centuries, this hall has been used for countless special events, from banquets and press conferences to swearings-in and military munitions distribution. Despite all that activity, the front doors to Doric Hall are opened on only three kinds of occasions—when a U.S. president visits, when a foreign head of state comes to call, and when a governor leaves office.

As you climb the stairs at the end of Doric Hall, you move out of the original Bulfinch building and enter the 1895 addition, designed by Charles Brigham. There, the small Bartlett Hall commemorates William Francis Bartlett, a Civil War general then only in his twenties, who was asked by both Virginia and Massachusetts to serve as governor when the war was over. He refused both invitations, and died at thirty-six. The next, larger room, once called the Senate Staircase Hall, was renamed the Civil War Nurses' Hall in 1985. It boasts Bela Pratt's dramatic 1914 sculpture of an army nurse in action, plus the best marble floors in the building (six types of exotic marble are inlaid there).

The Hall of Flags—also known as Memorial Hall—is a circular room surrounded by columns of Sienna marble. On display is a small sample of the more than four hundred flags once carried into battle by Massachusetts soldiers, from the Civil War to Vietnam. Though the hall once exhibited the original banners—many of them badly frayed and mended with mesh—those were moved to climate-controlled vaults in 1987. Despite the fact that these banners currently shown look deceptively real, they're actually just life-size backlit transparencies. It's hoped that the originals will some day be returned to display.

The loveliest mosaic at the State House is certainly the beautiful marble-work of the Grand Staircase Hall floor. The most curious display may well be the stained-glass window on the staircase landing, which shows the evolution of the State Seal. It seems ironic, of course, that a Native American is depicted on the official state emblem, considering their historical mistreatment in Massachusetts and across the nation. But the tale is even stranger than the image.

On the original seal, created in 1629–30, an "Indian" in a leaf skirt implores "Come Over and Help Us"—presumably asking to be educated and Christianized by the new English colonists. The London artist commissioned to draw the Native American had never seen one, so he apparently copied a drawing in Sir Walter Raleigh's book on Venezuela. According to Russell Peters's book *The Wampanoags of Mashpee,* the most recent incarnation of the State Seal Indian is not much more historically accurate. When Harvard anthropologist Charles Willoughby was commissioned to create a better emblem in 1897, he could not find an appropriate-looking model among the Mashpees of Cape Cod or the Ponkapoags in the Blue Hills. He found his "ideal" Native American at the Parker House in Boston—a tall, strong, long-haired, high-cheekboned man named Little Shell. As a result, Little Shell, an Ojibway from Lake Superior, became immortalized on the Massachusetts seal, along with the new state motto, "By the sword we seek peace, but peace only under liberty."

Since 1986, both the Native American and the suggestion of violence on the State Seal have been sources of controversy and complaint in progressive circles inside and outside the State House. Not only was Little Shell a nonnative of Massachusetts, he carries a bow and arrow as a disembodied arm wields a sword above him; the implication, say critics, is that the only good "Indian" is a dead one.

The other most controversial artwork in the State House is probably the giant clock suspended in the magnificent, newly renovated Great Hall. The cavernous hall itself—decorated in tricolored marble and topped by a vaulted skylight—was opened in 1990 for official state functions and receptions. The clock, designed by New York artist R. M. Fischer at a cost of $100,000, was commissioned in 1986. Unfortunately, it arrived at a time when fiscal belt-tightening was *de rigeur* in the Commonwealth—thereby minimizing local appreciation of the clock's unusual postmodern design.

Other than the golden dome, the two symbols most frequently associated with the State House are the pine cone and the Sacred Cod. The pine cone—often mistaken for a pineapple by visitors—is the gilded figure atop the dome. The cone was given this prominent position to remind citizens of the importance of lumbering in the state's economy. Lumbering in Massachusetts may sound an unfamiliar note, until you remember that the current state of Maine was part of Massachusetts until 1820.

The Sacred Cod, suspended in the public gallery above the House of Representatives, is part of a delightful fish story. The four-foot-eleven-and-a-half-inch good-luck Cod is carved from pine, and is older than the State House itself. Though the fish's exact age is unknown, it certainly existed prior to 1784. John Rowe, a well-known Revolutionary-era gentleman—merchant, selectman, representative, activist, and patriot—donated the Cod to the Old State House "as a memorial of the importance of the Cod Fishery to the welfare of this Commonwealth." Rowe himself is memorialized today in the downtown wharf which bears his name. He was remembered by his contemporaries for his actions and ideas—including the suggestion that tea be thrown into Boston Harbor. (Rowe himself was part-owner of one of those Tea Party ships.)

As the House of Representatives moved from the old to the new State House in 1798, the Sacred Cod was carried along. In 1933, the famous fish was carried a bit farther, when members of the Harvard Lampoon cod-napped him. He was stolen again, and found again, in 1968.

Both the House and Senate chambers, located on the third floor of the State House, are beautifully decorated rooms with public galleries and plentiful historic tales. Moreover, modern history is being made in those active chambers today—at least *some* of the time. Meanwhile, there are literally hundreds of other rooms in the State House where business goes on as usual day after day, from offices and storage areas to restrooms, hearing committee rooms, ceremonial and reception halls.

The Sacred Cod, Great Clock, and State Seal are not the only pieces of art in the State House. Quite the contrary; visitors soon discover that the historic building's interior and exterior provide a veritable museum of architecture, painting, sculpture, and odd artifacts. The problem with this museum—not unlike the problem with government and politics—is a dearth of femininity.

The State House's chambers, halls, and beautifully landscaped lawn, for example, are filled with marvelous busts and larger-than-life memorials to men who molded the state's growth. In 1990, a statue of President John F. Kennedy became the newest addition to an array that includes educator Horace Mann, orator Daniel Webster, patriot-governor John Hancock, Supreme Court Justice Louis Brandeis, and—boldly facing the State House from across Beacon Street—the valiant all-black 54th Regiment being led into battle by Robert Gould Shaw during the Civil War. Though the aforementioned all have strong local connections, representations of men less related to Boston history—like Washington, Lincoln, and David and Goliath—also abound.

The State House statue with the shiniest shoes is surely Daniel Chester French's bronze depiction of Governor Roger Wolcott (1897–1900), seated outside the House of Representatives Chamber on the third floor. A woman touched Wolcott's shoe with her lottery ticket in 1976, then reported that she had made a major win the following day. Many people, hearing variations on this urban legend, followed suit—in such numbers that the sparkling gold-toned shoes are now a much lighter shade than the rest of Wolcott.

But where are the women? Inside the State House there is only one, artist Bela Pratt's statue of an anonymous nurse aiding a wounded Civil War soldier. On the front lawn are two statues of brave, powerful seventeenth-century women, Anne Hutchinson and Mary Dyer; the first was banished from Massachusetts for her religious beliefs, the second was hanged for hers.

The halls and chambers of the State House fairly burst with faces and scenes from our past. Portraits of all the Massachusetts governors can be found in the building, mostly hanging about the hallways, with a few notable exceptions. Governor James Michael Curley (1935–37), for example, who frequently served as Boston's mayor as well, is suspended over the fireplace mantel in Governor William Weld's office. When Michael Dukakis held that office, that space was occupied by an image of Governor Samuel Adams (1794–97). Each incumbent governor is encouraged to place his favorite predecessor in that spot.

Among these paintings as well, women are hard to find. A nameless group of sorrowful soldiers' mothers graces one painting, and a beautifully lit image of Eleanor Roosevelt is usually on display outside the House Chamber; the latter is a Polaroid copy of an oil portrait known to be the First Lady's favorite rendering of herself. In addition, women are alluded to in the spread of the "Milestones on the Road to Freedom" murals in the House of Representatives chamber. In one image, Judge Samuel Sewall is seen repenting his part in the 1692 Salem witchcraft trials and regretting the innocent women and men hanged because of this "error."

Throughout the decades, the stunning State House has retained a substantial hold on the city. Nineteenth-century "Boston Brahmin" Oliver Wendell Holmes—who was known to have something to say about virtually everything—called the State House "the hub of the solar system." Over the years, faulty collective memory and overzealous egos have altered his statement to "Boston is the hub of the universe"; Holmes died in 1894, but Bostonians still call their city "the Hub" today.

If Boston is the hub, incidentally, the golden dome must be the hub-cap of the universe. At least mapmakers seem to see it that way. When you're driving along and spot a highway sign that reads, "Boston, 75 miles," the distance is not measured to the city limits or some arbitrary central location; it's the distance in miles to—you guessed it—the dome of the Massachusetts State House.

THE ESSENTIALS

ADDRESS: Main entrance at Beacon and Park streets, Boston. Bounded also by Derne, Bowdoin, and Joy streets.

TELEPHONE: Tour and other information, (617) 727-3676.

VISITOR INFORMATION: Open to the public 9:00 A.M.–5:00 P.M. daily. Free. Free thirty-minute guided tours available 10:00 A.M.–4:00 P.M., Monday–Friday, year-round except holidays. Special topic, foreign language, and group tours available with three weeks' notice. Guidebook translations available in ten languages. Entrances on Mount Vernon and Bowdoin streets are wheelchair accessible; take elevator to second floor.

9 USS *Constitution*

WITH MORE than a million guests each year, "Old Ironsides" is Boston's most frequently visited historical landmark. And with a two-hundredth birthday arriving in 1997, it is also the oldest fully commissioned warship afloat in the world. The ship's official name, of course, is USS *Constitution*.

Whether taking a guided tour of the ship or visiting the newly refurbished USS *Constitution* Museum, many first-time visitors to the Charlestown Navy Yard still inquire about the names. "Why was it named *Constitution*?" After the document, it seems, which was ratified a decade before. "Why did they call the frigate 'Old Ironsides,' when the ship is clearly made of wood?" Answering the latter inquiry takes a bit more explaining.

The nickname originated in the ship's heyday, during the War of 1812. A sailor—Yankee or a British, depending on your historical source—

"Old Ironsides," in the old Charlestown Navy Yard, is Boston's most frequently visited historic landmark.

watched shots from the British warship *Guerriere* bounce off the side planking of *Constitution*. He allegedly exclaimed, "Huzza! Her sides are made of iron!" an understandable error since the ship's wooden sides were painted black and appeared indestructible. The name "Ironsides" stuck. A good thing, incidentally, since *Constitution's* earlier nickname was the comical "Ship of Patches," after its frequently torn sails, which were constantly being stitched back together.

The fact that USS *Constitution* was built at all is somewhat amazing, since the leaders of the newly formed United States didn't even want to have a navy. The Revolution was a vivid but distant memory. The nation had created its first Constitution—the document, that is—and elected its first president. America was happily at peace, while Britannia continued to rule the waves with a proud navy of some 1,500 vessels.

But economic reality was about to alter American complacency. In the early 1790s, Barbary Coast pirates persistently preyed on U.S. merchant ships in the Mediterranean. President George Washington and Congress responded by ordering six frigates to be built in major ports along the eastern coast. From Portsmouth, New Hampshire, to Norfolk, Virginia, construction began on ships respectively named *Constitution, Congress, President, United States, Constellation,* and *Chesapeake*. Though construction was stalled midway (because of the threat of peace!), the ships were eventually built, and the U.S. Navy was born.

Constitution was built in Edmund Hartt's shipyard, where the North End's U.S. Coast Guard Support Center stands today. The design was developed by Joshua Humphreys, who got all the credit, and Josiah Fox, who did not. Colonel George Claghorn was appointed the ship's "constructor," and a masterful job he did. In the words of USS Constitution Museum secretary and historian Leon Kaufman, the ship was deliberately "overbuilt and over-sailed." In essence, that meant that while Constitution was much thicker, heavier, broader, and sturdier than other forty-four-gun warships of the period, it was exceptionally swift as well.

The ship's speed was enhanced by hull lines designed to be as svelte as those of the later clipper ships, and by close to an acre of flaxen sailcloth, spread over thirty-six sails. Its sturdiness came from superior strains of wood. Tall pines—felled in Unity, Maine, then towed to Boston—became the masts. The mainmast was 220 feet high, only a foot shorter than the Bunker Hill Monument. The frame used durable live-oak timbers from Georgia, while the outside was covered with New England white oak.

The omnipresent Paul Revere, who protected our State House dome with copper in 1802, sheathed Constitution's bottom in copper as well. Revere's bill, which covered spikes, rods, and other bronze and copper fastenings, was $3,820.33—a pittance compared to the total construction cost of $302,718.00.

The launching of such a phenomenal frigate should have been marked by festivities and delight. Instead it was plagued with disasters that some superstitious sailors considered bad omens. The launch was initially set for September of 1797, but Constitution quickly jammed as it slipped toward the sea. It wasn't until the ways were adjusted to a steeper incline—and the tide was adequately high—that a successful launching followed, on October 21, 1797. Equally ominous, according to Kaufman, was that Constitution was christened by a man, Captain James Sever. "All ships have been christened by women since Helen of Troy," explains Kaufman, "so many assumed Constitution to be a hard luck ship."

Despite the dubious start, USS Constitution proved more than a match for other nineteenth-century naval vessels. In eighty-four years of service, the heavily armed floating fortress won forty-two battles, captured twenty vessels, was never defeated in battle, and was never boarded by enemy troops save for prisoners of war.

Though her active wartime duties began soon after 1797—first with a quasi war against France in the West Indies, and later with the plundering pirates of the Mediterranean—Constitution earned her undying fame in the War of 1812. The biggest battles are the stuff history classes are made of:

- On August 19, 1812, under the command of Captain Isaac Hull, it had a glorious, victorious mid-Atlantic clash with HMS Guerriere, a captured French warship that became first the pride of Her Majesty's Navy and then the prey of America's expertly run superfrigate.

Throughout 1992 and 1993, USS Constitution *remained open to visitors during its extensive dry-dock and inspection period.*

- On December 29, 1812, under commanding Captain William Bainbridge, *Constitution* defeated the warship HMS *Java*, off the Brazilian coast, only five months after the defeat of *Guerriere*.
- Her last great fight of the war, when *Constitution* outmaneuvered and defeated HMS *Cyane* and HMS *Levant*, was on February 20, 1815, under the command of Captain Charles Stewart.

All of this was astounding, incidentally, since vessels in Her Majesty's Navy were not expected to be beaten in one-on-one encounters with ships of their own class.

War is generally not a laughing matter, but Old Ironsides' sailors did get some amusement during the 1812 battle with *Guerriere*. Leon Kaufman, who has lectured to USS *Constitution* crews on the ship's history for some three decades, explains that the rotund Captain Isaac Hull—said to be the finest sailor the ship ever had—was in charge of the frigate at the time. Officers' breeches in those days were skin tight, and when the fighting captain bent down to yell "Fire!" his pants split and the sailors howled with glee. That didn't prevent them from firing the ship's many stout carronades and long guns on command—and vanquishing *Guerriere* in an astonishing thirty-five minutes.

A less amusing, but equally strange detail of history concerns *Constitution* sailors who died at sea. The dead were stitched up in their sleeping hammocks with thirteen stitches, the last of which went through the seaman's upper lip. The reason, says Kaufman, was to make sure the sailor was really deceased; some illnesses, like epilepsy, can simulate death, and sailors were known to feign death to escape naval duties.

★　★　★

War was certainly not *Constitution*'s only mission, though war tended to dominate its early days. For many years and many long stretches, the ship was laid up in dry dock, awaiting or getting repairs—while serving as a symbolic inspiration to a growing world power. At other times, the active ship was involved in peacetime missions and humanist endeavors.

From 1835 to 1855 in particular, USS *Constitution* was involved in numerous battle-free voyages. One was a spectacular round-the-world journey under the volatile "Mad Jack" Percival, in 1844–45. Pope Pius IX stepped on board when the ship visited Naples in 1849. Today, we're used to pontiffs jet-setting around the globe; in 1849, however, Pius made headlines as the first pope to enter what was technically U.S. territory, the deck of Old Ironsides.

Constitution's last trip abroad was in 1878, when it carried American exhibits to the Paris World Exhibition. The vessel's last trip under the power of its own sails was in 1881—though "assisted" excursions followed, including Captain Gulliver's cruise of major American seaports, which began in 1931.

Old Ironsides saw duty as an antislaving ship from 1852 to 1855. As part of the African Squadron, *Constitution* was supposed to stop the capture of slaves off the West Coast of Africa, but proved no match for the fast, small schooners used as slavers. During a renovation of the ship in 1927, stores of hard-to-find, extremely durable live oak were found stored in Pensacola, Florida. The precious timber had been cut by the U.S. Navy in 1856, using slave labor, then left unused and forgotten. Hence, wood cut by slaves was used to refurbish an antislaving vessel.

It's impossible to give an exact figure, but no more than 18 percent of the wood on the ship we visit today is the original 1797 fabric. Almost two centuries of periodic renovation and repair have left few of the frigate's initial wooden or metal parts intact. Surprisingly, the few vestiges left of the old structure are probably under, not over, the water line. Briny seawater is a superb preservative, while fresh water and man-made acid rain will both quickly rot a ship. Part of the preservation process for *Constitution* once included packing salt between the vessel's ribs so that any fresh rainwater seeping in became a saline solution. This practice was stopped on the frigate after the 1970s, however, when the salt began to solidify and lose its effectiveness.

While preserving Old Ironsides for posterity seems imperative today, that sentiment wasn't always held. Some insiders have even half-kidded that *Constitution* defended the country more than the country defended *Constitution*. As early as 1830, less than two decades after its victories in the War of 1812, the first talk of scrapping the ship began. It was Oliver Wendell Holmes, Sr., a Harvard student at the time, who first came to the rescue. Though the decision to save the ship had reportedly already been made, Holmes stirred up popular support for the project when he published his famous poem "Old Ironsides" in 1830. Money was soon found, and refurbishing begun.

The next time the ship was in financial danger, in 1897, Representative John F. Fitzgerald—President Kennedy's maternal grandfather and later mayor of Boston—successfully lobbied Congress for repairs. Still, USS *Constitution* needed even more work to survive another century. By 1905, some had suggested Old Ironsides be used for naval target practice out at sea. The public protested again, and Congress appropriated $100,000 for more repairs.

The cycle was repeated in the late 1920s, when the ship's condition looked hopeless once more. This time, kids across America collected pennies and nickels in a people's campaign to save the ship. Ordinary citizens collected most of the money, while Congress made up the difference. The repair bill ran close to a million dollars.

Today the U.S. Navy has assumed full responsibility for the frigate, including all repair work. The last significant repair period was completed for the American Bicentennial in 1976. In 1992–93, minor repairs and an inspection were made in preparation for the two-hundredth anniversary of the ship's launching, October 21, 1997. For the first time in history, USS *Constitution* was open to visitors while under repair, during this recent dry-dock and inspection period. The next major overhaul is planned for the late 1990s, following the ship's own bicentennial bash.

Old Ironsides itself is open 365 days a year, and the forty-five-minute guided tours—given by friendly, eloquent sailors dressed in 1812 uniforms—are among the most interesting and informative given at any historical landmark. The nearby USS *Constitution* Museum is also a must-see. Housed in a renovated 1832 pump house and opened in 1976, it offers a broad glimpse of American life and culture in the Federal period. Throughout the year, teacher workshops, lecture series, living history programs, and guided tours for school groups are part of the museum's ambitious activities.

Thanks to a major renovation during the 1991–92 year, the museum now excels at visually demonstrating just how *Constitution* was constructed and sailed. Its hands-on displays are wonderful ways to understand sailing life at the turn of the nineteenth century. Equally wonderful is the museum's friendly, well-informed "living exhibit," model-ship builder Bill Bromell, who constructs meticulously detailed wooden ships in his shop while gladly answering questions for visitors.

Though folks come to see it every day of the year, Old Ironsides certainly gets its biggest photo opportunity every Independence Day. Since 1975, visitors have flocked to watch its gala July 4 "turnarounds" in Boston Harbor. These jaunts are not just pomp and circumstance, mind you. The turn rotates the ship's pier-side position 180 degrees, so that the elements wear on it evenly. Since *Constitution* hasn't been able to sail under its own power for eons, the ship is escorted by a tugboat.

Under normal circumstances, the tug could easily charge $2,000 a trip. The winning tugboat-bidder, however, usually charges in the neighborhood of one cent. How often do you get to tow a 204-foot-long national treasure?

THE ESSENTIALS

ADDRESS: Charlestown Navy Yard, Charlestown, Boston.

TELEPHONE: Boston National Historical Park, (617) 242-5601; Ship, (617) 242-5670; Museum, (617) 426-1812.

VISITOR INFORMATION: Ship open 9:30 A.M.–sunset daily. Free. Free guided tours, 9:30 A.M.–3:50 P.M. daily; self-guided tours, 3:50 P.M.–sunset daily. USS *Constitution* Museum, located across the yard, open 9:00 A.M.–6:00 P.M. daily in summer; 9:00 A.M.–5:00 P.M. daily in spring and fall; 10:00 A.M.–4:00 P.M. daily in winter. Small admission fee. Ship is not wheelchair accessible, though accessible walkways are available alongside; the museum is accessible, with entrance at rear. A full video "tour" of interior of ship can be seen in the museum.

10 The Freedom Trail

FROM A purely business perspective, its credentials are impressive: it's known as Boston's second most popular tourist attraction and one of the most innovative concepts designed in the history of American tourism. Most of its day-to-day fans are oblivious to such economic considerations—and simply know that Boston's popular Freedom Trail is red, revolutionary, and three miles long.

The *red* part is a long, thin line: a stretch of inlaid bricks and overlaid paint that meanders down select Boston sidewalks, and is spruced up twice a year by the Boston Department of Public Works.

The *revolutionary* aspect involves the sixteen sites linked by that line: from simple ground markers, eerie graveyards, and lofty old churches to majestic buildings, a rambling park, and a sturdy old naval frigate. In theory, at least, each of these historic landmarks played a significant role in America's rebellious beginnings.

Though *three miles* sounds intimidating at first, it's really not. Yes, the full Freedom Trail does connect downtown Boston to the North End, then goes on to the Charlestown Navy Yard and the Bunker Hill Monument. While that seems like something of a hike for inexperienced walkers, the overview of Boston history is well worth the effort. The trail itself— overseen at various points by National Park Service rangers, city rangers, U.S. Navy officers, site personnel, and plenty of tourists—is one of the safest strolls around. Moreover, you can walk any single portion of the three-mile strip you'd like. Three to four million people do just that each year.

Perhaps the best thing about the Freedom Trail is that it can be an inexpensive and entertaining educational experience for all ages; free self-

National Park Service rangers interpret the statue at Paul Revere Mall, in the North End loop of the Freedom Trail.

guiding maps are available, as are tours by National Park Service interpreters. Guidebooks are available in area stores, and private tours—like those given by Boston by Foot, which emphasizes architectural history—offer visitors other perspectives.

In some ways, the Freedom Trail is as old as Boston itself. The Common, for example, was marked off in 1634, only four years after the town was founded. A year later, Boston opened its first public school. By 1661, the town boasted three urban burial grounds, followed by numerous churches, homes, meetinghouses, and public buildings. Many disappeared with time. But others survived—and played a role in the start of the American Revolution.

Though the sites were there for centuries, it wasn't until 1951 that *Boston Herald-Traveler* journalist William Schofield offered his own "revolutionary twist" to these landmarks. In several editorials, Schofield noted that Boston had an unusual concentration of sites sacred to our nation's beginnings, but tourists often visited just two or three of these spots and missed the full story. Since so many of these landmarks were located within easy walking distance of one another, Schofield concluded, why not "connect the dots" with a walking tour—and call it the Freedom Trail?

Boston Mayor John B. Hynes picked up on Schofield's challenge, and the trail took shape. At first it was little more than a series of painted plywood markers. By 1953, forty thousand people were walking the Freedom Trail each year, so the city commissioned sturdier metal signs in their stead.

Under the care and guidance of local businessman and philanthropist Richard Berenson (1909–1990), the trail began to mature through the late fifties and sixties. As is still true today, Berenson and his colleagues' successes with the trail were the result of cooperative efforts between the public and private sectors.

In 1958, the Advertising Club of Greater Boston and the Greater Boston Chamber of Commerce were persuaded to adopt the trail as a permanent joint community service project. The John Hancock Insurance Company agreed to donate $10,000 for the first brochures. Businesspeople and bankers made charitable contributions. The city agreed to lay the paint-and-brick line. And the Freedom Trail Committee—which later became the Freedom Trail Foundation—was established, with Berenson as its chair.

By 1966, the first Freedom Trail information center was opened on the Common, distributing maps to the half-million visitors who were then annually taking the trail. Among that period's most unusual Freedom Trail fund-raising efforts was a 1967 bean-eating benefit, sponsored by the Boston Rotary Club. Some twenty-two thousand people paid $25,000 to eat nine tons of Boston baked beans, serenaded by an eleven-piece banjo band and veteran local TV personality Rex Trailer.

"Boston's Freedom Trail is unique in that it is probably the only do-it-yourself tour in the world that actually works," wrote a local columnist in the early 1970s, punctuating his statement with a tentative "Well, maybe!" Despite all the Freedom Trail's successes and support, all was not yet perfect.

Public toilets were rare, and tourists sometimes got lost. People argued about which sites were appropriate for the revolutionary route. The modern Boston surrounding the sites was a mess, as it moved from disrepair to citywide rebuilding projects. Several of the sites were closed on Sundays, and all had different visiting hours.

For better or for worse, the sixteen participating sites were, and still are, a mix of city, state, and federally owned units, along with buildings belonging to or managed by various churches, private nonprofits, and historic associations. Some of the sites' personnel and managers proved less cooperative than others in dealing with the groups created to oversee the trail. The Chamber of Commerce, the Advertising Club, and the original Freedom Trail Committee eventually assumed lower profiles, and they were replaced by today's maze of committees: the Freedom Trail Foundation, specializing in fund-raising and development projects; the city's Freedom Trail Commission, which oversees physical maintenance and policy making; the Council of Freedom Trail Sites, providing a forum for voices from each of the independently run sites; and the Greater Boston Convention and Visitors Bureau.

In 1974, thanks to the persistence and vision of Berenson, U.S. Congressman Joseph Moakley and others, yet another group joined the fray.

Boston National Historical Park, run by the National Park Service, was established. Today, the Park Service and its rangers are the most visible presence along the trail. The National Park Service Visitor Center, at 15 State Street, is a full-service resource for tourists, offering free maps, a bookstore, restrooms, and a dozen guided "Heart of the Freedom Trail" tours each day during the summer. The Park Service works cooperatively with several of the sites, and has helped procure millions of dollars in federal funding to revamp decaying historic structures. The Park Service also participates in active school programs with cooperative sites, like the popular "Tea Is Brewing" and "People and Places"—the latter geared to the fourth-grade curriculum in the Boston public schools.

"Without the National Park Service," says Warren Berg, vice-chairman of the Freedom Trail Foundation, "there would be no Freedom Trail. They make the whole greater than the sum of its parts."

Opinions vary as to the best way to walk the Freedom Trail. Some people enjoy looking at just the outside of each of the sixteen sites—which allows them to complete the trail in two or three hours. Others prefer to linger inside each structure, making the excursion last a full day or more. Guided tours, for the most part, tend to be ninety-minute "samplers" of specific portions of the trail.

Where's the best place to start? It depends. Many people begin at the Common, and end at "Old Ironsides"—an order followed by most guide-books. Others reverse the route, since parking is easier in Charlestown and the last tour group enters the ship at 3:50 P.M.; so if you make USS *Constitution* the last stop of the day, you might just miss the boat.

There are other approaches. Folks who come to the Boston National Historical Park Visitor Center for tours may begin at the nearby Old South Meeting House or the Old State House. Boston by Foot tours, on the other hand, often depart from the statue of Samuel Adams behind Faneuil Hall. Because the sites are not in chronological order, the starting point is immaterial from a historical point of view.

With all that in mind, here's a brief synopsis of the sixteen official sites. Many of them offer self-guided or interpreter-guided tours or talks inside. Small admission fees are charged at the Old South Meeting House, the Old State House, the Paul Revere House, and USS *Constitution* Museum. The others are either free or ask for optional donations.

The forty-eight-acre **Boston Common** is America's oldest green. Purchased in 1634 as common land for Boston's townspeople, it initially served as a cow pasture, military training field, and public hanging site. During the Revolution, British regulars camped there and trained there—and were buried there after the disastrous Battle of Bunker Hill.

The majestic, gold-domed "new" **Massachusetts State House** opened in 1798. Designed by the celebrated Boston architect Charles Bulfinch, its contents include the Sacred Cod and refurbished Hall of Flags.

The striking, white-steepled **Park Street Church,** built in 1809, stands on "Brimstone Corner"—which alludes to both the fiery sermons heard inside and the gunpowder once stored below. It was there that William Lloyd Garrison gave his first antislavery address and the song "America" was first performed.

Next door is the **Granary Burying Ground,** named for a huge grain-storage building that once fed the poor near this site. It's now an outdoor museum of funerary folk art and a veritable Who's Who of Revolutionary-era names, including Paul Revere, John Hancock, Samuel Adams, and the victims of the Boston Massacre.

When Paul Revere died in 1818, his demise was tolled by the "passing bell" at **King's Chapel.** The bell itself had been recast by Revere's own foundry in 1816, a sweet-sounding addition to this 1754 stone chapel. Built as New England's first Anglican church, and once the house of worship of choice for royal governors, King's Chapel became America's first Unitarian church after the Revolution.

The adjacent **King's Chapel Burying Ground** is filled with feisty seventeenth-century Puritans, who surely turned in their graves when the Anglicans set up shop next door. Despite the confusing similarity of their names, these two sites are unrelated.

On the sidewalk behind King's Chapel is the site of another "American first"—the colonial precursor to the famous Boston Latin School. Marked by a folk-art mosaic, the memorial to the **First Public School** rests near the bronze statue of its most illustrious dropout, Ben Franklin.

Farther down School Street is the **Old Corner Bookstore,** now, appropriately enough, a modern bookshop. Built in 1718 as an apothecary, it gained renown in the nineteenth century as a magnet for esteemed authors like Ralph Waldo Emerson, Henry Wadsworth Longfellow, Nathaniel Hawthorne, and Harriet Beecher Stowe.

Near the bookstore stands the **Old South Meeting House,** where several thousand rowdy revolutionaries assembled before descending to Griffin's Wharf for the Boston Tea Party in December of 1773. Despite centuries of wear and tear—including its conversion by British soldiers into a horse stable and riding school during the Revolution—the Old South has survived.

The newly renovated **Old State House,** built in 1713, was the first seat of the Massachusetts state government. Colonial patriot James Otis argued against the Writs of Assistance there, and the Declaration of Independence was first read to Bostonians from its balcony.

Below the balcony of the Old State House lies the trail's most treacherous stop, the **Boston Massacre Site.** A circle of stones on a traffic island marks the place where British regulars fired on a snowball-hurling colonial mob, killing five colonists. Sam Adams blatantly exploited the incident to fan revolutionary flames.

Across State Street and a short walk down Congress Street lies **Faneuil Hall.** Recently renovated and reopened in 1992, the 1742 building has long been known as the Cradle of Liberty—and as America's foremost historic meeting, market, and military hall.

From the Faneuil Hall Marketplace area—an extremely popular complex of shops, cafes, and quality fast-food stands—the trail loops under the elevated Central Artery to the North End, toward the **Paul Revere House.** Built in 1680, it's the oldest building in Boston, and the place where Revere lived when he made his famous ride of April 18, 1775. From the steeple of the Episcopalian **Old North Church,** the city's oldest standing house of worship, sexton Robert Newman hung two lanterns that same night, warning Charlestown citizens that the British were approaching Concord "by sea."

The North End's **Copp's Hill Burying Ground** was a final resting place for colonists, which irreverent redcoats used as target-practice site, cannon emplacement, and lookout. Across the harbor, in Charlestown, stands the soaring obelisk commemorating the Battle of Bunker Hill. Though it rests on Breed's Hill, where the battle was fought, it's called the **Bunker Hill Monument.**

In the nearby Charlestown Navy Yard, which was decommissioned in 1974, floats the Freedom Trail's most visited site, the mammoth USS *Constitution,* as well as the privately run USS *Constitution* Museum. Built in 1797, Old Ironsides won battles against the Barbary pirates, and against the British in the War of 1812. The recently redesigned museum is a perfect complement to a visit aboard the ship.

Despite four decades of improvement and change, the Freedom Trail is not yet perfect. A basic problem has always been the lack of a single agency to oversee the trail and all the sites on it. Not only is there no desk marked "The Buck Stops Here," there's no buck—no annual city budget, no endowment fund, and no large financial source to pay for major improvements.

Among the improvements needed are more restrooms—especially in the North End—and more explicit, perhaps multilingual, signs. Wheelchair access is still erratic, and road renovations can often create glitches along the way. A comprehensive urban design study would enable better planning of revitalization efforts. And a new, more modern visitor center—one that employed multimedia audiovisual presentations and other new technology to illustrate Boston history—would help enhance the Freedom Trail experience.

"The Freedom Trail remains a resource that deserves more recognition," says John Burchill, superintendent of Boston National Historical Park. Whether that's a threat or a promise, it bodes well for Boston's historic future.

THE ESSENTIALS

ADDRESS: Three-mile red line begins on Boston Common, ends at the Navy Yard and Bunker Hill Monument in Charlestown.

TELEPHONE: Boston National Historical Park Visitor Center, (617) 242-5642; Greater Boston Convention and Visitors Bureau, (617) 536-4100.

VISITOR INFORMATION: Trail itself always there for self-guided walking tours. National Park Service offers free maps, and free daily ninety-minute tours, from April through November, starting at Boston National Historical Park Visitor Center, 15 State Street, Boston. Maps and information also available at Greater Boston Convention and Visitors Bureau information kiosk near the Park Street subway station on Boston Common. Freedom Trail sites open roughly 9:00 A.M.–5:00 P.M. in summer. Admission to most sites free; some have nominal fees. Trail fairly wheelchair accessible if curb cuts not blocked; minor rerouting necessary in the North End; all Freedom Trail sites are at least partially accessible, some with assistance; Visitor Center has wheelchair-accessible restrooms.

From Here to Eternity: Houses of Worship and Homes for the Dead

*I*N THE eighteenth century, during the stormy years that preceded the Revolutionary War, Boston gained a reputation as a center of political sedition. Just a century before, however, the same town was known for its religious repression—a product, pure and simple, of the Puritan presence.

When the Puritans of the Massachusetts Bay Colony first settled Boston in 1630, they were seeking religious freedom. Liberated from the shackles of the Church of England, the colonists began establishing their own houses of worship. Unfortunately, they also created a Puritan theocracy as intolerant as the Anglican society from which they had fled. Their meetinghouses—used for both town and church matters—were created in a simple, stark fashion, rather than the ornate architectural styles associated with Anglicanism and Roman Catholicism. Harvard College, founded in Cambridge in 1636, was intended to train the colony's ministers. Boston Latin School, today a public school for academically outstanding high school students, prepared young men to go to Harvard.

Meanwhile, church attendance was mandatory, sermons were long, and burial was an altogether unholy affair. Throughout the colonial period, corpses were buried in dismal downtown graveyards like King's Chapel, Copp's Hill, and the Granary. Not until 1831, with the advent of Mount Auburn Cemetery in Cambridge, were burial grounds designed as centers of eternal peace and bucolic calm.

As various groups of Puritans broke off to colonize other areas around Boston, their first order of business was building a meetinghouse. That house immediately became the First Church—like the First Church in Roxbury, begun in 1632—a naming practice which ultimately created a plethora of "First Churches" throughout New England. When schisms within a particular church occurred, groups would create Second and Third churches. The dissident Third Church of Christ, for example, broke from Boston's original First Church over a theological issue known as "the halfway covenant." They established their own independent meetinghouse in 1669, and by 1729 built the structure still known and loved today as the Old South Meeting House.

Some dissidents came from within the church. Anne Hutchinson preached a "covenant of grace" and the equality of men's and women's souls. For these heresies she was banished to Rhode Island (see Chapter 26). Some dissidents came from outside the church. If they appeared to accept the Puritan faith, as did the "praying Indians" of "apostle" John Eliot, their lives might be saved; if they refused to convert, however, they might be hanged on Boston Common. Such was the tragic fate of Quaker Mary Dyer, as well as countless Native Americans, supposed witches, pirates, and other so-called infidels.

Despite that early Puritan stranglehold, other religious groups filtered into Boston and eventually prospered. By 1685, much of the town was either Congregational (the later generations' name for Puritan), Baptist, or Quaker. By 1688, even the Anglican church had gotten its first real foothold in the Hub. The original King's Chapel was built on the corner of School and Tremont streets, displacing part of the town's first Puritan graveyard. The rapidly growing Anglican congregation of King's Chapel spawned two more of Boston's most cherished churches as well. In 1723, their parishioners helped build Christ Church in the North End—today popularly known as the Old North Church. In 1733, a third Anglican church, called Trinity, absorbed the next overflow. That building was the granddaddy of the magnificent 1877 Trinity Church which graces Copley Square to this day.

The last great change for these churches began near the end of the eighteenth century—and was partly inspired by ideals unleashed in the Revolution. In 1785, under the guidance of the Reverend James Freeman, the Anglican King's Chapel became the first official Unitarian church in America. Buoyed by the popular liberal preachings of William Ellery Channing, Unitarianism swept through New England, which explains in part why so many structures built as Puritan churches are Unitarian-Universalist today.

Meanwhile, Boston's rapidly growing community of free blacks was asserting its independence as well. African-Americans had always been allowed in white churches, but only tucked away in the back galleries, out of sight of both congregation and preacher. By the early nineteenth century, this too began to change. Free Boston blacks built their own African Meeting House in 1806. Today it's the oldest standing black church in the nation. Other African-American citizens joined their white comrades in protesting segregated churches like the Charles Street Meeting House, which was eventually purchased by a Black Baptist congregation (see Part 5, "The Many Faces of Boston," for these and related stories).

Boston churches and their congregations changed hands, shape, styles, and neighborhoods throughout the nineteenth and twentieth centuries. The influx of Irish immigrants in the mid-nineteenth century, for example, created numerous Catholic churches, while newly arriving German and Eastern European Jews built or adapted synagogues near their new homes (see Chapter 39 on the Vilna Shul). Old houses of worship sometimes succumbed to one of Boston's periodic "Great Fires," or adapted to different uses as their congregations moved to larger structures in more fashionable, and more convenient, parts of town.

The end result for Boston? A mosaic of engaging structures and sites with an endless stream of tales, both secular and religious, to share.

11 The First Church in Roxbury

STANDING ATOP a lightly wooded hill overlooking John Eliot Square, the First Church in Roxbury is a stunning sight. Prim, grand, and gracious—and guarding an enviable panoramic view of Boston proper—the white clapboard meetinghouse looks like the quintessential New England village church.

It *is*, in fact, just that. But the First Church in Roxbury also boasts an unusually distinguished past. Dating back to 1631, it is the third-oldest congregation in the present-day city of Boston. And though four previous church buildings stood on this site, the 1804 structure we see today is the Hub's oldest wooden-frame church. John Eliot, famous for his ministry to the "Indians," preached and taught here, in one of the building's more primitive incarnations. William Dawes began his own famous "midnight ride" here, to warn patriots that the British were coming, while Paul Revere made a parallel ride from Charlestown. Revere himself left his mark here, in the form of a huge church bell cast in his family's Canton foundry. That bell still hangs in the belfry—as impressive an ornament as the church's Simon Willard clock and Hook & Hastings organ.

Only the best was good enough for Roxbury's very first church.

The first people to come to the First Church were the Puritans of the Massachusetts Bay Colony, who arrived on the eastern shores of Massachusetts in 1630. In the course of the first year, small groups broke away from this core, dispersing into seven distinct communities. On the north shore they had already founded Salem, and on the south, Dorchester. In between were the Puritan settlements of Boston, Medford, Charlestown, Watertown, and Roxbury.

William Pynchon led one such group into the craggy land on the neck of the Boston peninsula. Because of the hilly uplands, ledges, and the distinctive textured rock they called puddingstone, the settlers named their town Rocksbrough, also spelled Rocksborough, or Rocksbury. The town, incorporated on September 28, 1630, included 10,686 acres. The town center developed in a small area of high ground at modern John Eliot Square. Since a meetinghouse was essential to Puritan life—providing a space for both town and church matters—and since church attendance was mandatory, work on the first First Church building began immediately.

Though records on this period are few, historians believe that the original meetinghouse, completed in 1632, was a simple log cabin with a thatched roof and clay floors. The first pastor was the Reverend Thomas

The community-centered First Church in Roxbury looks like the quintessential New England village church.

Weld, an English university graduate descended from an ancient Saxon family, and an ancestor of William Weld, who became governor of Massachusetts more than three and a half centuries later.

Known to his Roxbury flock as "a painful preacher"—then a term of respect—Weld helped to edit the original *Bay Psalm Book,* the colonies' first collection of metrical versions of the psalms, which became more popular than any other English psalter. He was also a member of the first board of overseers at Harvard College, founded in 1636. Less laudable from a modern perspective is the fact that Weld took active part in the 1637 sedition trial of Anne Hutchinson; as a result of her "unorthodox" religious views and these subsequent trials, Hutchinson was banished from the Commonwealth. The large Weld family also owned slaves, as did other rich, seventeenth-century Roxbury landowners like the Dudleys and the Williamses.

In less than a decade, the Reverend Weld returned to England, eventually becoming chaplain to Oliver Cromwell.

The most famous preacher to emerge from the First Church was Weld's colleague and successor, John Eliot (1604–1690), long remembered as the saintly "apostle to the Indians." Eliot worked alongside Weld as church teacher and editor of the *Bay Psalm Book,* then stayed with the First Church for fifty years after Weld's departure. In 1645 he helped establish the "Free Schoole in Roxburie," later known as the Roxbury Latin School.

Unlike most of his contemporaries, Eliot believed that New England's Native Americans were people—people who could and should share the Puritan gospel and covenant. One of his rationales may seem curious today: Eliot believed these natives were part of the Lost Tribes of Israel, and that their language included traces of Hebrew, the true tongue of God.

In a day and age when many Puritans thought nothing of killing or enslaving American Indians—or hanging Quakers simply because of their beliefs—Eliot's mission, begun in 1646, was clearly radical. He learned the native language, taught many Native Americans the English alphabet, translated the Bible into Algonquin, and began setting up communities for Christian Native Americans. The first such town was founded in Natick in 1651, and the second at Ponkapoag, on the modern site of Ponkapoag Golf Course in the Blue Hills Reservation.

Today we realize that imposing the white man's culture and religion on these Native Americans showed a cruel lack of respect and recognition for their culture. In Eliot's world, however, it was an earnest attempt to civilize and save "the heathens." John Eliot has been memorialized in the area in a variety of ways, including Eliot Square, Eliot Street, Eliot Hall, and the Eliot School in Jamaica Plain. His remains were buried in what's now known as the Eliot Burying Ground, on the corner of Washington and Eustis streets in Roxbury.

One interesting footnote to the Eliot story: According to historian Samuel Eliot Morison, the "Indian Bible" had trouble with words or concepts for which there was no Algonquin equivalent. For instance, apparently the native word for "virgin" was little-known and little-used, hence wherever that word appeared in the text, Eliot translated it using a more common Algonquin term that meant "a chaste young man."

During Eliot's tenure at the First Church in Roxbury, the congregation outgrew its first structure and built a bigger one, in 1674. This second house was razed in 1741 and replaced by an even larger, more elegant church building. Throughout this period, the First Church maintained its role as both civic center and religious meetinghouse. Therefore it was not unusual that the third First Church stored grain in its loft and gunpowder in the roof beams and steeple. That gunpowder led to disaster when, in 1743, a footwarming stove in one of the pews set the church ablaze only two years after it was built.

The fourth First Church emerged from the rubble in 1746, and survived the rigors of the Revolution—despite a cannonball that blasted through its belfry during the siege of Boston. In 1803, that sturdy structure was torn down, and its timber sold for $600, so that the beautiful white Federal-style building we know today could be built. Many irate parishioners complained of the decision to build yet another First Church when the last one was still sound. One mused in his diary, "Whether every generation grows wiser or not, it is evident they grow more fashionable and extravagant."

This fifth and present meetinghouse, dedicated June 7, 1804, was unarguably both fashionable and extravagant. The design was adapted from

Timothy Palmer's First Unitarian Church in Newburyport; architect William Blaney oversaw the Roxbury construction. Built on mortared rubble stone and granite, the structure was braced with heavy timber walls covered with wooden clapboard. The classical front entrance had finely arched doorways and a beautiful Palladian window. Directly above, a storied steeple rose in five sections, from clock tower to belfry, attic to dish-cover dome, finally ending in a swallowtail-banner weather vane. One reviewer called it "a virtual museum of Federalist architecture and antique decorative art." And that was true, both inside and out.

The interior was more ornate than the Newburyport meetinghouse on which it was based. It included multiple columns, white box pews with mahogany armrests, and a curved symmetrical pair of stairs leading to either side of the gallery. Among the furnishings were a grand chandelier, the Paul Revere bell, and two clocks designed by the famous clockmaker Simon Willard. Though the interior underwent major remodelings in 1835, 1857, and 1888, the exterior has remained essentially unchanged.

In 1876, a modest parish house, Putnam Chapel, was built behind the white clapboard church. Though most of that building's historical elements were lost in a devastating 1983 fire, the Parish House is still the center of First Church daily activities.

For more than 360 years, the five different structures that have housed the First Church in Roxbury have been a living stage for the play of Boston history. In the seventeenth century, the acts included preaching Christianity to the Native Americans, creating the *Bay Psalm Book* and the "Indian Bible," establishing America's first Protestant Sunday school, and helping to build centers of education like Roxbury Latin School and Harvard College.

During the eighteenth century, First Church naturally became a stage for scenes from the War for Independence. As noted earlier, William Dawes began his famous ride there. Moreover, because of its elevated location and unencumbered view of nearby Boston, Eliot Square was frequently used for militia training and musters after 1762.

Patriot general John Thomas, who commanded the First Brigade, under Major-General Artemus Ward, made his headquarters at the Dillaway-Thomas House, across Roxbury Street on Eliot Square. The grounds and meetinghouse of the First Church itself were occupied by patriot troops. To help minimize the inevitable devastation—which reached its height during the eleven-month British siege of Boston—the First Church parish committee removed the pews and the bell. As it happened, British cannonballs periodically punctured the church, the area in and near John Eliot Square was severely damaged, and many of Roxbury's woodlands were cut for firewood.

As the nineteenth century and the new republic dawned, so too did theological reforms. The Congregational church of colonial days declined—mired as it was in Puritan severity and Calvinist conservatism—while the liberal ideas of William Ellery Channing and the Unitarian movement found increasing favor with Boston churchgoers. This movement eventually transformed Protestant religion in New England, and the Reverend Eliphalet Porter quietly steered Roxbury's First Church through the first and roughest periods. Today, the First Church embraces Unitarian

Universalism, and its congregation includes members who are black and white, gay and straight, old and young, female and male, and from a variety of ethnic backgrounds and economic classes.

Recent decades have seen equal doses of sorrow and joy at Roxbury's aging First Church. In 1954, Hurricane Carol tore off the church's bell tower. Meanwhile, congregations declined, neighborhoods changed, tensions rose, and internal problems hurt the church. The area was victimized by vandalism and arson. Between 1978 and 1983 alone, three major fires ravaged Eliot Square. As a result, Putnam Chapel was gutted, the meeting-house suffered major water damage, and the famous Hook & Hastings organ, purchased in 1883, was rendered inoperable.

Happily, a 1990 matching grant from the Massachusetts Historical Commission's Preservation Projects Fund has helped fund $170,000 worth of exterior rehabilitation. Funds were also raised to minimally refurbish the chapel. And while it would take $150,000 to fully restore the organ, enough money has already been collected to make it playable.

One item that has survived intact it is the Simon Willard wall clock which was hung in the church in 1806. Although the clock now in the gallery is actually a replica of the original, the switch was not the result of vandalism or fire; in 1970 the rare original was moved to the Willard Clock Museum in Grafton, Massachusetts, where it may be viewed today.

Inside the church and in the chapel next door, much work remains to be done: paint is peeling; fabrics are frayed; access ramps need to be built. Despite its condition, "the community likes the building," explains the Reverend Elizabeth Ellis-Hagler, senior minister at large and executive director of the Unitarian Universalist Urban Ministry. "It's a symbol for beautiful things."

So bit by bit, with help from parishioners and friends, grants, donations, and rental fees, the work will be done. Meanwhile, the First Church's first priority is building and sustaining a community of faith and action. Its staff reaches out to community youth and helps develop programs like the "We Care Committee." Members of Alcoholics and Narcotics Anonymous regularly meet in Putnam Chapel, and celebrate "sober dances" on Friday nights. Special programs include three full-time outreach programs for youth, plus community speak-outs, AIDS healing services, and benefit concerts by the likes of Pete Seeger, Jane Sapp, and Odetta.

"The events here that are most sacred to me are ones meant for people who don't have a place, to have a place to come to," says Ellis-Hagler. "First Church is only important as it is filled with people."

THE ESSENTIALS

ADDRESS: John Eliot Square, Roxbury, Boston; bounded by Dudley, Roxbury, and Putnam streets.

TELEPHONE: (617) 445-8393.

VISITOR INFORMATION: Church open for services, late spring through early fall, and special events; call for details. Free, except for ticketed events which charge admission. Occasional tours given; call for information. Parish House open Monday–Friday, 8:30 A.M.–4:30 P.M.; also open evenings for youth outreach programs. No easy wheelchair access in church or upper hall of chapel; access plans currently being developed.

12 King's Chapel

MAYBE GEORGE Washington slept here. Then again, maybe not. But it really doesn't matter—since so many *other* historically significant events have taken place within King's Chapel's dark granite walls.

For starters, the downtown chapel with the "sawed-off" steeple is an architectural wonder. Built in 1754—around and on top of its congregation's previous church—King's Chapel was based on a "mail order" design and crafted with the first granite dug from the not-yet-famous Quincy quarries. Its original organ was the first to be permanently installed in a church in British America, while the chapel's exceptional musical programs included the American debut of Handel's *Messiah*. The building served as the first Anglican church in New England and later as the first Unitarian church in America (explaining, in part, the church's unique formal liturgy and its Unitarian-Universalist congregation's continued use of the Anglican-based *Book of Common Prayer*).

Tucked away in its subterranean chambers are the tombs of a multitude of colonial souls, while upstairs, King's Chapel's religious services have inspired and consoled a broad spectrum of humanity, including British redcoats, plundering pirates, Boston Brahmins, repentant prisoners on their way to the hangman's noose, and a host of everyday people. Throughout it all, the chapel's chiming bells—especially the sweet-sounding one recast by Paul Revere in 1816—have tolled the ends of major wars and the deaths of prestigious leaders.

As for George Washington, who knows if he dozed off here? He did come to a concert at the chapel in 1789, and sat in the eminently comfortable, regally decorated, boxed-off Governor's Pew. "And his sleeping here," muses longtime church member Dr. Rudolph Toch, "I infer by the circumstances!"

You can find King's Chapel on the corner of Tremont and School streets. It's interesting to note that the story of King's Chapel—and, in many ways, the story of colonial Boston—actually begins with those three simple words: King's, Tremont, and School.

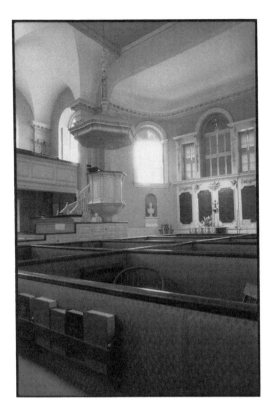

Beautiful King's Chapel was New England's first Anglican and, later, America's first Unitarian house of worship.

Tremont, for example, is a contraction of Trimountain, or three mountains. When the Puritans of the Massachusetts Bay Colony arrived in Boston in 1630—escaping, among other things, the oppressive "popery" of the Church of England—they found a pear-shaped peninsula with a distinctive mountain ridge running through its center. Three hills made up this ridge, individually known as Pemberton Hill, Mount Vernon, and Beacon Hill, and collectively known as the Trimountain. The colonists called their peninsula Trimountain for a brief period before changing its name to Boston. As for the three hills, Beacon was eventually pared down some sixty feet and used for landfill in Boston's mudflats, while the other two disappeared altogether.

School Street, once called Latin School Street, was named for Boston's—as well as America's—first public school, built in 1645; it's commemorated by a folk-art memorial set in the sidewalk behind King's Chapel. When the original small wooden chapel was replaced by today's larger stone structure, its congregation literally snatched land away from the Latin School property. In return for this land, King's Chapel built the displaced school a new home where the Parker House hotel stands today. (Boston Latin School still exists; its current home is in the Fenway.) Among the Latin School's alumni were Samuel Adams and John Hancock, men who would eventually rebel against English sovereignty in the colonies.

The name King's Chapel comes from the British monarch James II (not, as a visiting child once surmised, from Martin Luther King, Jr.). It was during James II's brief reign (1685–89) that Britain began tightening its control over the American colonies. Part of that crackdown meant building a church for loyal Anglicans living in Boston—a group which included royal governors, British soldiers, and certain local merchants.

It was difficult for King James and his Boston emissaries to buy land for the Anglican church, especially since those emissaries were the despised Royal Governor Edmund Andros and the detested Reverend Robert Ratcliffe, Boston's first Anglican minister. The Puritans, as noted earlier, had deliberately left the Church of England six decades before, and their descendants were understandably loath to sell precious downtown Boston real estate to support an Anglican establishment.

Rather than face failure, the resourceful Governor Andros expropriated a prime parcel of land at the intersection of Tremont and School streets. The land was already in use—as a burying ground owned by the city. Perhaps assuming that it would be easier to dislodge the dead than the living, the governor seized the land by eminent domain. By 1688, many of the dead were presumably reinterred elsewhere, and the original King's Chapel built on part of that site. The portion of the burying ground that remained, incidentally, is still owned by the city (and legally unconnected to the adjacent King's Chapel). An ironic twist, since the Puritan men, women, and children interred there would have been outraged at the idea of spending eternity next to an Anglican church.

Though christened as King's Chapel, the original wooden church was renamed Queen's Chapel during the reign of Queen Anne (1702–14). It was not long before the building (by either name) was bursting at the seams with a growing congregation; less than sixty years after its construction, plans to build the larger, more elegant granite church we know today were already in the works.

Building funds, as ever, were hard to come by, despite the chapel's royal connections. Fortunately, in 1749 the talented Peter Harrison of Newport, Rhode Island, agreed to design a Georgian chapel for the Anglicans for nary a shilling. In the mid-eighteenth century, architecture was still a gentlemen's hobby, not a paying profession, and Harrison was ably supported by his wealthy wife.

Designing King's Chapel, as it turned out, was an easy job. The church's building committee mailed its size requirements and a request for "Symmetry and Proportion" to Harrison. Harrison, who had a sizable architectural library to draw from, mailed back detailed plans, which borrowed liberally from the designs of certain London churches, including Sir James Gibbs's St. Martin-in-the-Fields, in Trafalgar Square. It's not clear whether Harrison, who later gained fame for his Newport mansions, ever saw the empty site. But the builders in Boston employed his plans, ultimately with great success. In order to keep the church open as much as possible during the five-year construction process, the workers built around the old wooden structure, gaily passing leftover segments out the new windows as they progressed.

The exterior of the new chapel was rough-hewn granite from Quincy (then Braintree), the first use of the stone that would later be used in the Bunker Hill Monument, the Parker House, Quincy Market, Fort Warren, and other Boston buildings. Since the Quincy quarries were yet to be dug, surface granite was used, shaped into four-foot blocks by a process of heating the stone and then dropping cannonballs on it.

Two major exterior sections deviated from Harrison's plans. Due again to lack of funds, the steeple was never finished—thereby giving it the distinctive, truncated "half-steeple" look we see today. Money was also lacking for the front portico and its twelve twenty-five-foot Ionic columns. Those were added in 1789—after the Revolution, when the chapel had evolved into America's first Unitarian church—but added on a tight budget. Since rock was costly, the massive columns were built of wood, then disguised as stone. A close inspection reveals the wooden beams underneath, with some chinks corroding away, gnawed by the elements.

Though Harrison gave King's Chapel a rustic and dark exterior, the Georgian interior was all brightness and light. Harrison's design lined the galleries with matching pairs of Corinthian columns, which draw the eye up to the vaulted arches. King's Chapel tour guides often bring visitors to one particular such column on the edge of Pew 24. There a small door opens on one side, revealing a shallow closet where the pew's owners could store personal belongings; on the other side, a similar hatch exposes the enormous tree trunk from which the column was hewn.

Echoing the ceiling's upward sweep is the wineglass-shaped pulpit, complete with sounding board above, and a reading and clerk's desk below. The 1717 pulpit—like the communion table in the chancel behind—is among the objects remaining from the original wooden chapel. Over the centuries, church leaders from virtually every faith have spoken from the elegant, elevated podium. Thanks in part to the chapel's excellent acoustics, a microphone has never been necessary to spread the Word all the way back to the organ and choir loft in the rear gallery.

Above the chancel is another Georgian touch, Harrison's fan-shaped Palladian window. Behind the central shutters lies hidden a perennial point of contention, a German-made glass window painted with the image of Christ. Donated by merchant and banker John Amory Lowell during the Civil War, the image was considered an inferior artwork by many Unitarian parishioners. "It's terribly ghastly . . . and not even real stained glass," confided one longtime church member while awaiting the chapel's weekly Wednesday noontime service. Though the glass panel has been covered in various ways for much of its life—some claim it's simply to keep irritating light from seeping in—the Reverend Carl Scovel, King's Chapel's minister, insists that the Christ image will not be removed. "It would be wrong to remove a symbol of Christ," he explains.

Representations of Christ—whether poorly executed or expertly done—are not often found in Unitarian churches today. Though the church has Protestant roots, contemporary Unitarian Universalists often shy away from using formal Christian ceremonies and symbols. This Unitarian church, however, is unique—as its guides will explain in detail—at once "Unitarian in theology, Anglican in liturgy, and congregational in church government." Though occupation by the Church of England and the link with the British crown officially ended after the American Revolution—when the Reverend James Freeman helped pioneer changes in liturgy and doctrine that made King's Chapel America's first Unitarian church—the chapel has retained reminders of its historic Anglican roots.

As a result, many items reflecting the congregation's Anglican heritage are still in use. The antique communion table donated by British monarchs William and Mary, for example, is employed for monthly communion services. Within the comfortably cushioned wooden box pews can generally be found a Holy Bible and a hymnal, along with a self-published *Book of Common Prayer;* the latter is an Anglican/Episcopal text, adapted for King's Chapel's use and revised nine times by the parish so far. Royal crowns and miters adorn the handsome loft organ, and the Governor's Pew, once dismantled as an affront to democratic seating, was rebuilt in 1928. Furthermore, the name King's Chapel remains, although it was changed to Stone Chapel from 1776 to the 1830s, due to ardent anti-British sentiments.

In recent decades, a gradual democratization has helped to dispel the chapel's old aura of wealth and Brahminism. A century ago, well-to-do parishioners bought pews for exclusive use by their families. Owners would outfit their pews with shelves, umbrella stands, fabrics, stools, and varied seating arrangements. Today the church owns these pews, which are open to all. And women are gaining power and position in the church now—not unusual, of course, for Unitarian Universalists.

Although its religious history fascinates, visitors to King's Chapel will find other interesting items as well. In the rear gallery, for example, sits the chapel's sixth organ, built by Charles Fiske. This wonderful mechanical-action instrument, housed in a walnut-stained oak case, closely resembles its eighteenth-century predecessors. The chapel's active musical life includes sixty concerts per year, thanks largely to world-renowned musical director Daniel Pinkham. Present-day musical endeavors build on a foundation strongly established in the past. The American premiere of Handel's *Messiah*, for example, took place at King's Chapel in 1786. The Handel and Haydn Society, formed in 1815, made its American debut there as well.

King's Chapel also honors dozens of men and women with memorials. Thirty-five commemorative plaques are displayed on walls and floor surfaces, and an obelisk dedicated to the slain Frenchman Saint Sauveur is on display in the front courtyard. There are people buried in the chapel, too, in vaulted tombs within a large basement chamber scattered with boxes, files, old furniture, maintenance supplies, and heating pipes. The crypt, which was closed to future interment by an 1890 city act, includes twenty sealed family tombs, plus a common "Strangers' Tomb." Tours are by special arrangement.

Some 200,000 people a year now visit King's Chapel, a popular and lovely stop on the Freedom Trail. But clearly, King's Chapel harbors a lot more of interest and import than immediately meets the eye.

THE ESSENTIALS

ADDRESS: 58 Tremont Street, corner of Tremont and School streets, Boston. Parish House at 64 Beacon Street, Boston.

TELEPHONE: Parish House, (617) 227-2155; King's Chapel, (617) 523-1749.

VISITOR INFORMATION: Unitarian Universalist Christian services every Sunday at 11:00 A.M., followed by special guided tour. Services also on Wednesdays, 12:15 P.M. Concerts each Tuesday, 12:15 P.M. Reading aloud, Thursdays at 12:15 P.M. Open to the public Patriots' Day through Labor Day, 10:00 A.M.–4:00 P.M., Monday through Saturday; Sunday, noon–4:00 P.M. The rest of the year, open 10:00 A.M.–2:00 P.M., Tuesday through Saturday; Sunday, noon–2:00 P.M. Self-guided tours always available; special guided tours may be arranged with one day's notice. Free; donations encouraged. Main floor is partially accessible by wheelchair; no accessible restrooms.

 The Old North Church

GRANTED, THE building popularly known as the Old North Church will forever be remembered for its association with patriot Paul Revere and his daring "midnight ride" of April 1775. Revere, that ride, and the church were all memorialized and immortalized by Henry Wadsworth Longfellow, in his narrative poem of 1861, "Paul Revere's Ride."

Still, the Old North, located on the Freedom Trail in Boston's North End, has many other, less widely touted claims to fame—claims that continually draw in curious visitors from around the world. The 1723 Georgian-style brick building, with its lofty white spire and grand peal of eight angelic bells, is renowned as Boston's oldest standing house of worship and an architectural treasure. Moreover, the structure's rich history includes British generals, benevolent pirates, toppling steeples, seminal Sunday schools, community outreach programs, and a wealth of art, architecture, and artifacts from Anglican, British, and American history.

Old North's long and wide-ranging story is partly the result of the fact that unlike so many other historic churches, it was never burned down, torn down, converted to condominiums, or made into a museum. "The place was fifty-two years old when the lanterns were placed in the steeple," explains the Reverend Dr. Robert W. Golledge, vicar of Old North. "And I'm proud that it's still in its original business—the business of being a church."

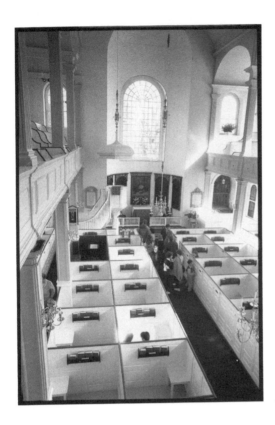

Active Christ Church in the North End is best known as the Old North Church of Paul Revere fame.

While it's true that none of the Old North staff *expect* visitors to come in knowing much more about the church than the Revere legend, at least the popular patriot has enticed visitors in. "I like to say Paul Revere was my original P.R. man," muses the vicar. "I take it as an opening."

Long before the Old North Church was constructed, the Puritan town of Boston had two major centers. One was around the main wharf and the Town House on the site of today's Old State House, and the other was the North End, Boston's first real neighborhood. Because it was surrounded by water and wharves, the North End's inhabitants included many wealthy English families, merchants, and middle-class tradespeople. And because most early Bostonians were Puritans, most of the churches and meeting-houses created were also Puritan—though they later evolved into Congregational churches. Other Bostonians, however—including government and military officials—belonged to the Church of England, and attended services in the Anglican King's Chapel.

By 1722, the Anglican congregation had outgrown the King's Chapel building, and a site for a second Boston church was sought in the bustling North End. The land the congregation purchased was part of Nathaniel Henchman's pasture in the old Mill Field. It seemed ideal, surrounded as it was by busy wharves, shops, spacious homes, gardens, inns, taverns, cattle pastures, a windmill, and even a burying ground on Copp's Hill. Moreover, the Reverend Dr. Timothy Cutler, a Harvard graduate and Yale's first president, seemed the perfect person to get the new church started.

The Old North Church was established as Christ Church in Boston, which remains its official name. For the past two centuries, however, its popular name has prevailed. According to local custom, the oldest church in the North End was generally called "Old North." Though that title presumably belonged to several other buildings before Christ Church, one in particular causes confusion to this day. The Old North Meeting House, across from Paul Revere's home on North Square, was the church served by the famous Puritan preachers Increase and Cotton Mather. That church was burned by the British for firewood in 1776.

Though the architect of Christ Church/Old North may never be known, the inspiration for its 1723 design is presumed to be Sir Christopher Wren's early eighteenth-century London churches. Records do show that Anthony Blount, and later William Price, oversaw the twenty-two-year struggle to build the simple yet magnificent Georgian structure, with its high, vaulted ceiling and New England touches.

While panes for the tall sash windows were imported from England, most of the building materials were domestic. Wood was shipped from York, Maine (then part of Massachusetts), from the same forests that provided masts for the Royal Navy. Red bricks, laid in an English Bond pattern, came from Medford kilns. Master builders Thomas Tippin and Thomas Bennett were aided in the construction process by laborers whose wages included free beer, a common practice at the time.

The Old North's cornerstone was laid April 15, 1723. When Dr. Cutler preached the first sermon, on December 29 of the same year, the church was hardly completed. Rough-hewn temporary floors and pews filled the main floor. Most of the church's distinctive features—from the brass chandeliers and cherubim-decorated organ to the 197-foot spire and peal of bells—would be added during the next two decades and beyond.

- The exceptionally tall box pews, for example, were purchased and decorated by individual families in early days. In 1806, these were replaced by more compact slip pews, then returned to their original box form during the major reconstruction of 1912. Though originally heated by footwarmers, these pews were later warmed by stoves; not until 1861 was the first furnace installed in the building.
- The two ornate brass chandeliers above the center aisle, gifts of an admiring English sea captain named William Maxwell, were first lit on Christmas Day 1724. Each is topped by a dove of peace.
- A new tracker-action organ with cowbone keys, dedicated in 1992, sits in the upstairs gallery, in a 1759 organ case. Decorating the gallery are four trumpeting cherubim donated by Captain Thomas James Gruchy of the privateer *Queen of Hungary* in 1746; the angels had been on their way to a Roman Catholic church in Canada when Gruchy plucked them as booty from a passing French vessel. (The captain's pirating activities were widespread; widespread, too,

Old North sexton Al Mostone, the last child born in the old Paul Revere House, holds a replica of the lantern that warned colonists "the British were coming" in 1775.

were suspicions that a tunnel led from his house on Salem and Charter streets down to the wharves, enabling his smuggling to continue unseen by local authorities.)

Though the modern-day exterior of the Old North Church is said to be much like its eighteenth-century form, the interior has changed with various ages and fashions. Major restorations occurred in 1806 and 1912, while minor alterations have been ongoing. Only since 1912, for example, has white been the church's dominant color, and the wineglass pulpit has periodically drifted from the left to the right, to the center front. As mentioned above, the pews were changed from box style, to slip, then back to box.

Meanwhile, additional buildings and courtyards have been annexed or improved over the years. A series of peaceful gardens, including the 1934 Washington Memorial Garden, are still maintained by the Beacon Hill Garden Club. The 1715 Ebenezer Clough House, now used for meetings, social gatherings, and classes, was saved from demolition and acquired by the church in 1958. The gift shop structure was built as a chapel for Italian Protestants in 1918. The shop, incidentally, doubles as a mini-museum in its rear section. Among its treasures are authentic Tea Party tea, the original "Vinegar Bible" of King George II, and the sword of Civil War Colonel Robert Gould Shaw.

★ ★ ★

The steeple of Old North is one of Boston's most famous landmarks. The two lanterns hung there in 1775, warning colonists across the river of the British approach, guaranteed its place in history, but plenty of other great stories are also associated with the well-known spire.

Hoisted in August of 1740, the steeple was a late addition to the church. On top of the 197-foot structure was placed a seven-foot weather vane fashioned by Shem Drowne, who also created the famous grasshopper above Faneuil Hall.

Though the original weather vane remains in place, the steeple has been repaired several times and replaced twice. During the Great Gale of October 9, 1804, and during Hurricane Carol of August 31, 1954, the wooden steeple was toppled off its square brick tower. The 1806 replacement—often attributed, without evidence, to Charles Bulfinch—was fifteen feet shorter than the original. When the 1806 steeple blew off in 1954, it was replaced with a faithful copy of the 1740 original.

The bells in the steeple were imported from England by Old North's first pastor, Timothy Cutler, in 1744. That same peal of eight magnificent bells still rings from the Old North belfry. A fifteen-year-old neighborhood boy named Paul Revere was part of the first guild of bell-ringers at the church, in 1750.

Only seven years later, a most bizarre event occurred above the belfry. Contemporary accounts report that a local eccentric named John Childs "flew" from the top of the steeple three separate times, once firing a loaded pistol in mid-flight. According to former museum curator Bud Millett, "Pictures sometimes show him wearing Leonardo-type wings. But one story says Childs constructed a sizable umbrella with a small opening at the apex, a prototype of the parachute. Finally, the town fathers ordered he cease and desist, since the spectacle caused people to take off from their labors."

The next major event at the steeple occurred on the night of April 18, 1775, an event still memorialized, celebrated, and reenacted at the Old North's annual Lantern Ceremony. The essence of the tale: Paul Revere and several other couriers were dispatched from Boston to Lexington and Concord, to warn colonists that "the British were coming" to seize a cache of colonial military stores hidden in the countryside. A crucial part of their message was to report the method of attack; would the British approach Concord by land, first marching the long route down Boston Neck to Roxbury, or by sea, launching their boats into the Charles River from the foot of Boston Common, then rowing upstream to Cambridge? If Revere and his colleagues were captured before delivering their message, the lanterns in the steeple of Old North would serve as a back-up system, alerting Charlestown citizens to the danger.

After secretly meeting with his friend Paul Revere—and receiving his final instructions—twenty-three-year-old sexton Robert Newman sneaked out of an upstairs window of his house near the Old North Church. He moved quickly and quietly, since British soldiers were quartered in his home and regulars patrolled the street. As Revere began his journey, first traveling in a rowboat to Charlestown, Newman crept up to the steeple and quickly flashed two lights across the bay. Once finished, he raced downstairs, climbed out the sash window to the right of the sanctuary, and eventually clambered back into his bedroom. Though he was arrested the next day for generally suspicious behavior, he was released due to lack of evidence; the British soldiers lodging in Newman's home agreed that he'd gone up to bed early and never left the house.

The exposed wooden window in the front of Old North today—decorated with a replica signal lantern—is the window through which Newman escaped. Though long ago bricked over and used as a display alcove for a bust of George Washington, this window was rediscovered during restoration work in 1989.

When Dr. Cutler preached the first sermon at Old North in 1723, he carefully chose words from the prophet Isaiah: "My house shall be called a house of prayer for all people." Throughout the following centuries, Old North has attracted quite a variety of worshipers and visitors, despite the tension and turmoil that openness sometimes caused.

One of the great ironies of history, for example, is that Old North served both sides during the War for Independence. British general William Gage watched the Battle of Bunker Hill from the Old North steeple—the same one from which the two signal lanterns had been hung. Major John Pitcairn, who led the British expedition to Lexington and Concord, was buried in the crypt below the church following his death at Bunker Hill.

Similarly, Old North's neighborhood has been home to a wide variety of people over the years. In 1903, when longtime Old North sexton Albert Mostone was born, his neighbors were Irish, Italian, and Jewish immigrants. Mostone was born in nearby North Square, in his great-aunt's apartment—in a run-down tenement that was owned and inhabited by Paul Revere from 1770 to 1800. Mostone has the distinction of being the last child born in that historic home before it was transformed into the museum it is today. Since the 1980s, the North End neighborhood has primarily housed a mix of traditional Italian families and more recent arrivals, young professional couples attracted to the area's waterfront, proximity to the financial district, and new luxury condominiums.

The church itself continues to maintain a reverent focus on both the dead and the living. The basement of Old North is a historic graveyard, with some 1,100 people buried in thirty-seven sealed tombs. Meanwhile, a new columbarium has recently opened in an adjacent basement chamber, which accommodates the cremated remains of about 720 others.

The living are represented in Old North's growing congregation, which includes many of the North End's new young professionals. In addition, the church offers music programs, daily interpretation for visitors, a gift shop and museum, a new archive room, and programs like the educational Old North Foundation. It continues to open its doors to all, from scurrying schoolchildren and fall-foliage bus tourists, to Roman Catholic cardinals, U.S. presidents, and Her Majesty, Queen Elizabeth II.

The "Third Lantern," which hangs in the "Newman Window," is another symbol of the Old North's commitment to the living future. It is a faithful replica of one of the 1775 signal lanterns, which rests in the Concord Museum. While the first two lanterns sparked the Revolutionary War, the third one represents continued striving for freedom and a renewed hope and effort to create America's unfinished dream.

"The American promise will never come true completely," says Dr. Golledge, "but it's our duty to try and try again."

THE ESSENTIALS

ADDRESS: 193 Salem Street, North End, Boston.

TELEPHONE: (617) 523-6676. Gift shop, (617) 523-4848.

VISITOR INFORMATION: Open 9:00 A.M.–5:00 P.M. daily, except Thanksgiving and Christmas Day. Free; donations encouraged. Sunday services at 9:00 A.M., 11:00 A.M., and 4:00 P.M. Clough House only open by special arrangement. Talks by church personnel given regularly for tourists; call for details or to arrange tour group visits. Main floor of church is wheelchair accessible, with assistance; first floor of Clough House similarly accessible; no accessible restrooms.

Trinity Church

ARCHITECTURALLY SPEAKING, its credentials are impeccable. Designed by renowned Boston architect Henry Hobson Richardson in the late nineteenth century, the building is still recognized as a masterpiece of Boston ecclesiastical architecture. Moreover, it's often said to be Richardson's personal best—and among the greatest works of architecture, either secular or religious, in the United States.

Its name is Trinity Church. And for those familiar with the ever-changing Boston skyline, the vision of Trinity is a constantly warm, yet wondrous, sight.

Today, the rustic Romanesque structure and its imposing towers are reflected on the glass-sheathed John Hancock tower by day, then illuminated by the play of the lights of Copley Square by night. During the winter holidays in particular, the lights seem to take on an ethereal glow. Entering the church's Victorian interior is described by some as a religious experience as well. Barrel vaults and a massive central tower lift toward the heavens, flanked by bold murals, stained-glass windows, and bas reliefs depicting an encyclopedic array of Christian saints and biblical stories.

To those who know the church intimately, however, such architectural glory is just a part of the Trinity experience. The ministers of this nationally renowned "preaching church" have provided spiritual guidance and inspiration for more than two centuries. Trinity's long line of influential Episcopalian preachers has included Samuel Parker, Alexander Mann, Theodore Parker Ferris, and the inimitable Phillips Brooks.

Giving has also been a part of the Trinity tradition. Under the recent direction of the Reverend Stephen Wade, the church's extensive outreach programs have included sponsoring a hospice and coordinating volunteer opportunities for parishioners through an AIDS support committee, pris-

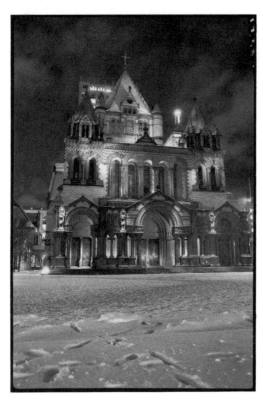

Trinity Church, the architectural masterpiece of H. H. Richardson, is particularly vibrant during the Christmas holiday season.

oner pre-release programs, local literacy projects, and shelters for battered women and the homeless.

But understanding how this building and congregation came together requires us to look back, heeding the Reverend Phillips Brooks's words of a century ago: "A parish, which for years has filled a place and done a work like ours in Boston, cannot forget its past."

Since the original Boston settlers of 1630 were Puritans, so too were the town's first religious meetinghouses. Still, as early as 1688, King's Chapel was built to accommodate members of the Church of England. Christ Church, later known as Old North, became Boston's second Anglican parish in 1723. A decade later, the congregation at King's Chapel agreed that yet a third house of worship was needed in the rapidly growing port town.

The decision to create Trinity Church was formalized in 1733, in a meeting at Luke Verdy's tavern. Curiously, the spot chosen for the church was the site of another popular tavern—the Pleiades, or Seven Star Inn, at Summer and Hawley streets near the present Filene's department store.

Bustling, commercial, downtown Summer Street may seem an odd location for a house of worship today, but it made sense in 1733. At the time, the avenue was lined with large orchards, splendid mansions, bountiful gardens, and cow-filled pastures. The first Trinity Church, completed in 1735, was a wooden, barn-like box with neither steeple, tower, nor porch. The interior was somewhat more elegant, with Corinthian columns and a few fine paintings. Among Trinity's first parishioners was wealthy merchant Peter Faneuil, the patron of Faneuil Hall. General George Washington became one of the church's most distinguished visitors, in 1789.

During the American Revolution—when churches associated with Tory sentiments were viewed as enemy outposts by many colonists—Trinity was the only Anglican church that remained open in Boston. Christ Church closed in 1775, and the ministers of both King's Chapel and Trinity fled north to Halifax during the British evacuation of 1776. But Trinity's assistant minister, Samuel Parker, kept the parish doors open, wisely agreeing to delete prayers for the British king from the church's liturgy. He also endorsed the patriot cause.

By 1828, a second, larger Trinity Church was built on the same Summer Street site. The "great, gloomy old thing," as Phillips Brooks fondly remembered it, was a massive stone building that succumbed to the Great Fire of 1872. Brooks had been Trinity's rector for three years when the building burned, along with much of downtown Boston. As he fled the flames, Brooks managed to save some of Trinity's books and robes.

According to the Reverend Spencer Rice, Trinity's rector from 1982 to 1992, Brooks "made another save" that day—one with an amusing twist. It seems that Boston jeweler Mr. Shreve, owner of the still-extant firm of Shreve, Crump, and Low, met Brooks on the street during the fire. He was afraid that his exclusive store's jewels and precious metals would be destroyed. "Brooks, being a large man, offered to fill his oversized coat with Shreve's goods. He stuffed the coat, ran out to safety in the street—and was immediately arrested for being a looter!"

Though the second Trinity Church was lost, the congregation remained together. Temporary services were held in an MIT lecture hall, where the New England Mutual Life Insurance building stands today. Moreover, even before the fire broke out, the hard-working, wealthy, growing congregation had agreed to build a grander church in the newly landfilled area of town known as Back Bay. The reasons for the move were simple: in only three years of preaching in Boston, the charismatic Brooks had attracted significantly larger crowds to Trinity services. In addition, the Summer Street location had become less appealing; the street was now crowded with shops and businesses, and putrid odors were emanating from the church's basement tombs.

Trinity Church was not the only cultural institution seeking greener pastures in Victorian Boston. No sooner had acres of Needham gravel been hauled in to fill the Back Bay's marshes and mudflats, than many of Boston's cultural and religious institutions set up new homes on the new land. In the broad open area known as Art Square—renamed for Boston artist John Singleton Copley in 1883—those buildings included a short-lived Peace Jubilee Coliseum, the original Museum of Fine Arts, and the *New* Old South Church. Between 1877 and 1895, two of Boston's greatest architectural masterpieces added the crowning touches to Copley Square:

H. H. Richardson's new Trinity Church and Charles F. McKim's Boston Public Library.

The magnificence of the Copley Square Trinity Church has always been credited to the architect, Louisiana-born Henry Hobson Richardson (1838–1886). Still, the splendid church that stands there today resulted from a variety of forces and factors—including the social and religious beliefs of Phillips Brooks; the wisdom of Brooks's closest friend, Robert Treat Paine; the talents of people like stained-glass artists John LaFarge and Margaret Redmond, sculptor Augustus Saint-Gaudens, and architects Stanford White and Charles F. McKim; the benificence of countless parish members; and the exigencies of a mushy foundation.

According to current building manager Richard Merrill, the choice of H. H. Richardson as architect was a result of the Harvard old-boy network. In 1872, six firms were invited to submit designs for the new church. Of those six, Richard Morris Hunt was the most prestigious, but Richardson was selected—by a building committee that included several of his old pals from exclusive Harvard clubs.

Despite the popularity of Gothic styling in American churches of the day, Richardson's plans were Romanesque and eclectic. A onetime student of the Ecole des Beaux Arts in Paris, Richardson borrowed many of his design ideas from the churches of the eleventh-century French Aquitaine, but added a distinctly American touch: the heavy building was made largely from light-colored Dedham granite and red Longmeadow sandstone, playfully mixing colors as well as textures. To Richardson, this styling was rugged, rustic, and individualistic, like the American character. To Brooks, the "Richardsonian Romanesque" style was far preferable to Gothic design, which he equated with late medieval Catholicism, flamboyance, and corruption.

Richardson's original contract called for a $200,000 building. By the time Trinity opened in 1877, the bill had reached an astounding $750,000, around $7,200 of which was Richardson's salary. Theological, musical, political, physical, and financial considerations were all incorporated into the final church design—a happy marriage of art and exigency. For example, three exquisite stained-glass windows by John LaFarge, valued today at $13 million, grace the back of the nave. Richardson once considered a rose window for that space, but decided it would be too Gothic.

The architect's original design also called for a cathedral-style ceiling for the church interior. That was altered to hanging barrel vaults, which provided better acoustics for preaching as well as for choral and organ music. According to musical director and organist Brian Jones, "Trinity has a big sound, and it's relatively resonant for an American church." In general, says Jones, Americans like "carpeting, curtains, and cushions," which tend to deaden sound. Trinity is thankfully sparse in all three.

Richardson's plan suggested that the church be filled with numbered pews, which were traditionally purchased for use by wealthy parish families. Phillips Brooks, however, threatened to quit unless free galleries were added for "the people." The galleries were added, the people came, and Brooks stayed. Eventually, in the 1940s, the practice of selling private pews was abandoned altogether.

The tall central tower of Trinity, modeled after that of the cathedral in Salamanca, Spain, proved another change from Richardson's design; it's substantially shorter, due to sheer physical necessity. The current tower, with a ceiling height of 103 feet, weighs approximately 12.5 million pounds. Richardson's original plans would have made the tower taller and heavier, which would surely have sunk the whole structure.

Because it was built on landfill—as was the whole of Back Bay—Trinity was constructed on a foundation of four massive granite pyramids with thirty-five-foot-square bases. Below the foundations of the church and its adjoining parish house, a subterranean safety net of 4,502 wooden piles was laid. Since those piles must be kept saturated to retain their strength, the water table and piles have been monitored continually throughout Trinity's history. Though it was feared that the piles were rotting in the mid-1930s, they remained intact. It was not until the construction of the adjacent John Hancock Tower in the early 1970s, in fact, that Trinity's foundation was seriously threatened. Trinity sued the Hancock company for $4 million in damages in 1975, explaining that the work had actually twisted the church, cracking parts of its foundation, walls, and some precious stained glass, and damaging a LaFarge mural. When the case was finally settled in 1987, Trinity received $11.6 million—the damage award plus twelve years of accumulated interest.

Another major change from the original Trinity was the addition of a magnificent marble altar, bronze candlesticks, gilded bas reliefs, and a suspended, hand-carved cross, all of which have graced the chancel since 1938. For doctrinal reasons, Phillips Brooks thought a simple communion table and his own pulpit were sufficient for his church of 1,500 seats and his standing-room-only Sunday crowds; the chancel was not refurbished until forty-five years after his death.

In his free time, bachelor Brooks—who carried three hundred pounds on his six-foot-four-inch frame—loved fast horses, fishing, billiards, and food. In the pulpit, he loved God, art and literature, dramatic language, and moving mountains. When Brooks preached, everyone listened—young and old, female and male, poor and rich. "He spoke like a machine gun," explains Spencer Rice. Contemporaries even timed him, estimating that he delivered 213 words per minute at full speed.

Brooks died in 1893, two years after his appointment as Episcopal bishop of Massachusetts. His original pulpit was replaced by the current Robert Treat Paine memorial pulpit in 1916. Nevertheless, the rector was remembered at Trinity in a variety of ways, some of them controversial. Twenty years after the building was completed, architect Hugh Shepley added a front porch and towers to Trinity. No one objected to the subjects of nine of the large statues on the porch—they were heroes of Jewish and Christian history like Moses, Abraham, and saints Matthew, Mark, Luke, and John. Not everyone was appreciative, however, when Brooks's image was added as the de facto tenth "saint" in 1925.

In 1909, a sculpture of Brooks, by Augustus Saint-Gaudens, was placed on the Boylston Street side of Trinity Church. On a positive note, says Trinity's Stephen Wade, "Brooks is facing outward, rather than inward at the church. That's significant because Trinity has had a remarkable history of community outreach from the start." On the negative side, of course, is the fact that Brooks has been accused of attracting more attention than the gentleman standing behind him. The gentleman is Jesus Christ.

In some ways, the Reverend Phillips Brooks was a hard act to follow. His immediate successor at Trinity, Reverend E. Winchester Donald, is reported to have said, "Someone must leap into the gulf. Why not I?" Fortunately for the congregation, he did take that leap, and several succeeding generations of rectors and parishioners have as well. Today, Trinity continues to contribute mightily to the Greater Boston and Episcopal communities.

The Trinity choir, for example, grew from a quartet to a chorus of men and boys at the turn of the century. Today, Brian Jones leads an integrated crowd of seventy members, several of whom are paid professionals. Trinity offers free lunchtime organ concerts every Friday from early fall through late spring, and musical preludes at Sunday services. The cathedralesque sound of the organ, refurbished in the early 1960s, is partly due to the fact that the three-keyboard console runs two organs, offering a stunning "stereo" sound. This sound is evident on several Trinity recordings, including the 1991 "Sounds of Trinity" and the popular Christmas collection "Candlelight Carols."

Trinity's musical program is particularly well attended during the winter holiday season. Its traditional candlelight carol service is held on the Sunday before Christmas each year, while the Trinity choir's annual presentation of Handel's *Messiah* occurs two Sundays before Christmas. It's interesting to note that the church has a historical connection to holiday music as well: Phillips Brooks penned the lyrics to "O Little Town of Bethlehem"; and John H. Hopkins, an assistant minister at Trinity from 1831 to 1832 and the great-grandfather of Phillips Brooks's wife, Harriet Rice, wrote "We Three Kings of Orient Are."

Amidst all this vibrant energy, it's no surprise that other parts of the church's life remain vital, too. During the 1980s, for instance, the congregation of Trinity tripled (of the church's 6,000 members, more than half live outside Boston proper). How can this unusual surge be explained? Partly by the influx of young professionals into the Boston area, and the Trinity staff that help make the people and the programs all work.

And, in the words of building manager Richard Merrill, Trinity has a "great location, great building, great city, great music! Trinity Church is very dignified. But it's also very accessible."

THE ESSENTIALS

ADDRESS: Copley Square, Boston, facing the McKim building of the Boston Public Library on Boylston Street.

TELEPHONE: (617) 536-0944.

VISITOR INFORMATION: Church and parish house open daily 8:00 A.M.–6:00 P.M. daily. Holy Communion services offered Wednesday, 12:10 P.M. and 5:30 P.M. Regular Sunday services at 8:00 A.M., 11:00 A.M., and 6:00 P.M. Tours given following 11:00 A.M. service. Free. Call about events, seasonal services, and special tours. Wheelchair ramps to church and parish house available on Boylston Street side, near the Phillips Brooks statue; ushers on duty near door for Sunday services; call in advance for assistance at other times; church restrooms are wheelchair accessible.

15 The Granary Burying Ground

IN 1816, a bell was hung in the tower at King's Chapel. It was a wonderfully resonant bell, the largest ever cast in the family foundry of Paul Revere. Two years later, that same bell tolled as the eighty-three-year-old Revere joined many of his prestigious Revolutionary-era colleagues in final reunion. John Hancock, James Otis, Sam Adams, Robert Treat Paine, the family of Ben Franklin, and the five victims of the Boston Massacre, of course, were already dead. But in 1818 Revere joined them all, ready to spend eternity in a soggy little plot of land off Tremont Street.

That soggy little plot was better known as the Granary Burying Ground. And the old patriot's funeral cortege was among the last to terminate there, since the two-acre graveyard had already been considered full decades before Revere's interment. But the end of in-town burials in no way signaled the end of pedestrian traffic through the graveyard.

Quite the contrary, in fact.

Today the colonial-era Granary Burying Ground, located next to Park Street Church on the Freedom Trail, attracts an astonishing 3,000 visitors daily during the busy summer months. Curious onlookers come to see the 2,345 grave markers and 137 tombs still standing—or slumping, as the case may be. Many of those stones are decorated with intricate examples of the American folk art of funerary stonecarving: cryptic verse and deathly images of skulls, crossbones, winged cherubs, and urns. Boston city rangers offer periodic tours, and explanatory plaques guide guests through the graveyard's history. That history includes the burial ground's most famous residents: Paul Revere and his colonial cohorts, three signers of the Declaration of Independence, nine governors of Massachusetts, and a woman some call the real "Mother Goose."

When the Puritans of the Massachusetts Bay Colony arrived to settle Boston in 1630, life was tenuous at best. The town's first burying ground (known popularly today as King's Chapel Burying Ground, although the Puritan graveyard had no connection with the Anglican church built five decades later) was nearly full thirty years after its opening. In 1659 and 1660, two new burying grounds were opened, one at Copp's Hill in the North End, and the second on the edge of Boston Common.

Modern visitors may find it hard to imagine that this third Boston burial ground, now known as the Granary, was once part of Boston Common. Secluded behind an iron fence and neo-Egyptian granite gates, and

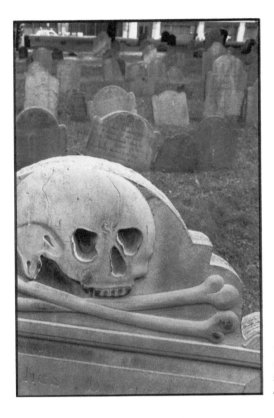

The Granary Burying Ground on Tremont Street is a virtual Who's Who of colonial Boston history.

shielded from the busy strip of Tremont Street between Park and Beacon, today's tree-shaded Granary Burying Ground is surrounded by tall buildings on three sides. Immediately blocking the graveyard from the Common, moreover, is the graceful Park Street Church and the two-way traffic of Park Street.

During the seventeenth and much of the eighteenth century, however, none of these barriers or paved byways existed. Boston Common, opened for the common use of local citizens and grazing cows in 1634, stretched beyond today's forty-eight acres. Modern Tremont and Park streets were but primitive pathways to and through the Common, and Park Street Church was not built until 1809.

During those early years, the buildings of the Common formed the graveyard's neighborhood. Since the Common was public ground, it was used for everything from pasture and public gallows to public buildings. During the Granary Burying Ground's first century, its neighbors included an almshouse for the poor, a bridewell (prison) for criminals and the insane, and a workhouse for the dissolute and indigent. The graveyard itself was also periodically rented out for grazing bulls, cows, or pigs.

Before the Park Street Church was built, a long wooden building occupied its site. From 1737 until the American Revolution, the building was used to store grain that was sold cheaply to the poor. In 1796, the famous eyesore was removed to Commercial Point in Dorchester and converted into a hotel. Though the granary itself is long gone, the name Granary for the burying ground remained.

The two acres borrowed from the Common for that burial ground (also known, during various eras, as the New, the South, the Central, and the Middle Burying Place) were fed by underground springs and plagued by poor drainage and spongy soil; the constant moisture, combined with the New England weather, decomposed bodies quickly.

Despite the convenient rate of decay, the graveyard was evidently full to the brim by 1738—when John Chambers and other local gravediggers complained that they were forced to bury the dead four deep. Despite that unholy glut and an increasingly sickening stench, bodies were interred one upon another in the Granary Burying Ground for another 141 years. Not until 1879 did the board of health close the downtown graveyard for good. By then, 12,000 or more anonymous souls rested below.

The crowded, difficult conditions reinforced a number of burial practices that twentieth-century men and women find unusual at best. Family members and friends, for example, were used to sharing or reusing existing tombs. Seventeenth-century diarist Samuel Sewall noted that his family tomb at the Granary had some forty occupants even before the American Revolution began.

The case of the Sullivan-Bellingham tomb, however, was not a family matter. In 1782, Judge James Sullivan expropriated the tomb in which Governor Richard Bellingham had lain since 1672. Custom dictated that if a family died out or could no longer care for its tomb, Boston selectmen could offer the space to whomever would provide needed repairs. When Judge Sullivan entered Bellingham's tomb, he found the late governor's remains floating in the water-soaked vault. Undaunted by the mess, Sullivan cleaned up the premises, became governor himself, and died in 1808. The Tomb of the Two Governors still bears the names of both Bellingham and Sullivan.

In another custom unusual by modern standards, the earliest burials at the Granary rarely included coffins. The dead were merely wrapped in a pall or linen cloth, with perhaps some lime thrown in on top. Lime is a caustic substance whose many uses include curing hides and treating sewage—both of which would have proved useful in a primitive graveyard.

While wealthier families often bought the tombs or vaults that extend around the periphery of the graveyard, poorer men and women placed slate gravestones in the site's central section. The oldest stone is the 1667 marker of John Wakefield, though his was hardly the first body interred.

Originally, these chiseled slate markers were randomly scattered about the graveyard's center, presumably over the bodies they commemorated. The markers generally included a headstone and a footstone—making each gravesite resemble a bed—and were placed facing east, so that the dead could face the rising sun on Judgment Day. The inscription on the headstone was directed away from the body, presumably to prevent readers from standing on top of the deceased.

Beginning around 1830, the Granary Burying Ground's gravemarkers were shuffled two or three times, ending up in the neat rows we find today. Needless to say, the interred were not shuffled along with them, inspiring

Oliver Wendell Holmes's remark, "Epitaphs were never famous for truth, but the old reproach of 'Here *lies*' never had such a wholesale illustration as in these outraged burial places, where the stone does lie above and the bones do not lie beneath."

Though many sources suggest this straightening was necessitated by new lawn-mowing devices, historian Blanche Linden-Ward disagrees. Linden-Ward explains that the symmetrical stone lineup began as part of a general beautification of the site during the 1830s, which included the laying of paths and planting of trees and shrubs. Such renovations were in turn inspired by the early nineteenth-century development of Beacon Hill into a "dense, elite residential and cultural area," and by the lavish new garden cemetery that had opened in Cambridge in 1831—Mount Auburn.

Throughout the centuries, the Granary Burying Ground remained an accessible, though sometimes under-appreciated, outdoor museum of history and folk art. The headstones and tombs alone provide a telling glimpse of early America's changing views of life, death, and eternity.

During the Puritans' first century in Boston, for example, life was especially harsh, and their view of death was bleak. Hence death's heads, winged skulls, crossbones, and soul effigies were often carved into these slate stones by talented local artisans. Linden-Ward finds the area to the right of the imposing Franklin family obelisk particularly rich in early iconography, including the stern skulls carved on the gravestones of Deborah Cobham, Lydia Green, Jonathan Belcher, and Sally May.

As Boston life became easier and Puritan ways faded, the stonecutters' symbols started to emphasize spiritual regeneration over physical decay. Cherub faces and harvest scenes appear on later stones, while urns and willows—classical Greek and Roman motifs—emerged during the Republican era that followed the Revolution.

The Granary's greatest renown comes from its harboring the remains of more famous colonial-era heroes than any other Boston burial ground. Countless guides and guidebooks relate tales of the elaborate funeral corteges, crowds of thousands, bold oratory, and general pomp and circumstance that accompanied the funerals of men like Sam Adams, John Hancock, James Otis, and Boston Massacre victim Crispus Attucks. When Paul Revere died in 1818, he became one of the last of these colonial heroes to join the historic downtown graveyard. The robust Paul Revere's death came so much later than the deaths of other patriots that he missed inclusion in his family plot, and almost missed burial in the star-studded Granary altogether.

Equally interesting are the tales of who, or what, is not in the Granary, or *might* not be there, as the case may be. Ben Franklin is not there, for example. Although the Granary's twenty-one-foot Franklin obelisk memorializes his family interred below, Franklin himself is buried in Philadelphia. Peter Faneuil, benefactor of Faneuil Hall, is there, but the original inscription on his tomb has been changed; it used to read "P. Funel," but was "corrected" in later years.

"Mother Goose" may be in the Granary, but her gravestone is nowhere to be seen. Boston's Mother Goose was Elizabeth Foster (d. 1757), the second wife of Isaac Goose (also known as Vergoose). Elizabeth raised and told stories to her ten children and ten step-children, and may have had her stories for children published. No one knows if Elizabeth was *the* storyteller of nursery rhyme fame, since serious contenders for that title predate her in France and perhaps in England as well; but the gravemarker of Mary Goose, Isaac's first wife, is often mistakenly claimed as Mother Goose's own.

The great orator Wendell Phillips (d. 1884) was once in the burying ground, next to his father, Boston mayor John Phillips. But when Wendell's widow, Ann Terry Greene, died two years later, his body was moved to her gravesite in Milton. Another migratory corpse was General Joseph Warren, who began eternity in the common grave where he died, at Bunker Hill. Warren's body was exhumed and spent 1776 to 1824 in the Minot family tomb at the Granary Burying Ground. Exhumed again, the body was brought to a Warren family tomb under St. Paul's Church on Tremont Street, then to a family vault at Forest Hills Cemetery in Jamaica Plain, in 1855.

Legend has it that the remains of John Hancock may not be all there, since his hand was severed by grave robbers the night after he was interred in 1793; others suggest that when his tomb lay open during some nineteenth-century construction on a nearby wall, someone made off with Governor Hancock altogether.

All of these stories of exhumation, alteration, and grave robbing point to the fact that American concepts of death and burial have significantly altered over the centuries. Not until the 1830s, in fact—with the advent of garden cemeteries like Cambridge's Mount Auburn—did Americans begin thinking of cemeteries as places to remember and visit the departed, rather than just to dispose of the dead.

The Granary began to respond to these changes in attitudes in the 1830s and 1840s, though most of its burying days were done by then. It was after 1830, for instance, that the gravestones were neatly realigned, numerous trees and winding paths were added, a new iron fence was built, and a bold granite Egyptian gateway was constructed at the entrance. The latter is generally credited to Solomon Willard, designer of the Bunker Hill Monument, though historian Linden-Ward believes it was designed by Isaiah Rogers.

The Granary Burying Ground experienced no major changes or concerted overhauls in the twentieth century until a burst of enthusiasm and funds in the 1980s and 1990s. Today the old graveyard is beginning to recover from those years of constant use and little maintenance. Thanks to the Boston Parks Department's 1985 Historic Burying Ground Initiative and the newly formed Friends of the Granary, an organization made up of abutters to the site, much-needed repairs and restoration of the site and stones are in the works. In the spring of 1991, for example, the Friends of the Granary funded a new pathway system and a wheelchair-accessible entrance at Tremont Place. As part of its restoration activities, the Parks Department installed a new signage system to tell the history of the site and show where famous people are buried. In the last few years, stones have been repaired and reset, inventories taken, ranger tours begun, and a master plan for restoration developed.

According to Kathy Kottaridis, project manager for the Historic Burying Grounds Initiative, the city's $6.1-million program to restore its sixteen historic graveyards will also rebuild the historic granite walls and entry along Tremont Street, repair gravestones and tomb markers, and deal with landscaping, erosion, and other problems.

The old Revere bell at King's Chapel still tolls, by the way. Hopefully, with such ambitious restoration projects underway, that bell will never have to toll the end of the Granary Burying Ground—one of Boston's great historic treasures.

THE ESSENTIALS

ADDRESS: 83–115 Tremont Street, between Park and Beacon streets, Boston.

TELEPHONE: Boston Parks and Recreation Department, (617) 635-4505; City Park Rangers Office, (617) 635-7378.

VISITOR INFORMATION: Open during daylight hours, 365 days a year. Free. Call City Park Rangers Office for information about changing seasonal tour schedules. Wheelchair-accessible entrance at Tremont Place, around the corner, off Beacon Street; access throughout graveyard much better since 1991 improvement of paths; main Tremont Street entrance includes four steps.

16 Mount Auburn Cemetery

IN 1962, President John F. Kennedy complimented that year's Nobel Prize winners with the following observation: "I think this is the most extraordinary collection of talent, of human knowledge, that has ever been gathered together at the White House, with the possible exception of when Thomas Jefferson dined alone." If you take Kennedy's quote and replace "White House" with "any American cemetery," you've got a perfect description of Mount Auburn Cemetery in Cambridge. Although neither Kennedy nor Jefferson is buried there, the 87,000 *other* resident souls—reposing amidst one of New England's prettiest landscapes—constitute quite stunning company.

Interred and memorialized in varied spots around Mount Auburn's 174 acres of rolling hills and winding pathways are dozens of historical movers and shakers known throughout the world: Christian Science founder Mary Baker Eddy, poet Henry Wadsworth Longfellow, actor Edwin Booth, architects R. Buckminster Fuller and Charles Bulfinch, painter Winslow Homer, and social reformers Julia Ward Howe and Dorothea Dix are but a few who come to mind.

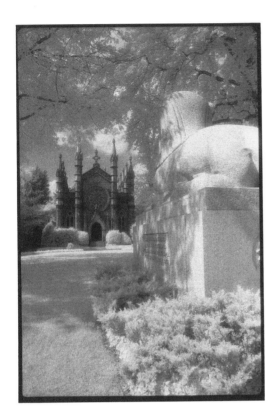

A sphinx commemorating the American Civil War faces Bigelow Chapel at Mount Auburn Cemetery, America's first rural garden cemetery.

There are also multitudes of celebrities whose Boston-area legacies may be better known than their own names—including the founders of Babson College, Star Market, Mount Auburn Hospital, Hood Milk, the Gardner Museum, the Massachusetts Society for the Prevention of Cruelty to Animals, and the John Birch Society. The individuals who invented overnight delivery service, the elevator, and "the Gibson Girls" are all buried at Mount Auburn, too, as is the woman who may have inspired "Mary Had a Little Lamb."

It's an impressive roster indeed. Still, Mount Auburn Cemetery has always been more than a beautifully maintained Who's Who of the rich and famous. Unlike its aristocratic European counterparts, the cemetery began as, and remains to this day, a democratic burial ground—open to people of all social levels, religions, races, and political persuasions. Observing the gravestones and memorials of everyday people—with their changing art, architecture, and inscriptions—provides visitors with a fascinating firsthand glimpse of American social history.

Furthermore, Mount Auburn has been a center of horticultural experimentation and creative landscape design since its founding in 1831. As such, it has continually attracted nature lovers, landscapers, horticulturists, gardeners, historians, photographers, and other artists, and proved a popular oasis for migratory birds and avid birdwatchers.

★   ★   ★

Mount Auburn is probably best known as the first garden cemetery in the United States. For the two centuries before it was founded, life in the Boston area may have been hard, but death was even worse.

The Puritans who first settled New England were an apocalyptic lot who warned of fiery postmortem fates in their sermons and disposed of their dead accordingly. The bodies of Boston's dead were buried in urban graveyards that quickly became overcrowded. Their slate headstones were often decorated with such cheerful designs as a skeletal death's head or the Grim Reaper. Many church lots were ill-kept, foul-smelling dens of decay, and blamed as a cause for epidemics. Burial "in perpetuity" was not yet in vogue—meaning new bodies were often dumped on top of old ones, sometimes marked and sometimes not. City graveyards often had distinctive pockmarks, since thin wooden caskets crumbled with age, causing the earth above to collapse into the interred remains.

Historian Blanche Linden-Ward, author of *Silent City on a Hill: Landscapes of Memory and Boston's Mount Auburn Cemetery* and other treatises on historic graveyards, tells of a spine-tingling, though not unusual, incident: a nineteenth-century Bostonian passing by Tremont Street's old Granary Burying Ground apparently gazed into James Otis's open tomb and observed how the tree roots wound through the famous patriot's skull! The deceased clearly had neither privilege nor privacy.

By the early 1800s, however, romantic new attitudes about death and the afterlife were coming into fashion. Instead of focusing on eternal damnation, many began to think of death as an ethereal repose. In gravestone art, ominous skulls gave way to cherubs, willows, and urns. The concept of a perpetual resting place for human remains—a pleasant, marked, permanent home for a single body, or for loving companions—also emerged.

Meanwhile, philanthropist-merchant George Brimmer had purchased Stone's Woods, on the rural outskirts of Boston—an ample chunk of woodland on the Cambridge-Watertown line. Harvard students often strolled and studied there, and had nicknamed the spot "Sweet Auburn," from a reference in Oliver Goldsmith's popular poem "The Deserted Village." Brimmer wanted to save the land from development, and eventually sold it to the Garden and Cemetery Committee of the Massachusetts Horticultural Society.

That committee included Dr. Jacob Bigelow, a physician, botanist, and Harvard professor who helped found the Massachusetts Institute of Technology and popularized the word *technology*. It also included Henry A. S. Dearborn, a retired army general, civil engineer, and the first president of the Massachusetts Horticultural Society.

Bigelow and Dearborn wanted to create a garden cemetery—a spacious, peaceful, rolling, "natural" park embellished with flowers, trees, and ponds, where the dead could rest intact and the living could wander, ponder, and pray. The landscape design was inspired by British pleasure parks and the Parisian estate-turned-cemetery called Père Lachaise. Initially, the committee sold a hundred burial plot subscriptions, at $60 each, to interested citizens. Then, with the necessary funds in hand, they purchased Brimmer's seventy-two acres for $6,000 in 1831. Those acres became the Mount Auburn Cemetery, and a revolutionary new era in American graveyards had begun.

Mount Auburn quickly became the "in" place for burial and to visit, both nationally and internationally. Moreover, the popularity of this and the other rural cemeteries that followed proved a major inspiration to the parks movement of the mid and late 1800s (see Part 6). As Mount Auburn grew in fame and size—with twelve land purchases from 1835 to 1944—its commitment to being a garden remained steadfast. By the late twentieth century, only a handful of hearty oaks remained from the original woods; around them, however, Mount Auburn horticulturists continually planted native trees and shrubs, interspersed with many nonnative experiments. Hills were leveled, topography periodically changed, and plantings altered from era to era. Marshlands were filled in, or sometimes reshaped, to create the cemetery's major bodies of water: Halcyon Lake, Auburn Lake, Conse-cration Dell Pond, and Willow Pond.

Buildings were also added as funds allowed. The Egyptian Revival entrance gate came first, built on a budget in wood in 1832, then rebuilt with durable Quincy granite a decade later. The nondenominational Gothic Revival Bigelow Chapel and a circular, Norman-style observation tower named for President George Washington came next.

The initial statuary purchased for the cemetery—presumably the first of many projected art acquisitions—comprised four majestic statues of Ameri-can heroes that stood in Bigelow Chapel. When plans changed, the four were moved first to the cemetery's administration building, and then, as space was needed, to Harvard University. (John Adams and John Winthrop now stand in the Great Hall of Harvard's Memorial Hall, James Otis in Sanders Theater, and Joseph Story, a U.S. Supreme Court justice and Mount Auburn's first president, in Langdell Hall at the Harvard Law School.)

Everyone has a favorite monument at Mount Auburn. Some like the neo-Egyptian symbols, which became popular in America not long after Napoleon's 1798 invasion of Egypt and the deciphering of the Rosetta Stone. At the cemetery are many such examples, from the great fifteen-foot sphinx, dedicated to the preservation of the Union and the ending of slavery, to countless obelisks.

On the nineteenth-century monuments, classical symbolism predomi-nates, with mausoleums, cenotaphs, and miniature temples galore. Histo-rian Barbara Rotundo, who offers periodic walking tours of Mount Auburn, will gladly point out many popular symbols of the time: ascend-ing angels, urns (representing the soul), flames (eternity), doves (the holy spirit), winged hourglasses (time flies), oak or ivy (everlasting), and sheaves of wheat (fulfilled life), to name but a few. Though sentimental Greek-inspired, full-figure sculptures appear in many places, incidentally, Ma-donnas and crucifixes do not. Both the anti-Catholic sentiment in Boston in the mid-nineteenth century and the insistence of many in the Roman Catholic hierarchy that their own be buried in consecrated church grounds ensured this result.

Around some family plots today you'll find ornate cast-iron gates and fences, granite staircases and curbings. These are vestiges of the extrava-gance of the mid-nineteenth century at Mount Auburn; as the popu-larity of the cemetery grew, so did the popularity of elaborate memorial decorations. Plots acquired hedges, ivy-draped fences, and even curbs.

Cast-iron "lawn furniture" was placed on some plots, while fountains were added to cemetery lakes, sometimes surrounded by exotic palms and warm-weather flora. The latter, incapable of surviving harsh New England winters, were protected from the cold in "half-hardy" greenhouses.

After the Civil War, the popularity of such clutter diminished. By the end of the century, cemetery officials had removed many such difficult-to-maintain embellishments. Private plot gardeners were banned, and "perpetual care" contracts with the cemetery began. Mount Auburn Cemetery began to return once again to a policy promoting more modest, natural beauty.

Mount Auburn was a haven for birds even in the nineteenth century. In the late Victorian period, avian enthusiasts were known to eagerly blast birds from treetops with their guns, then bring them home for study and identification. Although birdwatchers pulled such stunts in other nearby locations, like Fresh Pond, no such hunting took place on Mount Auburn grounds. Fortunately for the birds, one Ludlow Griscom pioneered a different method of avian study in the late 1920s, chronicling the flights of his feathered friends using binoculars and notepads rather than firearms. Griscom, who frequented Mount Auburn, is buried near one of the best birdwatching areas in the cemetery, the deep, mysterious, wooded spot called Consecration Dell.

Other good areas to observe the wealth of migrating land birds that pass through Mount Auburn are Auburn Lake and Washington Tower—older, more settled sections of the grounds, where the trees are taller and the growth wilder. More than two hundred species of birds have been seen at Mount Auburn, including thirty-six species of wood warblers. Prime viewing times are spring days, from early morning until 11:00 A.M.

Mount Auburn Cemetery is not an arboretum per se. Still, the well-maintained and plentiful collection of trees, shrubs, and flowers creates an urban forest, thoughtfully planted and spaced for landscape appeal rather than scientific order. Under the guidance of resident experts, the cemetery grounds sparkle with a varied selection of predictable and unexpected colors, textures and scents from plants both native and exotic. Among the nearly four thousand trees (many labeled for easy identification) are maples, oaks, and beeches, as well as flowering shrubs and trees like crabapples, magnolias, azaleas, and mimosas. Flowers—including snowdrops, daffodils, lilacs, and roses—also bloom at Mount Auburn, from March to August.

The single most tenacious urban legend associated with Mount Auburn Cemetery concerns Mary Baker Eddy, founder of the Christian Science Church, whose beautiful pillared temple is the centerpiece of Halcyon Lake. Historian Blanche Linden-Ward assures us that the story is "totally lore," though based on a shred of truth. That shred: When the religious leader-writer died in 1910, her body was placed in a receiving tomb while her memorial was under construction. To avoid foul play—vandals, body-snatchers, and the like—a watchman was assigned there, and a phone hooked up by the temple, for use should an emergency arise. The legend grew, of course, that Eddy had ordered the phone so that she could check in from Eternity. No, she didn't call. And yes, the telephone is long gone.

Today, visitors can hear stories like this one from tours sponsored by the Friends of Mount Auburn Cemetery, a membership organization founded in 1986 to promote the appreciation and preservation of Mount Auburn. It publishes a wonderfully readable newsletter, *Sweet Auburn,* and offers lectures, tours, and walks on varied aspects of Mount Auburn's unique history, horticulture, art, architecture, and ornithology.

One popular tour offered by the Friends of Mount Auburn Cemetery includes the cemetery's famous women—women like historian Hannah Adams, Franklin Delano Roosevelt's secretary Missy LeHand, Mount Auburn Hospital founder Emily Parsons, cooking authority Fannie Farmer, reformer Dorothea Dix, reformer and poet Julia Ward Howe, poet Amy Lowell, art collector Isabella Stewart Gardner, and Josephine Saint Pierre Ruffin, an early activist for black and women's rights.

People wishing to set up eternal residence in Mount Auburn today have fewer options than in the past. Surprising as it may seem, room for casket burial still exists, and Mount Auburn's staff continues to lay out new interment space. As the years have passed, however, these spaces have become more limited, while providing memorials that do not detract from the spacious, historic landscape has become increasingly difficult. Mount Auburn's trustees have made clear their commitment to preserve and enhance the cemetery's horticultural character.

For those who wish to be cremated, on the other hand, there is still plenty of room. Space is available either in a niche in the Story Chapel columbarium or in the ground. The cemetery also runs its own modern crematory behind Bigelow Chapel. It performed 887 cremations in 1992, mostly for interment elsewhere. In New England, according to the Cremation Association of North America, cremations are performed on approximately 17 percent of the deceased.

Pax vobiscum.

THE ESSENTIALS

ADDRESS: 580 Mount Auburn Street, on the Cambridge-Watertown line.

TELEPHONE: Business Office, (617) 547-7105; Friends of Mount Auburn Cemetery, (617) 864-9646.

VISITOR INFORMATION: Gates open 8:00 A.M.–7:00 P.M. daily during daylight savings time; 8:00 A.M.–5:00 P.M. rest of year. Office open Monday–Friday, 8:30 A.M.–4:30 P.M.; Saturday 8:30 A.M.–12:30 P.M. Free. Brochures, maps, program schedules, and other information available at both the gatehouse on Mount Auburn Street and the nearby office. No bicycling, picnicking, skateboarding, jogging, skating, or rollerblading; open for "passive recreation" only. No dogs unless kept inside cars. Grounds, restrooms, and office are all wheelchair accessible.

PART III

The Athens of America: Arts and Entertainment in Boston

NE OF the most cherished epithets ever bestowed on Boston is "the Athens of America." Though most would agree the appellation was eventually well deserved, it took the town centuries to earn it. Ancient Athens, of course, was known as a center of early democracy and a wellspring of art, theater, poetry, literature, and finely tuned athletes.

Puritan Boston may have been an efficient, self-disciplined, hardworking machine, but a center of culture and the arts it was not. Musical instruments, including organs, were long forbidden in Puritan meetinghouses. Theater presentations were strictly prohibited, since, according to the Massachusetts legislature of 1750, stage plays "tended to increase immorality, impiety and contempt of religion." Museums were essentially an unknown entity, at least until the success of Charles Willson Peale's museum in Philadelphia, begun in 1785. And artists were initially employed primarily for more practical purposes, like building furniture and carving tombstones.

By the first decades of the 1800s, however, all that began to change, and Boston began to grow. The founding of the Boston Athenaeum in 1807 heralded the beginning of one of Boston's finest libraries. Moreover, the Athenaeum's patronage of the arts and artists helped lay the foundation for the Boston Museum of Fine Arts, first opened in 1876. As Bostonians became devotees of the arts, they brought back countless treasures from their travels abroad. The collections at the M.F.A., the Gardner Museum, and the museums of art at Harvard College all profited and prospered from these sojourns.

Meanwhile, the world of music took a giant step forward with the creation of the Boston Music Hall in 1852, touted as the city's first real concert hall. When philanthropist Henry Lee Higginson founded the Boston Symphony Orchestra in 1881, he rented the Music Hall as a performance space. Twenty years later, Higginson built his orchestra a more permanent home—Symphony Hall. Over in Cambridge, Harvard College fostered cultural growth on a variety of similar fronts. One of the city's favorite concert stages, Sanders Theater, was built as part of Harvard's Memorial Hall in 1876. In addition to the aforementioned art museums, Harvard established and nurtured on-campus museums throughout the nineteenth and twentieth centuries, in fields as diverse as botany, geology, minerology, comparative zoology, archaeology, and ethnology.

Legitimate theaters began to emerge in Boston in the decade after the Revolution, then flourished for much of the nineteenth century. By the turn of the twentieth century, a building boom was in full swing. The stages most closely associated with the downtown theater district today—the Colonial, the Shubert, and the Wilbur—were all opened between 1900 and 1914. Fast on the heels of live theater entertainment came motion pictures and the early movie palaces; one of Boston's best live performance venues, the Wang Center for the Performing Arts, began as a movie house called the Metropolitan Theater in 1925.

It's interesting to note that aside from those downtown theaters, much of the art and cultural life that flowered in nineteenth- and twentieth-century Boston depended on landfill and reclaimed land. Symphony Hall, for example, was built on the wild frontiers of Huntington Avenue. The Museum of Fine Arts first opened in the former marshland of Copley Square, then moved to the former marshland of the Fenway in 1909. The Fenway also hosted other centers of arts and entertainment in the early 1900s: the Gardner Museum, originally known as Fenway Court, opened in 1903, while Fenway Park, the home of Boston's indigenous baseball team, the Red Sox, celebrated its opening day in 1912.

One final note: we included the history of Park Street Station in this section because (a) there was nowhere else to put it, (b) public transit is a good way to access all these sites, and (c) the Park Street subway stop is, after all, an entertaining place.

17   The Museum of Fine Arts

SOME PEOPLE still think that an art museum is a building filled with paintings, paintings, and more paintings. And to some extent, that vision is true. Boston's Museum of Fine Arts (M.F.A.), for example—one of the city's oldest and most revered cultural institutions—does have a world-class collection of oil paintings. But since first opening to the public on July 4, 1876, this "jewel of Boston museums" has been much more than that.

Today, the M.F.A.'s array of more than a million objects is divided among nine curatorial departments and ranges from tiny painted shards of pottery, Greek vases, Indian fertility goddesses, and Peruvian tapestries to a full-fledged Japanese garden, the silverwork of Paul Revere, the contents of ancient Egyptian tombs, and exquisitely furnished period rooms from American and European history.

"The M.F.A. is a repository of memory through vision," says Jonathan Fairbanks, curator of the Department of American Decorative Arts and Sculpture. "Objects do speak to those who are willing to listen."

Oil paintings, of course, "speak" as well. And the museum's impressive collection is clearly multilingual. Nineteenth-century French painters are represented in legion force, and works include Vincent van Gogh's *Postman Roulin*, Auguste Renoir's *Bal de Bougival*, Paul Gauguin's *D'ou venons nous? . . .* and thirty-eight works by Claude Monet—the largest collection of Monet's work outside of France. Well-known paintings by Mary Cassatt and Georgia O'Keeffe are here, too, as well as gems by Gentile Bellini, Pablo Picasso, El Greco, and Winslow Homer.

Bostonians are particularly proud of the paintings of American Revolutionary patriots in the M.F.A. collections, which portray local heroes and represent local artists of international renown. The best known of these are Gilbert Stuart's unfinished portraits of Martha and George Washington—the latter being the 1796 rendering reproduced on our dollar bill. Other colonial men and women depicted include John Hancock, Paul Revere, and Joseph Warren, all painted by John Singleton Copley, as well as Stuart's oil of Rachel Walker, Mrs. Paul Revere.

Still, the tale of Boston's proudest museum—located on the outbound reaches of Huntington Avenue—is more than a mere delineation of its vast and varied art treasures.

The M.F.A.'s story began a little more than one hundred years after colonial Bostonians helped incite the American Revolution. In the early nineteenth century, Boston's principal repository of fine art was not a museum at all. The Boston Athenaeum, a private club incorporated in 1807 and located on Beacon Street since 1849, acted as a combined library and art gallery for the rapidly growing city. By the 1860s, however, the skylighted top floor of the Athenaeum was overflowing with art. Its members decided to focus on the Athenaeum's role as a scholarly society and research library, and to find other quarters for its art.

At the same time that an Athenaeum committee was seeking alternative gallery space, Boston was creating a new neighborhood by filling in its Back Bay. Once a foul-smelling section of mill-dam mudflats, the "new" Back Bay soon became a haven for institutions of culture, learning, and religion. By the turn of the century, the streets around Copley Square boasted such illustrious structures as Trinity Church, the Boston Public Library, and the New Old South Church.

Years of efforts by the well-connected Fine Arts Committee of the Boston Athenaeum finally paid off in 1870. On February 4 of that year, an act of the Massachusetts legislature established the Trustees of the Museum of Fine Arts, who were instructed to build a city art museum. They were awarded a 91,000-square-foot lot in Art Square (renamed Copley Square in 1883). As it turned out, this land grant was essentially the beginning and end of substantial city support for the Museum of Fine Arts. Instead, private citizens built the M.F.A. and filled it with collections. Contribu-

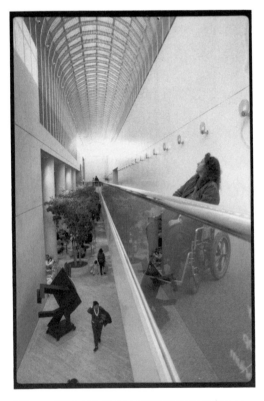

Renowned as the "jewel of Boston museums," the Museum of Fine Arts is also exceptionally accessible to those with special needs.

tions to the $230,268 construction project ranged from modest gifts of thirty-five cents to the $25,000 donated by Mrs. T. Bigelow Lawrence, the wealthy widow of an Athenaeum benefactor.

The museum's first home, an ornate Ruskinian Gothic structure at the corner of Dartmouth and Saint James streets, was designed by John H. Sturgis and Charles Brigham. The extravagant red-brick and terra cotta building, with depictions of the "Genius of Art" and "Art and Industry" adorning the exterior, was opened to the public for America's centennial, July 4, 1876. Its first exhibits were largely composed of works loaned by the Athenaeum, including the Stuart portraits of George and Martha Washington, and Thomas Crawford's marble statue *Orpheus and Cerberus.*

Despite an opening-day moral controversy, solved by masking the private parts of "explicit" classical casts with fig leaves, the museum proved a success. With a paid staff of six in 1876—compared with more than five hundred in 1993—the M.F.A. welcomed thousands of guests. In 1877, annual visitation was 158,446. By 1895 that number had grown to 301,315.

By the turn of the twentieth century, only twenty-four years after the M.F.A. first opened its doors, the vast array of incoming art collections had outgrown the museum's Copley Square home. Despite additions in 1879 and 1889, a move to larger quarters was essential. A site was finally chosen on Boston's newest frontier, a dirty, marshy area known as the Fenway, which had been transformed in the 1880s to an "arboreous state" by the work of landscape architect Frederick Law Olmsted. As had happened earlier in the Back Bay, distinguished cultural institutions—such as the Isabella Stewart Gardner Museum, Symphony Hall, and the Massachusetts Historical Society—began building in this newly attractive rural outpost of the congested Hub.

Guy Lowell was chosen to design the new fine arts museum in 1907, assisted by R. Clipston Sturgis, Edmund M. Wheelwright, and D. Despradelle. Working with more than 500,000 square feet of land, Lowell and associates created much of the massive granite neoclassical building we know as the M.F.A. today. The Huntington Avenue facade—with its Ionic temple portico and two flanking wings—was designed as the main entrance, partly as a convenience to visitors whose streetcars stopped in front. The Huntington Avenue doorway was overshadowed as the museum's main entry after I. M. Pei's modern West Wing was added in 1981. Most recently, economic constraints have closed the Huntington entrance altogether.

By the time the museum's Fenway home opened in 1909, the cost for building, land, and improvements, moving, and installation was a staggering $2,887,968.75. The move from Copley Square to the Fenway, however, was surprisingly uneventful. Two horse-drawn carriages made repeated trips between the sites to transport the collections. No guards were hired to protect the art, and nothing of value was broken or damaged in the process.

Almost immediately the 1909 building was expanded. Between 1911 and 1915, the Evans Wing was added, increasing exhibit space by 40 percent. That wing was funded by a single gift from Mrs. Robert Dawson Evans, whose husband, a rubber and copper-mining magnate, died when thrown from a horse in 1907. Between 1928 and 1988, other additions included the Decorative Arts Wing, the George Robert White Wing, the modern West Wing—which houses the museum shop, three restaurants, Remis Auditorium, education offices, and modern art galleries—and finally, Tenshin-en, the Japanese "Garden of the Heart of Heaven."

Cyrus Dallin's equestrian sculpture *Appeal to the Great Spirit*—which has essentially become the symbol of the M.F.A.—was placed in front of the Huntington entrance in 1913. The fourth of four Dallin statues depicting the attitude of Native Americans toward the intruding Europeans, this work was purchased for the museum by public subscription. Though the Native American rider is clearly from the Plains, Dallin created the work in the Boston suburb of Arlington Heights.

Over the decades, a great number of families have contacted museum offices, explaining how it was their horse, their relative, or their close friend who was *the* model for Dallin's landmark sculpture. Jonathan Fairbanks has an ample file of these claims, some or all of which may be true, depending on how many different models posed for *Appeal to the Great Spirit*. According to Fairbanks, it was, and still is, quite common for sculptors to use several models in the course of creating one statue.

Another piece of art that is considered part of the fabric of the M.F.A. is the array of murals, moldings, enrichments, painted decorations, and bas reliefs that decorate the great rotunda. The entire area, including skylights and columns, was built, then completely rebuilt at great cost to accommodate the artistic schemes of John Singer Sargent. From 1917 to 1925, Sargent executed the work, primarily in London, though occasionally from his Newbury Street studio. His models for the demi-goddesses above the library entrance were three touring Ziegfeld Follies chorus girls, who were performing at Boston's Colonial Theatre at the time.

While commissioned artists like Dallin and Sargent were compensated for their labors—and art purchases were periodically made—the Museum of Fine Arts has always needed loans and gifts to fill its galleries. Though the nucleus of the 1876 exhibit was Athenaeum artwork collected over the previous fifty years, this was augmented by art borrowed from individuals and the city of Boston. Paintings composed a portion of these early loans, as did plaster casts, pottery, porcelains, textiles, embroideries, tapestries, and other decorative arts objects.

For its first fifteen years, the museum depended primarily on such loans. Gifts were a second source of art, followed by outright museum purchases afforded by "special funds." J. M. W. Turner's painting of a flaming *Slave Ship*, for example, was a loan from Miss Alice Hooper; it was purchased by the M.F.A. in 1899 from the painting's subsequent owner. Stuart's unfinished Washington portraits were loaned to the museum for more than a century before finally being purchased from the Athenaeum in 1980. Wealthy donors and the bequests of art patrons provided many of these gifts and special funds.

The museum was also blessed by the contributions of globe-trotting Bostonians, who helped create priceless collections during the M.F.A.'s formative years. According to the late historian Walter Muir Whitehill, whose definitive two-volume history of the museum was published in 1970, Edward Perry Warren was one of several friends of the M.F.A. who proved to be "the right collector in the right place at the right time." Warren's particular expertise was classical art, which both he and John Marshall purchased in travels across Europe in the 1890s. Their acquisitions formed the foundation of the museum's department of classical art.

Similar turn-of-the-century expeditions formed the basis of other museum collections. In the 1880s, for example, Edward Morse, Ernest Fenollosa, William Sturgis Bigelow, and Dr. Charles D. Weld brought a wealth of Japanese artwork to Boston, and helped begin what's now known as the Asiatic Arts Department. During the first decades of the twentieth century, archaeologist George Reisner helped fill Boston's art museum with more Egyptian Old Kingdom treasures than exist anywhere outside of Cairo, through a series of excavations cosponsored by the M.F.A. and Harvard University.

Though many of the museum's finest holdings were acquired with deliberate thought and meticulous research, others were discovered through strokes of fate. For instance, the M.F.A. contains a replica of the subterranean burial room of Egyptian Queen Hetep-heres; the original was literally stumbled upon in 1925, when an expedition photographer's tripod leg sank into the ground, uncovering a secret staircase to the tomb.

In another serendipitous discovery, an original Gentile Bellini painting of a doge of Venice (doges were the tiny republic's chief magistrates) was found by a Boston woman while cleaning her attic in 1937. Assuming it was a cheap imitation, she donated it to Morgan Memorial Goodwill Industries. Luckily, that charitable organization brought it to the M.F.A., which verified the painting's authenticity and worth.

One of the museum's treasures is the diminutive gold and ivory statue of a Minoan snake goddess. Though the details are hazy, the statuette reportedly arrived in a cigar box carried by a Cretan peasant who was traveling from Piraeus to Boston in 1913. A Greek-speaking Bostonian on the same vessel saw the artwork, broken into hundreds of tiny slivers and fragments, and directed the peasant to the M.F.A. The gracious Mrs. F. Scott Fitz, mother of a museum trustee, donated the appropriate funds, allowing the goddess to be purchased and painstakingly reconstructed by the M.F.A. staff.

As the M.F.A.'s collections grew, departments gradually formed, each with its own specialty and curatorial staff. Today the museum has nine: Classical; Asiatic; Ancient Egyptian, Nubian, and Near Eastern; European Decorative Arts and Sculpture; American Decorative Arts and Sculpture; Paintings; Prints, Drawings, and Photographs; Textiles and Costumes; and the newest addition, Contemporary. The Nubian gallery, opened in April of 1992, is one of the museum's newest permanent exhibits; it is dedicated to the art and culture of ancient Nubia, an African region that once encompassed southern Egypt and northern Sudan.

Though each department has its highlights, those interested in Boston history will take particular pleasure in areas featuring American paintings and American decorative arts and sculpture. A series of fully furnished period rooms recreate eighteenth- and nineteenth-century New England parlors, from the dark rustic charm of the 1704 Brown-Pearl House of West Boxford, to the opulent, hand-polished luxury of heiress Elizabeth West's rooms at her 1801 estate, Oak Hill. (Oak Hill was demolished in the 1920s to make room for the construction of the North Shore Shopping Center in Peabody, twenty miles north of Boston.)

Among a multitude of acquisitions relevant to Boston history are some of the museum's best-known pieces. The silver Liberty Bowl, created by Paul Revere and commissioned in 1768 by the Sons of Liberty, commemorates the brave resistance of the Massachusetts legislature to British tyranny. The unfinished Stuart portraits of George and Martha are eminently popular, but not always present. Since 1980, the first First Couple have been jointly owned by the M.F.A. and the National Portrait Gallery in Washington, in an arrangement that allows them to rotate between the institutions every three years. (They'll be in Washington until May 1995.)

Since its earliest decades, the M.F.A. has been concerned with educating Bostonians about art and with making its collections accessible to as many people as possible. As early as 1877, a "School of Drawing and Painting" was run within the old museum; a more structured entity, today's Museum School, became a part of the museum in 1901. In 1907, docents—or nonstaff teachers—began offering museum visitors information on the collections; some claim that the M.F.A. was the first to use such guides, though other museums quickly followed suit. Various efforts to reach all social and economic classes were periodically launched—including free daily access, free concerts, and even a storyteller who freely interpreted art for "slum children" from 1911 to 1919. Though much of this was apparently done in earnest, the notion persisted for decades that the M.F.A. was a haven only for the white and the wealthy.

Today's museum staff has made an even greater effort to mold the prestigious institution into what Director Alan Shestack calls a user-friendly facility. The museum education department oversees and sponsors programs for the community, schools, and the public, offering art classes, scholarships, "artful adventures," parent-child programs, hands-on activities for youngsters, concerts, and films. More brochures are being written, and more labeling is appearing everywhere, in both special exhibitions and permanent collections. Interpretation and guided tours, by volunteer gallery instructors and members of the volunteer Ladies Committee, are available several times a day. The museum's accessibility to the disabled is comprehensive—and arguably the best in Boston.

"Our real commitment is to attracting, winning, and sustaining a more diverse audience," says Director of Education Bill Burback. "When museums started, the objects, the collections, were the most important things. Now, I think museums have a different sense of responsibility and commitment—to the visitors' experience with the objects.

"But we do still love the objects!"

ADDRESS: 465 Huntington Avenue, Boston.

TELEPHONE: (617) 267-9300.

VISITOR INFORMATION: Open 10:00 A.M.–4:45 P.M., Tuesday–Sunday; 10:00 A.M.–9:45 P.M., Wednesday; closed Monday. Moderate admission fee; free every Wednesday, 4:00–10:00 P.M. Daily tours, both of the entire museum and of specific collections, begin at the information desk; call for details and times. Excellent, exceptionally well-conceived wheelchair access throughout building, including restrooms, elevators, and gift shop.

18 The Isabella Stewart Gardner Museum

IT'S SURROUNDED by a wrought-iron fence and a stark brick exterior— hardly the stuff that would inspire passing drivers to stop and stare. From the outside, neighboring institutions along the Fenway—like Emmanuel College, Simmons College, and various buildings of the Museum of Fine Arts—look far more impressive. But once inside the luxurious neo-Venetian palace of art treasures, quirky antiquities, and floral extravagance known as the Isabella Stewart Gardner Museum, visitors inevitably become enchanted.

Historian Henry Adams once described the Gardner, which opened in 1903, as "peace, repose or dream, rather like opium." Decades later, architect I. M. Pei would characterize the museum as "an oasis of calm and beauty." Actress Katharine Hepburn added a most important footnote to these rather ethereal analyses: "It's great fun," she insisted of the curious Fenway palace, "and it's a fascinating creature that it's all about."

That "creature," of course, was Mrs. Isabella Stewart Gardner, known to posterity as the founder and creator of the Gardner Museum, and to her peers as Boston's *most* improper Bostonian. Gardner was a patron of the arts and a flamboyant social leader in a conservative Victorian age. She was also a learned collector, a world traveler, a multilinguist, a music lover, an accomplished social dancer, and the alternately beloved and belittled talk of the town.

Contemporary accounts suggest that Belle, as Isabella was called, had a certain individualistic spirit and energy even in her earliest years. Her original home was New York City. Her father was a Stewart, boasting a family lineage that traced back to the Stewarts of twelfth-century Scotland. Their money came from Irish linen, Pennsylvania iron, and well-invested inheritances.

The beautifully flowered central courtyard of the Isabella Stewart Gardner Museum is a seventy-nine-foot tall glass-roofed atrium.

In later years, her character was alternately described as "charming," "flirtatious," "whimsical," and "imperious." Morris Carter—director of the museum from 1924 to 1955, and Mrs. Gardner's biographer in 1925—described her as "a fascinating, frail, delicate little creature, delightful to everybody, but determined to lead her own life." Today, being a strong, free-thinking woman is almost acceptable. A century ago, it was essentially scandalous.

Belle met her future husband's family through a connection with a childhood friend. The Gardners of Boston had money from sailing ships, railroads, and investments. They also had a son they called Jack, presumably to avoid confusing him with his father, the senior John L. Gardner. Belle and John L. Gardner, Jr., courted and fell in love, then married when she was nineteen. The couple eventually moved into one of the Gardner family homes at 152 Beacon Street, soon expanding into 150 Beacon as well.

If the new "Mrs. Jack" was initially unpopular with the female socialites of Boston, it was perhaps partly because a New Yorker had married a tall, dark, rich, eligible Boston bachelor. She was also a good dancer, and an avid, educated listener—both of which were terribly attractive to men, married and single. Despite the petty jealousies that ensued, Mrs. Gardner did have many female friends.

Though she was born in 1840, a year after the invention of the camera, the best pictures of Isabella Stewart Gardner are paintings and sketches, including ten scattered throughout the museum. Mrs. Gardner's favorite was the life-sized John Singer Sargent painting in the Gothic Room; it depicts Belle as many of her early friends remember her—small, slender, and rather plain-looking, with her distinctive string of pearls wrapped around her waist. If Belle was plain, however, she was not self-conscious about it; moreover, her contemporaries continually marveled at the beauty of both her voice and her complexion.

Why Mrs. Jack began traveling and collecting art work, and finally built a home for her treasures, is a complex question. As a teenager, she had confided to a friend her childhood dream of creating a palace for the people. The death of her two-year-old son Jackie in 1865 probably provided the impetus for making that dream become reality. The loss of her only child put Belle in a deep depression, a so-called nervous breakdown that left her bedridden for months. As an antidote, Jack took his wife on extended visits to foreign lands. The "therapy" worked then, as it would with later family crises. Belle loved many cultures and countries, though the exquisite ornamentation and Renaissance artwork of Venice took center stage in her heart.

Meanwhile, Mrs. Jack had become friends with many members of Boston's cultural elite, who sustained her interest in art. Among them were Henry James, Henry Adams, James McNeill Whistler, John Singer Sargent, art history professor Charles Eliot Norton of Harvard, and the soon-to-be-famous art critic Bernard Berenson. Belle helped support young Berenson when he graduated from Harvard in 1887. He traveled to Europe and purchased art for her there, writing her with descriptions and prices, then awaiting her response. Among the paintings he acquired for her were several Rembrandts, two Botticellis, two Raphaels, a Rubens, a Degas, and a Titian, all of which are displayed at the Museum today. Because of the predilections of both Bernard and Belle, most of these purchases were of works by Italian Renaissance painters. The Gardner collection as a whole is strongest in Italian Renaissance, seventeenth-century Dutch, and nineteenth-century American works.

The deaths of loved ones continued to haunt Belle's life; several of Jack's relatives passed on early, as did Belle's three siblings, her father, and, quite unexpectedly, Jack himself. With no husband, no heirs, and a heightened sense of her own mortality, Mrs. Jack plunged headlong into buying and building. She had ample financial resources for this pursuit: she inherited $1.6 million after her father's death in 1892, and received another $2.3 million when Jack died in 1898. These funds may seem inadequate for establishing a major art collection today; at the time, however, Mrs. Gardner purchased many museum items for as little as $5 or $10. Other works were comparatively expensive, but still affordable: she bought Titian's painting *The Rape of Europa*—a priceless piece now displayed in the Titian Room—for $100,000. Today it's considered one of the most important Italian Renaissance paintings in America.

★ ★ ★

It was inevitable that the collection would eventually outgrow the Gardner house on Beacon Street. Jack and Belle had actually discussed building a museum to display Belle's accumulating treasures years before Jack's death. Though Belle had wanted a site in their Beacon Street home, Jack pushed for a spot in the Fens, a once-marshy area that had recently been reclaimed, and that Jack predicted would become "the new Back Bay."

Jack was wrong; the Fenway area never did become as prestigious as the Back Bay. Nevertheless, Mrs. Gardner began furiously building on the wide-open Fens site shortly after her husband's death, selecting Willard T. Sears as architect. Since construction was hidden behind a high brick wall, since Mrs. Gardner would not talk to reporters, and since many of her workmen spoke only Italian, myths about "Belle's folly" were favorite fodder for gossips and tabloids around the world. "WEIRD WALL SHUTS MRS. 'JACK' GARDNER PALACE IN FROM THE WORLD: Whim of a Woman!" cried a headline in one June 19, 1901, edition of the *Boston Herald*.

Behind that "weird wall," Mrs. Jack was building her own eclectic version of a Venetian palazzo. While the interior design was based on Belle's interpretation of an ornate fifteenth-century Italian palace turned inside out, the exterior resembled a simpler northern Italian villa. Because of the soft, moist land below, pilings were sunk beneath the heavy stone walls. The center courtyard, however, originally had no pilings. Hence, it sank; you can still see that the lower stairs were added to the original top steps of all four entrances.

As Fenway Court took shape, Belle occasionally bolted off to Italy to buy staircases, balustrades, lace, furniture, ironwork, and other furnishings. She also changed her plans in the middle of the building process—to the chagrin of her workers, who would sometimes characterize her as whimsical, mad, or an egomaniac. In fact, the periodic changes were relatively minor; in the same era Frank Lloyd Wright would be dubbed a genius though he tore down walls he had just erected.

Isabella Stewart Gardner's eccentricity—and her unwillingness to spoil a good story by telling the truth—spawned many urban legends in her time, some of which contained kernels of truth. Although she did not walk her pet lions on Beacon Street, as in one favorite tale, she did pet a toothless old lion and escort it around a traveling zoo that was located on the Boylston Street side of Boston Common in 1897. She did collect exotic trees for her grounds and courtyard, but she did not, as legend had it, greet guests while perched in mimosa trees. She did not have multitudinous affairs with men, although she had many male admirers. Scholars think that if she ever did have such a liaison, it was with author F. Marion Crawford, with whom she spent considerable time in the early 1880s. Belle's husband was apparently tolerant of whatever did, or did not, transpire.

And no, she did not dismantle an extant Venetian palace and bring it back, stone by stone, to build her museum. No Venetian prince would ever have built as Mrs. Jack did; though Fenway Court used many Venetian palace parts, those parts were often chronologically, regionally, and archaeologically unrelated.

Contrary to popular gossip, there's no evidence that Belle liked to lie naked on a bear rug in front of Titian's *Rape of Europa;* moreover, she was never the puppet of Bernard Berenson, and actually rejected many of his recommendations for art acquisitions. She did, however, attend a concert at Symphony Hall wearing a headband that read, "Oh, You Red Sox."

In her construction methods, her art and artifact acquisitions, and the way she arranged them together, Mrs. Gardner followed no rules. She did what she pleased, and even engraved the motto "C'est Mon Plaisir" over the main entrance to Fenway Court (today the museum's exit).

Inside, Mrs. Gardner's dream is both a visitor's delight and a conservator's nightmare. The museum's collections include 290 paintings, 280 pieces of sculpture, 60 drawings, 130 prints, 460 pieces of furniture, 240 ceramic and glass objects, an archive of more than 6,000 letters, and a library of 2,300 volumes focused on the museum collection. The collections are spread throughout the building—four floors comprising thirty-one rooms, chambers, and hallways. Paintings are often placed back-to-back by an open window, with viewing chairs planted on either side. Antique tables, chairs, and glorious clutter occasionally obstruct the view of other artwork. Rare medieval choir stalls, statues, and art objects are open to public affection, unprotected by pedestals, glass cases, or rope barriers. Precious textiles are placed under or draped over objects, as if they were common tablecloths. Enormous medieval tapestries hang free from the walls. Many paintings are hung directly across the room from bright, broad windows overlooking the beautifully flowered central courtyard—a glass-roofed atrium seventy-nine feet tall.

One favorite, and typically eclectic, museum area is known as the Spanish Cloister. The featured painting is the huge *El Jaleo* (1882), a vision of a Spanish dancer by American artist John Singer Sargent. The cloister—so named for its architectural design as a covered passage on the side of a courtyard—also includes Mexican wall tiles, Boston-made floor tiles, a French medieval portal, three Roman sarcophagi, and Egyptian wood-carvings.

The Gardner Museum was first opened to visitors, as Fenway Court, on January 1, 1903. Mrs. Gardner made her personal living quarters on the fourth floor of the building—in spaces now used for storage and administrative offices. During her lifetime, she opened her museum home to the public for two weeks each spring and fall, limiting tickets to two hundred per day. Her fee was $1, a sum which she thought would make the public appreciate the visit more.

While Belle was alive her museum changed constantly. For example, the current Spanish Cloister and the Tapestry Room above it—where concerts are now held from September through May—were originally one huge, two-story music room, until Mrs. Gardner altered it in 1914. She also loved regular changes of the floral displays throughout the courtyard and on the surrounding grounds. The seasonal plantings continue to this day, facilitated by the acquisition of seven greenhouses for the museum site in the 1970s. Among popular favorites are the courtyard's rare orchids and its tumbling nasturtiums, which grow from the second story down, sometimes reaching twenty-five or thirty feet in length.

In her will, Mrs. Gardner specified that the museum, its contents, and their general arrangement should remain the same as in her last year of life, which turned out to be 1924. If the rules were broken, she stipulated, the museum would see its end—with its treasures auctioned off in Paris and the proceeds given to Harvard.

Therefore, the Gardner now features the same works of art, displayed in the same places, decade after decade; objects disappear only occasionally for rest, travel, or in-house conservation. Although such sameness is unusual for a major museum, many visitors find the Gardner a comfortable, familiar "home"—as well as a place where you can always make new discoveries.

Some changes have taken place since Mrs. Gardner's death, necessitated by the changing demands time places on any institution. A two-story administrative wing was added in 1932—exempt from the will's conditions since it was outside the original home and museum. A small gift shop and a cafe were added in 1972 and 1978, as a service to visitors. The greenhouses were additions of the 1970s, while installing a climate control system throughout the museum is an ongoing project of the 1990s. In 1992, the new Special Exhibitions Gallery was also opened in the 1932 annex, allowing the museum both to showcase items from its permanent collections and bring in significant traveling exhibitions.

Other changes result from the ongoing conservation of Gardner treasures—a scientific and artistic process made more difficult by the museum's setup, which often subjects the works to excess light, heat, humidity, air pollution, and the wear and tear brought on by thousands of friendly visitors. A dedicated staff of professional conservators works daily in the annex, painstakingly making repairs to antique tapestries and other pieces, repairs that often take years to complete. Incidentally, virtually all the Gardner's conservation work is done in-house, with the notable exception of work on paintings.

Reparations can't be made, however, for the greatest heartbreak of recent Gardner Museum history: the robbery of March 18, 1990, which resulted in the loss of thirteen objects, including priceless paintings by Vermeer, Rembrandt, and Manet. Two thieves disguised as police officers talked their way past college-age security guards, dismantled the Gardner's alarm system, and then made what was touted as the "biggest art heist in history." The objects taken were estimated by some to have a value of $200 million, and a million-dollar reward was offered for information leading to the recovery of the stolen art.

Despite the years, periodic problems, and that singular tragedy, Isabella Stewart Gardner's dream of creating a "palace for the people" remains very real today. Classical music concerts—a part of the Gardner heritage for decades—are still held in the Tapestry Room on weekends from September through May. Meanwhile, the Gardner staff is working to revitalize their existing educational programs to reach more youngsters than ever, while developing a new lecture series and an artist-in-residence program. In so doing, they are working to recreate the flourishing intellectual and cultural center that Isabella Gardner established at the turn of the century.

What more appropriate place than Belle's Venetian palace?

THE ESSENTIALS

ADDRESS: 280 The Fenway, Boston; offices at 2 Palace Road, Boston.
TELEPHONE: (617) 566-1401; concert information line, (617) 734-1359.
VISITOR INFORMATION: Open 11:00 A.M.–5:00 P.M., Tuesday–Sunday;
   open some holidays: call for details. Moderate admission fee; extra
   charge for concerts. Tours Friday at 2:30 P.M. Wheelchair accessible;
   staff assistance required for use of elevator to second and third floors.

19 Harvard University Museums and Memorial Hall

YOU DON'T have to be a student to reap many of the benefits of Harvard
University. America's oldest institution of higher learning—founded in
1636—has eight museums open to the public on its Cambridge campus.
The tickets are cheap, even free on Saturday mornings. Exhibits range from
stunning blown-glass flowers to triceratops skulls, and from Monet's *Char-
ing Cross Bridge* to Native American totem poles. The museums themselves
vary in style from Victorian "cram'n'jam" setups to spacious, climate-
controlled, interactive rooms with theatrical lighting and sound. Equally
appealing is geographic convenience: the three Harvard University Art
Museums, the four Harvard Museums of Cultural and Natural History,
and the Semitic Museum—as well as Harvard's architectural marvel, Memorial Hall—can all be found within a few short blocks of one another.

The Harvard University Art Museums are at or near the corner of Broadway and Quincy streets, a five-minute walk from Harvard Square. Combined, these three museums house a world-class art collection, featuring
150,000 objects from East and West, and from ancient to modern times.
One ticket admits you to all three.

The Fogg Art Museum, founded in 1891, is the eldest. In its early days,
the Fogg primarily housed art reproductions. Since 1927—when it moved
into the familiar Georgian red-brick building at 32 Quincy Street—the
museum has become a treasure house of European and North American
originals, and has served as a vital source for art education.

The Fogg's central courtyard is a grand, two-story adaptation of the
sixteenth-century Church of the Madonna de San Biagio at Montepul-
ciano, Italy. Surrounding this centerpiece are galleries and halls that contain masterpieces by Giotto, Fra Angelico, Rembrandt, Ingres, Renoir,
Rodin, Whistler, Picasso, and Rothko. A decorative arts gallery—
including silver, furniture, and wondrous old clocks—was added in 1989.

The Busch-Reisinger Museum, which occupied nearby Adolphus

Harvard University Museums and Memorial Hall   111

Busch Hall from 1921 to 1987, is now located in the new Werner Otto Hall; its entrance is on the second floor of the Fogg. The only museum in America devoted to Germanic art, the Busch-Reisinger's early benefactors included Kaiser Wilhelm II and Adolphus Busch, the St. Louis beer magnate. Founded in 1901, the museum was housed in a Harvard gymnasium before the more ornate Busch Hall was built. Anti-German sentiment prevented the new building from opening until 1921, and closed it entirely during World War II.

Longtime curator Charles Kuhn expanded the Busch-Reisinger's collections between 1931 and 1968, acquiring Expressionist works by Klee, Munch, and Kandinsky, as well as Max Beckmann's startling *Self Portrait in Tuxedo* and the *Actors* triptych, two of the gallery's most riveting pieces.

The sleek, striped Arthur M. Sackler Museum, at 485 Broadway, is a recent addition to Harvard's art museums. Dedicated in 1985, the spacious Sackler highlights ancient and Eastern treasures once housed in the Fogg. Rare Persian and Indian miniatures, Japanese prints and ceramics, Greek vases, ancient Chinese jades, and Buddhas are among the beautifully displayed collections. A museum shop is on the main floor.

The Harvard Museums of Cultural and Natural History share one building, with entrances at 24 Oxford Street and 11 Divinity Avenue. As with

Memorial Hall, Harvard University's Victorian Gothic "secular cathedral," has literally played host to cabbages and kings.

the art museums, a single ticket admits one to all four. Although they double as tourist attractions, the collections of all these museums were acquired for use as in-house teaching tools—a purpose they still ably serve to this day.

The most popular exhibit at any of these museums is undoubtedly the display of glass flowers in the Botanical Museum. Formally known as the Ware Collection of Glass Models of Plants, and created by artists Leopold Blaschka and his son, Rudolph, between 1887 and 1936, the three thousand exquisitely blown and hand-shaped flowers are unique. Apparently only the Blaschkas had the patience, or the expertise, to create every pistil, stamen, petal, and stem of 850 plant species in such intricate detail.

Next door to the Botanical Museum is the Museum of Comparative Zoology, also known as the M.C.Z. or the Agassiz Museum. Begun in 1859, this Victorian-era wonderland of halls and chambers is packed with fossils, skeletons, and stuffed creatures of every size and shape. The largest figures include skeletons of the giant sea serpent kronosaurus, the "Harvard Mastodon" (a historic skeleton from Hackettstown, New Jersey, presented to Harvard in 1846), and the first type specimen of the dinosaur triceratops ever described by science. Smaller items include two golden Chinese pheasants given to George Washington by the Marquis de Lafayette, which, after they died, were driven by stagecoach to Charles Willson Peale's museum in Philadelphia and stuffed with pepper as a preservative. (Peale's museum was touted as the first popular museum in America. When it closed in 1850, half its collections were purchased by showman P. T. Barnum, while half went to the Boston Society of Natural History. In 1913, portions of the latter collection—including the Washington pheasants—were acquired by Harvard.)

The Mineralogical and Geological Museums have a similarly nostalgic feel. Though most of the display cabinets are flat-topped, wood-and-glass Victorian-era cases, they've been spruced up with pastel paints and matching rugs. The venerable Geological Museum was established in 1784, and its impressive collection—including gems, minerals, ores, and meteorites—is the oldest and largest in the United States. One of its first curators was John Webster, who was hanged in 1849 for the murder of another faculty member, in the macabre George Parkman case.

The newest museum in the building is the Peabody Museum of Archaeology and Ethnology, founded in 1866. Its ground-floor Hall of the North American Indian was reopened in 1990 following a ten-year, multi-million dollar renovation. Today it's a colorful, interactive, state-of-the-art exhibit, highlighting ten Native American cultures and five hundred artifacts, from a fearsome Crow warbonnet to delicately woven baskets (see Chapter 40 for more information).

The Peabody includes three additional floors of exhibits. While the galleries dedicated to the American Southwest and Oceania have old-fashioned decor and presentation, the artifacts themselves are interesting—though more to curious academics than casual museum-goers. In stark contrast is the newly redesigned third floor, which opened in December of 1992 with the long-term exhibit "Encounters with the Americas." The "hook" of this new hall is the Columbian Quincentennial of 1492. Rather than praise or damn Columbus and the "Age of Discovery," the exhibit uses 1492 as a dividing line from which to observe five specific South and

Central American cultures, past and present. The question of how five centuries of encounters between east and west forged a complex cultural mosaic in the New World is explored through a variety of beautifully presented objects, from huge plaster casts of Classic Maya monuments to modern displays chronicling the plight of the Amazonian tropical forest.

The Harvard Semitic Museum, established in 1889, is located in the classical-style building at 6 Divinity Avenue. Late nineteenth-century Germans coined the word *anti-Semitic* to mean anti-Jewish, but the term *Semitic* actually applies to both Jewish and Arab language and culture in the Near East. This small museum delves into Near Eastern cultures, largely through ongoing archaeological digs and displays of relevant photos. There are no permanent exhibits, though some displays do run for long periods.

Although it's not technically a museum, no tour of the area would be complete without a visit to Harvard's Memorial Hall. New England novelist Jane Langton clearly spent time in the engaging old structure—then used it as the setting for her chilling 1978 mystery, *The Memorial Hall Murder*.

> *The building rose above him like a cliff face, mass piled upon mass, ten thousand of brick laid upon ten thousand. It was ugly, majestically ugly. Augustly, monumentally ugly. It was a red-brick Notre Dame, a bastard Chartres, punctured with stained-glass windows, ribboned around with lofty sentiments in Latin, finialed with metallic crests and pennants, knobbed with the heads of orators. . . .*
>
> *The colossal edifice contained a theater and a great hall and a memorial transept and a lecture room and radio station and a lot of small offices and classrooms, but now in its gloomy grandeur it was a mausoleum as well. When it had been erected in the 1870s it had been intended as a half-secular, half-sacred memorial to young graduates who had died in the Union cause in the Civil War. Now it was an actual coffin. . . .*

All things considered, Memorial Hall—Harvard's own 1874 Victorian Gothic "secular cathedral"—was an ideal location for Langton's fictional murder. To this day, it is filled with memorials to the dead, endless Latin inscriptions, marble busts, dark wooden walls, cavernous chambers, and an unfathomable maze of basement rooms. Overhead hover a series of catwalks, gargoyles, medieval-looking stained glass, chandeliers, and vaulted ceilings.

But there's much more to its story than that. Since its grand opening more than a century ago, Harvard's very adaptable hall has catered not only to murder mystery writers, but quite literally to cabbages and kings. The building's best-known chamber is Sanders Theater, an intimate hybrid of theater and lecture hall that has hosted everything from Elizabethan drama to Gilbert and Sullivan, the Boston Symphony Orchestra to Pete Seeger, Prince Charles to Jesse Jackson, Igor Stravinsky to John Cage, and Social Analysis 10 to Foreign Cultures 48. Across the hallway from Sanders is Alumni Hall, also known as the Great Hall, which served as a major Harvard dining area until 1925—and which will return to that dining function late in 1995. In between, it's been used sporadically for rehearsals, final exams, blood drives, book sales, dances, and receptions.

Dividing the two—much like the transept of a cathedral separating the choir (Sanders) from the nave (Alumni)—is the memorial hallway itself, lined with the names of the dead and lit by two stained-glass windows. Although it serves today primarily as an intermission vestibule and a convenient passageway for Harvard students on cross-campus jaunts, this section is the least understood and perhaps the last appreciated of the building's three major chambers; yet it's the transept itself that best reflects why Memorial Hall was created in the wake of the American Civil War.

Hundreds of young Harvard students and graduates had marched off to battle in the bloody War Between the States. By the war's end in 1865, a committee of fifty Harvard alumni was actively planning a structure to honor those who had died for the Union cause. The two-acre site they chose was a wide-open playing field nicknamed "the Delta," which Harvard had acquired in 1816. To rationalize using such a large lot, the new structure would have to fill other needs of the college as well as serving as a memorial; it was proposed that the building contain an academic theater for literary festivals, a dining hall large enough to serve commencement dinners, plus dozens of meeting- and classrooms.

Two Harvard graduates, William Ware (class of 1852) and Henry Van Brunt (1854), won the design competition for Memorial Hall. The architects modeled Sanders Theater after Oxford University's Sheldonian Theater, then combined elements from London's Westminster Hall and the dining halls at Cambridge and Oxford universities for the rest of the building. The final structure was more than twice its originally planned length, and cost more than twice the initial budget of $150,000. Of the $390,000 finally spent, an astounding $368,980 was contributed by alumni.

Save for a missing clock tower—which was lost in a 1956 fire and never replaced—Memorial Hall's exterior looks much as it did in Ware and Van Brunt's day, particularly after the extensive renovations of the late 1980s. What Memorial Hall does not look like, however, is any other Harvard building.

Its architects designed the structure in the Ruskinian, or High Victorian, Gothic style. Popular in England in the 1860s, such Gothic Revival buildings typically have animated silhouettes, massive and assertive shapes, an overflow of finely crafted details, and, most distinctively, a multitude of colors. In Memorial Hall's case, the predominant red brick is interspersed with stripes of black, tar-dipped brick and buff sandstone. A similar polychrome motif stretches to the roof, which has been likened to both "streaky bacon" and a Navajo blanket.

Although Memorial Hall resembles a cathedral in many ways, both in design and in decorative touches, architect Van Brunt denied throughout his lifetime that the structure was meant to be churchlike in any way.

Less than four years after the cornerstone was laid in 1870, Memorial Hall opened its doors to Harvard's festive June commencement activities. Sanders Theater would not be complete until 1876, and the tower not set in place until 1878, but the sparkling new dining hall and memorial vestibule were dedicated and opened on June 23, 1874.

The vestibule is literally and figuratively the heart of Memorial Hall.

Twenty-eight white marble tablets solemnly list the names of 136 Harvard graduates and students who died in the Civil War, and the battles in which they fell—including Gettysburg, Antietam, and Fredericksburg. There's a longstanding controversy over the fact that those listed are all Union men, while some 64 slain Harvard Confederates remain unnamed to this day. Among those memorialized is 1860 medical school graduate Benjamin Franklin Peirce—whose name may have inspired the full name of the "Hawkeye" character on the beloved television series "M★A★S★H."

The vestibule has other pop culture connections as well: it was there Langton's fictitious victim fell prey to a fatal bomb blast in *The Memorial Hall Murder,* and it was there actor Christopher Reeve pondered the memorial tablets while playing southern Civil War veteran Basil Ransom in the 1984 film version of Henry James's *The Bostonians.*

The sixty-foot tall vestibule's ecclesiastic feel—and its popular name, Memorial Transept—comes primarily from the two gorgeous stained-glass rose windows that dominate its north and south entrances. Though the aura is sacred, the messages are quite secular. The newly refurbished north window, originally designed by Donald MacDonald in the late nineteenth century, lists all the virtues in Latin, explains Louise Ambler, a Fogg Museum curator who was active in the recent restoration. "If you read the Latin . . . carefully," she adds, "you'll see that one word is meaningless. It was reassembled incorrectly during the repair."

The south window was donated in 1898 by Martin Brimmer, class of 1849. The window's designer, Sarah Wyman Whitman, is affectionately dubbed "our wild woman of stained glass" by architect Peter Riley, who helped coordinate Memorial Hall's restorations of the late 1980s. Whitman included some 35,000 pieces of glass in this work, some sandwiched six layers deep in order to create certain color effects. The north window, by contrast, contains a mere 7,800 segments.

The rest of Memorial Hall's veritable museum of nineteenth-century American stained glass graces the high walls of cavernous Alumni Hall. When the 165-foot dining hall was completed in 1874, all eighteen of its windows were filled with plain white glass. Between 1879 and 1902, however, seventeen of those spaces were filled with stained glass, primarily donated by alumni classes, and designed by well-known artists like Whitman, John LaFarge, Frederic Crowninshield, and the Tiffany Glass Company.

The windows portray scenes of war, peace, bravery, morality, and enlightenment. The historic personages depicted on them are hardly Harvardians, though most were learned "soldiers" of some sort. Generally standing in pairs, with a scene or inscription below, the characters are as diverse as Pericles, Leonardo, Shakespeare, Charlemagne, Christopher Columbus, and Joseph Warren. (The last was a local fellow and a beloved patriot, who died at the Battle of Bunker Hill.)

A break from that standard, posed pattern—and one of the Hall's most moving pieces—is the famous Battle Window, designed by John LaFarge and donated by the Class of 1860. Twelve members of that class died in the Civil War, including Robert Gould Shaw, who led the black, all-volunteer

54th Regiment commemorated in bas relief on Boston Common (see Chapter 34).

Above these stained-glass scenes is the Hall's great hammerbeam trussed ceiling, inspired by the medieval halls at the colleges of Oxford and Cambridge in England. Down below is a gallery of marble busts and rippling oil paintings, depicting soldiers, statesmen, and Harvard sons of the Civil War era. Amidst them are large rectangles that at first glance appear to be medieval tapestries. Not so, explains Ambler as she draws us closer: "See, they're more like beach mats, and painted as if they were stage sets." The origins and artists of these painted grass mats are not documented.

The rest of Alumni Hall is a vast open space, once filled with long dining tables and hungry Harvard students—a use it will resume by the fall of 1995. Henry James once commented on the curious irony of the space's dining use, calling Memorial Hall "the great bristling brick Valhalla . . . that house of honor and hospitality which . . . dispenses . . . laurels to the dead and dinner to the living." Following its retirement as a dining hall in 1925, Alumni Hall's use was limited for several decades. Like the rest of Memorial Hall, it was frequently rented by non-Harvard individuals and organizations, which helped the building pay for its own upkeep.

Now, thanks to a $12-million grant from the Walter H. Annenberg Foundation, the Great Hall (which will be renamed for Annenberg's late son, Roger) and the rest of the building will soon undergo major renovations. Meanwhile, the basement area of Memorial Hall—for years the home of WHRB radio plus a flurry of little classrooms and offices—will house a Harvard "common," or informal student center. The latter is thanks to a $7-million gift from Katherine Bogdanovich Loker.

Renovations are also slated for Sanders Theater, the other half of Memorial Hall, which has always been a strange sort of place as performing stages go. It has no real marquee. It has no green room, though performers can use nearby rooms to rehearse. There are no individual seats in the audience, just rows of cushioned wooden pew-like benches, marked by one of the strangest numbering systems ever devised. And there's no way to move the built-in risers off the stage. Still, Sanders Theater, named for the alumnus who bequeathed $56,000 for its completion, has long been extolled as a magical, surprisingly intimate theater with excellent sight lines. With 1,224 seats, it remains Harvard's largest theater, roughly comparable in size to the Berklee Performance Center and Jordan Hall in Boston.

Despite the fact that it was created for literary festivals and academic lectures—which still take place there—Sanders has seen it all. In recent years, classical and acoustic music groups of all sizes have shown a particular fondness for the space. Folk music legend Pete Seeger wrote in a 1974 letter to the newspaper *Harvard Today*, "Sanders Theatre is one of the greatest auditoriums in the country. . . . The very reverberations which make it difficult for lecturers and some music make it ideal for singers. It's like singing in a bathtub."

While modern halls are too often sterile, Sanders has character in abundance. Above the stage is an enormous inscribed panel, heralded as the "queen" of Harvard's Latin inscriptions by historian Mason Hammond. The panel chronicles the 1636 founding of Harvard College "here in wooded and uncultivated places." Down below, stage left and right, are marble statues of Josiah Quincy—the Boston mayor and Harvard president—and colonial-era orator James Otis. The marble Otis, like the statues of John Winthrop and John Adams which guard the inner entrance at Alumni Hall, were moved to Memorial Hall from Mount Auburn Cemetery in 1936. A John LaFarge stained-glass portrait of the Greek goddess Athena, posed in a classic mourning motif, looks down from the balcony. Below LaFarge's masterpiece are what some consider the best seats in Sanders, by the way—the C, D, and E sections of the mezzanine.

Memorial Hall and its unusual chambers are wonderful places to wander through, or to settle down in for a show or special event. But if you're thinking of renting out any part of the hall, be forewarned of one unusual restriction: no helium balloons are allowed. Once trapped in Memorial Hall's High Gothic trusses, they may never escape, even if deflated. Legend has it that tiny bits of colored rubber still rest in the eaves up yonder.

THE ESSENTIALS

Harvard University Art Museums

ADDRESS: 485 Broadway and 32 Quincy streets, near Harvard Yard, Cambridge.

TELEPHONE: (617) 495-9400.

VISITOR INFORMATION: Open 10:00 A.M.–5:00 P.M., Tuesday–Sunday. Small admission fee. Free Saturday, 10:00 A.M.–noon. Call for details on free weekday docent tours, available at each of the three museums. Wheelchair access to the Sackler and its restrooms via ramps and elevators; Fogg/Busch-Reisinger accessible via back door; advance arrangement with security office preferred; call (617) 495-4040.

Harvard Museums of Cultural and Natural History

ADDRESS: Entrances at 24 Oxford Street and 11 Divinity Avenue, Cambridge.

TELEPHONE: (617) 495-3045.

VISITOR INFORMATION: Open 9:00 A.M.–4:30 P.M., Monday–Saturday; 1:00 P.M.–4:30 P.M. Sunday. Small admission fee. Free Saturday 9:00 A.M.–11:00 A.M. No regularly scheduled tours, though special group tours can be arranged for a fee. Call ahead to arrange wheelchair access.

Harvard Semitic Museum

ADDRESS: 6 Divinity Avenue, Cambridge.

TELEPHONE: (617) 495-3123.

VISITOR INFORMATION: Open weekdays, 11:00 A.M.–5:00 P.M. Free; small admission for special exhibits. Tours given in conjunction with special exhibitions; call for information. No wheelchair access.

Memorial Hall

ADDRESS: Located at the junction of Kirkland, Quincy, Cambridge, and Oxford streets, Cambridge.

TELEPHONE: Box office and recorded information on events, (617) 496-2222; Memorial Hall director's office, (617) 495-4968.

VISITOR INFORMATION: Memorial Hall offices and building doors open Monday through Friday, 10:00 A.M.–6:00 P.M. Free. Building also open other hours for events. Hall is included in general campus tours, available through Holyoke Information Center, (617) 495-1573, or Harvard Admissions Office, (617) 495-1551; free. Wheelchair access via ramp on Kirkland Street entrance; accessible restrooms.

20 Symphony Hall

ANY "LIVING legend" that's almost a century old and still going strong must be doing something right. And such is the case with the beloved Boston landmark known as Symphony Hall. The simple, stark, shoebox-like building—home to the Boston Symphony Orchestra and the Boston Pops—has dominated the busy intersection of Huntington and Massachusetts avenues since the turn of the twentieth century. And though its dull, neo-industrial exterior has been the subject of endless jokes, the structure's overall design has made Symphony Hall one of the most acoustically perfect performance spaces in the world.

Such acoustic excellence is quite appropriate, of course, given that the building has been full of music since the first symphony concert was held there on October 15, 1900.

Symphony Hall was the brainchild of Civil War veteran, philanthropist, and amateur musician Henry Lee Higginson (1834–1919). His decision to commission the construction of a permanent home for the Boston Symphony Orchestra in 1893 was not altogether surprising; the fabulously wealthy Higginson had also founded the B.S.O. in 1881, and sustained it for years thereafter. To this day, Higginson is commemorated in both an enormous John Singer Sargent painting at the Massachusetts Avenue entrance, and a bust by Bela Pratt in the Hatch Memorial Room, the building's original entrance foyer. Though Higginson was a colonel when honorably discharged from the Union Army, he preferred to use his former title, Major. The scar on his right cheek—apparent in both pieces of art—was incurred during a private scuffle over a horse.

When Higginson began plans to build a home for the B.S.O., he believed that the orchestra's old residence—the 1852 Music Hall, located on Hamilton Place where the Orpheum Theatre stands today—was going to be demolished. Hence, he would call his building the *new* Boston Music Hall. As it turned out, the old Music Hall was not demolished as planned, but Higginson made the discovery too late to warn his builders. As a result, the railings along the new building's marble staircases are decorated with BMH medallions, and the exterior lacks any prominent sign identifying it as Symphony Hall—unless you count the small I.D. plaque added by the Bicentennial Commission in 1976. According to Martha (Pat) Burnham Humphrey, a former Symphony Hall artist and author, some interior fixtures actually were stamped with the words "Symphony Hall" in the early building—the metal toilet paper holders in the restrooms. When those fixtures were removed during a later building renovation, some 300 symphony fans bid to take the precious powder-room souvenirs home.

The architect of choice was Charles Follen McKim, of the acclaimed New York architectural firm of McKim, Mead, and White. Architect McKim's original drawings for Symphony Hall's exterior had much more "frosting"

Symphony Hall, home to the Boston Symphony Orchestra and the Boston Pops, has been filled with music since October 15, 1900.

than the somewhat Georgian, very basic red-brick and limestone-trim exterior we see today. His other major works—including the Boston Public Library, the gates and fence at Harvard Yard, and New York's Pennsylvania Station—all had their share of ornate ornamentation. During Symphony Hall's construction, however, the funds simply ran out, and the McKim trimmings were never added.

Moreover, the building's main entrance, now on Massachusetts Avenue, looks less impressive than the architect imagined. McKim actually designed the structure's lavish front doors to open onto Huntington Avenue. Unfortunately, Huntington was widened during the 1930s, forcing the primary entrance to be switched to the Massachusetts Avenue side. Although the exterior Huntington Avenue doors have remained shut since then, the gorgeous main marble staircases with the BMH medallions can still be seen inside.

Symphony Hall's main auditorium, known simply as the Hall, is about one-quarter the size of an average football field. Overall, the motif is simplicity, with touches of gold and crimson on surfaces of wood, brass, and leather. The aisles, once covered with terrazzo tile, now have industrial-strength red runners; lovely plush carpets would have absorbed too much sound and been harder to maintain. The wall areas are decorated with a flat pattern of panels and statues, which *Boston Globe* architecture critic Robert Campbell once compared to "a Robert Adam wallpaper; it is like a light pencil sketch of a room rather than a heavy oil."

While the chairs are turn-of-the-century originals, they're kept in good condition by the basement repair shop. Though these seats' firm wooden frames and thin leather padding have always elicited some complaints about comfort, their acoustic qualities are superior. On the arms of more than 350 of them are gold plaques that have been purchased by patrons for $6,000 each; such endowed seats became a renewed tradition during the orchestra's 1980–81 centennial campaign. The practice of endowing seats hearkens back to the first years of Symphony Hall, when seats were "auctioned off" to socialite bidders; these men and women would add their bid price to the cost of a twenty-four-concert season ticket. Patrons who "bought" seats were given first priority on those spots the following season—which began the tradition of passing down seats within a family. Who bought what seat, incidentally, made great news in the society pages of all the Boston papers of the day.

The most elaborate ornamentation in the Hall is on the gold-leafed proscenium, which bears the name Beethoven on the top. Though eight other cartouches spread out from Beethoven's name, they are conspicuously blank. Beethoven—acknowledged as the father of orchestral music—was apparently an uncontroversial choice for commemoration; since agreement could not be reached on whom else to include, the remaining frames were left empty.

Several other fascinating features are scattered about the large hall:

- The four small chandeliers in the Hall have 71 bulbs each, and the fifth one in the middle has 110. Any of the twenty-five-watt bulbs that burn out are replaced when the chandeliers are lowered from the ceiling hydraulically, which happens twice a year.

- A clock was added at center stage in 1942, though it's often concealed by a small set of doors. The clock's raison d'être is that since 1942 the B.S.O. has been unionized, which means every minute counts.

- If you see a piano on the stage floor, it's likely to be a Baldwin (visiting artists, however, are always permitted to rent or bring another brand if they don't want to use the "house piano").

- The sixteen statues of mythical and real-life heroes in the balcony nooks may look like marble, but they're really plaster with a marbleized finish. The scantily clad figures created a scandal in the eyes of certain proper Bostonian ladies when the Hall first opened. (Wealthy art patron Isabella Stewart Gardner was one of the few symphony-goers who understood the uses of nudity in art and approved of the statuary.)

- Patrons in floor row Q are actually sitting on one of Symphony Hall's three elevators. That particular elevator is a hydraulic lift used to stow away all the seats and risers during the Christmas and Pops seasons, when food and drink are served on cafe tables on the floor. Once the risers and seats are removed, the upwardly sloping back half of the Hall flattens out, assuring that foodstuffs don't slip off the 241 tables hauled in for the festivities. (The tables themselves won't slip—they're bolted to the floor.)

- From 1930 until 1942 the atmosphere during Pops concerts was downright frivolous; the stage was decorated to look like an outdoor garden, replete with green and gold decor and lovely lattice work. The deadly Cocoanut Grove fire of 1942—a downtown Boston blaze which claimed 490 victims—put an end to that decor; Symphony Hall decided the festive greenery was a potential fire hazard.

- At the back of the stage you can see a facade of the original forty-eight organ pipes. More than five thousand other pipes lurk behind that facade, added when the instrument was replaced in 1950. The new organ was made locally by the Aeolian-Skinner Organ Company, and inspected during construction by a variety of experts including the Nobel Prize–winning physician, organist, and Bach authority Albert Schweitzer. When the new organ made its Symphony Hall debut on November 14, 1950, the concert was a benefit for the Albert Schweitzer Hospital, located in what was then called "French Equatorial Africa." That year was a perfect "birth" year for the instrument, since it marked the fiftieth year of Symphony Hall and the two hundredth anniversary of the death of J. S. Bach, considered the greatest of all composers for organ. At the time of the new organ's installation, Symphony Hall's organist was the world-famous E. Power Biggs. Today it is played considerably less than in Biggs's heyday. This is partly due to the slim repertoire of new works for organ, and partly to aging and deterioration of the instrument. According to the Symphony Hall press office, funding is currently being sought for repairs.

For fans of all kinds of music, Symphony Hall has proven to be a stellar listening room for almost a century. Internationally known B.S.O. conductors, like the late Serge Koussevitsky and the current conductor, Seiji Ozawa, have led the full orchestra through scores of classical treasures; stars like the late Arthur Fiedler and composer John Williams (of Hollywood film score fame) have conducted the Boston Pops in its lighter musical fare, featuring guest vocalists from the worlds of pop, rock, Broadway, and jazz. Meanwhile, successful Hall rentals have ranged from the rocking folkabilly of Nanci Griffith to the *a cappella* gospel of Sweet Honey in the Rock, and from the topical folk tunes of Joan Baez to the syncopated reggae of Casselberry-Dupree. Barbershop quartets once sang here on Sunday afternoons. Even plays were performed here from time to time; in 1971, Dame Judith Anderson appeared as Hamlet on the Symphony Hall stage, and twenty years earlier, Agnes Moorhead, Charles Laughton, Cedric Hardwicke, and Charles Boyer read from Shaw's *Don Juan in Hell* on the same boards.

One of the keys to the Hall's tremendous success with all kinds of acts and audiences is its unusually good sight lines. Unlike many venues with larger balcony overhangs, Symphony Hall has only six seats with views blocked by support columns (and those, according to the management, are only "slightly obstructed"). The total seating capacity is 2,625, reduced to 2,371 during Pops concerts.

A major Symphony Hall appeal, of course, is the acoustic excellence—the origins of which take us back again to the late 1890s. Acoustics was more a matter of luck than science before the turn of the century. When noted Harvard physics professor Wallace Clement Sabine reluctantly agreed to take on the challenge of making Symphony Hall the perfect spot for orchestral music, he became one of the first to apply scientific principles to an artistic problem. Architect McKim had planned to shape the Hall like a rounded Greek theater; Sabine recommended he replace that design with a simple shoebox shape. The resulting box-within-a-box design—with hallways and offices surrounding the Hall—created an air space to serve as a sound buffer, keeping out noise from the busy surrounding streets.

Just how good are the acoustics? According to a 1981 article by Robert Campbell, acoustical scientist Leo Beranek set out to discover the finest concert hall in the world in the 1960s and eventually considered fifty-four halls in sixteen countries; after polling numerous conductors, performers, and music critics who rated the halls on an elaborate scale, Beranek concluded that Boston's Symphony Hall was Number One.

It's not simply a matter of McKim's shoebox-in-a-box design, however. Multiple layers of brick, tile, steel, and plaster were used when Symphony Hall was built. Though these measures were intended to protect against fire—making Symphony Hall the first major structure in Boston built with fireproofing in mind—the layers also helped insulate the Hall from outside street noise. Inside the Hall, furnishings also continue to contribute to the near-perfect acoustics. There are no lush carpets, drapes, or billowy cushioned seats to absorb the sound; oak floors, leather seat covers, and plaster walls provide a more neutral background. The stage is built with its floor, ceiling, and walls all sloped outward in the shape of a giant truncated "horn." And the baffled ceilings lack domes and arches that could turn sound around or jam it up in a corner. Moreover, there are just enough nooks and statues to avoid broad, flat, bounce-the-sound surfaces.

The acoustics, incidentally, are calibrated for a full house of patrons; during rehearsals and auditions, when the sound might reverberate and echo unduly, a huge burlap curtain is hung from ceiling hooks directly above row F, to stifle the excess vibrations. You can see those hooks up near the hanging microphones that are used for recording, radio or television broadcasts, and for other performers who rent the Hall—never for amplification of orchestral performances. Insiders tell us, incidentally, that the sound is best when there are at least a thousand people in the audience.

Though the Hall is the heart of the Symphony Hall structure, interesting items exist all around the building. Plaques and tributes are found throughout the hallways, listing various benefactors over the past century. A hallway plaque on the Massachusetts Avenue side is a memorial to eight musicians "who were drowned, still playing as the *Titanic* went down, April 15, 1912." (None, it seems, were in any way connected to the B.S.O.; Isabella Stewart Gardner just wanted it displayed there, and her clout made it happen.)

The Cohen Wing, an adjacent building annexed in 1980–81, was once the home of a bowling alley and two ballrooms. The building, renovated in 1990, houses several B.S.O. offices, the Tanglewood Music center, conference and function rooms, the switchboard, a handsome new display of the prized ancient instrument collection, and an enlarged Symphony Shop. The multitude of ever-changing chambers in the original building still contains offices, green rooms, locker rooms, workshops, libraries, conference rooms, storage areas, practice booths, and lounges.

New additions to the building include a wheelchair-accessible restroom, and a patron lounge named in honor of Leo Beranek, longtime Symphony supporter, former chairman of the board of trustees—and the man who "proved" Boston's Symphony Hall was acoustic perfection.

THE ESSENTIALS

ADDRESS: 301 Massachusetts Avenue, Boston.

TELEPHONE: Symphony Hall main number, (617) 266-1492. SymphonyCharge ticket sales, (617) 266-1200.

VISITOR INFORMATION: Administrative offices open Monday–Friday, 9:00 A.M.–5:00 P.M. Building open other hours for concerts and events. Tours available by advance arrangement; call for information. Wheelchair ramp and accessible restroom available at west entrance, in the Cohen Wing.

The Colonial Theatre

THE HANDSOME, intimate Colonial Theatre is not only one of the most popular stages in town but also the oldest continuously operating legitimate theater in Boston. As such, it has seen a sizable slice of stage history. Today, it hosts theater pieces that run from intimate dramas like *Driving Miss Daisy, A Soldier's Play,* and *Children of a Lesser God* to elaborate musicals such as *La Cage Aux Folles, Grand Hotel,* and the most recent incarnation of *Guys and Dolls.*

On its opening night of December 20, 1900, however, the Colonial staged a very different kind of spectacle—a high-tech biblical blockbuster.

"Nothing So Beautiful, Pictorially and Mechanically, Ever Seen Before on a Boston Stage," proclaimed a *Boston Globe* sub-headline about the opening of *Ben Hur.* The hyperbolic comment may well have been true. In the heroic melodrama's most widely touted scene, the lush Colonial stage was bursting with period props and tunic-clad actors, backed by an enormous panorama of the Roman Coliseum. Meanwhile, four hydraulic lifts elevated a dozen frisky horses from their basement "stable." Hitched to ornate Roman chariots, the steeds galloped across the stage for the show's climactic chariot race—prevented from plunging into the audience by an ingenious treadmill built into the stage boards.

While memories of that turn-of-the-century production have since faded away, the beloved Colonial has not.

That the Colonial Theatre has flourished for close to a century is due in part to the beauty of its classically inspired building. Historian Douglas Shand Tucci called it "as sumptuous and elegant as any of the productions its proscenium has disclosed." Part of its endurance is surely due to its charming intimacy, superior sight lines, and excellent acoustics—the latter thanks to Thomas A. Edison, whom the Colonial's management hired to improve the sound in the theater's early years.

"It is said that no work of construction in the city of Boston for a long time has aroused so much interest among builders and capitalists as that on the Colonial," read a *Boston Globe* analysis of February 14, 1900. The location was Boylston Street, across from the historic Boston Common, originally the site of the Boston Public Library. (Once the library was moved to its present home in Copley Square, its old Boylston Street structure was leveled, allowing the Colonial to slowly emerge in its place.)

The sight must have been a fascinating one for curious Bostonians. Workmen could be seen below ground level, driving yards of hydraulic tubing into the earth—tubes which would later hook up to those four

Boston's Colonial Theatre was the stage where actors like Danny Kaye, Jane Fonda, and Barbra Streisand got their first breaks and first major critical recognition.

famous rear-stage elevators. Above ground, enormous mounds of dirt were eventually replaced by a ten-story building. Though relatively plain on the outside, it would soon be filled with fine, functional business offices and one gem of a theater.

Funds for the $1.5-million venture came from the estate of Frederick L. Ames, an industrial entrepreneur and enlightened philanthropist who had died in 1893. The architect was Clarence H. Blackall, whose design credits eventually included the Wilbur and Metropolitan (today's Wang) theaters, the Kenmore and Braemore hotels, the Little Building, and Tremont Temple Baptist Church. Credited as the first architect to make a building entirely framed in steel, Blackall also founded the Boston Architect's Collaborative.

Though the Ames family chose to call their theater the Colonial, the lavish interior work executed by Blackall and his colleagues was hardly colonial in style. Instead, classical motifs filled room after room, inspiring one Boston critic to gush in 1900, "It glitters like a Venetian jewel box . . . with examples of the art of Pompeii, Florence, Rome and Italy employed!"

Visitors to the theater entered through the seventy-foot-long box office vestibule lined with Italian marble walls and frescoes; the floor was a magnificent crescent-design mosaic of forty thousand tiles. While reviewers likened this spacious, simple entrance hall to Pompeii, the adjoining foyer was compared to a lavishly ornate Louvre gallery. The luxurious ladies' lounge, in turn, was "suggestive of the throne room of the Fontainebleau Palace near Paris."

If the allusions were exotic, so too is Blackall's Colonial. The theater has actually changed very little in its more than ninety years, thanks in part to an ambitious $750,000 restoration in 1960. The "Louvre-style" foyer, for example, still features giant plate mirrors, ceiling paintings, cupids, bucolic landscapes, bronze staircases, gilt ornamentation, and intricately carved wood designs—the latter by John Evans and Company. Such visual ebullience—with its fruits, cupids, palms, and lutes—continues in the fan-shaped auditorium. There, two wrap-around balconies, three chandeliers, imposing columns, pearl-necklace lights, and a grandiose dome frieze threaten to distract the viewer from the stage. Painter Herman Schladermundt created the ceiling's allegorical male figures representing Tradition, Truth, and Inspiration, as well as the female figures in the adjoining circles—Epic Poetry, History, Tragedy, and Comic/Pastoral Verse.

Even the expansive backstage areas at the Colonial are a story wonderland. More than three dozen dressing and chorus rooms are spread out over long hallways and endless flights of stairs. The tiny, cluttered prop room is a veritable museum of theatrical glossies, autographs, buttons, posters, graffiti, and other memorabilia. The hovering fly floor—the loft far above the stage from which scenery is lowered and raised—is strung with so many lines of heavy hemp that it looks like a reunion of clipper ships. The stage basement has been so sawed, reshuffled, and rebuilt to accommodate the trap-doors and distinctive underbelly mechanics needed for different productions that it resembles an oversized shanty from Tobacco Road.

"Blackall had a great intellectual capacity," says writer and historian Bettina A. Norton. "He was attuned to the business community, and aware of multipurpose uses of buildings. He thought of the theater audience—of layout, sight lines, comfort, and circulation patterns—along with using fine materials. Blackall was also an excellent architectural journalist. In fact, he probably wrote many of the newspaper reviews that ran on the Colonial when it opened!"

If the architectural splendor of the Colonial Theatre set it apart from other Boston theaters before and since, so did its use. Some theaters were built to accommodate other kinds of entertainment—vaudeville, motion pictures, opera, or exhibitions—as well as plays. But, though the ten-story Colonial did contain rooms for business offices, the sumptuous space at its core was constructed for "legitimate theater," pure and simple; moreover, its layout and seating capacity of close to 1,700 made it ideal for both musical and dramatic productions.

Legendary Boston drama critic Elliot Norton fondly remembers his earliest visits to the Colonial in the 1910s and early 1920s. "While I was still in school I saw some of the musicals. Then, of course, came Ziegfeld's revues. Revues had no plot—just songs, dances, and sketches, all held together by the music and the same performers. They were enormously ornate, elaborate, and beautiful. His shows cost $100,000, maybe $150,000, and they advertised they had the most beautiful girls in the world. There were 'ponies'—small girls who danced. And 'showgirls'—tall ones who just paraded. I remember the highest paid showgirl was named Gladys Glad."

The Ziegfeld revues the young Norton and his peers saw at the Colonial featured many legendary talents in the history of music and comedy. Fred and Adele Astaire, W. C. Fields, Fanny Brice, Will Rogers, Bob Hope, Eddie Cantor, and Ed Wynn all performed there, as Flo Ziegfeld sculpted his annual Follies into final form before taking each show and its performers to New York.

From the 1920s through the 1970s, in fact, Boston—like Philadelphia and New Haven—was well known as a "tryout town," where producers and directors polished and perfected Broadway-bound plays, using the Hub's sophisticated audiences as a barometer of their successes. The Colonial hosted an ample share of these previews. *Porgy and Bess,* for example, celebrated its world premiere at the Colonial in 1935. "The original production was sung from end to end," recalls Elliot Norton. "It was an opera. All the drama critics loved it, and all the music critics hated it. Later on, it became a success, when they introduced spoken dialogue instead of sung dialogue. It has since been restaged as a fully sung opera."

Richard Rodgers and Oscar Hammerstein opened a musical called *Away We Go!* at the Colonial in 1943. In Boston, Rodgers and Hammerstein revised the show and successfully revitalized its slow-starting second act. The production later became a hit under the name of the song that opened Act II—*Oklahoma!* Another Rodgers and Hammerstein favorite, *Carousel,* began in Boston's Colonial as well.

An enormous oval onyx table once located in the Colonial's sumptuous ladies' lounge was often used for such revisions, incidentally. When the great German director Max Reinhardt directed Thornton Wilder's *The Merchant of Yonkers* at the Colonial in 1938, for example, Wilder did an immediate rewrite in the lounge. (The table disappeared when the theater last changed owners in 1981; members of the departing Jujamcyn Corporation apparently walked off with the famed piece of furniture, along with much of the Colonial's archival material.) Wilder's Boston rewrite failed, and the play was turned into a comedy called *The Matchmaker;* under a new director, it starred Ruth Gordon and again opened at the Colonial. Unfortunately, only the third and final version of the play will be remembered—the musical comedy *Hello, Dolly!*

Some well-known actors and actresses—including Danny Kaye, Jane Fonda, and Barbra Streisand—got their first real breaks and their first major critical recognition at the Colonial. An impressive number of internationally renowned stage stars have performed there as well, including Ethel Barrymore, Ethel Merman, Gertrude Lawrence, Frederick March, Henry Fonda, Paul Robeson, Helen Hayes, Paul Muni, Ethel Waters, James Earl Jones, Julie Harris, and Katharine Hepburn. Still, fame never guaranteed artistic or commercial success, nor even an easy run. When English star Nicol Williamson opened in *Hamlet* at the Colonial in 1969, for example, he threw a fit and walked off the stage, disgusted by what he considered to be the mediocrity of his own performance.

Williamson's was but a minor eruption compared to the day when Edward Albee's *Who's Afraid of Virginia Woolf?* came to town in 1963. Albee was ordered to cut some allegedly obscene words from his original script. When the playwright complied, drama critic Kevin Kelly chided him in the *Boston Globe*. After Albee replied with an explanation of his actions, an illegal censorship pact between certain city officials (the so-called city censors) and local theater management was exposed, and the American Civil Liberties Union took action. It was the beginning of the end of stage censorship in the city, which had made "banned in Boston" an international joke.

The Colonial's long life has seen four major owners, under whom a multitude of management teams and lessees have operated with surprising continuity. The Ames family of New York, who built the theater, maintained it from 1900 until the Great Depression. The Depression—plus the success of early films, and other factors—drastically reduced the number of legitimate theaters in America, from an estimated four thousand in 1900 to some four hundred in 1932. The Colonial was saved from possible demolition when purchased by the Shubert Organization in 1934. (The Shuberts saved many such theaters across America during the Depression, buying out what others could no longer maintain.)

As a result, the Colonial became one of seven Boston stages owned by the New York–based entertainment empire, from 1934 through 1956. Antitrust legislation forced the Shuberts to break up their Boston theater monopoly, however, and the Jujamcyn Corporation purchased the building and owned it from 1957 to 1981. Under this ownership, extensive renovations were made, while Boston waned as regular tryout town. Since 1981, the theater has been owned by realtor Martin S. Berman, and is currently leased to the 106 Boylston Street Corporation. The ride has been worth it: Boston's Colonial Theatre is now one of the last independent commercial theaters in the United States.

The mid and late 1980s were not the best of times for Boston theater in general. For one thing, pre-Broadway tryouts had clearly shifted to other American cities, including New York itself. Still, while the theater district suffered some ominous dark periods, the decade also had its bright points. The 1980 production of the musical *Annie,* for example, was the Colonial's longest running show ever. The Colonial also hosted the premiere of two award-winning musicals: *La Cage Aux Folles* in 1983, and Tommy Tune's *Grand Hotel* in 1989. In 1988, *Cabaret* became the production with the highest weekly gross in Colonial history, only to be superseded by *Man of La Mancha* in 1992.

If you are planning to attend a performance at the Colonial, be prepared to pay significantly more than turn-of-the-century Bostonians did for tickets. During opening week in 1900, the Colonial's best orchestra seats sold for $2.00. By 1925, these seats averaged $3.30. Top tickets for the 1992–93 productions of *Evita, The Secret Garden,* and *Guys and Dolls* went for $55.00. Unsold seats on the day of performance, however, are often available for half-price at the Bostix booth in Quincy Market—as are tickets for most Boston shows.

One final note of trivia on that two-dollar-a-seat debut show of 1900: When *Ben Hur* opened at the Colonial, its stars included William Farnum and William S. Hart, both of whom went on to later fame as cowboys in the silent movies. Farnum's brother Dustin costarred as well, and one of his avid fans later named her infant son after him. Yes, it was Dustin Hoffman's mom.

THE ESSENTIALS

ADDRESS: 106 Boylston Street, Boston.

TELEPHONE: (617) 426-9366.

VISITOR INFORMATION: Box office hours vary with production. No tours. Main Boylston Street entrance is flat and wheelchair accessible, as is ladies' lounge; unisex wheelchair-accessible restroom; reduced ticket prices available on wheelchair spaces in orchestra; call in advance to arrange specifics.

The Shubert Theatre

ASK BOSTON theatergoers about the character of downtown stages, and they're bound to respond with a variety of strong opinions. Some will rave that the Wang is the biggest, the Charles is the funkiest, or the Colonial is the coziest in town. Others reminisce that the finest theater ever conceived and constructed in the city was the old Opera House; sadly, it was razed in 1957 to make way for Northeastern University dormitories.

Still, close to the hearts of many Bostonians—and located in the heart of Boston's theater district on Tremont Street—is a living monument to the history of the twentieth-century American stage. The grand old Shubert Theatre, built in 1910, was once one of seven Boston theaters owned or operated by the New York–based Shubert brothers, one of the most powerful theater families in U.S. history. Over the years—and especially during the decades when Boston served as a major pre-Broadway tryout town—the Shubert has hosted a variety of theater greats, from Richard Burton and Maurice Evans to Angela Lansbury and Gertrude Lawrence. Today, due to antitrust legislation of the 1950s, the active Shubert is the only Boston theater the Shubert Organization still owns. But it's a gem of a remnant—especially since its sorely needed $1.4-million renovation of 1980, which gave the old structure a gleam reminiscent of its heyday.

Back on opening night, on January 24, 1910, some critics raved more about the city's newest playhouse than about the notable production of Shakespeare's *The Taming of the Shrew*. "NEW PLAYHOUSE CHARMS

THRONGS: Shubert Theatre Opening Made Brilliant Event" read the *Boston Globe* headlines. In smaller print was a postscript about the performance: "Sothern and Marlowe Seen in 'Taming of the Shrew.' " The *Globe* critic acknowledged his—and the crowd's—overriding interest in the new building, designed by architect Thomas James. He was even willing to ignore the fact that the plush backs to the chairs had not yet arrived—since the glorious Shubert had wide, comfortable seats, great sight lines, an unusually wide and deep orchestra pit, a beautiful, picturesque lobby, a speedy coat-check system, a spacious foyer, and near-perfect acoustics.

Contemporary theatergoers, accustomed to more spacious foyers, pits, and lobbies, might not agree with that generous assessment. Nevertheless, the charm of such old theaters remains, notes Elliot Norton, the dean of Boston theater critics. "They were created for audiences of a previous time," he explains. "But they have a warmth and an elegance that makes them something special. When you go in you feel this is going to be a special event. You're going to be lifted out of the street world and into an exotic world. Another kind of world. A place in which you live in another way."

Catherine and David Shubert must have noticed the entrepreneurial genius of their sons Lee, Sam, and Jacob J. (J. J.) quite early in the game. As kids, the Shubert boys sold papers in the streets. As young adults, they

Boston's Shubert Theatre was built and owned by the New York–based Shuberts, one of the most powerful theater families in U.S. history.

began working in—and eventually operated—theaters in their hometown of Syracuse, New York. Though the family had begun in poverty—one sister reportedly died of malnutrition—the three sons went on to become America's leading theatrical producers and managers, powerful business-men who eventually leased or owned theaters in almost every major city in the United States and held a virtual monopoly on the world of the legitimate theater.

Lee, born in 1875, was the eldest. Next year came Sam, "boyish in appearance and short in stature," who was known among colleagues as "Peanut." J. J.—who later became a major presence in the Shubert's Boston holdings—arrived in 1880. By 1900, the brothers hit Manhattan, buying, selling, and producing their way to the top. They effectively battled the all-powerful entertainment syndicate of Klaw and Erlanger. They brilliantly booked the finest talent available in the world—paying Sarah Bernhardt in gold, for example, to make her first American appear-ances. In their heyday in 1927, the Brothers Shubert owned or operated 110 theaters across the United States and booked productions into a thousand others. Until 1956, they controlled all seven of Boston's legiti-mate theaters.

What part brother Sam could have played in building the Shubert theater empire is mere conjecture now. Sam was the first to arrive in New York City, pulling Lee behind him. Only after Sam's death in 1905 did J. J. join Lee in the Manhattan business. Sam was twenty-nine when he was killed in a fiery Pennsylvania train crash. Newspapers across the nation reported the train's explosion, Sam's rescue through the flaming train window, and his death a day and a half later.

Though we know that Sam was considered a shrewd businessman, many photos and accounts of him also portray "Peanut" as a sensitive artist, a devoted brother, and a passionate theatrical impresario. When Lee and J. J. built their Boston theater in 1910—completing construction in less than five months—it was named the Sam S. Shubert Theatre in their brother's memory. Sam's picture still hangs in the foyer. In fact, Lee and J. J. sent framed photos of Sam to all their theaters—and charged the theaters ten dollars for each. Throughout their lives, Lee and J. J. ran the growing Shubert empire together with utmost skill, all the while maintaining a fierce sibling rivalry. After Sam's death, they rarely saw one another, communicating primarily through messengers.

Except for the Shubert's facade, which underwent a few alterations because of the widening of Tremont Street in 1926, much of the theater still looks like it did when it opened in 1910. There have, of course, been a few changes, mostly related to modern convenience and monetary considera-tions. Restrooms, bars, and coatrooms have been reshuffled, and former doorways have been blocked off. The old standing-room space at the back of the orchestra section is gone, replaced by three cramped rows of seats. The addition of three more rows in the front of the orchestra section caused the size of the orchestra pit to be reduced, forcing most of the musicians under the lip of the stage. The antiquated Shubert cooling system—a fan blowing over a bin of block ice—is gone, though the gargantuan old boiler still sits in the basement, across from the small, efficient steam heaters that replaced it.

Backstage, the sets are bigger than in the old days. The set-up takes much longer than when house carpenters used to build the sets. Longtime house workers explain that the Shubert's backstage quarters are too cramped for some of the bigger modern musicals. Among the various chambers, halls, offices, and storage areas in that backstage area are fourteen small dressing rooms, plus a large wardrobe center.

Acoustics and amplification are also far different than in the early days of legitimate theater—at the Shubert as well as most other large stages. For decades, actors depended on good lungs, vocal training, and fine acoustical design to ensure that their words reached their audiences. In recent times, however, microphones have been added as acoustic "crutches." The cast of a recent Shubert production of *Cats* used small lapel mikes to amplify their vocals; seventeen cast members of *Les Misérables* used wireless mikes placed in their hair. (The mike transmitters were fastened under clothing on the actors' backs.)

It's surely no surprise that an even more drastic change has come in the price of theater tickets. In 1925 a seat at the Shubert cost $3.30. Local motion picture "palaces" at the time charged seventy cents for admission; you could stay there all day, catching three or four films for the price of one. Both theater and film prices had increased more than 800 percent by 1993, when a balcony ticket for a popular musical like *A Chorus Line* at the Shubert cost $30.00.

As the twentieth century progressed, theater became a big business in America, the Shuberts became a big name in theater, and New York City became the production center of note. Since Manhattan's opening-night critics and crowds were known to be ruthless, producers often sought educated tryout towns to smooth out their productions before opening on Broadway. For decades—until tryouts became too costly to mount and other cities promised better deals—Boston was a major pre-Broadway stop. According to Elliot Norton, a typical pattern for a new play might be three days in New Haven, two weeks in Boston, then off to Manhattan. During the trial period, actors could be switched, lines or whole plays rewritten, and songs composed or deleted.

Among the major stars and productions Norton remembers passing through the Boston Shubert were Mary Martin and Ezio Pinza in Rodgers and Hammerstein's *South Pacific* ("Everybody loved the show," Norton says, noting that many Bostonians hated one song which had an antiracist theme—"We were pretty racist here at that time"); Richard Burton and Julie Andrews in *Camelot* ("She was charming and he was very exciting"); Burton's first appearance in America, in a small role in *The Lady's Not For Burning* (1950); John Gielgud's first and grandest Boston performance in *Hamlet* (1936); Laurence Olivier in *The Entertainer* (1958); Maurice Evans's first U.S. performance as Romeo to Katharine Cornell's Juliet (1935); and Burton's controversial 1964 *Hamlet*, directed by Gielgud and performed in rehearsal clothes ("[Burton] admitted he used to play forty different characters in the course of one production . . . and people still weren't paying any attention to him, at any rate many of them weren't—Liz Taylor was in the audience!").

Among the audience favorites at the Shubert—from a box-office perspective—were the 1925 production of *Rose Marie,* which ran for twenty-nine weeks, and *Evita* and *Cats,* which each had twenty-one-week runs in the early 1980s.

Needless to say, Boston audiences didn't enjoy every New York tryout. When Angela Lansbury opened with *Mame* in 1966, and when *Dreamgirls* premiered in 1981, it's reported that producers could not even give tickets away before opening night. So much for audience prescience!

Incidentally, though Boston audiences were often willing to watch the kinks being worked out in shows, the so-called Boston city censors posed a unique problem for many theatrical productions from 1907 through the mid-1960s. They censored "risqué" lines, lyrics, outfits, and scenes, in a dubious practice that brought the phrase "banned in Boston" worldwide notoriety.

One of Elliot Norton's favorite anecdotes about pre-Broadway tryouts at the Shubert involves that "enormously exciting, brilliant" play of 1951 called *The King and I.* During the brief Boston run, apparently, Rodgers and Hammerstein decided they needed three more songs to round out the show—including one that would fit Gertrude Lawrence's limited vocal range. Hammerstein found a discarded love song, originally penned for *South Pacific,* and wrote new lyrics to suit the tale of Anna and the King of Siam. The song, "Getting to Know You," wasn't sung for opening night in Boston, but it was well integrated into *The King and I* by the time it left the Shubert, and it became Lawrence's signature tune.

Critic Norton estimates that American legitimate theater was at its finest from roughly 1930 to as late as 1975. During those decades, however, a variety of phenomena chipped slowly away at theater audiences. Increasing ticket prices, the advent of "talkies," television, VCRs, and rock concerts all took their toll, as did the decline of good plays, good theater writers, the value of a dollar, and U.S. education.

The Shubert monopoly also eroded during these years, most dramatically after 1956 antitrust legislation. In Boston, the Shuberts held onto Sam's namesake, letting their other six houses go. The Copley, Plymouth, and Majestic theaters became movie houses; the Boston Opera House was sold to Northeastern University and demolished; and the Wilbur and Colonial theaters yielded to other ownership or management.

Lee Shubert died in 1953, and J. J. in 1963. J. J.'s son John was intended to run the organization, but he suffered a fatal heart attack on a train a year before his father passed on. Today, Bernard B. Jacobs and Gerald Schoenfeld are the president and chairman, respectively, of the Shubert Organization and the Shubert Foundation. Shubert owns or operates seventeen theaters in New York and six others across the country.

Some longtime Shubert employees openly admit they respect their new bosses more than the old. (J. J. Shubert in particular seems to have been unpopular, while "down-to-earth" Lee was clearly their favorite.) The Shuberts, of course, were bound to be hated for their power, fortune, and monopoly over American theaters. They were also feared because they were known to try to censor critics who wrote unfavorable reviews of their productions. Elliot Norton remembers discovering he was on the Shuberts' "hit list" as early as a year after he started reviewing in 1934. The

Shuberts' tactics for taming Norton were direct. They tried to have him fired by his editors, with no success. They also banned him from their theaters; but the critic just went out and bought his own tickets.

On the positive side, the Shuberts helped break up the early Klaw and Erlanger theater monopoly. Equally important, critics agree, was the fact that the Shuberts single-handedly helped pull American theater through the rough Depression years by purchasing, and producing in, many theaters that might otherwise have demolished. Without their work, American legitimate theater—and theater houses—might have disappeared in the 1930s, and Boston would be much the poorer today.

THE ESSENTIALS

ADDRESS: 265 Tremont Street, theater district, Boston.
TELEPHONE: Box office, (617) 426-4520.
VISITOR INFORMATION: When shows are being produced, the box office open Monday, 10:00 A.M.–6:00 P.M.; Tuesday–Saturday, 10:00 A.M.–8:00 P.M.; Sunday, noon–8:00 P.M. No tours. Main Tremont Street entrance and restrooms are wheelchair accessible; reduced rates for wheelchair-accessible seats in orchestra; call in advance for more information.

23 Fenway Park

ONE OF the most apt descriptions of Boston's favorite ball field is also the most succinct. "Fenway Park is a lyric little bandbox of a ballpark," noted novelist John Updike. "Everything is painted green and seems in curiously sharp focus, like the inside of an old-fashioned peeping-type Easter egg."

Calling the park small and somewhat antiquated is an endearment, of course, not an insult. First opened in 1912—and tied with Detroit's Tiger Stadium as the oldest major-league ballpark in the United States—Fenway is both a remnant and a reminder of golden baseball days gone by. In the early years of the twentieth century, it was among the nation's largest ballparks. Today it's the smallest—and the last single-deck stadium in the major leagues.

As the twentieth century evolved, professional baseball eventually became a world of domed mega-stadiums with symmetrical sides, multiple decks, plastic grass, mascots in animal suits, constant canned music, vaguely visible ballplayers, and electronic cue cards imploring fans to "Cheer!" or shout "Charge!" Not so at Fenway. Unlike most other fields, Fenway Park

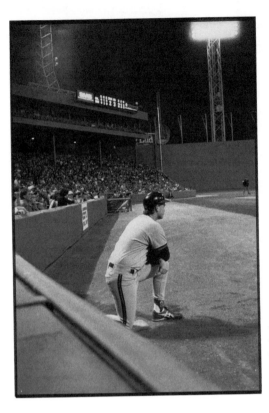

First opened in 1912, Fenway Park is tied with Detroit's Tiger Stadium as the oldest major league ballpark in the United States.

was never razed, rebuilt, or replaced. Instead, Boston's beloved ballpark has worked to balance old and new—growing and changing with the times, while keeping most of its cozy, intimate charms intact. To this day, those distinctive charms include live organ music, a hand-operated scoreboard, honest-to-goodness live bluegrass, and a looming left-field wall known to generations of fans as the Green Monster.

It may not be the original "Field of Dreams," but Fenway's flock of avid fans think it's about as close as you can get.

Since its birth in 1912, Fenway Park has played home to more than the landlord Red Sox and that infamous fast food called the Fenway Frank. Boston's other major-league baseball team, the National League's Boston Braves, used Fenway Park in 1914 when their own Braves Field was under construction. (The Braves abandoned the city for Milwaukee after 1952, and eventually landed in Atlanta.)

Throughout its history, the park has also been used on occasion for such diverse fare as revival meetings, concerts (the 1973 Newport Jazz Festival), memorial services (for the World War I armistice), basketball exhibitions (the Boston Celtics and the Harlem Globetrotters), soccer games (the Boston Beacons), and football games. Three pro football teams, in fact, called Fenway home for several years at a stretch: the Boston Redskins, now in Washington, D.C.; the Boston Yanks, now the Indianapolis Colts; and the Boston Patriots, now the New England Patriots of Foxborough, Massachusetts. The park is still used for amateur baseball games as well.

But the reason Fenway Park was built—and the reason it stands today—was to accommodate Boston's longstanding love affair with the Red Sox. The Sox were founded in 1901 and quickly recognized as an important franchise in the newly formed American League. According to sports historians Dick Johnson and Bob Bluthardt, the Sox tried out a variety of names—including the Pilgrims, the Puritans, and even the Plymouth Rocks—before deciding on Red Sox in 1907. The name was partly a tribute to a club named the Red Stockings, which had played in the 1870s, and partly a description of their own red-colored stirrup socks. The Red Sox's first field was the old Huntington Avenue Grounds, now part of Northeastern University. That old-fashioned, multipurpose space had a capacity of ten to fourteen thousand; the larger numbers came when fans stood on the field during the game, a popular practice in the early days of baseball.

Fenway Park itself was the project of John I. Taylor, an early Red Sox owner and son of *Boston Globe* publisher General Charles H. Taylor. John Taylor was also involved in the Fenway Realty Company, a group developing the reclaimed marshland area known as the Fenway.

The plot Taylor purchased for the team's new home was a strangely skewed piece of land in that once-marshy Fenway area, tightly lodged between existing streets and conveniently located near the Boston trolley line. The park Taylor built there struck a balance between old-fashioned wooden ballparks and their more modern concrete-and-steel counterparts. Though today's visitors are impressed by the park's politely industrial red-brick exterior, the decorative mosaics and diamond designs on the outer walls, and the tons of concrete that underpin the rambling interior, fans in 1912 were most astonished by another innovation—eighteen whizzing turnstiles that made entry and egress a simple operation.

No one knows for sure whether the park's legendary asymmetrical interior angles were dictated by the adjacent streets or the shape of the lot, or were simply the way the field was placed. The result, in any case, was a field bordered by seventeen facets and barriers, and governed by numerous regulations as to how many bases a hitter takes when his ball ricochets off this or that wall, pole, screen, scoreboard, or bevel.

Two Fenway quirks in particular have become part of Red Sox lore. Before 1934, a ten-foot hill along the left-field wall served as a viewing spot for fans and a warning to players that the back wall was imminent. The fans were rarely in danger of being hit by a ball, incidentally: until 1920, homers of any sort—over the left-field wall or anywhere else—were relatively rare, since the old rag "dead ball" was still in use. The hill's greatest historic moments came with the career of outfielder Duffy Lewis, who played for the Sox from 1910 to 1917. Lewis became famous for successfully scampering up and down the left-field embankment to make spectacular catches; the incline was named Duffy's Cliff in his honor. Since that cliff proved an exasperating stumbling block to scores of unknowing outfielders, however, it was removed during park renovations of 1934. Today, a gravel track provides players the warning that The Wall is near.

During that same modernization of 1934, the park's original wooden left-field wall was replaced by a significantly larger, thirty-seven-foot-high concrete-and-tin barrier. The Wall became popularly known as the Green Monster—and has proven to be the nemesis and obsession of sluggers ever since. Hit a high fly ball over the top, for example, and you've scored one of the shortest home runs in any major league ballpark. If you miss the top and hit The Wall instead, a line drive that might have been a homer anywhere else could end up a mere double.

John Taylor named his park Fenway—"It's in the Fenway, isn't it?" was his laconic explanation—and officially opened it on April 20, 1912. Though Fenway's debut and the Red Sox's eleven-inning, 7-6 victory over the New York Highlanders (Yankees) were major news, Boston's newspapers failed to give the story much space on the front page. Writers were too busy reporting the sinking of the *Titanic* that week.

After Taylor sold the park, also in 1912, the Red Sox and Fenway Park eventually fell into disarray. Among the park's many problems was owner Harry Frazee, who bought Fenway in 1917 and siphoned off its profits to support his entertainment business, including a new musical called *No, No, Nanette*. Among the worst of Frazee's follies was trading Babe Ruth to the New York Yankees in 1919—for $100,000 and a $300,000 mortgage on Fenway Park. (The Sox won the World Series in 1912, 1915, 1916, and 1918, but never again after Ruth's trade; legend says that "the curse of the Bambino" remains on Fenway Park to this day, apparently unbroken by exorcism rites offered by comedian "Father Guido Sarducci," aka Don Novello, in 1992.) As if Frazee's activities weren't destructive enough, a major fire illuminated and eliminated the wooden left-field bleachers in 1926. Then came the Great Depression.

In 1933, Fenway Park's fortunes took a turn for the better. Four days after his thirtieth birthday brought him an inheritance of $7 million or more, Thomas A. Yawkey, "the savior of the Sox," bought the ball club and the park. By 1934, Yawkey had already begun rebuilding the team and renovating Fenway at a cost of two million Depression dollars.

Yawkey's physical improvements resulted in much the same park we see today. Concrete bleachers replaced the old wooden ones; the grandstand was enlarged and seating increased; the facade was sandblasted; Duffy's Cliff was leveled and the Green Monster built; a larger scoreboard with traffic light–style signals plus American and National League scores was featured; and the entire park was painted its distinctive shade of green.

Yawkey officially reopened his "new" Fenway Park on April 17, 1934. The park began serving beer for the first time in 1934 as well—a tradition that continues to this day, often in conjunction with that historic hot dog the Fenway Frank.

According to Dick Johnson, curator of the Sports Museum of New England, "Thomas Yawkey did for sports in this city what Henry Lee Higginson did for music." (Higginson was the founder and patron of the Boston Symphony Orchestra in 1881, and the man who financed the orchestra's permanent home, Symphony Hall, in 1900.)

Though the much respected and loved Yawkey died in 1976, his memory and name live on in Fenway. Among the memorials was the renaming of Jersey Street, where the park's front facade is located; since 1977 it has been called Yawkey Way. His widow, Jean Yawkey, remained general partner and president of the Red Sox until her death in 1992, and was the first woman elected to the board of directors of Cooperstown's National Baseball Hall of Fame and Museum. Another tribute to the Yawkeys is covertly ensconced on the hand-operated scoreboard; descending between the R and the P on that board are the initials of Thomas and Jean Yawkey, written in Morse code.

The peculiar logistics, size, and shape of Fenway Park have been blamed for altering the course of ballgames since Fenway history began. The short distance to The Wall—an "official" 315 feet that many outside experts claim measures no more than 309 feet—can increase homers, for example. Before a 1974–76 renovation, The Wall also gave Red Sox outfielders a definite home-field advantage; old pros like Carl "Yaz" Yastrzemski had mastered the art of altering their catching stances depending on whether the ball ricocheted off the bouncy cement at the bottom or the deadening metal above. The park's angular corners and smaller-than-average foul areas—not to mention the glaring afternoon sun, whipping wind, and occasional pigeons colliding with balls—have also altered the course of plays and even games over the decades. As a result, baseball scores are apt to change mercurially in Fenway. As Dick Johnson says, "It's like a pinball machine in there."

On the other hand, the players have sometimes changed the park as well. Charismatic Sox slugger Ted Williams, for instance, is credited with moving the bullpen from the right-field corner to the front of the right-field bleachers after his rookie 1939 season. Williams was a powerful left-handed batter, and Fenway wanted to make the most of his hits. The area where Williams could slam his homers free and clear after the bullpen move was dubbed Williamsburg—Boston's counterpart of Yankee Stadium's Ruthville.

Various renovations have changed the park slightly since Williams's day. Skyview seating was added on either side of the press box in 1946. That press box was replaced in 1988–89 by the 600 Club, a plush, glass-enclosed section of 610 stadium seats; a new broadcast booth and press box was then installed on top. Large ads once posted across The Wall were painted over in 1947 to improve ball visibility, while portions of the center-field bleacher section were occasionally roped off during day games to avoid the blinding reflections of fans' white shirts. Between 1974 and 1976, safety padding was added to the outfield walls, plastic red and blue seats appeared in the stands, and the club's first huge electronic message board was installed above center field. That board was replaced by a color "videoboard" in 1987–88.

During those same 1974–76 park renovations, The Wall was again modernized and recreated in fiberglass. Fenway Park's longtime official charity, the Jimmy Fund of the Dana-Farber Cancer Institute, benefited from the last wall change, incidentally: green sheet metal from the old facade was clipped into snapshot-sized rectangles, mounted on wood, then sold to fans in a fund-raiser for cancer research.

One final change at Fenway—and perhaps the most noticeable—has been the price of tickets. On opening day in 1912, bleacher seats cost twenty-five cents and "pavilion" seats half a dollar. In 1993, the price of bleacher seats was $7, reserved grandstand seats $10, and box seats ranged from $14 to $18. But, as legions of longtime fans—from comic Frankie Fontaine and Mrs. Calvin Coolidge to former Speaker of the House Tip O'Neill and novelist Stephen King—would surely testify, it's a small price to pay for the Fenway Park experience.

THE ESSENTIALS

ADDRESS: 4 Yawkey Way, Kenmore Square, Boston.
TELEPHONE: Ticket office, (617) 267-1700; administrative offices, (617) 267-9440; tours, (617) 236-6666.
VISITOR INFORMATION: Open to ticket holders during home games, April through September. Call ticket office for schedule. Tours available May through September; moderate admission. There are 101 wheelchair spaces, along with 101 companion seats, available throughout the park; special facilities are also available for hearing-impaired and visually impaired persons.

24 Park Street Station

ITS ADMIRERS see it as a wondrous gem lodged in the center of Boston—"the epitome of Beantown," "the hub of the Hub," and "the melting pot of the whole system." Its detractors view it as just another downtown dungeon—a necessary byway for zipping from here to there.

Most people probably don't think about Park Street Station at all. They just use it, take it for granted, count on its being there day after day and decade after decade. On an average weekday, an astonishing 105,000 people enter, exit, or make trolley transfers at Park Street Station, using 4,711 cars on 2,359 trains.

What they're missing, however, is a sense of this subway stop's historic significance. First opened in 1897, Park Street was one of the four original stations in the Tremont Street Subway, the first subway in the United States. Since 1964, both the station and its headhouses have been honored with National Historic Landmark and National Historic Civil Engineering Landmark status.

Park Street Station was also the nucleus of a system that grew from a half-mile downtown strip to one serving seventy-nine cities and towns in the Greater Boston area. Though the system itself has changed and grown

Park Street was one of the original underground stations of America's first subway system.

over the last century—and has been known by a variety of names ("the El," the M.T.A., the M.B.T.A., and "the T")—Park Street Station has remained as one of four junction points at the center of the T. Park Street trolleys can transport riders in, around, and far away from Boston's downtown in a matter of minutes. On its top level are Green Line cars, which travel west to Boston College and Brookline, and north to East Cambridge. From the platform down below run Red Line trains, which go north to Cambridge and Somerville, and south to Boston neighborhoods like Dorchester and Mattapan, and suburban Quincy and Braintree.

Given all those accomplishments, it's certainly no surprise that Park Street Station and the surrounding system have been heralded in sonnet, song, film, and legend. Nineteenth-century poet Oliver Wendell Holmes was one of the first to wax poetic about the Hub's first subway, in "The Broomstick Train." A. J. Deutsch penned an eerie, science-fiction tale about a Cambridge-bound train disappearing into thin air, in a 1950 story called "A Subway Named Mobius." The Kingston Trio had a smash hit with "M.T.A.," a song about a man named Charlie who got trapped on Boston's underground by a five-cent fare hike. Both Joanne Woodward and Robert Urich have performed in Park Street Station, during respective filmings of the movie *See How They Run* and the television series "Spenser for Hire."

In 1972, Boston College professor Brian Cudahy wrote an entire book,

Change at Park Street Under, about the history of Boston's subway system and its trains. In 1979, there was even a short-lived television comedy series called "Park Street Under," whose main claim to fame was inspiring yet another Boston-based sitcom, the long-running "Cheers."

That a simple downtown subway stop should prove so uplifting is quite logical to George Sanborn, the official librarian of the Massachusetts Bay Transportation Authority: "Whenever you think about Boston, sooner or later you get back to Park Street. Whenever you talk about Boston, Park Street eventually enters the conversation. There's no other place like it. Many of the other stations are—well—sterile, bland. But Park is fascinating. It has a distinctive ambiance. There's that mosaic mural by Lilli Ann Rosenberg, a pictorial representation of Boston through the ages, as it revolved around Park Street. And there are the people who use it everyday—the mainstream of humanity.

"No matter what goes through Park Street, whatever changes are made at Park Street, it always remains Park Street."

In the early days, Boston had no need for an underground rapid-transit system. When legs wouldn't do, horses, cows, and tethered carts were enough to transport colonial people and their colonial possessions around the town's narrow, winding streets and alleys. Little by little, however, the scale of Boston life began to change. In 1800, only one in thirteen Americans lived in cities; by 1895, that number had increased to one in three. In Boston and other urban centers, congestion and overcrowding became serious problems, and improving public transportation a major issue.

As a result, Boston introduced its first horsecars in 1852. For two decades, these horse-drawn streetcars provided both reasonable transportation and a good source of revenue through the sale of fares, inside advertising cards, and horse manure. In the 1870s, however, horsecars were dealt a double blow. A virulent equine influenza, the "Great Epizootic," spread throughout horsecar stables in the eastern states in 1872, disabling or destroying great numbers of animals. Moreover, inventors were beginning to experiment with alternative power sources for streetcars, including steam, compressed air, naphtha, mechanical legs, cables, and even giant clock springs.

It was not until 1888, when engineer Frank Sprague equipped the streetcars of Richmond, Virginia, with electric motors, that urban mass transit really arrived. One year later, Boston's West End Street Railway—one of the largest horsecar companies in America—went electric. The remaining horsecars were slowly phased out; the last one ran in Boston on Christmas Eve, 1900.

As the 1890s unfolded, Boston's new electric trolleys proved so successful that they created even greater problems. The city streets became crammed with tracks, wires, feeds, posts, crossings, and junctions that offended the eye and periodically immobilized the town. One observer noted that between 5:00 and 6:30 P.M., a man could walk down Tremont Street from Scollay Square (near today's Government Center Station) to Boylston Street on the roofs of streetcars without ever touching the ground. Tremont itself was four lanes wide—three of which were covered by trolley tracks. (Brooklyn, New York, had a similar trolley glut—so much so that their baseball team was called the Brooklyn Trolley Dodgers, a name that was later shortened.)

Politicians and citizens alike argued about the most logical solution to the surfeit of electrified surface trolleys. The two strongest factions agreed that public transport must be taken off the streets: one group insisted on elevated tracks, while the other espoused the "European transit system"— subterranean trolley tunnels—which had already proven successful in Glasgow, Paris, London, and Budapest. After prolonged debate, the subway idea prevailed, although elevated streetcar tracks were added on Boston's periphery beginning as early as 1901.

The corner of Tremont and Park streets was a logical starting point for the initial leg of America's first subway. The area was part of Boston Common, a place Bostonians had used for cow grazing, military drills, public meetings, hangings, and other festivities since 1634. A variety of buildings had graced that broad corner in times past, including a granary, a workhouse, and the still-standing Park Street Church.

Nevertheless, when the Boston Transit Commission was created in 1894 to plan the subway, and when Chief Engineer Howard A. Carson began construction on March 28, 1895, tempers ran high. Some people worried the digging project would tie up traffic. Others feared damage to the Common, inspiring Mayor Nathan Matthews to remark that Boston's eleventh commandment seemed to be "Thou shalt not touch the Common."

Despite public fears, the commandment was disobeyed for almost three years, as laborers dug up clay, gravel, and sand along the Common's Tremont Street edge, from the Park Street intersection to the far corner of the Public Garden. Working with teams of a hundred workers doing ten-hour shifts, the crews hauled out tons of dirt, using steam-driven carts on overhead trestles, then dumping the unwanted soil at the end of the Common, where the baseball field exists today.

Despite inaccurate or nonexistent utilities maps, beds of quicksand, and accidental explosions—like the one at the corner of Boylston and Tremont that killed nine workers—work went on. Work went on, too, though some one thousand colonial cadavers were inadvertently exhumed; the bodies were reinterred in the northwest corner of the Common's burial ground, facing the Colonial Theatre on Boylston Street.

Work went on and persistence won out: the first leg of the Tremont Street Subway was ready to open on September 1, 1897. The total cost of that first subway line was $4,404,958.25, substantially under the original estimate of $5 million. Of that expense, $350,000 was for Park Street Station itself. The subterranean streetcar stop was constructed using steel beams, brick, and concrete masonry. Though the steelwork on the roof was left exposed, the walls were lined with white porcelain brick or tile, and the supporting steel columns were encased in concrete and painted white.

The original station was on the level of the modern-day Green Line; the Red Line's "Park Street Under" was not added below until 1912. In a space about half the size of today's upper level station there were four tracks, two island platforms, two loop tracks for return cars, plus a space for disabled or extra cars. Stairs with patent safety treads led up to four headhouses on the street level, two of which are still in use today.

Those boxlike headhouses were designed by Edmund Wheelwright of the architectural firm Wheelwright and Haven. The kiosks' walls were made from granite brought in from Deer Island, Maine. Their roofs were glass, and the exterior details were neoclassical, featuring decorative dentils and pilasters, high, brass-screened windows, and—in 1897—no doors in the doorways.

Wheelwright's careful design was not appreciated by contemporary critics or the press, who complained that the entrance cubes looked like mausoleums.

Those critics had nothing but good to say about the opening day of the subway, however. In the wee hours of September 1, 1897, crowds began to assemble at both the Boylston and Park Street stations. Back in the western suburb of Allston, where the first car would begin its journey, an overflow crowd of 175 jammed into the 50-person streetcar. By the end of the day, 100,000 riders would make the same trip.

Conductor Gilman T. Trufant and motorman James Reed—both West End Street Railway veterans—guided Car #1752, an open-bench four-wheel trolley, on the inaugural run. "All aboard for Park Street!" was the cry as the trolley traveled on preexisting surface tracks from the Allston car barns, across the River Street Bridge to Pearl Street in Cambridge, then across the Harvard Bridge, toward an incline that began at the Public Garden. Swinging off Boylston Street, the car descended underground, arriving at the Park Street platform at 6:02 A.M. to cheers and waving flags.

That first strip of Boston subway was only six-tenths of a mile. But little by little, the subway expanded—extending throughout downtown, over to Cambridge, out to South Boston and East Boston, and beyond. Sometimes it grew underground and sometimes above ground, on the elevated lines built outside the busy city center. (The elevated lines were much cheaper to construct than their underground counterparts, but considered too great an obstruction and eyesore to place in congested downtown areas.) The fares grew, too—from five cents in 1897 to eighty-five cents in 1993. Incidentally, the first subway riders paid their fares with tickets; coins were used later, starting in 1915. Of the payment methods in use today, tokens were introduced in 1951. The T pass, allowing for a month of subway rides, was first used in 1974, and the Boston Passport, allowing for either three or seven days of unlimited public transportation travel, in 1989.

The Boston Elevated Railway Company, which built and operated most of "the El," was a private stockholder corporation that took control of all the Boston transit lines and stations in 1922. In 1947, the whole system was transferred to a public agency created by the Massachusetts legislature—the Metropolitan Transit Authority. The M.T.A., which served fourteen cities and towns, was replaced in 1964 by a larger transit group, the Massachusetts Bay Transportation Authority. The M.B.T.A., which still exists today, expanded the service district to seventy-eight, then seventy-nine communities.

Under the M.B.T.A., Boston's four historic streetcar lines were labeled with the color codes we know today. The original Boylston-Tremont trolley subway became the Green Line. The Cambridge-Dorchester line, begun in 1912, became the Red Line; the 1901 Main Line El became the Orange; and the 1904 East Boston line the Blue. Since each of the four lines was developed at different times by different groups, their equipment was never made interchangeable. Hence the complex history of subway and elevated rapid-transit vehicles in Boston—from the earliest trolleys to sophisticated PCCs, LRVs, Pullmans, Type 7s and Kinki Sharyos—has four different versions: one for each line. Each line has its own idiom as well. People still throw around terms like trains, cars, streetcars, and trolley cars, referring to all sorts of different vehicles. Technically, however, Green Line cars are light rail vehicles, and they're run by operators; Red Line cars are heavy rail vehicles, also called trains, and are run by motormen.

What all the T's vehicles do have in common is 550 volts of direct current, provided today by the local utility company, Boston Edison. For decades, however, Boston's subway system had its own power plants and generated its own electricity; during the Great Northeast Blackout of November 1965, the M.B.T.A. kept running, while the New York City subways stopped dead in their tracks. The T's generating plants were eventually deemed expensive and impractical, and phased out between 1977 and 1981.

Another major change of the past two decades has involved personnel, both at Park Street and throughout the entire M.B.T.A. Women are on the job everywhere now—making up roughly one-quarter of all T staff. The subway's personnel for its first seven decades were essentially all male. Not just any men, mind you. As far back as 1901, the company outlined strict standards for its employees: "Our conductors must be presentable, for the very appearance of some men gives offense quickly in a cultured community. These men must have all their fingers and thumbs, and now-a-days must have all their toes. . . . [They also need] a reasonable number of either real or artificial teeth."

Park Street Station itself has changed and improved since 1897. The Red Line platform was added in 1912, and the Green Line's track-and-platform space was enlarged twice. Two of Park's original four street-level headhouses are gone, while newer additions—such as elevators, escalators, computerized systems, and a little-known concourse to the Orange Line—have made the station a bit more modern. Save for a single donut concession stand by the Lechmere-bound trains, all of the vendors that used to crowd the Green Line platform have disappeared, leaving the platforms free for their most important components: token booths, an information booth, and people.

Though the whole M.B.T.A. system doesn't operate out of Park Street as it once did, the station still acts as "Emergency Backup for Central Control," from a spartan chamber hidden behind the long mural. That mural, a 1978 mosaic by Lilli Ann Killen Rosenberg, is located on the Green Line level near the entrance; it's a creative and colorful collage that incorporates ceramic and found objects—like railroad spikes, horseshoes, hammers, and wheels—into a fanciful city scene filled with tidbits about Boston and its famed subway system. The only artwork on the Red Line, below, is a pair of praying hands set in the arches above the track, executed by Ralph Helmick—the artist who created the Arthur Fiedler bust on the Charles River Esplanade.

Today, Park Street bears few signs of the crisis it experienced in the 1970s. Racial tension, fanned by the busing crisis, led to sporadic friction and fights, generally quelled by T personnel. A December 1975 fire, which presumably began in a "greasy spoon" fast-food stand near the Lechmere track, caused significant interior damage. Old and unreliable equipment led to constant breakdowns and delays; ongoing financial shortages caused the T to shut down entirely on December 6, 1980, for a period of twenty-six hours; and a major renovation of the station in the late 1970s proved architecturally controversial at best.

Fortunately, better equipment and more dependable streetcars have arrived since then, and a $6–7 million renovation, executed in 1992 and 1993, has given the station a cleaner, brighter environment, improved signage, some historical commentary, and better wheelchair access to platforms.

Another improvement has been a more lyrical one. "There was a joke among the guys in the mid-1970s," says Ed Manning, the superintendent of surface lines. "We said, If we can't provide them service, we'll give them music to soothe their nerves!" Hence, the official policy of inviting musicians to play in Park Street Station—and eventually throughout the T—began. Kevin McNamara, a folk-rock musician who has played the crowds at Park since 1978, reports that subway gigs are fine experiences. It's true that noise and constantly changing audiences are inherent problems, and that street-corner shows attract higher contributions than their subway counterparts, "but it's great training in winning over an audience," says McNamara. "Plus you can work out new music. Who's going to know if you play the same song all day?"

During late 1993 and early 1994, the newest planned additions to Park Street and other M.B.T.A. stations were thirty-inch MetroVision video screens offering commuters information on news, sports, weather, and M.B.T.A. service, as well as more controversial stuff: ads. Since most of this info-tainment has no audio component, it is hoped that the street musicians will still occupy center stage on the Red Line platform.

Meanwhile, with sweet melodies in the background, the constant crush of humanity continues to swarm in and out of Park Street Station, day after day. And the same old questions are asked of T personnel with clocklike regularity.

"How do I get to Harvard?"
"How do I get to Fenway Park?"
"How do I get to the M.F.A.?"
"How do you get to the other side?"
"Excuse me, but where's 'Cheers'?"

THE ESSENTIALS

ADDRESS: Intersection of Park and Tremont streets, Boston.

TELEPHONE: M.B.T.A. customer service and travel information, (617) 722-3200.

VISITOR INFORMATION: Park Street Station, and subway lines in general, are open from approximately 5:00 A.M. to 1:00 A.M. daily. Small fee. No scheduled tours. Green Line trolleys not yet wheelchair accessible; Red Line accessible via elevator in kiosk at Tremont and Winter streets, plus raised platforms at Park Street Under that allow patrons to wheel directly (though with some difficulty) onto trains. No public restrooms.

PART IV

Athens Two:
Literary Boston

he cultural awakening of Boston that began in the second
quarter of the nineteenth century continued through the time
of the American Civil War. That flowering involved not only
the arts and entertainment, but the literary world as well.

It was two of Boston's nineteenth-century literary lights, in fact, that
gave Boston its nicknames "the Athens of America" and "the Hub of the
Universe." William Tudor, a founder and the first editor of the *North
American Review,* and an original Athenaeum member, is credited with
making the first comparison to Athens, in a letter of 1819. Oliver Wendell
Holmes called Boston "the hub of the solar system" in his 1858 work *The
Autocrat of the Breakfast Table,* and later generations expanded that phrase to
include a much larger chunk of the heavens.

To make books and literature available to Bostonians, libraries were
needed. In the first half of the nineteenth century, the area's prime book
repositories were Harvard College and the Boston Athenaeum. Books
were therefore within the reach of only a relative few. By 1854, however,
the Boston Public Library opened its doors, making waves as the first free
municipal library in America. Creating new books and literature required
that there be book publishers. And though publishers had existed in
Boston long before, it was the firm of Ticknor & Fields, lodged at the Old
Corner Bookstore, that revolutionized Boston and American publishing in
the mid-nineteenth century.

Jamie Fields in particular drew the area's finest authors to the Old
Corner Bookstore building. The shop's location, at the corner of Washington and School streets, became known as "Parnassus Corner," yet another
reference to the era's classical cultural inspirations and aspirations. The road
that led from Washington Street to the new State House on Beacon Hill
became the regular haunt of numerous literary luminaries, from Harriet
Beecher Stowe, Louisa May Alcott, and Margaret Fuller to Henry Wadsworth Longfellow, Ralph Waldo Emerson, and Charles Dickens. Nearer

the State House, on Beacon Street, was the Athenaeum, where many read, researched, and assembled. At the intersection of Beacon, Tremont, and School streets were two of Boston's finest hotels, the Tremont House and the Parker House. The latter became the festive center of the literary "Saturday Club" during the second half of the nineteenth century.

Downtown theaters were also a part of the nineteenth-century literary world. Stages like the Tremont Theatre (now Tremont Temple Baptist Church), the old Music Hall (now the Orpheum Theatre), and the long-gone Boston Museum and Howard Athenaeum were popular sites for presenting plays and musical events to Boston audiences; but literary readings by poets and authors—as well as inspired orations by reformers like William Lloyd Garrison and Frederick Douglass—were just as likely to draw large crowds. A perfect microcosm of the intermingling of arts and other aspects of culture that occurred during this period was the Boston Museum, which opened on Tremont and Bromfield streets in 1841. Concerts, plays, and lectures were offered in its upstairs performance space, while the first floor housed a museum that included both paintings and stuffed animal specimens.

Many of the writers, poets, and philosophers associated with the flowering of nineteenth-century Boston actually lived outside of the city. Henry David Thoreau and other Transcendentalists preferred a pastoral existence, viewing city life as a "menacing artifact." Little towns like Concord—and in Thoreau's case, a tiny cabin by Concord's Walden Pond—were sometimes deemed more appropriate homes. Still, plenty of the literati stayed right in the Hub, often in stylish enclaves like the Back Bay, Beacon Hill, and the Hill's private, cobblestoned block known as Louisburg Square. In-town locations, after all, made "Athens" all the more accessible.

The Boston Athenaeum

FEMINIST JOURNALIST Margaret Fuller studied here, and so did philosopher Ralph Waldo Emerson. Statesman Daniel Webster happily whiled away the hours in these chambers, as did essayists, authors, and poets like Oliver Wendell Holmes, Lydia Maria Child, Amy Lowell, and Henry Wadsworth Longfellow. Filmmaker Ken Burns burrowed through antique photographs and Confederate imprints, assembling materials for his television documentary series "The Civil War." Here, too, amidst a sea of library stacks and shoulder-to-shoulder neoclassical busts, historian Doris Kearns Goodwin wrote *The Fitzgeralds and the Kennedys,* and historian David McCullough researched his biography of Harry S. Truman.

Few proper Bostonians would be surprised to hear that the place where these nineteenth- and twentieth-century movers and shakers all hunkered down was the Boston Athenaeum. What's more surprising to some is that the Athenaeum, renowned as Boston's first library and first real art museum, has served scholars and ordinary folk alike in its nearly two centuries of existence. While this Beacon Hill institution is indeed a private library, qualified scholars are invited to use the research facilities for free, and nonmembers are welcome to visit the art gallery and to join free weekly tours. Those tours, incidentally, won *Boston Magazine*'s 1989 award for "Best Out-of-Body Experience"—a citation that still perplexes and amuses Athenaeum staff.

The Athenaeum began in 1805, when fourteen Boston gentlemen formed the Anthology Society, their own literary and dining club, to edit the *Monthly Anthology and Boston Review.* Within its first year, the society set an even more ambitious goal: to create an institution with "a reading room, a library, a museum, and a laboratory" for its members. They opened to subscribers in 1806, and incorporated as the Boston Athenaeum on February 17, 1807.

Why *Athenaeum?* Defined as "an institution or society for the promotion of literary and/or scientific learning," the term also evokes the classical Greek word *athenaion,* a temple dedicated to the goddess Athena, where poets read their works aloud. Some Anthology Society members were certainly familiar with the Athenaeum and Lyceum of Liverpool, England, as well.

While simultaneously working on other projects, such as creating the *North American Review* in 1811 (a periodical still published today), the Athenaeum's founders went about finding a home for the books and artwork they had begun to collect. After housing the collection briefly in buildings on Congress and Tremont streets, members bought the Rufus Amory House, next to King's Chapel Burying Ground, in 1809. In 1822, when that space proved too small, they moved to a new home on Pearl Street, made from two separate houses combined by architect Solomon Willard.

Once collections overflowed yet again, the Athenaeum's present structure was built at 10½ Beacon Street, and opened to great fanfare in July of 1849. Its Italianate, neo-Palladian style was chosen by Edward Clarke Cabot, who won the Athenaeum's design competition.

In many ways, Cabot's Athenaeum looked much as it does today: a dignified exterior of dark sandstone, with Corinthian pilasters defining tall, arched window bays and a central entrance. Inside, long, high-ceilinged rooms are filled with little balconies, alcoves, and nooks, and packed with an eclectic, easily accessible collection of books. To this day, 90 percent of the 700,000 volumes remain on open stacks.

Unlike the modern Athenaeum, the 1849 building had only three floors—two for art galleries and a third for books. To no one's surprise, the collections continued to exceed available space. Sometimes this was dealt with in a small way; in 1888, for example, the entrance foyer's monumental Sumner staircase was sacrificed to make room for new stacks. Other times, physical expansion came in a big way. During 1913–14, Henry Forbes

Created as Boston's first library and first art museum, the Boston Athenaeum is still a wonderful place to read, browse, and research.

Bigelow choreographed a total renovation and fireproofing of the Athenaeum, adding two more floors to Cabot's original building. The result was today's five-story structure.

In the beginning, the Athenaeum tried to be all things to all people. Its art gallery accumulated and exhibited treasures by American artists such as Gilbert Stuart, John Singer Sargent, Washington Allston, Chester Harding, Thomas Crawford, and John Frazee. It also supplied studio space, moral support, and financial backing for working artists. Meanwhile, its library became one of the five largest in America. With 50,000 volumes by 1851, its collection equaled that of the Library of Congress.

Later in the nineteenth century, the Athenaeum's role changed. The Boston Public Library opened in 1854, and in 1876 the Athenaeum helped to establish the Boston Museum of Fine Arts, lending it many of its first exhibits. No longer inspired to be *the* library and *the* art museum of Boston, the institution gradually committed itself to more limited, and more specialized, acquisitions and goals. In particular, the printed word took precedence over art.

Nevertheless, artwork—including spectacularly fine or wonderfully curious nineteenth-century paintings and sculptures—is still displayed throughout the building. A second-floor gallery with changing exhibits is a favorite attraction for visitors.

The paintings and sculpture on view—gently crammed into every available wall, pedestal, and corner—are primarily the work of American nineteenth-century artists. Artwork connected to Athenaeum history has also deliberately been kept, making the place look like "a big family house." Among the more extraordinary pieces in the library's possession are several paintings by Gilbert Stuart, Giovanni Panini's *Interior of St. Peter's, Rome,* and Luca Giordano's *Golden Age.* Among the pieces most requested in duplicate form—for display, research, or publication outside the Athenaeum—are Jean Antoine Houdon's busts of Washington, Lafayette, and Franklin; Chester Harding's painting of Daniel Webster; and Allan Crite's painting *Harriet and Leon.* (Crite is a pioneering twentieth-century African-American artist and art historian based in the Boston area.)

As the Athenaeum reduced its role as art museum over the decades, it sold many works of art. Perhaps the most regrettable loss was Thomas Crawford's marble statue *Orpheus and Cerberus,* which was loaned to Boston's Museum of Fine Arts in 1872. A century later, in 1975, the statue was purchased by private individuals and donated to the M.F.A., where it's still on prominent display. The M.F.A. and the Smithsonian Institution jointly acquired Gilbert Stuart's unfinished portraits of George and Martha Washington from the Athenaeum in 1980, in a $4.9 million sale that stipulated that the first "first couple" be shared by the Museum and the Smithsonian's National Portrait Gallery. (The "sharing" process is simple: three years in Boston, followed by three years in Washington, *ad infinitum.*)

Not all of the nonbook objects at the Athenaeum can be classified as art. Among the stranger items in its special collections are a breastplate and sword from the battlefield at Waterloo, and shoes purportedly owned by President McKinley's wife. The Athenaeum's more scholarly highlights include a superb group of Confederate States imprints, eighteenth- and nineteenth-century Boston newspapers, and one of the finest groupings of nineteenth-century prints in the nation. An engaging and beautifully printed book, *Boston Lithography, 1825–80,* assembled by staff members Sally Pierce and Catharina Slautterback, based on historic lithographs housed in the Charles E. Mason, Jr., Print Room, was recently published.

The Athenaeum's present emphasis on reading and research is readily apparent—if only because books are lodged in every conceivable cranny of the building. The basement includes conservation and photo labs, engineering shops, and movable compact shelving. The first floor features a new book display, a children's room, and an elegant periodical reading room, with magazines spread out in nineteenth-century fashion. The second floor—with its chandeliers, well-trod oriental rugs, and polished old tables—functions as a hall for musical events, poetry readings, and lectures when not used for general reading, research, and the display of fine arts periodicals. Technical services now dominate the third floor, while the main catalogues and reference department fill much of the fourth. Two of the building's most fascinating spaces are the Trustees' Room on floor four, and the fifth, uppermost level, a peaceful, cathedral-like reading room reserved for members only.

When Athenaeum members come here to read, they're sometimes seeking books that plenty of other libraries have—and sometimes books that are nowhere else to be found. Obscure, out-of-print titles are, after all, an Athenaeum specialty. Some of the books are in fragile condition, but most remain in unusually usable shape, thanks largely to the Athenaeum's conservation department.

Among the most prestigious volumes are those from George Washington's library, purchased from Mount Vernon in 1848, the Schoolcraft Collection of books in Native American languages, and volumes from the King's Chapel theological collections. Among the most surprising resources—especially to those who view the Athenaeum solely as a serious research library—is one of the finest collections of detective fiction in the country.

The most infamous book is certainly the autobiography of an executed nineteenth-century highwayman, which, following his request, was bound in his own skin. Once on display, the autobiography has been tactfully tucked away from the public eye.

The library has 700,000 volumes in all, a number increasing at the rate of 5,000 per year. In 1991, more than 22,500 of those volumes were circulated to various readers. When not in use by members, the books are borrowed by hundreds of other institutions, both private and public, and accessed by a growing number of computerized inter-library loan networks. (Though about three-quarters of their books are still catalogued according to the Athenaeum's peculiar in-house Cutter classification system, all acquisitions since 1978 use the modern Library of Congress method.)

In its earliest years, the Athenaeum was essentially a gentlemen's reading room for wealthy white Bostonians. The resulting nineteenth-century biases were reflected in the book classification system developed by Athenaeum librarian Charles Ammi Cutter. According to the Athenaeum's current reference librarian, "It's an alpha–numeric system that is logical and user friendly. But 'Class D' lumps together books on education, the poor, women, and slavery."

It was not long, however, before demographic changes in Athenaeum membership began to take place. In the 1820s, when women were often excluded from colleges and private libraries, writer Hannah Adams was allowed to study here. Granted, the woman renowned as America's first full-time professional female author was locked in the library at lunchtime to pursue her studies "in modesty." But she did get in, and was awarded permanent free access by 1827.

Once Adams got her foot in the door, others followed. In 1856, the Athenaeum became the first library in America to hire a female staff member. Nineteenth-century African-American sculptor Edmonia Lewis was among the artists supported by the institution, as was Gilbert Stuart's daughter, Jane. A higher percentage of paintings and sculpture of and by women was accumulated—and is still displayed at the Athenaeum—than in most other historic buildings in Boston.

Despite these inroads by women, and despite the fact that many of its members were ardent abolitionists and reformers, conservatism remained a strong force at the Athenaeum; when member Lydia Maria Child wrote "An Appeal in Favor of the Class of Americans Called Africans"—an immediatist tract that angered gradualists in abolitionism—she found her privileges mysteriously revoked.

Today, the Athenaeum remains a curious mix of conservative and liberal, of old and new. "A lot of people still think this is an old gentlemen's club," muses Ann Wadsworth of the Athenaeum's Research Department. "Actually, there still are a few old gentlemen here who think that!" Alongside them, and heartily welcomed by the Athenaeum, are those not accommodated in the past. In 1850, one might have been shocked to find a woman wandering through the second floor art gallery with her baby stroller, preschoolers enjoying story time downstairs, or a well-attended lecture on Native American or black history. But today they're all a matter of course. Members can no longer smoke in most spaces as they once did, but they can still bring in well-behaved dogs.

And, yes, the tradition of afternoon tea is still maintained one afternoon a week. Indeed, the best of the nineteenth century remains alive and well at 10½ Beacon.

THE ESSENTIALS

ADDRESS: 10½ Beacon Street, Boston.
TELEPHONE: (617) 227-0270.
VISITOR INFORMATION: Building open 9:00 A.M.–5:30 P.M., Monday–Friday, year-round. Open 9:00 A.M.–4:00 P.M. Saturday, September through May; closed all regular holidays. Free tours Tuesday and Thursday, 3:00 P.M., or by arrangement; reservations required. Wheelchair-accessible walkway to right of front entrance; assistance needed via movable ramp once inside vestibule; elevators available to all floors; accessible restroom on first floor.

26 The Old Corner Bookstore Building

IT'S BEEN more than a century since the editor of New York's *Home Journal* observed that, with a little exaggeration, all of Boston could be said to pass through the Old Corner in a day. That's a bit far-fetched, of course. Still, anyone versed in Boston's literary history knows that the quaint brick building at the corner of School and Washington streets—affectionately known to generations as the Old Corner Bookstore—has been a mecca for avid readers, illustrious men and women of letters, and other curious Bostonians since the mid-nineteenth century.

Between 1845 and 1865 in particular, when the shop was run by the prestigious publishing team of Ticknor & Fields, the guests on any given day might range from Norwegian violinist Ole Bull and popular American actresses Charlotte Cushman and Fanny Kemble, to authors like Harriet Beecher Stowe, Henry David Thoreau, and Nathaniel Hawthorne. British novelist Charles Dickens passed frequently through the shop's portals, as did local literary heroes such as Oliver Wendell Holmes, Henry Wadsworth Longfellow, and Ralph Waldo Emerson.

When you add to this group a broad array of doctors and lawyers, ministers and midwives, artists and professors, abolitionists and librarians, and just plain people, it becomes clear why the intersection of School and Washington sometimes looked a bit like Grand Central Station. What's more, it was nicknamed "Parnassus Corner," after the sacred Greek mount where the Muses and Apollo once held forth. If Boston was "the Hub of the Universe," the bookstore was arguably the cultural "hub of the Hub," at least during the tenure of William Ticknor and Jamie Fields.

But the history of the Old Corner Bookstore neither started, nor ended, with Ticknor and Fields. Today, for example, the building houses the busy Globe Corner Bookstore, which specializes in books about New England and world travel. During the winter holiday season, the shop is also the downtown headquarters for the *Boston Globe*'s Santa, a charity that purchases toys for children with money contributed by *Globe* readers. The building itself, a site on the Freedom Trail, is owned and managed by Historic Boston Incorporated, a nonprofit group that helped save the old bookstore structure from demolition in 1960 and continues to assist preservation efforts for other Boston landmarks. Historic Boston, the Globe Pequot Press, the Liberty Bank, the Body Shop, Copley Flair, and other businesses have offices in various sections of the complex.

The corner on which the Old Corner Bookstore sits is considered a prime downtown location. Oddly enough, that was also true in 1630, the year

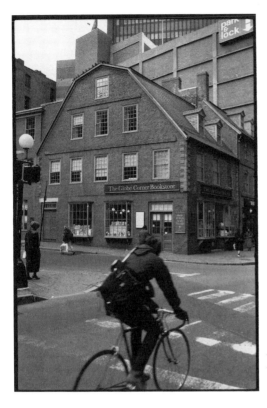

Internationally acclaimed nineteenth-century publishers Ticknor & Fields put the Old Corner Bookstore on the literary map of America.

Boston was settled by the Massachusetts Bay Company. Many of the first colonists constructed crude homes near the freshwater spring that bubbled up where Spring Lane is found today. Boston's first church, market, and town house (the last term meant a public building, not a private family condo, at the time) were all built within two blocks of the future site of the Old Corner Bookstore.

A prominent East Anglican Puritan named Isaac Johnson was the original owner of the bookstore site and several surrounding acres. But Johnson and his equally prominent wife, Lady Arbella Fiennes, failed to survive the severe Boston winter. Anne Hutchinson, her husband, William, and their children, who arrived in Boston on September 18, 1634, subsequently built a home on the half-acre corner lot that Johnson had once owned. The spot was clearly at the heart of the village, where "the street leading to Roxbury" met "the lane leading to the Common." The prestige of the area was also evidenced by the Hutchinsons' immediate neighbor: Governor John Winthrop lived across the street, a circumstance that Mrs. Hutchinson would soon learn to regret.

Hutchinson became a popular, powerful woman, respected as a midwife and as the spouse of an established merchant. She was also a brilliant thinker and a leader of the controversial Antinomian sect, which took issue with prevailing Puritan thought. Hutchinson argued that both men and women could find true spirituality in the personal and the mystical—

thereby challenging the Puritan establishment's academic foundations, their religious disciplines, and the authenticity of their "learned clergy." She also attracted more and more ardent female followers to the prayer meetings she held in her home. Such mysticism and feminism combined as a formidable affront to the eminently rational, all-male Puritan hierarchy.

As a result, Winthrop and his colleagues were incensed. In 1637, the General Court of Massachusetts banished Hutchinson for heresy. Like most religious refugees of the time, she fled to Rhode Island, along with her family and several friends. After her husband died, Hutchinson and her fourteen children moved to Long Island, where they were killed in 1643 by Siwanoy Indians who were quarreling with the area's Dutch settlers.

Two year's after her death, Governor Winthrop waxed philosophical about women like Hutchinson, whom he thought suffered from excess intellect—from too much reading, writing, and thinking; such a woman would have had a less troubled life, wrote Winthrop in his journal, "if she had attended to her household affairs and such things as belong to women, and not gone out of her way and calling to meddle in such things as are proper for men, whose minds are stronger."

Following the Hutchinsons' forced departure, their house passed through a variety of owners. An apothecary named Dr. Thomas Crease bought the home in 1707, then lost it in the Great Fire of October 2, 1711, which swept away hundreds of downtown shops and residences. By 1718, however, the apparently well-to-do Crease had built a solid brick structure in its stead. Though the interior has been altered over the centuries, the building's shell remains essentially unchanged today.

Like many of his contemporaries, Crease built his progressive English-style house with a shop on the ground floor and his residence above. The structure had stately sides of rose-red brick, and a sloping gambrel roof. On the School Street side, string courses of brick were laid as decorative bands dividing the building's three stories. Squared blocks of Connecticut sandstone, used as quoins, added both visual flair and an air of importance to the exterior corners. Today the building remains one of Boston's oldest brick structures, and a rare surviving example of eighteenth-century brick, gambrel-roofed domestic architecture.

For a hundred years after Dr. Crease built his dream house, a series of pharmacists and physicians lived upstairs while selling their wares on the busy street level below. In 1817, ownership fell to Dr. Samuel Clarke, father of the celebrated liberal thinker and Unitarian minister at King's Chapel, the Reverend James Freeman Clarke.

During this period, little changed at the Old Corner building except the address. When Crease bought the property in 1707, the intersecting streets were known as "the main street leading to Roxbury" and Schoolhouse Lane (Boston Latin School had been lodged up the street since 1645). In 1708, a town committee officially named them School Street and Cornhill. Though School Street has maintained its 1708 designation, Cornhill became Washington Street in 1824. After Washington Street was lengthened in 1875, the Old Corner building became Number 283. Two-hundred-eighty-three Washington remains its address to this day, though the current tenants use One School Street as the address for their bookstore.

★   ★   ★

The biggest changes to the structure at School and Washington came in 1829, when young Timothy Harrington Carter obtained a lease from building owner George Brimmer. Carter was a former bookseller's apprentice from Lancaster, Massachusetts, who harbored ambitious ideas about the future of book publishing. He envisioned the old Crease house as an ideal location for the world of books, and spent $7,000 to alter the aging pharmacy and private residence into a modern commercial space.

Carter added projecting, small-paned windows to the ground floor, giving the shop what's been called a "Dickensian London touch." He also rebricked that first story and lowered the floor three to four steps to street level. On the School Street side, where Thomas Crease once had a garden, Carter added a brick extension to his structure, creating the area where the Liberty Bank resides today. The corner apothecary was transformed into a bookshop, while the extension housed seven printing presses, first run by Canadian horses and later by steam.

Carter set himself up as a silent partner, with brother Richard Carter and Charles Hendee as booksellers (a fourteen-year-old youngster named James T. Fields, from Portsmouth, New Hampshire, was hired as an apprentice not long thereafter), and the Old Corner Bookstore was officially born, with Carter & Hendee as the first of ten firms of booksellers and publishers to be housed there over the next seventy-five years.

In 1833, Carter & Hendee were replaced by Allen & Ticknor. When John Allen left that company in 1837, William D. Ticknor continued his book business alone. The consistent thread through these three original firms was one building—the Old Corner Bookstore—and one apprentice, the bright, witty, charming, versatile, and ambitious Jamie Fields.

While carefully and cheerfully scrutinizing his employers, other publishers and booksellers, artists, authors, and the book-browsing public, Fields developed a vision of the Old Corner as a magnet for the authors who were then creating the first body of truly American literature. Many of these writers, including Hawthorne, Thoreau, Emerson, Longfellow, and Whittier, lived in New England. Ticknor came to believe in Fields's vision. In 1842 he made Fields a junior partner, and by 1845 the firm was officially known as Ticknor & Fields.

Before promoting Fields, Ticknor had a shop that was solid but nondescript, with no real specialty or personality. As with many booksellers of the day, he also published works now and then—generally at the authors' risk and expense. But with the ideas, personality, and push of Fields, and the financial backing of John Reed, Jr., Ticknor & Fields eventually ushered in a whole new era of Boston book publishing.

Fields wanted to publish and sell fine American and English literature, and his tactics were brilliant. At that time, authors were neither bound by legal contracts to a single publisher nor protected from later "pirate" editions of their work. Hence there was little sense of loyalty or obligation between author and publisher. It was also customary for authors to be paid in a standard lump sum for their manuscripts. To lure authors and secure exclusive American publishing rights, Fields formulated the royalty system, which gave authors both the standard manuscript sum and 10 percent of retail sales. He also secured ownership of prestigious magazines like the *North American Review* and the fledgling *Atlantic Monthly,* for which his writers became the literary backbone.

Fields was a master of promotion, as epitomized by the lucrative American lecture tour he organized and publicized for Charles Dickens in 1867–68. He was also a huckster who planted publicity in periodicals, "bought" reviewers, wrote his own glowing reviews under false names, and fabricated accolades for his stars. Equally important, he became the friend, protector, literary counselor, and guardian of his flock of writers. While the more solitary Ticknor occupied a counting room at the back of the shop's book-lined sales floor, Fields held court in a cozy rear nook behind a green curtain. There, explains William S. Tryon in his 1963 book *Parnassus Corner,* Jamie Fields blossomed. "In what appeared to be hopeless confusion he wrote his letters, read his manuscripts, and entertained his friends. Amid whispered consultations, endless talk and bright anecdotes, jokes and shouts of laughter, Fields was creating something new in the literary and business world of America."

While Fields gained everlasting renown as the man who put the Old Corner Bookstore on the literary map of America, some of his peers have been less heralded by history. His wife, Annie Adams Fields, for example, helped consolidate Ticknor & Fields's literary relations by hosting salons for authors in the Fields home on Charles Street. She also supported the work of many of the women writers of her time, in part by bringing together luminaries like Willa Cather and Sarah Orne Jewett.

Meanwhile, tenants who worked in other parts of the building attracted nineteenth-century patrons as well. Bookbinder George Gould, printer Isaac Butts, bootmaker Isaac Waitt, and the toy-vending Calender family had shops in the corner complex for years. So did the famous Boston hairdresser William Dudley, and Mrs. Abner Haven, whose popular, packed coffee-room was known by contemporaries as serving "perfect toast," thick lemon pie, and "an exhilarating boiled coffee suspected of brandy infusion."

By the turn of the century, much had changed at the Old Corner Bookstore building. After William Ticknor died in 1864, Jamie Fields assumed sole ownership and moved the business to more spacious quarters on Tremont Street. The firm's descendants later merged with the Riverside Press, established by Henry Houghton in 1852, which evolved into Houghton Mifflin and Company. (In 1979, that company restored the Ticknor & Fields imprint as a tribute to its predecessor.)

The last booksellers to inhabit the corner building departed in 1903, though they used the name Old Corner Bookstore for their new, larger space on Bromfield Street. On Christmas Eve of 1979, that Old Corner Bookstore—then owned by Doubleday Books—closed its Bromfield Street doors and the business, a victim of competition from huge bookstore chains.

In the decades after 1903, the building at the corner of School and Washington went through a variety of incarnations, from haberdashery to photo supply store. By 1960, the nearly unrecognizable, deteriorated structure hosted a pizza parlor and was plastered with billboards advertising "15 cents, Sliced Crispy Pizza" and the Boston Five Cents Savings Bank. Meanwhile, urban renewal was taking its toll on Boston. Certain developers viewed the Old Corner Bookstore building as worthless—and a prime space for a downtown parking garage.

In response to the threat of demolition, a public-spirited group of Bostonians—including Athenaeum director Walter Muir Whitehill and John Codman, chairman of the Beacon Hill Architectural Commission—organized the nonprofit organization Historic Boston Incorporated. With encouragement from the city of Boston, generous contributions of some $100,000 from dozens of private donors throughout the country, and a bank loan, H.B.I. took title to the Old Corner building on December 30, 1960. The cost was $275,000 for the entire L-shaped complex, which included both the expanded 1829 bookstore building and the attached Andrew Cunningham House (ca. 1722) at 277 Washington.

Historic Boston's goal was to prove that small, historic, commercial buildings did not have to be turned into museums exempt from city taxes and that such structures could contribute to the city's tax base without sacrificing their historic uses and appearances. Hence, between 1960 and 1985, hundreds of thousands of dollars were used in restoring the building's exterior to its mid-nineteenth century look and modernizing its interior to accommodate contemporary needs for retail sales and office spaces. In the beginning, Historic Boston needed help to make this possible.

In 1965, the *Boston Globe* provided the answer. It lent Historic Boston money to repay its bank loan, and agreed to restore the corner building in exchange for a long-term lease. For two decades, the *Globe* used the ground floor for in-town classified advertising offices, which were located amidst a mini-museum of the bookstore's history. *Globe*-owned companies like the Globe Pequot Press and the Globe Corner Bookstore became tenants. Though the press and the bookstore have not been affiliated with the *Globe* since 1989, they still rent space, and continue the building's history of housing fine booksellers and publishers. The *Globe* itself maintains office space in the Old Corner building.

As downtown commercial real estate values soared in the mid-1980s, hthe Old Corner building's value also increased. As a result, it became the oil well, the nest egg, the endowment, and the home of Historic Boston Incorporated—supporting preservation projects in all parts of the city and providing a source of credibility for a society engaged in business transactions to preserve Boston's cultural heritage.

Today, hundreds of folks still bustle and browse through the old brick building at the corner of School and Washington. It's ironic that probably few of them know they're in a structure that needed saving less than four decades ago and is now dedicated to saving others. How many realize, moreover, that they're standing on a spot that was once home to radical Puritans, revolutionary publishers, crispy sliced pizza . . . and a potential parking garage!

THE ESSENTIALS

ADDRESS: Corner of School and Washington streets, Boston.

TELEPHONE: Globe Corner Bookstore, (617) 523-6658 or (800) 358-6013; Historic Boston Incorporated, (617) 227-4679.

VISITOR INFORMATION: Bookstore open 9:00 A.M.–7:00 P.M., Monday–

Friday; 9:00 A.M.–6:00 P.M. Saturday; noon-6:00 P.M. Sunday. Free. Varied hours for other businesses in building. No interior tours, though the building is included on many Freedom Trail tours. Ground floor is wheelchair accessible, though awkward due to small space. No public restrooms.

 The Boston Public Library

"BEAUTY AND the Beast" aren't only in fairy tales. They're also affectionate nicknames for that massive duet of buildings in bustling Copley Square officially known as the Boston Public Library. "Beauty," of course, is the McKim building, an elegant 1895 structure with an ornate facade inspired by the Italian Renaissance and a magnificent interior decorated by some of the country's leading artists. "The Beast" is the library's mammoth, modern, unadorned 1972 addition, designed by architect Philip Johnson.

John Doherty, assistant director of the Boston Public Library, offers an insider's perspective on this curious architectural non sequitur. "McKim is 'the palace' . . . and Johnson was built to be a workable library, a fusion of a good architect and a librarian," he explains. "And we're blessed to have them both."

Indeed it's true. While the old McKim building resonates with marble staircases, majestic columns, vaulting arches, and artistic treasures, the modern Johnson structure sparkles with wide-open spaces, wheelchair accessibility, functional design, and optimal light and ventilation. All things considered, an odd couple with conveniently compatible traits.

But architecture isn't everything—especially to an institution that's busy welcoming two million visitors a year. When it first opened its doors in 1854, the Boston Public Library was already the talk of the town. Though often touted as "America's first free public library," it was, more precisely, the first *major* free municipal library in the country. Still, it was and continues to be a quiet innovator. During the twentieth century, the B.P.L. pioneered in circulating paperback books and in offering services for elders. During the nineteenth century, it was the first public library to allow patrons to borrow materials, the first to issue an annual report of library trustees, and the first in the nation to develop branch libraries.

A major cultural and educational center for Boston since the turn of the century, and a National Historic Landmark since 1973, the B.P.L. currently sponsors some dozen free lectures, concerts, films, exhibits, and programs every week. Moreover, it's home to 6.1 million books, its own publishing house and conservation lab, plus ninety special collections and

Majestic Bates Hall in the Boston Public Library, the first major free municipal library in the country.

two million archival items, which include such diverse artifacts as a gold medal awarded to George Washington, the first book printed in the United States, and the memorabilia of comic Fred Allen—all kept in various chambers, nooks, and cases scattered about the two buildings.

Meanwhile, a tea room, a bookstore, and an efficient new connector between the McKim and Johnson buildings will soon grace the two-acre site, as part of the McKim's $50 million restoration and renovation campaign, already well under way.

In the 1840s, when the idea of a free public library in Boston began to take shape, the area already had two large book repositories—the Harvard College library, open to Harvard students and faculty, and the privately run Boston Athenaeum. Every proper nineteenth-century Bostonian had an Athenaeum card, it seems, since it was deemed as important a status symbol in Victorian Boston as a season subscription to the Boston Symphony or a family plot at Mount Auburn Cemetery.

So why did certain Brahmins and their colleagues—including such diverse characters as Athenaeum trustee George Ticknor and a quirky, controversial French visitor known worldwide as Monsieur Alexandre the Ventriloquist—want a free library, too? Part of their rationale, admits the library's director, Arthur Curley, was reactive: Boston was being flooded by new waves of immigrants, many of whom were illiterate; it was assumed that a public library would help provide the education needed for these recent arrivals to become responsible, law-abiding, job-holding Bostonians. A second motive was more idealistic—the desire to create a cultural center accessible to all, where knowledge could be disseminated without charge. Such a concept was fully in keeping with Boston's longstanding status as a center for progressive thought and action. The motto "Free To All" is still visible on the keystone of the McKim building's central arch, above Minerva's helmeted head.

The city was finally convinced to found this much-discussed public library in 1852; in 1854, its doors opened on Mason Street, one block off the Tremont Street side of Boston Common, though a move to larger quarters on Boylston was necessitated only four years later. In 1895, the very mobile Boston Public Library made one more move, to a Copley Square lot donated by the state. (Its former Boylston Street site was used for a zoo, which was in turn supplanted by the Colonial Theatre.)

Architect Charles Follen McKim, of the New York architectural firm McKim, Mead, and White, was commissioned to build the Copley Square "palace" for $1,165,000. In the end, he spent more than two-and-a-half times that amount. The results were then—and still are today—appropriately lavish.

Built on pilings driven through slippery blue clay to the bedrock beneath, McKim's structure was a magnificent jewel. The granite Italian Renaissance Revival facade, replete with chiseled dolphins, laurel wreaths, medallions, and lofty windows, took inspiration from three magnificent models: Bibliothèque Sainte-Genevieve in Paris, Tempio Malatestiano in Rimini, and, somewhat less glamorously, the Marshall Field Wholesale Store in Chicago. The entrance was guarded by Art and Science, in the form of two heroic female figures sculpted by Bela Pratt.

Inside, the vaulted Roman entrance hall was tiled with colorful mosaics. The noble stairway, crafted from yellow Sienna marble veined in black, was guarded by marble lions. The main reading room upstairs, called Bates Hall after a major library benefactor, was designed like a cavernous Roman bath, filled with oak tables and bookcases, and lavishly decorated with Italian Renaissance embellishments. All of these figures, flourishes, and decorative motifs remain intact to this day.

Suffice it to say that from room to room and hallway to hallway, the majesty and the cost of the Copley Square palace kept escalating—escalating, that is, until the money ran out. As a result, notes retired research supervisor Joseph O'Neil, the rear of the McKim is much more "pedestrian" than the front.

Architect McKim spared no expense for the artists he employed to decorate the library's walls, halls, and galleries. The Parisian painter Puvis de Chavannes, for example, created the series of murals that top the Grand Staircase, including a main panel entitled *The Muses of Inspiration Welcoming the Spirit of Light*. The imagery was Greek and the attitude typically Victorian. The crowd of hovering, gift-giving Muses were depicted as girls, while the object of their adoration, Enlightenment, was shown (in a decidedly unenlightened fashion) as a nude boy. The aging de Chavannes didn't come to Boston, incidentally, but made his murals in his Paris studio, then shipped them stateside. As with all the other murals in the library, his works were painted on canvas, then permanently adhered to the walls with white lead.

John Singer Sargent is also represented on the library's walls. Though best known for his portraits of the nineteenth-century rich and famous, Sargent decorated the gallery above de Chavannes's with an unusual series on the history of religion. Sargent created quite a stir in Boston when he depicted Judaism as a wounded, suffering being, in contrast to the triumphant pose of Christianity. He also created a stir when he died unexpectedly in 1925. His central panel, *The Sermon on the Mount*, had not yet been painted. To this day, that middle space has been left blank, though we have a sense of Sargent's intended imagery, based on his rough sketches, or cartoons, which are displayed in a chamber off the Wiggin Print Gallery.

Other conspicuously blank walls in the McKim are found in the archways and the Boylston Street end of Bates Hall. London-based painter James McNeill Whistler was supposed to paint the framed horizontal panel at the hall's end, but that contract fell through. Painter and stained-glass artist John La Farge was then offered the commission, but declined it—and no other artist was ever hired. Given the difficulty of altering a National Historic Landmark today, the space will probably remain blank forever.

To no one's surprise, virtually all the engraved names, statues, and busts throughout the McKim are tributes to men. One important exception is in Bates Hall, where feminist Lucy Stone and physician Elizabeth Blackwell are commemorated with busts. Another exception, in a backhanded sort of way, is the ceiling mural in the Elliott Room. According to Joseph O'Neil, each of the winged female figures in *The Triumph of Time* was modeled after a Boston debutante of the day. "See that lantern jaw?" O'Neil asks as he points to one angel. "I bet she's a Saltonstall!"

The library's Venetian-inspired, open-air courtyard is a favorite green oasis for the city-worn and the study-weary. But the central fountain is no longer decorated with another famous piece of art once associated with the Boston Public Library—Frederick MacMonnies's *Bacchante*. When the statue was installed in 1896, an immediate furor arose; it was allegedly immoral (*Bacchante* was naked, and maybe even a strumpet) and promoted intemperance (the statue represented a celebrant of riotous intoxication). National and local periodicals weighed in with their opinions, some serious and others more tongue-in-cheek. In the latter category was the *Boston Globe,* which recommended that McKim replace *Bacchante* with "a nice moral statue—of a Sunday school teacher, say."

Eventually, the Puritan ethic won out, and *Bacchante* was banned in Boston. McKim donated the statue to the Metropolitan Museum of Art in New York, though the Boston Museum of Fine Arts still owns a bronze replica. As part of an ongoing restoration project, negotiations are now underway to return *Bacchante* to its original home, ideally by the time of the McKim building's centennial in 1995.

It's curious that *Bacchante* was banished while the seal of the B.P.L.—featuring two beautiful nude boys with a shield, an open book, a batch of dolphins, and laurel—survived, albeit amidst another uproar. Some speculate that the seal, or its most prominent version above the McKim's central outdoor archway, may simply have been too hard to remove.

The most unusual artwork in the McKim building may well be the intricately composed miniature dioramas created by Louise Stimson (1890–1981). Stimson was born in Brooklyn Heights, New York, but spent forty years as an artist in Concord, Massachusetts. She created almost fifty historical dioramas between the 1940s and the 1960s. The project reportedly began as a way to amuse Stimson's older sister, who was bedridden for most of her life. Fortunately, many of the final products—including *The London of Charles Dickens, Alice in Wonderland, Arabian Nights* and *Printmakers at Work*—were donated to the library. Each three-dimensional scene, fabricated from cardboard, paper, and other accessible household sundries, is a "living picture" representing an episode from a famous book, or imagining the creation process of well-known art prints. As you move from one scene to the next, you'll find—in Alice's Wonderland words—that Stimson's dioramas get "curiouser and curiouser." They are arguably the best conversation pieces in the library.

The art and architectural glories of the Boston Public Library are appropriately matched by its seemingly infinite resources. The library's 6.1 million volumes—with 250,000 new books added each year—rest on some 65 miles of bookshelves. Each floor of stacks is an acre in size, and holds nearly a million pounds of books on more than 22,000 shelves. Meanwhile, the library stores nearly 10 million patents, 3 million government documents, 120,000 musical scores, 8,500 sixteen-millimeter films, 400,000 archival drawings, 75,000 prints, drawings, and watercolors, 350,000 maps, 400 on-line databases, and 4.5 million units of microfilm—making the B.P.L. the largest public research library in New England.

Appreciating certain Boston Public Library attractions, however, requires some special inside knowledge. For example, assistant director John Doherty loves the archives of old architectural drawings and bridge plans stowed in the Johnson building's upper floors. He speaks proudly of the architectural wonders of the Johnson addition, constructed for $24 million in 1972: its curious "hanging floors," innovative indoor "bridges," and sturdy beams allowing optimum open space and flexibility, and better service for the public. Today, the Johnson building serves as the general library, enabling the McKim building to house research collections.

Other staff members are thrilled by the changes brought on by new library technologies such as audio-visuals and the widespread use of microcomputers. The B.P.L. has a state-of-the-art printing operation, an in-house conservation lab (begun in 1982), and sophisticated services for people with special needs.

It's perhaps surprising that so-called antiquated technologies have held their own at the B.P.L. as well. An old pneumatic tube system, for instance, which takes book request slips to and from the stacks, proved as practical in the 1990s as the day the library opened. Research books themselves travel from the stacks to the circulation desk via a conveyor belt built in the 1950s (some believe the old "miniature railway" system the conveyor belt replaced functioned far better).

★ ★ ★

Today, though it bears the city's name, the Boston Public Library is open to all residents of the state. Moreover, neighborhoods are serviced by its twenty-five smaller branch libraries and the downtown Kierstein Business Library. In its ongoing efforts to reach the widest possible audience, special facilities have been developed in the Johnson building to accommodate children, young adults, non-English-speaking people, senior citizens, and the physically handicapped. Some forty-two languages are represented in the mezzanine-level foreign language section. More than a hundred and thirty copies of the classic Boston children's book *Make Way for Ducklings* are on hand, including one in Braille.

It's a far cry from the nineteenth century, when no such amenities existed. Kids, in particular, were *persona non grata* at the original B.P.L. Old rule books explain that in 1854, no one under the age of sixteen was welcome. By 1896 the age minimum was lowered to twelve. The 1896 book also warned that "all annoying and disagreeable behavior, such as hawking, spitting on the floor, humming, whistling, whispering, is strictly prohibited."

Come to think of it, not a bad idea at all.

THE ESSENTIALS

ADDRESS: Copley Square, Boston.

TELEPHONE: (617) 536-5400.

VISITOR INFORMATION: Open 9:00 A.M.–9:00 P.M., Monday–Thursday; 9:00 A.M.–5:00 P.M., Friday and Saturday; closed Sundays and all legal holidays. Free hour-long tours of the art and architecture of the B.P.L. given Mondays at 2:30 P.M., Tuesdays and Wednesdays at 6:30 P.M., Thursdays and Saturdays at 11:00 A.M.; call to confirm times and details. Johnson building completely wheelchair accessible; McKim building accessible only with assistance; restrooms accessible in Johnson building; those in McKim building are being made accessible as well.

The Parker House

ITS GUEST rooms are not as luxurious or spacious as those found at Boston's Ritz-Carlton or Four Seasons, nor does it share those hotels' splendid aerial views of the Public Garden; but the Omni Parker House is arguably the grande dame of Boston hotels and *the* downtown hotel of choice for historic-minded Bostonians. And it's not simply because it's the only Boston hotel directly on the Freedom Trail.

The historic Parker House, the "grande dame of Boston Hotels," was home to the Saturday Club and the Parker House roll.

Located at the junction of Tremont and School streets, the Parker House—now part of the international family of Omni hotels—is the oldest of Boston's elegant inns, as well as the oldest continuously operating hotel in America. One of its great claims to fame is as the nineteenth-century meeting place of the Saturday Club, a monthly gathering of literary giants such as Ralph Waldo Emerson, Nathaniel Hawthorne, and Henry Wadsworth Longfellow. The Parker House is also celebrated for its contributions to American cuisine—most notably, the fluffy Parker House roll, invented in Parker kitchens by a nineteenth-century German baker named Ward.

First opened by Harvey D. Parker in 1855, the historic hotel has had more than its share of famous patrons over the decades. Mayor James Michael Curley, Senator John Fitzgerald Kennedy, and art patron Isabella Stewart Gardner regularly dined there. Authors Charles Dickens and Willa Cather each lived there for a time; actress Charlotte Cushman and one of Jimmy Hoffa's lieutenants *died* there. Other prestigious lodgers have ranged from Sarah Bernhardt, Joan Crawford, and Elizabeth Cady Stanton to Ulysses S. Grant, John Wilkes Booth, and William "Hopalong Cassidy" Boyd. Prestigious guests were occasionally matched by prestigious staff; Malcolm X reportedly once worked there as a waiter, and Ho Chi Minh was employed as a kitchen worker. As if all that weren't impressive enough, that nineteenth-century man of letters Oliver Wendell Holmes even penned some light verse about the place. Which is all meant to suggest that the Parker House has enough history and charm to last a lifetime.

In colonial Boston, there were no hotels in the contemporary sense of the word. Instead, local taverns and inns provided rest stops for weary travelers—colonial males, for the most part, whose major interest seems to have been the quaffing of multitudinous pints of beer.

As these precursors to the modern hotel developed beyond simple taprooms and inns, however, they began to call themselves "houses." One of the most luxurious of these lodging and dining houses, built on the edge of Beacon Hill in 1828, was the Tremont. Over the next twenty years, competitors emerged around Boston—including the American House, the Shawmut, the Adams, and the handsome Revere House.

In 1825, a twenty-year-old farm boy named Harvey D. Parker arrived in Boston Harbor, on a packet from Maine. With less than a dollar in his satchel, Parker immediately sought employment. His first job, as a care-taker for a horse and cow, brought him eight dollars a month. A subsequent vocation as coachman for a Watertown woman provided even higher earnings.

Whenever Parker and the coach were in Boston, the young man ate his noonday meal at John E. Hunt's dark cellar cafe at 4 Court Square. He became so enamored of the cafe that in 1832 he purchased it for $432. After renaming it Parker's Restaurant, he began to attract a regular clientele of lawyers, newsmen, and businessmen, who appreciated Parker's combination of excellent food and perfect service. In 1847, Parker chose John F. Mills as a partner. And by 1854 he was ready to embark on a grander enterprise.

Parker wanted to build a new, first-class hotel and restaurant, and wanted to build them a stone's throw from the successful Tremont House. The site Parker purchased on April 22, 1854, was on School Street, just southeast of the Tremont-Beacon junction where the Tremont House stood. Parker's lot already had a lodging of sorts—a decrepit boarding house known as the Boylston Hotel, which had once been the fine 1704 mansion of John Mico. Parker razed the old structure and built in its stead a glorious five-story, marble-fronted hotel he initially called Parker's. (After a series of negotiations and sales over the next two decades, Parker eventually owned the bulk of the land bordered by Tremont, School, and Bosworth streets and Chapman Place.)

Despite the nearby competitor, the location was ideal. Once a narrow lane flanked by wooden homes, barns, gardens, orchards, shops, and the famous Boston Latin School, School Street had already developed into a classy, much-traveled thoroughfare by the mid-nineteenth century. Next-door to Parker's was the granite Horticultural Hall (on the former site of Boston Latin, America's first public school), which Parker purchased and demolished in 1860 to create his lofty east wing. (The Massachusetts Horticultural Society subsequently moved Horticultural Hall twice; the second site, facing Symphony Hall, became its permanent home in 1901.) Across School Street was King's Chapel; next to it, a French Empire-style city hall would be built in 1865. At the other end of School Street was the 1829 Old Corner Bookstore, a magnet for poets, authors, and philosophers. And just a brief walk up School and Beacon streets was the seat of state government. That Parker's became situated on the "hot line" between the State House and City Hall was a fortuitous accident, perhaps—but it ensured regular governmental clientele for more than a century.

The excellence that came to be associated with Parker's in-house restaurants was no accident at all. In a day when a good Boston cook could be hired for eight dollars per week, or $416 a year, Parker paid a gourmet French chef named Sanzian the astonishing annual salary of $5,000. The investment paid off; Sanzian's versatile menu drew continual accolades and large crowds. In another innovation, Parker implemented the "European plan," which separated charges for food and lodging, allowing guests more flexibility. Moreover, though most hotels of the era had fixed dining hours, Parker made food available at any time during the day or evening. Added to his business acumen was Parker's attitude. He was the ultimate host, lavishing personal attention on every detail.

On May 31, 1884, after guiding his hotel and restaurants to world renown, Parker died. The Maine farm boy who had arrived in Boston with less than a dollar in 1825 had a net worth of $1,272,546.94 when he drew his last breath. His hotel's fame is documented in the *King's Handbook* of 1885, which described Parker's as one of the finest restaurants in the United States, with "a central location, sumptuous equipment, and ancient prestige." Gentlemen, the book explained, were provided a great dining room and fine basement billiard room; ladies had their own cafe; politicians and businessmen were provided a rendezvous; and the 260 well-designed guest rooms ranged from $1 to $5 a night, with luxury suites at $8 to $12.

Fine food, superior service, fair prices, elegant surroundings, and an ideal location all brought the Parker House a clientele that included poets, philosophers, politicians, and performers. Many nineteenth-century actors were familiar with the neighborhood before the hotel was even built. The popular Tremont Theatre (1828–43), which later became the Tremont Temple Baptist Church, was around the corner, and several other legitimate stages were but a few blocks away. In the nineteenth century, Parker's guests included world-class actors such as Sarah Bernhardt, Adelina Patti, Ellen Terry, Charlotte Cushman, Richard Mansfield, Henry Irving, Augustin Daly, and Edwin Booth.

One of the theater-world guests Parker rarely discussed was actor Edwin Booth's younger brother. John Wilkes Booth arrived at the hotel in April 1865, visiting Boston while his sibling performed on a downtown stage. While residing at Parker's, John Wilkes practiced his pistol aim in a cellar shooting gallery at the corner of Chapman and School streets. Eight days after departing, he assassinated President Lincoln at Ford's Theatre in Washington.

Retired bellman John Brehm, a Parker House employee from 1941 to early 1993, remembers another type of performer who frequented the hotel: "In the 1940s we still had 'permanent guests'—guests who lived here for months, or years, at a time. All the hotels did, until it was phased out in the decade after the war. In the forties and fifties burlesque queens stayed here, because we were the nicest hotel in the area, and so close to Scollay Square, the Old Howard, and the Casino." (Boisterous Scollay

Square and its popular, seedy burlesque theaters all disappeared in the 1960s, before and during the construction of Government Center.) "I recall one woman named Lois de Fee, who was huge—six-feet-four-inches tall—and walked her little Pekinese dog on a twenty-foot leash!

"They were all good tippers."

Brehm was also a bellman when powerful, charismatic politicians from Mayor James Michael Curley to Senator John Fitzgerald Kennedy paid regular visits to the hotel. According to Brehm, Curley lunched daily in the main dining room, and tipped silver dollars. Kennedy chose the Parker House to announce his candidacy for the U.S. Congress in 1946.

Until the construction of Boston's new city hall and Government Center in the late 1960s—which left the hotel off the new path from city hall to the State House—political "power breakfasts" and meetings were part of the Parker fabric. So too were reporters and editors from old Newspaper Row, legal eagles from Pemberton Square courthouses, financiers from the banks near Post Office Square, students from Harvard, and traveling baseball umpires. Brehm even recalls the visits of Red Sox slugger Ted Williams, who was once engaged to a woman who worked in Parker's now-defunct Paul Revere Room. Many of these famous men, women, and events are depicted in the historic photos on the walls of one of the hotel's restaurants, the basement-level Last Hurrah! Other memorabilia from the Parker House past are displayed in glassed cases in the main lobby.

Of all the famous guests, the most illustrious certainly came as part of the nineteenth-century Boston men's social gathering known as the Saturday Club. Originating in the Literary Club and the Magazine Club, two private associations of the mid-1850s, the Saturday Club began as a small group of friends who held festive roundtables on the last Saturday afternoon of every month. Philosopher Ralph Waldo Emerson, poet and *Atlantic Monthly* editor James Russell Lowell, and scientist Louis Agassiz were soon joined by novelist Nathaniel Hawthorne, poets John Greenleaf Whittier and Henry Wadsworth Longfellow, diplomat Charles Francis Adams, historian Francis Parkman, sage-about-town Dr. Oliver Wendell Holmes, and many others.

The Saturday Club's afternoons were taken up with poetry readings and book critiques, gossip and discussions, seven-course meals, and free-flowing elixirs. Visiting British novelist Charles Dickens, who resided at the Parker House during his 1867–68 American lecture tour, joined club members for their November 30, 1867, meeting. The colorful Dickens, who died two years later, preened and practiced his animated talks in front of a large mirror which now rests in the mezzanine level hall by the Press Room. Artifacts from his stay were long kept on display in the Dickens Room. Today that room is used for meetings and dining, but it still holds the marble fireplace mantel Dickens used. Other famous guests—from Hawthorne to Holmes and John F. Kennedy to Martin Luther King—are likewise remembered in meeting room names along the mezzanine level.

Though the Parker House still maintains the nineteenth-century charms, comforts, and fine foods that Dickens and the Saturday Club enjoyed, much has changed. When Harvey Parker died in 1884, only his wife, Julia Ann Parker, survived him. His original partner, John F. Mills, had passed away, as had both of Parker's sons—one at the age of ten, and the second lost at sea at age twenty-four. Per the instructions of Parker's will, the building was leased to his later partners, Edward O. Punchard and Joseph H. Beckman, who added a new wing, annex, and elaborate exterior decorations. Roxbury grocer Joseph Reed Whipple, who had worked under the supervision of John F. Mills, took over in the 1890s. Though Whipple died in 1912, the J. R. Whipple Corporation bought the hotel from the trustees of the Parker estate in 1925.

To the horror of many, the Whipple Corporation demolished Harvey Parker's old "marble palace," and built in its stead the "new" Parker House—essentially the one we know today—which opened on May 12, 1927. Designed by G. Henri Desmond of Desmond & Lord, the 1927 version was arguably more beautiful than its predecessor. Built fourteen stories high, with polished Quincy granite on the exterior, it featured lush, ornamented public chambers with oak paneling, plastered ceilings, crystal chandeliers, bronze-detailed doors, and 800 guest rooms. Even today, the lobbies—with their dark little enclaves resembling private clubrooms—retain a comforting nineteenth-century beauty.

Through the hotel's subsequent owners—Glenwood Sherrard in 1933, the beloved Dunfey family in 1968, and most recently, the Omni Hotels subsidiary of Wharf Holdings Ltd. of Hong Kong—the Parker House has had its ups and downs, its changes, additions, and alterations. Beginning in 1927, the old basement billiard room was converted to casual restaurants like the English Grille Room, and, in its current incarnation, The Last Hurrah! The mezzanine-level lobby lounge, landing, and reading library gave way to the cozy Parker Bar. The magical rooftop terrace of 1935—closed in 1969, when taller downtown buildings outstripped its height and blocked its aerial view—now hosts special functions as the only rooftop ballroom in the city. The spirit of the Saturday Club was even rekindled in the New England Circle, private evening gatherings begun by the Dunfeys in 1974 and continuing to this day.

Bowing to modern needs for space, the 800 guest chambers of 1927 have been restructured into 535 larger, though sometimes oddly shaped, rooms and suites. Chambers that once featured four-channel radios now have eighteen-channel color television sets. Room furnishings, decor, utilities, and services have been upgraded and adapted in each new era, while the staff that Brehm recalls included 600 in 1941 has shrunk to 334. The faces of Parker House wait staff have changed, too—from mainly Irish, to predominantly African-American, to today's multicultural mix—though their attentiveness and hospitality have remained constant.

Executive chef Joseph Ribas, who has trained such local culinary stars as Lydia Shire of Biba and Jasper White of Jasper's, makes sure that fine food is still available at Parker's, in its restaurants or via room service, from 7:00 in the morning to 11:30 at night. Aromatic Parker House rolls are still served, piping hot and free of charge to diners. (Their ingredients became public knowledge after 1933, the year Franklin and Eleanor Roosevelt requested the recipe be sent to them in Washington.) Another "historic" specialty is Boston cream pie, which was perfected and popularized at Parker's in the late nineteenth century. Since chef Ribas is now emphasizing regional cuisine, featuring plenty of seafood, yet another probable Parker first is on the menu—scrod. According to legend, the term *scrod* was coined in the

Parker kitchens. Scrod is not a type of fish; the word is used for cod or other white-fleshed fish that are either the youngest, freshest, or smallest of the day's catch.

Granted, the glitterati may flock to more modern and pricier luxury hotels today, but the Parker House still attracts a down-to-earth crowd of businesspeople, vacationing families, and conference-goers, and its restaurants continue to draw local professionals and politicians. Tourists, of course, are enamored by its gentle aura of historic import and its convenient location on the Freedom Trail. And who knows how many are enticed to visit by these words from Oliver Wendell Holmes's "At the Saturday Club," written a century ago:

> *Such feasts! The laughs of many a jocund hour*
> *That shook the mortar from King George's tower;*
> *Such guests! What famous names its record boasts,*
> *Whose owners wander in the mob of ghosts!*

THE ESSENTIALS

ADDRESS: 60 School Street, corner of School and Tremont streets, Boston.

TELEPHONE: (617) 227-8600 or (800) THE-OMNI.

VISITOR INFORMATION: Open twenty-four hours a day, 365 days a year. Food is available 7:00 A.M.–11:30 P.M., either via room service or in one of the hotel's restaurants. Call hotel for room prices. No tours available. Lobby is wheelchair accessible at Tremont Street entrance; passenger elevators access most areas, though service elevator is needed to reach the ballroom and The Last Hurrah!; accessible guest rooms and restrooms are available.

Louisburg Square

SINCE THE mid-nineteenth century, the green garden of Louisburg Square has been a welcome surprise among the endless red brick of Beacon Hill. One of Boston's finest residential neighborhoods, the square is neatly lodged between Pinckney and Mount Vernon streets—a shady urban oasis filled with handsome Greek Revival houses, facing a meticulously maintained private park and cobblestone roadway.

Lyrically lovely as it may be, Louisburg Square is not just another pretty

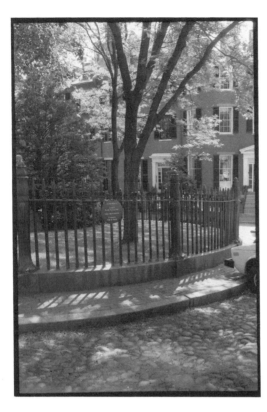

The red-brick Greek Revival–style houses of Louisburg Square were the residences of many of Boston's finest writers.

place. For starters, this short Beacon Hill block has been home to some of Boston's finest writers. In recent decades, those residents have included Robin Cook, author of medical thrillers such as *Coma* and *Brain*, and Pulitzer Prize–winning poet and playwright Archibald MacLeish. A century ago, historian John Gorham Palfrey, author of *The History of New England,* lived at Number 5. William Dean Howells, novelist and editor of *The Atlantic Monthly,* lived first at Number 16, then at 4, from 1882 to 1884. Howells frequently entertained and discussed literature with novelist Henry James at Number 16, and began writing his master work, *The Rise of Silas Lapham,* while residing on the square.

The most popularly renowned of the Louisburg literati is certainly Louisa May Alcott, who, along with her father, Bronson, lived at Number 10 between 1885 and 1888. Louisa had already won fame and fortune from her writings, especially *Little Women,* which literally rescued her family from poverty. The relocation to Louisburg Square was both evidence of her success and the last of her many moves; she died in the spring of 1888, two days after her father's demise.

A second major significance of the square is its history, in some respects, older than that of the town itself. That history may have begun with William Blackstone (or Blaxton), the first European to settle in the place that became Boston. Blackstone was an eccentric Anglican clergyman who arrived on the Shawmut peninsula with Robert Gorges's expedition in 1623, and remained when the others returned home. He settled on a hill (Beacon Hill), found a freshwater spring on a spot some historians identify as modern Louisburg Square, and enjoyed a hermit's life, drinking, reading from his large library, and riding his white bull across what would later be called Boston Common.

Blackstone's freshwater fountain became the source of wonderful urban legends for centuries to come. In the late nineteenth century, Dr. Edward Everett Hale said that every resident of Louisburg Square claimed to have the original Blackstone spring in his cellar. In Robert McCloskey's ageless 1941 children's tale *Make Way for Ducklings,* however, Mr. and Mrs. Mallard pondered raising their ducklings in the square, then abandoned the thought since "there was no water to swim in." Clearly, things had fairly well dried up by the middle of the twentieth century.

But let's return again to 1630. Governor John Winthrop and the Puritans of the Massachusetts Bay Colony had settled in nearby Charlestown, but were disturbed by its impure waters. Blackstone invited Winthrop et al. to share the Shawmut peninsula and partake of its potable springs. The Puritans came—and proceeded to found the town of Boston. The eccentric Blackstone soon became claustrophobic, and moved to the more rural countryside. Despite the "overcrowding" that offended the hermit in 1630, the area we now know as Louisburg Square—like much of Beacon Hill—remained open pasture for Boston's first 150 years. It eventually became part of the farmland owned by painter John Singleton Copley.

When the new state house designed by architect Charles Bulfinch was being planned on the slopes of Beacon Hill, developers saw the potential to turn the rest of the hill's rural acreage into fine residences. In 1796, a syndicate called the Mount Vernon Proprietors bought Copley's farm for $18,450. At the time, Bulfinch sketched street plans for Beacon Hill, which included a large square inspired by the quaint residential squares of London. Thirty years later, surveyor Stephen P. Fuller drew up the manicured streetscape of Louisburg Square, possibly based on Bulfinch's earlier plans. Whatever the source, the London look was still there, so much so, in fact, that when Hollywood filmmakers wanted to replicate Russell Square for their filming of William Thackeray's *Vanity Fair* in 1915, they chose Louisburg Square as their shooting location.

When the hillside square was finally developed, between 1826 and 1847, it was called Louisburg (pronounced as the English "Lewis," not the French "Lou-ie"). The name allegedly commemorates a 1745 battle, in which Massachusetts colonials helped capture the "impregnable" French-Canadian fortress of Louisburg, thereby securing the Atlantic seaboard for England. (That victory's exact connection to the square is unclear. One legend says that Blackstone's grandson was killed in the battle. Others offer a more ironic interpretation: that Louisburg Square, like the French fort, was built to be impenetrable by the outside world.)

Between 1834 and 1847, a variety of housewrights built the stately rowhouses we see today—orderly lines of harmonious, shoulder-to-shoulder, brick homes. Though each had its distinct characteristics, trends did occur, partly because the structures were often built in pairs or larger multiples. The houses at Numbers 2 through 22 generally have three stories and bow fronts. The upper, odd-numbered side of the square features more flat-faced, four-story structures. Red-brick exteriors, iron fencing, stone front steps—and in later years, shutters and gas street lamps—all added to these buildings' charms. As with most Beacon Hill residences, the homes were built fairly narrow and multileveled, with staircases connecting the floors.

In 1844, when all but a few lots had been filled, the homeowners formed the Proprietors of Louisburg Square—a prototypical civic association that functions to this day, and which includes several adjoining houses on Pinckney Street. Annual dues are used for maintenance of the private way, the partly cobbled, partly paved strips connecting Mount Vernon and Pinckney. Dues also cover the promise of two parking spaces per home and the care of the fenced central park. From 1844 to the present day, incidentally, Louisburg Square has remained a city within a city, a privately-owned property which issues its own parking tickets and tows away transgressors.

Despite plant diseases, storms, and the noxious fumes of city life, the oval park at the square's center is still lush and green, filled with grand old elms, honey locusts, rhododendrons, mountain laurels, and other plants and flowers. The garden also includes two small, semi-obscured Florentine marble statues, one of Athenian statesman Aristides the Just, the other of Christopher Columbus. The statues were donated by ship owner and merchant Joseph Iasigi, who lived at Number 3 in the mid-nineteenth century. Suffice it to say that the statues' artistic merits and historic relevance have eluded critics for decades.

Over the years, a fascinating and eclectic group of people molded Louisburg Square into a unique Beacon Hill community. And for generations they maintained its distinctive holiday traditions, from strolling carolers and handbell ringers to candle-lit windows and informal open houses. Granted, purists will say that Christmas Eve street-caroling began at the nearby Church of the Advent early in the nineteenth century, then spilled onto Louisburg Square and the rest of Beacon Hill. West Cedar Street residents claim to have originated the concept of the candle-lit window in the 1890s. Still, all these traditions were somehow more compacted, more noted and noticeable, in the brief block of Louisburg Square. One person to notice was poet Sylvia Plath, who lived a block from the square in 1958. Though her poems were often impassioned and angry, one of her lighter verses saluted the hill's off-key Christmas carolers and odd, violet-paned windows.

Just who were the square's residents over the years? Some were Brahmins and bluebloods with recognizable family names such as Cabot and Vanderbilt. Some were students, writers, artists, judges, and other professional people. Some were celebrities who were just passing through. Singer Jenny Lind, for example, renowned in the nineteenth century as "the Swedish Nightingale," was married at Number 20, in the townhouse of Samuel Gray Ward. Ward was, among other things, a founder of Boston's prestigious Saturday Club and Union Club, and a prominent banker who raised the cash for the United States to buy Alaska from Russia. (He was not, however, the brother of Julia Ward Howe—that was a different banker, also named Samuel Ward.) Another famed guest was the future King Edward VII of England, who made merry at Number 19, in an 1860 bash touted as "the grandest party in Boston in the nineteenth century." The home belonged to Boston's Civil War–era mayor, Frederick Lincoln.

The "family" that lived in Louisburg Square the longest was the Anglican convent of the Society of Saint Margaret, whose gentle, social service–oriented sisters occupied Numbers 13 through 19 for more than a hundred years before leaving for Roxbury in 1990.

Today, about half of the Louisburg Square residences are single-family homes. The rest have either been split and made into condominiums, or are owner-occupied, with the owner residing in a portion of the house and renting out the rest. Economic reality has clearly caused the latter: homes that might have sold for $18,000 in the late Victorian era soared to $3 million by 1990. Hence both purchase prices and city taxes on these sites are astronomical.

Despite its aura of impenetrability, the square has seen a bit of disruption, much like any other residential neighborhood. The first such intrusion was probably in 1850, when overzealous boys knocked off one of Columbus's fingers; barricades were periodically put up at the street's ends in the last half of the nineteenth century to prevent such transgressions. In 1962, the square was more seriously shaken when a young female resident from a reputable family fatally shot her errant boyfriend, in the gory episode known as the Debutante Murder. Though Albert de Salvo never murdered anyone on Louisburg Square, the self-avowed Boston Strangler apparently cruised the area during his notorious 1962 to 1964 spree: two of his female victims were killed only blocks away. By the 1990s, the tremors were more cosmetic than cataclysmic: when Celtic co-owner Don Gaston installed a high-tech satellite dish at his Number 14 home in 1991, you'd have thought, from the accompanying uproar, he'd applied vinyl siding to his brick abode.

Despite these fusses—some petty, some real—the allure of Louisburg Square remains. What's changed since the early 1980s, however, is the profile of its residents. Skyrocketing real estate prices have meant that mostly millionaires buy homes on Beacon Hill today. And while high-income residents have pretty much ensured that the historic homes remain in good condition, many of these newcomers—young, rich, and seldom home—have let the sense of community and the beloved holiday traditions slide away. Nevertheless, according to one longtime resident, "the Hill is still quite cohesive for a city."

With its beautifully maintained grass and trees, its prim homes, and its textures of brick and cobblestone, Louisburg Square looks much as it did a century back, save, of course, for the autos. Very few residential neighborhoods in Boston—or anywhere else, for that matter—can truthfully say the same.

THE ESSENTIALS

ADDRESS: Between Pinckney and Mount Vernon streets, Beacon Hill, Boston.

VISITOR INFORMATION: Louisburg Square is a private roadway and residential area. Square itself accessible twenty-four hours a day, 365 days per year, free; homes are generally open only by personal invitation of a resident. Several local tour groups, however, offer seasonal guided tours of Beacon Hill that include Louisburg Square; among the best are Boston by Foot, (617) 367-2345; recorded tour information, (617) 367-3766; and the Historic Neighborhoods Foundation, (617) 426-1885. Moderate tour fees. Wheelchair access often difficult, due to rough surfaces.

30 Walden Pond

EACH YEAR, more than half a million people visit Walden Pond State Reservation, a beautiful wooded site that spans 304 acres in the suburban towns of Concord and Lincoln. Many, of course, come simply to enjoy the swimming, picnicking, hiking, fishing, boating, skating, and cross-country skiing available on the lake and surrounding woods. Walden Pond, after all, has served Greater Boston as a popular recreation area since the end of the Civil War. Today the area's many offerings have expanded to include ten miles of established trails, summer-season lifeguards, and a pond stocked with thousands of rainbow and brook trout provided by the state's Fisheries and Wildlife Division.

Still, recreation is hardly the only reason to visit this bucolic retreat. Since the late nineteenth century, scholars, poets, social activists, nature lovers, and rugged individualists have taken the half-mile trek to one specific spot on a far, wooded corner of the pond. Their pilgrimage ends at the site where writer and philosopher Henry David Thoreau once lived in a rustic cabin—a sojourn chronicled in his 1854 classic, *Walden*. A replica of Thoreau's tiny cabin stands near the entrance of the reservation's parking lot, sparsely furnished with bed, desk, chair, and woodstove, but purists and pilgrims insist on seeing the original site, too. Some drop commemorative stones on the cairn that Bronson Alcott and Mary Adams began there in 1872. Others stare and ponder the rough outline of the long-gone cabin's foundation, wondering at the life and thoughts Thoreau engaged in there between 1845 and 1847.

All of this is meant to suggest that there's a lot more at Walden Pond than initially meets the eye.

It's perhaps appropriate that Walden Pond has served as a stage for so many different types of players over the years, since it's located in a natural amphitheater. First-time visitors are often stunned by the site's dramatic

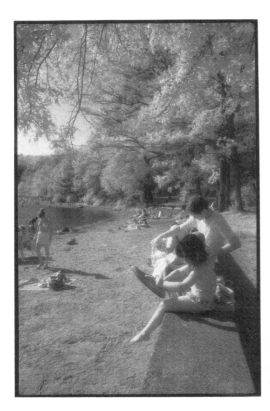

The pond that inspired Thoreau's Walden *has been a popular recreation area since the end of the Civil War.*

bowl-like form: woods and paths descend to smooth blue-green waters, and the pond's warm, flat sandbars suddenly give way to chillier depths of up to a hundred feet. The shape is actually a "kettle hole," molded during the end of the Ice Age some ten thousand years ago, when an enormous chunk of ice broke off from a retreating glacier. Streams of melting water gradually surrounded the glacial remnant with gravel and sand deposits, forming the steep sides of today's basin. Emerson Cliff, a wooded hillside to the left of Walden Pond's main beach, is a glacial outcropping created during that period. The hill was named for Ralph Waldo Emerson, who bought the land in 1844 for a mere eight dollars an acre to protect the woods from timbering.

Though Native Americans had passed through the area for several thousand years, leaving plenty of arrowheads, artifacts, and a network of paths still used today, it's likely that no major villages were established at Walden. The pond's waters were too still and sterile to satisfy their needs, and a large fishing village already existed in nearby Concord. Native American legends do tell of a large hill on the site where Walden Pond rests today. It's probably not a geographical error, but a story dating back to the Ice Age—before the hill made of ice melted down into today's basin.

Seventeenth-century Europeans also left Walden Pond essentially unsettled. Its glacial legacy gave the Walden area dry, sandy, acidic soil, unsuitable for farming. Settlers did build a few homes within a half-mile of

Walden Pond—perhaps eight of them by 1800, according to historian Dick O'Connor of the Thoreau Lyceum. But the land was clearly best suited to use as woodland and pasture.

The names of various sites and paths on Walden trail maps today reflect people and events from its long history. Thoreau's name lives on in a sandy cove near his cabin site, while his famous backyard bean field survives as a path. Wyman Meadow was a wetland owned by a local potter named Wyman, and Red Cross Beach reflects a group who gave swimming lessons there during the 1950s. In the 1840s, Irish laborers built the old Fitchburg Railroad (which still carries commuters from north central Massachusetts to Boston today); their rustic temporary huts are remembered in Shanty Town Path. Ice Fort Cove was where a nineteenth-century ice company stored blocks of Walden Pond ice awaiting shipment to India. And nearby Brister's Hill commemorates former slave Brister Freeman, one of several free black residents of the area in the early 1800s.

The origin of the name Walden itself remains a matter of conjecture. It may, as Thoreau suggested, have simply described the "walled-in" pond. Or it may have been brought from Saffron Walden, England, which had many connections to Concord through the Minots and other old New England families. The pond may have been named for Walden, a mythical Native American woman who survived the traumatic transition of the site from melting glacial hill to pond. Some historians note that it could simply be a corruption of "wald" or "wold," common Old English words for forested areas. Finally, one Major Waldren—a trader with Native Americans in the area—may have been commemorated, albeit in a misspelled fashion, in the Walden name.

The man who made Walden famous was the multitalented, Harvard-educated Henry David Thoreau, who moved into a ten-by-fifteen-foot hand-hewn cabin by Walden Pond on July 4, 1845. He was twenty-eight years old when he came to Walden, and would spend two years, two months, and two days reading, writing, walking, and thinking in spartan semi-solitude.

Ironically, though history and world literature have forever linked Thoreau and Walden, it was not so in the mid-nineteenth century. Thoreau's widespread fame emerged only in the socially conscious, antimaterialist, environmentally aware decade of the 1960s, a century after Thoreau's death at the age of forty-four. In 1847, Walden's most famous citizens were Ralph Waldo Emerson and Frederic Tudor. Emerson was already a prestigious essayist and local landowner by then; it was he who gave his friend Thoreau the parcel of land on which to build a cabin. "Ice King" Frederic Tudor had expanded his international ice-export business to Walden in 1847, when the new Fitchburg Railroad line offered him easy access from pond to port. Thoreau actually enjoyed the fact that Walden ice might go to India; he loved the Indian philosophers, and kept the Bhagavad Gita, the sacred Hindu text, close at hand. Close by, too, was his copy of the Greek epic poem *The Iliad*.

In his book *Walden,* Thoreau related his observations, thoughts, and encounters with nature and society, based on the journals he had kept while living at the pond. "I went to the woods because I wished to live deliberately," he explained, "to front the essential facts of life and see if I could not learn what it had to teach, and not, when I came to die, discover that I had not lived." Like his colleague Emerson, Thoreau argued that studying nature and knowing oneself were one and the same. Both believed that the Divine was located in the human soul, and that the self, as the source of the Divine, could perceive the Divine in the rest of the world. Such thoughts were part of the nineteenth-century idealist philosophy known as Transcendentalism.

Despite these philosophical contributions, Thoreau's nineteenth- and twentieth-century detractors have periodically labeled him a shiftless hermit, hippie, freeloader, fraud, or misanthrope, who lived in a cabin to save money and escape the responsibilities of a working adulthood. More often than not, however, Thoreau is today admired as a pioneer of passive resistance and wilderness preservation, and as an inspiration to Martin Luther King, Jr., Mahatma Gandhi, Leo Tolstoi, and environmentalist John Muir.

Anne McGrath, curator of the Thoreau Lyceum, rebuffs those who would call Thoreau a hermit, lazy, or free of responsibility; instead, she views him as "the most practical man alive." McGrath explains that while living at Walden, Thoreau welcomed visitors, walked into town, and earned money surveying, selling vegetables to neighbors, and even lecturing. He had made improvements in his father's pencil-making business and built his own home in the woods using building skills learned with his father. Because Thoreau borrowed an ax, cut nearby pines for his frame, and bought boards from the shanty of a neighboring Irish railroad worker, he was able to construct his house for just $28.12. (The Thoreau house replica, in the park's parking lot, was built in 1986 at a cost of $7,000.)

On many issues, Thoreau was a thinker ahead of his time. He had few class pretensions, decried corporal punishment of schoolchildren, and doubted the benefits of succumbing to the world of business and material accumulation.

Anne McGrath suggests that if his brother John hadn't died, Thoreau might never have come to stay at Walden, nor immortalized that stay in his book. Certainly, Thoreau wanted to learn to simplify his life, appreciate nature, "live deliberately," find peace and quiet, and work on his writing career; but he also needed to recover from the loss of his beloved older brother. John had died in Henry's arms three years earlier from a freak accident, a straight-edge razor cut that had led to tetanus. (Henry himself suffered from psychosomatic lockjaw afterward.)

Like Thoreau, Walden Pond, the cabin, and the woods have attracted their share of misconceptions. Many people believe, for example, that the area was a wooded wilderness in Henry's day. In fact, woodsmen had collected so much lumber by 1845 that fewer trees stood there then than do today. Massive planting efforts by the state and by concerned citizens like the group Walden Forever Wild have helped bring the shoreline back to its original splendor; still, more money and staff are always needed.

Walden Pond itself was rumored to be bottomless until the skillful surveying of civil engineer Thoreau put that idea to rest. Some suggested that Walden was fed by a huge system of underwater rivers that traveled from New Hampshire's White Mountains to Cape Cod; but Walden is so deep simply because it intersects the water table.

By 1945, the exact location of Thoreau's cabin was a mystery. Roland Wells Robbins, a Thoreau enthusiast and amateur historian, excavated the old foundation and several artifacts in that year. The house itself, of course, had long since disappeared. The popular account of its fate generally goes like this: Thoreau first gave his cabin to Emerson, who sold it to his gardener, who moved it from the site as a home for *his* family. The gardener, however, abandoned his family and the cabin—the latter of which sank into the cellar hole he had dug for it. Two farmers finally bought Thoreau's house, dragged it away with oxen and used it for grain storage. In 1868, the roof was transferred to a pig sty, while the sides became first a stable and finally scrap lumber.

True, half-true, or largely apocryphal, it makes a fine tale.

The Walden Pond area had started to suffer from misuse and overuse even during Thoreau's time. The Fitchburg Railroad began rumbling through Walden Woods in 1844, leaving the abandoned shanties of railroad construction workers in its wake. Meanwhile, ice and wood from the area were regularly hauled away and sold for profit. Between 1866 and 1902, a railroad excursion park called the Picnic Grounds—a pleasure park that city dwellers came to by train—brought thousands of visitors tromping through Ice Fort Cove. Swings, bathhouses, dancing and speaking pavilions, boat rides, concession stands, a baseball diamond, and a cinder track for runners and bicyclists, drew both rich and poor out to Walden. Famous speakers on popular topics like spiritualism drew crowds as large as those that gathered for church picnics and chowder parties.

By 1922, part of Walden Pond had become a park; eighty acres had been donated to the state by private landowners—an area since quadrupled by several land acquisitions. Still, the abuse of Walden continued. By the 1930s, a sweltering Sunday might bring 25,000 bathers out to the pond, compared to today's daily limit of 1,000. In 1957, the woodland behind Red Cross Beach was bulldozed to make room for an expanded swimming program. Later years brought motorcycles, alcohol abuse, cars parked randomly along the roadsides, and a general lack of control.

By 1975, when management of the park was transferred from Middlesex County to the Massachusetts Department of Environmental Management (D.E.M.), Walden Pond had been literally loved to death, and drastic steps were required to save the area from recreational abuse and overuse. Specifically, parking and daily attendance quotas were established and vigorously enforced, dramatically reducing the number of people allowed into the park at any one time. Much of the pond's bank was restored and replanted, the buildings renovated, ugly concrete piers removed, and interpretive programs added.

The controversy over the appropriate use of Walden Pond State Reservation continues to the present day. Some groups want to ban all or some of the active recreation at Walden for the sake of historic and natural preservation. Others—angered when told that the parking lot and park are full for the day—want full recreational access restored. Meanwhile, a continuing shortage of state funding has cut park staffs and stalled improvement plans.

Beginning in the 1980s, large condominium and office development projects in parts of the surrounding Walden Woods—efforts condoned by the town of Concord—further threatened Walden from without. As a result, a variety of preservationists began a fight to save the land made famous by Thoreau's writings. Musician Don Henley, a former member of the Eagles, founded the Walden Woods Project in 1990, and helped choreograph a variety of rallies, walks, concerts and other fund-raisers and consciousness-raisers to protect the property from commercial development. The group's primary goal was to purchase the land and allow it to remain woodland. Among their fund-raising efforts was the publication of *Heaven Is Under Our Feet,* a book of essays by celebrities, authors, and environmentalists, dedicated to preserving the lands around Walden Pond. In 1992, Henley was named the Massachusetts Historical Commission's "Man of the Year" for his ongoing efforts. By 1993, the group's success was all but assured: commercial development on the land had been stopped, and the process of buying the woodland begun.

Through all the controversy, the park's interpretative staff continues to enlighten visitors to the pond's literary, historical, and natural past and present. Park interpreters are generally available to the public at the Thoreau house replica; the D.E.M. also offers special programs, and maintains a fascinating photo exhibit on the history of Walden Pond, in the park office building on Route 126.

Other resources for visitors curious about Henry David Thoreau include the Thoreau Lyceum, on Belknap Street in Concord, only a short drive from Walden Pond. The Lyceum is a respected learning center and the headquarters of the Thoreau Society, which operates a weekend bookstore at Walden Pond State Reservation from June through mid-October. The Lyceum also houses a research library, changing exhibits, a gift shop of New England crafts, and a bookshop featuring out-of-print and current books on Thoreau and other Transcendentalists. One permanent exhibit is a furnished replica of Thoreau's house at Walden Pond—similar to the replica which stands near the pond itself. Meanwhile, Thoreau's original bed, desk, and rocking chair are on display with other Thoreau artifacts in the Concord Museum, at the junction of Lexington Road and the Cambridge Turnpike.

THE ESSENTIALS

ADDRESS: Route 126, off Route 2, Concord; reservation spans parts of Concord and Lincoln.

TELEPHONE: Walden Pond State Reservation, (508) 369-3254; Thoreau Lyceum, (508) 369-5912.

VISITOR INFORMATION: Open 365 days a year, 5:00 A.M. until dusk. Staff hours 8:00 A.M. to dusk. Free, but parking fee in adjacent lot, limited to 350 spaces; visitors limited to 1,000 at a time. Call for details on guided walks and educational programs. No fires, camping, pets, alcoholic beverages, off-road vehicles, bicycles, motorcycles, novelty flotation devices, sailboats, or boats powered by internal combustion engines. Wheelchair access minimal; special parking spaces in lot; steep ramp to main beach accessible with assistance; main beach toilets accessible; phone ahead for special accommodations.

The Many Faces of Boston: Minorities, Immigrants, and Unsung Heroes

A S RECENTLY as thirty years ago, most histories of Boston—and most of the city's historic walking tours—gave the distinct impression that the town was created by and for white, Anglo-Saxon Protestants. A closer look suggested an even narrower vision: the Hub of the Universe seemed to consist of a small, select group of middle- and upper-class white males, many of whom could trace their family lineages back to Boston's seventeenth century. A jocular look at the legendary "Proper Bostonian" was provided by John Collins Bossidy, in a toast he delivered in 1910:

> And this is good old Boston,
> The home of the bean and the cod,
> Where the Lowells talk to the Cabots
> And the Cabots talk only to God.

Though Bossidy's rhyme was amusing, it was hardly a full picture of Boston history. Boston did begin as a Puritan colony, populated largely by immigrants from the British Isles. And despite the fact that religious controversies and schisms erupted constantly in colonial times, they generally involved Protestants arguing with other Protestants. Native American religions were disregarded, as were the accomplishments and contributions of local tribes. Women were invisible, disenfranchised daughters, mothers, and wives—except, of course, when they became outspoken heretics or witches. African-Americans were treated as second-class citizens, even after slavery was abolished in Massachusetts in 1783. And Catholics and Jews were rare indeed (when the Italian Judah Monis became the first Jew to teach at Harvard College in 1722, he converted to Christianity before teaching his first semester.)

As the nineteenth century unfolded, however, the many faces of Boston became harder to hide, more difficult to disregard. Boston's African-American community fought and won battles to abolish slavery in the United States and to gain equal status in churches, public schools, and the community. Women began entering the work force in greater numbers—inspired, in part, by the mill girls of Lowell—and started the first phase of the women's movement. Women and blacks began to emerge as writers, artists, orators, educators, reformers, and community leaders, sometimes side by side. Meanwhile, immigrants flooded into Boston as the century progressed. Irish Catholics, escaping the potato famine and British oppression, were one of the first and largest groups; they were soon followed by German Jews, French Canadians, Italians, Portuguese, Eastern European Jews, and many others. Though Hispanic and Asian immigrants were part of this move, they came in greatest numbers in the twentieth century.

Today, more and more histories of Boston—and more of our historic walking tours—reflect the lives and contributions of Boston women, minorities, immigrants, and other formerly unsung heroes. The development of the Black Heritage Trail in the 1960s, and the Boston Women's Heritage Trail in the 1980s, were sure signs of such growth. Even the prestigious Freedom Trail has significantly broadened its vision of Boston, both in tour guide information and in National Park Service programs offered on Boston history.

It's true that discovering the stories behind the many faces of Boston still requires work and exploration. But it's well worth the extra effort.

The African Meeting House

THE VOICE of Frederick Douglass? Ruth Batson, the dynamic former director of Boston's Museum of Afro American History, has been known to say she's heard the great abolitionist's voice when standing inside one of Boston's brightest historic lights, the African Meeting House.

"There's a feeling you get when you go into the meetinghouse," explains Batson of the oldest standing black church in the United States. "First you have to have the knowledge that in 1806 black people created that building. So you certainly must be captured by the spirit there. Now, Frederick Douglass happens to be one of my heroes—his oratory, his courage, the way he would say things. He took great risks in explaining the problems of his people. And his voice? Well, who can say what I can or cannot hear?!

"All kinds of voices were heard at the African Meeting House," Batson continues. "Children's voices. Abolitionist voices. Black voices. The voices of refugee slaves . . . Sometimes those voices were in agreement, sometimes in opposition."

Today the old structure—restored to its simple beauty and reopened to the public in 1987—is filled again with varied voices from Boston and beyond. The African Meeting House is a major stop on the Black Heritage Trail, a walking tour that explores the history of Boston's nineteenth-century black community. Moreover, unlike hands-off museum relics encased in glass, this sturdy historic building enjoys a contemporary life of its own.

"The meetinghouse is a means of drawing the people of Boston together," explains former museum director Marcus Mitchell. And it's true: celebrations, lectures, concerts, workshops, exhibits, and occasional church meetings all play a part in the new African Meeting House, as they did in the old.

The African Meeting House was built in 1806, at a time when the opportunities for African-Americans to worship were dismal, despite Massachusetts's reputation as a relatively welcoming state for blacks. African slaves first arrived in Boston in 1638. Some earned status as free men and women over the ensuing decades, and the American Revolution brought even louder cries for liberty. In 1783, slavery was declared illegal in the Commonwealth. According to the first federal census, of 1790, Massachusetts was the only state in the newly formed Union that recorded no slaves.

But freedom, it was soon discovered, had little to do with equality. By 1800, there were some eleven hundred free blacks living in Boston, first

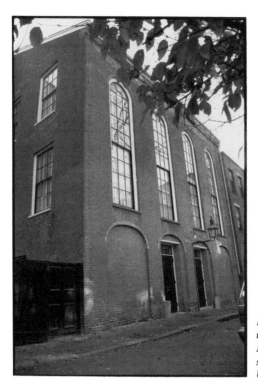

Built by African-Americans in 1806, the African Meeting House is the oldest standing black church in the United States.

primarily in the North End, and later in the West End and the north slope of Beacon Hill. Though blacks held a variety of jobs around the city—including a virtual monopoly on the barbering trade—they could not vote. Even worse, they did not have their own churches.

Boston blacks *were* generally allowed into the town's many white churches. But they were required to stay in the back galleries, out of sight of both preacher and white church members. Certain African-Americans avoided such indignities by worshiping in private homes; others attended religious meetings in Faneuil Hall, offered on Tuesday and Friday afternoons (never, alas, on Sunday).

According to James and Lois Horton's book, *Black Bostonians,* some proud locals tried to defy the segregated system. In the early 1800s, for instance, blacksmith James Easton and his family were forcibly thrown out of one area church after they refused to sit in the "black section." In response, Easton purchased a pew in a local white Baptist church. Their effort to block that sale having failed, some white members tarred Easton's pew. Undaunted, Easton hauled a clean carriage seat to his pew. Indignant whites removed the pew altogether. Easton's response? He and his family sat through services in the aisle.

Though creating a church specifically for black Bostonians was one obvious solution to this problem, the building of the African Meeting House wasn't simply a response to racism. The African-American community had grown and flourished. A meeting place where black self-expression could grow—where ideas could be exchanged and nurtured—was sorely needed.

When plans for the African Meeting House began to take shape, an appropriate black preacher was already available. Thomas Paul of New Hampshire had been attending religious meetings in Boston since 1789, when he was only 16. By 1805 he was an ordained Baptist minister. Soon after, he assembled twenty members and formed the First African Baptist Church.

Time clearly had come to build a permanent home for the church. But where? The North End, where most African-Americans lived, was too congested; the West End, on the other hand, was wide-open farmland at the time, a perfect place to build a religious meetinghouse, and to attract and absorb the expanding black population.

Funds for the meetinghouse project came from both black and white supporters. Cato Gardner, an ambitious, illiterate native of Africa, swiftly collected $1,500—an ample portion of the final cost of $7,700. A plaque above the African Meeting House's front door still reads, "To Cato Gardner, First Promoter of This Building."

The new meetinghouse—from its red-brick outer walls to its spiraling staircases and broad pine floors—was built almost entirely by free black laborers. Since funds were limited, plans for the facade were adapted from an existing town house design by Boston architect Asher Benjamin. The interior layout was simple and plain, though up-to-date. Many of the materials—including floorboards, pulpit, and trusses—were recycled items, presumably gathered from the nearby Old West Church, which was being dismantled at the time.

Just how economically was it done? The ornate and elegant new State House, built on Beacon Hill eight years earlier, cost $133,333. The naval frigate, USS *Constitution*, was constructed for $302,718 in 1797. The African Meeting House's total building budget of $7,700 equaled roughly what Paul Revere had been paid to lay copper on the *top* of the State House dome and the *bottom* of old Ironsides. Small miracles can indeed be made on a shoestring.

When the Reverend Thomas Paul and his Baptist congregation moved into the African Meeting House, it was a time for revel and revolution. The revolution in question began with a whisper, not a roar. Supportive white Bostonians who were invited to attend the dedication ceremonies on December 6, 1806, were given the superior floor seats, while black members sat up in the gallery. "No one would do that again," insists local historian and longtime State Representative Byron Rushing, "and they shouldn't have then! But they were so confident of their control of the space that they could do it." Besides, it was probably good public relations.

From the start, the African Meeting House was more than just a church building. It was a place where blacks could find solace from segregation and prejudice, and rejoice in their community, culture, and accomplishments. It was a place they could argue over hot, divisive issues: separate versus integrated schools; the proposed resettlement of freed blacks in Liberia or Haiti; and the effectiveness of violence versus nonviolence in antislavery protest.

By 1808 the meetinghouse basement was also housing a school for black children—children who were banned from attending white public schools. Archaeological evidence suggests that people may have lived there as well: a nineteenth-century trash pit, excavated in the backyard, was full of domestic debris like porcelain, glassware, and edible-animal remains—too much of it to be the result of church suppers.

The African Meeting House's most famous nineteenth-century connections—"the shouts heard 'round the world"—were certainly its abolitionist meetings, which earned the building such nicknames as "the Abolition Church" and "the Black Faneuil Hall." Boston's influential white activist William Lloyd Garrison founded the New England Anti-Slavery Society in a stirring speech delivered inside the meetinghouse in 1832.

"We have met tonight in this obscure schoolhouse," Garrison began, "our numbers few and our influence limited; but mark my prediction, Faneuil Hall shall ere long echo with the principles we have set forth. We shall shake the Nation by their mighty power." Although the twelve signers of the preamble to the society's constitution were white, an estimated quarter of the seventy-two signers of the constitution itself were African-Americans.

Often banned from speaking against slavery in public places, many other eloquent white reformers—including Wendell Phillips, Charles Sumner, and Angelina Grimké—addressed their supporters within the welcoming meetinghouse as well. Black speakers such as Frederick Douglass, William Nell, and Maria Miller Stewart also shook the rafters with cries for black freedom.

Douglass and radical activist Lewis Hayden were two of the black leaders who encouraged African-American enlistment in Union armies during the Civil War. The meetinghouse became their recruiting center for the renowned 54th Regiment—and served as the Union's celebratory send-off site as those valiant "colored" soldiers marched off to war.

Despite rumors to the contrary, the African Meeting House was never a stop on the Underground Railroad. Simply put, it was just too obvious a spot. Fugitive southern slaves *were* hidden elsewhere in Boston, as they followed the North Star, in the Little Dipper (known by some as the Drinkin' Gourd), while working their way toward the Canadian border. But many risky escapes *were* choreographed or aided by Bostonians who used the meetinghouse as their political base.

In the famous Abolition Riot, for example, brave black Boston women charged into a courtroom and bore fugitive slaves to a waiting carriage. On another occasion, Lewis Hayden stood with a torch and two kegs of gunpowder on his porch, threatening to blow his home sky high if slave-hunters tried to apprehend the fugitive hidden inside. Hayden's house on Phillips Street—another stop on the Black Heritage Trail—was indeed an Underground Railroad station.

As the nineteenth century progressed, so did the African Meeting House. Physically, the structure underwent a major facelift in 1855, and a major renovation in the 1980s restored it to that 1855 appearance—from color schemes and window layout to gaslight fixtures and the cinder-block pattern on the wallpaper. (No known photos exist of the building's earlier appearance.)

In historical references, the building's name periodically changed, too. It was sometimes called by names of the congregations which actively used the space, like the First African Baptist Church, or the First Independent Baptist Church of the People of Color of Boston. Others referred to it by location, alternately calling it the Joy Street Church or the Belknap Street Church (after Joy Street's former name). Its most popular nicknames, as noted before, were the Black Faneuil Hall and the Abolition Church.

Meanwhile, the building's uses changed as well. When students moved to the Abiel Smith School, and then, twenty years later, into integrated public schools, the meetinghouse basement was no longer needed as a classroom. Other black churches were founded in Boston, and the congregation begun by the Reverend Paul eventually split. His direct heirs include today's People's Baptist and Twelfth Baptist churches, now located in the South End and Roxbury, respectively.

By 1898, the African Meeting House congregation had outgrown its headquarters, and Boston's black population had largely migrated to other parts of the city. The building was sold to the Hasidic Jewish congregation called Anshei Libovitz, and remained a synagogue through much of the twentieth century.

In 1964, Sue Bailey Thurman and her husband, Howard Thurman (Boston University's first black chaplain, credited as the most influential black theologian of the twentieth century) founded the Museum of Afro American History. By 1965, the prototype Black Heritage Trail had been established. Seven years later, the museum was able to purchase the African Meeting House, which was designated a National Historic Landmark in 1974.

Only a year after the 1972 purchase, however, disaster struck. While struggling to solidify a dangerously rickety roof, a worker accidentally ignited a fire. The losses were massive: the meetinghouse's original pulpit and trusses and the old slate roof were destroyed, while the original pews were badly burned and damaged. (Most of these pews still lie in storage, awaiting further donations to the pew restoration fund.)

Thanks to aid from the National Park Service, the Museum of Afro American History forged ahead with the Meeting House Project in the 1980s. The building was finally refurbished and reopened to great fanfare late in 1987. Today, the museum has developed a broad range of educational and public programming related to African-American history and culture. Their projects include educational publications and workshops, changing exhibits, lectures, films, and performing arts presentations at the African Meeting House. Contact the museum or the National Park Service directly for current program information.

Meanwhile, the simple, stark, and proud old meetinghouse stands as a statement and an inspiration. As museum chair Henry Hampton explained during the festivities of 1987, "The re-opening of the African Meeting House is more than a rededication of bricks and mortar. It is a renewal of historic purpose."

THE ESSENTIALS

ADDRESS: 8 Smith Court, Beacon Hill, Boston.

TELEPHONE: Museum offices, (617) 742-1854.

VISITOR INFORMATION: African Meeting House open Monday through Friday, 10:00 A.M.–4:00 P.M. Free; donations encouraged. Tours are free; included as stop on Black Heritage Trail. Only ground floor and restrooms are wheelchair accessible; call about wheelchair access, being planned for sanctuary.

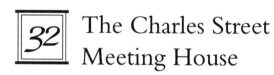

32 The Charles Street Meeting House

EVERYONE KNOWS that you can't tell a book by its cover. But rarely is the difference between a building's interior and exterior so pronounced as in the modern-day Charles Street Meeting House.

Inside the historic structure, which has graced the corner of Mount Vernon and Charles streets for more than 180 years, is a thoroughly modern complex of shops and offices, topped off by a home and office for the building's current owner, architect John Sharratt. There are sleek new staircases and elevators, several ground-floor retail shops, thirty up-scale, upper-level offices, and bright, boldly modern chambers punctuated by archways and large glass partitions.

On the outside, however, the simple, elegant, red-brick church building looks much the same as it did in 1807. Tastefully embellished with recessed arches, tall multipaned windows, fan-lighted doors, and a beautiful old clock tower, the structure often reminds viewers of the Old West Church on nearby Cambridge Street—which it should. Both churches were built in the early 1800s, and both designed in the Federalist style by the well-known Boston architect Asher Benjamin.

It's this exterior, of course, that suggests the years of history that have passed through the Charles Street Meeting House. When constructed in 1807, the building was designed to accommodate the word of God, not the world of commerce and industry. Between 1807 and 1980, four consecutive congregations—the Third Baptist Church, the First African Methodist Episcopal Church, the Universalist Church of America, and the Unitarian Universalist Association—called this structure home. Throughout those years, the meetinghouse also served as a community center that sheltered meetings, educational forums, and impassioned debates involving everyone from Sojourner Truth to Dr. Benjamin Spock, from the

Now privately owned by a Boston architect, the Charles Street Meeting House has a long history as a center of religious, cultural, political, and social life in Boston.

abolitionists to the Black Panthers, and from the Beacon Hill Civic Association to various gay, feminist, civil rights, peace, arts, theater, and dance groups. The ground-breaking *Gay Community News* had its first home at the Charles Street Meeting House. And so did the modest black heritage display that grew into the Museum of Afro American History.

As Boston entered the nineteenth century, water entered the area we now know as Charles Street; during high tide, in fact, the Charles River flowed right up to the base of Beacon Hill. In 1795, however, a group of Boston developers known as the Mount Vernon Proprietors began plotting to add more land, and more buildings, to Boston proper. With the aid of a rock-hauling apparatus touted as "the first gravity railroad," they began lopping off the top fifty feet of Beacon Hill, then carting the gravel down to the banks of the Charles for use as landfill.

By 1805, Charles Street was born—and appropriately named for the river it partly displaced. Only two years later, a handsome new Federalist-style church was constructed on one segment of this Charles Street landfill for the sum of $27,000. Apparently patterned after drawings from the popular copybooks of architect Asher Benjamin—which liberally integrated designs by the great Charles Bulfinch—the Charles Street Meeting House was built to accommodate the rapidly growing Boston Baptist community.

Back in 1765, there were only thirty-two Baptist churches in the area later known as New England. By 1795, that number had increased tenfold; 330 churches with 22,000 parishioners called themselves Baptist. It was the 337 members of the Third Baptist Church, recently departed from the First and Second Baptist Churches, who moved into the Charles Street Meeting House in 1807.

The structure those Baptists worshiped in presumably looked on the outside much like the building we see today. The exterior brick was laid in the stylish Flemish bond pattern, and the tall, white, wooden arches and paned windows helped make a fairly plain, square building appear unusually vertical. A beautiful balustrade with urn finials graced the porch roof, which was topped by a clock tower that was destined to signal time to all of Charles Street for generations to come.

Inside, a single vaulted chamber occupied most of the space. Slender Grecian columns supported the gallery around the sides and back of this auditorium, while a high wooden pulpit and draped curtains dominated the front. Dark box pews lined the wooden floors, with the organ console and pipes set in the rear.

When the church's first pastors preached there—beginning with the Reverend Caleb Blood and followed by the forty-two-year reign of the powerful Reverend Daniel Sharp—the congregation was actively engaged in the practice of baptism by immersion. Since the Charles then flowed right up to the riverside wall of the meetinghouse, where River Street runs today, baptisms may have been performed directly outside the church; other sources suggest that an inlet may have been cut so that the river flowed into the church itself, allowing baptisms to occur within its walls.

The Baptist congregation that first owned and inhabited the Charles Street Meeting House was mainly white. In an age when the best seats in the house—the mahogany box pews on the main floor of the church— were sold to wealthy churchgoing families, poorer members were relegated to seats in the backs of distant galleries. Included in the latter group were Boston's free black families, many of whom lived on the north slope of Beacon Hill.

Timothy Gilbert (1797–1865), a white parishioner of the Charles Street church, chose to challenge such segregation. Known by his peers as "the Grandest Abolitionist," Gilbert was a cabinet and piano maker who sold his wares in the South, then used his profits to fight Southern slavery. Gilbert's home, once located at number 2 Beech Street, was a hotbed of antislavery rhetoric and a stop on the Underground Railroad. At one time as many as six fugitives hid in Gilbert's home, on their way to freedom at the Canadian border.

In 1835, Gilbert decided to test the segregated seating policies of New England's white churches by filling his front-row pew at the Charles Street Meeting House with black Baptist friends. Though the antislavery elements of the church were delighted, the strong proslavery segments were not. Whether Gilbert was angrily expelled after the event, or whether he left voluntarily—as one biographer cautiously put it, "to seek a more congenial atmosphere [for] his anti-slavery opinions"—is unclear. But it is clear that Gilbert and many of his abolitionist friends left the Charles Street congregation soon thereafter to form the first truly integrated church in America, Tremont Temple Baptist Church.

Meanwhile, back at the meetinghouse, the issue of abolitionism was getting hotter and hotter. The Reverend Mr. Sharp allowed plenty of debate within the red-brick walls, and several major antislavery leaders—including Sojourner Truth, Harriet Tubman, Frederick Douglass, William Lloyd Garrison, Wendell Phillips, and Charles Sumner—found receptive audiences there.

By 1876, however, both the world and Boston's West End had changed significantly. The Civil War was over. Slavery had been abolished. Vast migrations from the South had swelled Beacon Hill's black population, and the white members of the Third Baptist Church had largely moved out to Back Bay. The white-run congregation sold their meetinghouse to the black members of the First African Methodist Episcopal Church, which maintained the sturdy brick structure for the next sixty-three years.

The Charles Street A.M.E. Church, as it came to be known, proceeded to become a major community leader in black religious, social, and cultural activities. The purchase of the Charles Street property alone, bought in 1876 for $45,000, was an impressive accomplishment for a congregation of only two hundred. The National Federation of Afro-American Women was organized there in 1895 (it later merged into the National Association of Colored Women). Sarah Gorham (1832–1894), the first woman missionary sent to Africa by the A.M.E. Church, left for Sierra Leone from the Charles Street congregation in 1888. Two of the church's pastors went on to become bishops.

As the twentieth century progressed, however, the church began to falter. Maintaining the big building proved to be a financial drain, and the black community had gradually moved from Beacon Hill and the West End to the South End and Roxbury. Hence, in 1939 the building was sold to a group of religious liberals known as the Charles Street Meeting House Society. The society sold the building nine years later to the Universalist Church of America and helped relocate the Charles Street A.M.E. congregation to the St. Ansagarius property in Roxbury, at Warren Street and Elm Hill Avenue. To this day, that large and active black community church proudly bears the name Charles Street A.M.E., though its address is 551 Warren.

During the Unitarian Universalist tenure at the meetinghouse, the building became a haven for a variety of local cultural, social, and political groups. Members of the gay community fondly remember the gay coffeehouse there, and the seminal years of the nation's oldest gay newspaper, *Gay Community News*. African-Americans established the first displays of the American Museum of Negro History in the meetinghouse, displays which later evolved into the Museum of Afro American History. Vibrant performances, meetings, lectures, rallies, debates, and support groups were all a part of the building's social fabric.

By the late 1970s, however, the aging building itself was in dire need of repair—much more repair than its owners could afford. No educational, religious, cultural, or charitable group could be found to buy and renovate the grand old structure. Hence, under the watchful eye of the Society for the Preservation of New England Antiquities—and just about everyone else who had ever loved or used the meetinghouse—architect John Sharratt was allowed to move in and to repair and renovate the space at a cost of more than a million dollars.

In order to save the meetinghouse, some compromises were necessary. Aside from ground-floor shoppers and visitors to the Charles Street offices, the building is not currently open to the public. Furthermore, the tall auditorium was carved up into multiple floors and smaller units, which were then rented out by Sharratt to help defray costs of renovation, exterior preservation, and high property taxes.

Although the changes were drastic, it wasn't the first time that the historic interior had been "compromised." A fire in the mid-nineteenth century had destroyed many of its original elements. Radical stylistic changes were also voluntarily imposed there in the 1850s: the floor was raised, box pews were discarded for slip-style benches and pseudo-Norman columns and arches replaced the early Grecian ones. The roof's pitch was changed, as were the windows and pulpit. Somewhere along the line, someone had even painted the exterior brickwork brown—a murky tint which was not blasted off until the 1920s.

Moreover, even the site was not really original. In 1921, when the city decided to widen Charles Street from fifty-five to sixty-five feet, most residents were forced to clip ten feet off the fronts of their buildings. Rather than chop up the meetinghouse—or, even worse, level it for a high-rise building or a parking lot—Beacon Hill residents and the Charles Street A.M.E. Church combined forces and finances to pick up the historic building and move it ten feet closer to the river. Architect Frank Bourne oversaw the stunning move, as well as subsequent changes and renovations to the structure.

Though many Bostonians are still saddened that some version of the old church interior was not preserved, no one can fail to be grateful for what is there. The principal architectural landmark of Charles Street is alive and well, its exterior restored to its splendid look of 1807. As travelers of the Black Heritage Trail know, it is a sparkling and proud chunk of history for new generations to watch, touch, and enjoy.

THE ESSENTIALS

ADDRESS: Corner of Mount Vernon and Charles streets, Beacon Hill, Boston.

TELEPHONE: Meeting House Offices, (617) 367-7171; John Sharratt Associates, (617) 227-0094; Black Heritage Trail and Boston African American National Historic Site offices, (617) 742-5415.

VISITOR INFORMATION: Interior of building open only to shop customers or office visitors. Offices open 9:00 A.M.–5:00 P.M., Monday–Friday. Some retail stores open weekends also. No organized tours, but building is discussed on Black Heritage Trail tours. Ground-level retail shops are wheelchair accessible; remainder of building is difficult because of steps by front door; once inside, all floors accessible by elevator.

33 The Abiel Smith School

IT'S A plain, box-shaped building on the corner of Joy Street and Smith Court—not the sort of place that would normally stop passersby in their tracks. But the old Abiel Smith School is more than the sum of its simple exterior parts: the sturdy red bricks, gabled roof, and twenty-four-pane window sashes that have held it intact for more than 150 years.

Today the building is headquarters for both the Museum of Afro American History and the Boston African American National Historic Site. School groups, Black Heritage Trail followers, and other tourists regularly visit the site by day, while veterans' groups periodically used the structure for nighttime meetings well into the 1980s.

Less immediately evident is the fact that this same structure was at the eye of a nineteenth-century storm. Built in 1834 as the first Boston public school to educate the city's African-American children, the Abiel Smith served Boston's black community for twenty long and frequently turbulent years.

In the decades preceding the Civil War, of course, the turbulence that most often comes to mind when speaking of Boston's black history is the argument over slavery. Boston in general, and Beacon Hill in particular, were known as hotbeds of abolitionism and antislavery sentiment. Next door to the Smith School, for example, at the African Meeting House, fiery abolitionists like William Lloyd Garrison, Frederick Douglass, and Angelina Grimké continually entranced exuberant antislavery crowds. Radical activists like Lewis Hayden, who valiantly aided fugitive Southern slaves on their Underground Railroad route to freedom at the Canadian border, lived only a short distance away.

Though abolitionism may have received the most press, the most pressing *civil rights* issue of the time concerned segregated schools. The debate over school integration, which so divided Boston in the twentieth century, actually began at the Smith School shortly after its dedication, on May 3, 1835. According to longtime state representative Byron Rushing, Boston's human library of black history, "Boycotting schools, setting up freedom schools in people's homes, the invention of the concept of 'separate but equal'—all these things seem so modern. But they all happened here."

And that's where the fascinating story of the Abiel Smith School begins.

Though their attitudes may not seem praiseworthy today, many white Bostonians of the late eighteenth century were proud of their "progressive," humanistic views on Boston's black population. Blacks had been

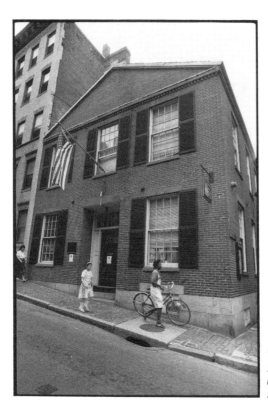

The fight to desegregate Boston's public schools began at the all-black Abiel Smith School.

enslaved in the city since their first arrival in 1638, only eight years after the founding of the Massachusetts Bay Colony; but by 1783, in the era of American Revolutionary idealism, slavery was legally abolished in the Commonwealth. In the first federal census of 1790, Massachusetts was the only state reporting no slaves.

Moreover, by 1800, Boston was home to almost 1,100 free African-Americans, making it one of the largest free black communities in North America. (Boston's total population at the time was 24,397.) Before 1800, many black men and women lived in the crowded, run-down North End. As the century progressed, however, they slowly began to migrate to the north slope of Beacon Hill.

Boston's growing black community may have been free, but it was clearly not equal. Though Boston's whites could pursue a wide variety of careers, blacks were often limited to a few vocations—as dock workers, shipbuilders, sailors, caterers, blacksmiths, servants, caretakers, street laborers, shopkeepers, barbers, and such. Jobs with higher pay or more prestige required more schooling. And while no law prevented Boston blacks from enjoying public education, blatant prejudice and outright abuse in the white-dominated schools effectively denied black children such benefits. Widespread public indifference allowed discrimination to continue. In addition, economics played a role. Poor families couldn't afford to send a child to school if help was needed at home.

Boston's black leaders were aware that education was essential if African-American families were to improve their lot. One such leader, Prince Hall, petitioned and pleaded for a decade before the city finally approved a private school for black children. Classes began in 1798, in the home of Hall's son, Primus.

Supported by white philanthropists, sometimes staffed by Harvard student-teachers, the Primus Hall school struggled along with erratic success. Finally, in 1808, a "real" schoolroom was created in the basement of the brand-new African Meeting House. Blacks and whites together had made education for black children possible in Boston, in the only way that seemed viable at the time—the de facto establishment of segregated schools.

The school that began in the basement of the African Meeting House eventually became known as the Abiel Smith School. Who was Abiel Smith? The details are scarce. We know he was a white philanthropist and business leader, and one of Boston's "merchant princes." On more than one occasion, Smith was asked by the eloquent black teacher, Prince Saunders, to contribute to the school. When Smith died in 1815, he left Boston close to $5,000 worth of shares in New England turnpikes and bridges, plus U.S. bonds, to be used "for the free instruction of colored children in reading, writing and arithmetic."

Though the written records are sketchy—a problem sadly true of much black history—it seems the African Meeting House school received some of these funds soon after, and was renamed the Abiel Smith School in appreciation. While the city agreed to allocate $200 per year for educating blacks—a sum that never increased, though student populations grew, and two more ad hoc black schoolrooms were created in the 1820s—students still had to contribute twelve and a half cents per week to help cover costs. Every Boston school relied partly on students' fees to meet costs, but, as ever, the poorest were hit hardest.

Eventually, overcrowding and intolerable conditions in the meeting-house basement convinced a reluctant school committee to apply Smith's legacy to building an actual schoolhouse for African-American children. Construction began on a parcel of land owned by Augustin Raillion, next to the meetinghouse. The mason may have been a man named Cushing Nichols, and the front door may have originally been on the left (as suggested by a site sketch in the 1849 *Boston Almanac*). The final cost of the building was $7,485.61 in 1834 dollars.

One year later, on May 3, 1835, the simple, two-story Abiel Smith School was dedicated, the first city-owned school building ever constructed for black Bostonians. It was not in the best section of Beacon Hill; wealthier folks lived farther up Joy Street, while the north slope housed stables and simpler lodgings. Moreover, the new school, like its predecessors, was a segregated or "race" school. Abiel Smith students were being taught the basics of reading, writing, and arithmetic; but, unlike their white counterparts, they were prohibited from instruction in advanced grammar.

The first-floor classroom, where museum offices sit today, was probably used simultaneously by two to five teachers and many dozens of students. In 1840 alone, the school had 263 students enrolled. The second floor—which now houses headquarters for the Boston African American National Historic Site—may have been another classroom or an auditorium. According to archaeologist Beth Bower, digs behind the African Meeting House have unearthed pieces of slate, slate pencils, toys, marbles, and ceramic cups—items that may well have been used at the Smith School, too. Beyond that, details of the school's operation and physical setup are not very clear.

What is clear, however, is that political battles and economic conditions made the Abiel Smith School fall rapidly from grace after its opening in 1835. A school committee report of 1847 decried the school's disrepair, overcrowding, and generally "deplorable" condition; special attention was called to the outhouses in its tiny backyard, accessible only "through a dark and damp cellar."

It's difficult to know today how conditions compared to those at other Boston schools. Contemporary reports, however, suggest that Smith School classrooms were more overcrowded, supplies more limited, teachers less educated, white headmasters more immoral, and facilities more marginal than in the dozens of white schools scattered about Boston by mid-century. Moreover, white students could easily walk to the nearest neighborhood school, while blacks had to travel to the Abiel Smith from throughout the city.

Compared to the best white primary or grammar schools of the period—like the majestic, three-story, 1824 Phillips School on the corner of Pinckney and Anderson streets, which now houses condominiums—the black-only Smith School was indeed a third-rate facility. Still, according to Stanley Schultz's book, *The Culture Factory,* the average Boston schoolroom of 1833 crammed one teacher and sixty-two students into a nineteen-by-twenty-six-foot space, and was often located in the densest, most rundown sectors of town.

For many of Boston's African-American citizens, the all-black Abiel Smith School—though not equal to its white counterparts—was an educational solution they could live with. For others, like black activist William Cooper Nell, separate was unacceptable, and equal education for blacks was essential. In 1840, Nell began to mount a campaign that would eventually bring an end to lawful school segregation in Boston.

Some historians suggest that Nell's drive to abolish black schools and end segregation came from one particular childhood event. As an honors student in the old Smith School when it was still housed in the basement of the African Meeting House, Nell had won the coveted Franklin Medal for scholastic achievement, along with top white students around the city. Because of his color, however, Nell was denied the prize and the special Faneuil Hall dinner honoring medal winners. Actually, Nell *was* permitted to attend the dinner—but only as a waiter!

Whatever the reason, Nell was a prime mover behind relentless petition drives and an eleven-year Smith School boycott, which helped the black school's attendance dwindle from 263 in 1840 to 50 in 1849. Meanwhile, powerful abolitionists like former senator Charles Sumner and black attorney Robert Morris added clout to Boston public school integration forces when they brought the case of *Roberts v. the City of Boston* to court.

The case involved a six-year-old student named Sarah Roberts, who was allegedly denied access to the five white public schools she had to pass on her way to the Smith School. Her father, printer Benjamin Roberts, sued the city for damages, testing the legality of segregated schools in Boston. In 1850, Judge Lemuel Shaw ruled against Roberts, arguing that Sarah did have access to a public school, the Abiel Smith, and that the school had in no way been proven inferior.

Though the battle was lost, the war was all but won. By 1855, aided by furor over the federal Fugitive Slave Law—which required that runaway slaves be returned to their owners—a bill to end segregation in Boston public schools passed the legislature and was signed by the governor. In the fall of that year, the Abiel Smith School was officially closed. The black children of Boston were finally free to attend the public school nearest their homes. (Despite Boston's pride as a pioneer in free education, incidentally, its school integration program came later than those in other Bay State cities, including Salem, New Bedford, Lowell, Cambridge, and Worcester.)

The old Smith School building continued to serve the city in less earth-shaking ways. First it became a city storage building, then, starting in 1887, veterans groups began using the structure as a meeting place. It was not until a century later that Boston's black community regained primary use of this important historic site.

Over its many years of civil service, the original Smith School underwent several physical changes. The old coal chutes to the basement have been cemented shut, and a brick wall separating the tiny schoolyard from the African Meeting House has eroded away. The ceiling downstairs may once have been supported by four pillars, which have since been replaced by a steel beam. The wonderfully ornate, arched tin ceiling upstairs is conjectured to be a Victorian addition, installed by black Civil War veterans of the famed 54th Regiment. (A comprehensive 1970 study by Elizabeth Amadon suggests that an earlier, arched plaster ceiling may be concealed beneath that Victorian tin.) Two modern restrooms were added to the upstairs in the twentieth century. New, too, in this century is the cellar bar—a reminder of the boisterous days when the United Service Organizations drank and partied down below.

Despite these cosmetic changes, the Abiel Smith School building probably looks much the same today as it did in 1835. Visitors can still see the bright brick walls, the brownstone lintels, the rows of large 12-over-12 sash windows, the two chimneys, and the gabled roof of the institution that first inspired, then infuriated black students in the decades before the Civil War. The substance, as well as the spirit, has survived the ages.

THE ESSENTIALS

ADDRESS: 46 Joy Street, at Smith Court, Beacon Hill, Boston.
TELEPHONE: Museum of Afro American History offices, (617) 742-1854; Boston African American National Historic Site headquarters, (617) 742-5415.

Visitor Information: Boston African American National Historic Site offices open daily, 9:00 A.M.–5 P.M. Museum's administrative offices open 10:00 A.M.–4:00 P.M., Monday–Friday. See Chapter 35 for tour information. Building not wheelchair accessible.

The Shaw/54th Regiment Memorial

It sits on the high corner of Boston Common, near the intersection of Beacon and Park streets. And for some, this imposing hunk of sculpted bronze, granite, and marble simply marks a convenient byway in a busy city. On the site are long, low benches, plus the shade of two soaring nineteenth-century elms. Moreover, the bus stops out front, unloading visitors on a perfect spot to view, photograph, or protest the State House, which sits majestically across the street.

Still, the most important thing at the corner of Beacon and Park is the "imposing hunk" itself—the Shaw/54th Regiment Memorial, widely acknowledged as Boston's most outstanding piece of public art. A commemoration of the first free black regiment in the Union Army, the bronze sculpture portrays Colonel Robert Gould Shaw and twenty-three black infantry volunteers. In this remarkable work, the three-dimensional figures of Colonel Shaw and his prancing steed emerge from a bas-relief background of marching men. As the monument's many visitors know, something else is quite remarkable about this statue—the temptation to grab the bronze colonel's three-dimensional saber. Fortunately, Shaw's blade has been made of rubber since the late 1980s, which generally ensures that the sword will spring back into place after curious passersby yield to the urge.

The Shaw/54th Monument, sculpted by Augustus Saint-Gaudens, is the first stop on Boston's Black Heritage Trail. As such, its tale is told daily by park rangers leading visitors on the fourteen-site black history tour. A century's worth of books, poems, and songs also have told the story of the 54th Regiment, works by men such as Luis Emilio, Lincoln Kirstein, James Russell Lowell, Robert Lowell, and Charles Ives. Most recently, the stirring Civil War tale of the white Bostonian Robert Gould Shaw and the brave black regiment he commanded was portrayed in director Edward Zwick's Academy Award–winning 1989 film *Glory*.

Henry Lee, president of the Friends of the Public Garden and Common, explains the monument's enduring popularity. "The odd thing about the Shaw/54th is that it's both a great work of art and important piece of history. It honors the memory of Shaw and the 54th Regiment, their courage and service. But it's also a symbol of something deeper, of black and white working together for liberty and equality. It's an eternal reminder of people of both races who gave their lives together in harmony: a source of conscience to whites, a source of pride to blacks. And it's a reminder to carry on."

The first free black regiment of the Union Army was formed about two years into the Civil War. Shortly after President Lincoln issued the Emancipation Proclamation, in January 1863, Secretary of War Edwin Stanton accepted a petition from Governor John Andrew of Massachusetts requesting permission to form a regiment of black soldiers in Boston. By May of that year, the 54th Regiment of Massachusetts Volunteer Infantry had been created—and was actively drilling and ready to march into battle.

It was not the first black regiment in America, but it was the first Union grouping of free black volunteers—soldiers fighting to emancipate their black brothers and sisters, end slavery, and perhaps even to prove their equal abilities to white Civil War soldiers. There was certainly an abolitionist sentiment supporting the 54th's formation: Boston was a hotbed of anti-slavery agitation, and the governor himself a staunch abolitionist. But those

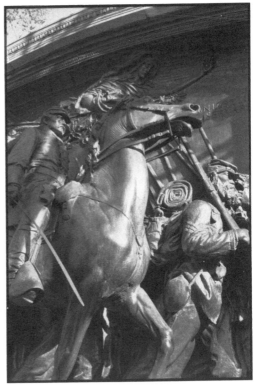

The Shaw/54th Regiment Memorial, commemorating the first free black regiment in the Union Army, is arguably Boston's finest piece of public art.

were not the only reasons. "The 54th was recruited in part because the Union was losing so badly by 1862," explains Marilyn Richardson, former curator of the Museum of Afro American History. "Blacks had volunteered for service before then, but were turned down. And, of course, there was a pay differential between white and black soldiers."

Black abolitionist Frederick Douglass played a major part in recruiting for the 54th. Much of that recruiting was done at the African Meeting House on Beacon Hill. Dozens of men from Boston's African-American population volunteered for the 54th, joined by hundreds of black volunteers from as far afield as Canada, the Caribbean, and Detroit. By the war's end, some 180,000 blacks had joined the Union forces, forming 10 percent of the total Union Army.

Selected as the 54th Regiment's commanding officer was Robert Gould Shaw, a twenty-five-year-old Bostonian and Harvard dropout. Son of a prominent abolitionist family, Shaw already had seen action in two battles. Despite initial misgivings and his recent marriage, he agreed to lead the 54th, and proceeded to train the men rigorously at Camp Meigs in Readville, near the modern-day neighborhood of Hyde Park.

The 1989 motion picture *Glory* both succeeds and fails in bringing the 54th Regiment to life. On the positive side was the film's faithful outline of the regiment's fateful story: the development of mutual respect and care between Shaw and the troops; the rampant racism in both Northern and Southern armies; the 54th's pride and military prowess; and their glorious departure march down Beacon Street, on May 28, 1863, hailed by 20,000 spectators as they headed toward the Boston docks.

The grisly battle scenes, including the regiment's final assault on Fort Wagner, South Carolina, are also surprisingly true to life, thanks largely to the contemporary Civil War reenactment groups who participated. It was during the futile night siege of Fort Wagner, on July 19, 1863, that Shaw and many of his men were slaughtered by Confederate troops. The soldiers in the enormous, impenetrable seaside fortress outnumbered their Union invaders two to one. Shaw's body was hurled into a mass grave, along with those of his black comrades. Shaw's parents later refused proposals to extricate the colonel's body and give it a special, separate burial; they were sure their son "Rob" would have chosen to remain with his men.

One of *Glory*'s main failures, however, relates to the African-American soldiers portrayed. Though the names and faces of the 54th's black soldiers—including two of Frederick Douglass's sons—were readily available, the film used fictional black characters instead. New Bedford Sergeant William Carney, for example, the first African-American to win the Medal of Honor, was not represented in the film. Carney was rewarded for brave combat and for saving the regiment flag as he barely escaped death on the Fort Wagner battlefield. "To tell the story of the 54th without Sergeant Carney," claims Marilyn Richardson, "is like telling the story of the Boston Massacre without Crispus Attucks," referring to the colonial African-American who was the first to die in that 1770 skirmish.

It's significant that both *Glory* and the 1897 bronze memorial dedicated to Shaw and the 54th leave the real black soldiers anonymous, while depicting Shaw clearly and well. In the case of the Shaw/54th Memorial, the renowned sculptor Augustus Saint-Gaudens claimed solid artistic reasons: he could fit only twenty-three black marching infantrymen in the final version of his intricately detailed, bronze bas-relief, though some one thousand once swelled the ranks of the 54th. In the artist's view those twenty-three black faces had to represent a broad array of physical types. (Saint-Gaudens was often seen pursuing black strangers walking in the streets near his New York City studio to convince them to model for his head studies.)

Creating a grand memorial statue to the martyrs of the 54th Regiment was a commission granted to Saint-Gaudens, but not an idea created by him. In 1865, some black veterans and citizens of South Carolina attempted to create a monument to Shaw near Fort Wagner itself. Though that plan failed, a group of Bostonians—including Governor John Andrew, Senator Charles Sumner, Colonel Henry Lee, and Joshua B. Smith (a former fugitive slave who once worked for the Shaw family)—began raising funds for a memorial in Boston.

"Talk about bureaucracy, and talk about taking a long time!" exclaims Henry Lee, great-grandson of the concerned Bostonian who helped raise money for the memorial. It took another nineteen years and a public subscription purse of $22,620.95 before young sculptor Saint-Gaudens was hired to begin the project. Another delay came from the artist: the memorial project was supposed to take two years, but Saint-Gaudens took fourteen. By the time the memorial was dedicated, many of those most intimately involved were dead—or precariously close to it.

Saint-Gaudens, who began his illustrious artistic career as a cameo cutter, was hired to create a classic equestrian statue of Shaw alone. Shaw's family objected, however, insisting the colonel be portrayed with his men. Saint-Gaudens then faced the challenge of creating an emotionally moving, physically animated army in bronze—not to mention fusing a bas-relief sculpture of twenty-three black infantrymen with a three-dimensional figure of Shaw on horseback. As a result, the artist spent many of those fourteen years thinking about, not actually modeling, the monument.

Dr. Edwin Gittleman, a University of Massachusetts professor and scholar of Shaw and the 54th, admires Saint-Gaudens's mix of realism and allegory in the memorial. "There's the symbolic floating figure on top holding poppies and an olive branch—death and peace. Then there's the photographic detail. Look at the men's knapsacks, and Shaw's tunic, filled with creases and wrinkles. It suggests a civilian soldier, not the spit and polish of a professional soldier. There are also more rifles than figures you can account for—though each rifle is accurately presented. This suggests the statue should be taken figuratively, not literally. Still, the memorial is accurate in a way that's almost obsessive, when compared to the free and easy style of the film."

Saint-Gaudens's stunning sculpture was cast in bronze and set in a marble and granite terrace fashioned by celebrated Boston architect Charles F. McKim for another $20,000. The structure was built around the two elms that still grace the monument's front porch. On Decoration Day, May 31, 1897, two hundred black Union veterans—from the 54th Regiment, the 55th Infantry, and the 5th Cavalry—triumphantly marched through Boston during a day-long gala celebration of the monument's official unveiling. A few surviving monument committeemen, like treasurer Edward Atkinson, were there. So too were illustrious speakers like the governor, the mayor of Boston, Colonel Henry Lee, and philosopher William James, who had two brothers who served as officers in the 54th.

Though contemporary accounts suggest that Booker T. Washington, founder and president of Tuskegee Institute in Alabama, gave the day's most electrifying oration, his words were not immortalized on the monument. Instead, the thoughts of white men—like poet James Russell Lowell, Harvard president Charles W. Eliot, and former governor John Andrew—were inscribed on the stone. The names of the 54th's white officers were listed, but nary one black soldier was named.

That error was not rectified until 1984, when the names of the black infantrymen of the 54th killed at Fort Wagner in 1863 were added to the back of the memorial. An early-1980s campaign by the Committee to Save the Shaw/54th was the fund-raiser behind that long-overdue inscription. Eventually collecting some $200,000, the Save-the-Shaw Committee also helped restore the badly deteriorating memorial, and provided an endowment for ongoing maintenance. The effort also helped save many of Boston's other historic memorials, by inspiring the city's Adopt-a-Statue program, which began in 1987.

Visitors can learn more about the memorial today from a variety of sources. The Shaw/54th is the first of fourteen stops on the Black Heritage Trail walking tour, given by park rangers from the Boston African American National Historic Site. The free tour visits many Beacon Hill sites connected to black social and political history in Boston, including Underground Railroad stops, a gambling house, the first integrated public school, and the homes of famous citizens.

Across the street from the Shaw/54th Memorial is the State House Hall of Flags, where a detailed photographic replica of one of the 54th's flags is on display, open free to public viewing. The State House has three of the 54th's original flags—including the one Sergeant Carney saved in battle—stored in a controlled environment in the Massachusetts State Archives at Columbia Point. It is hoped that eventually these original flags, along with other state flags, will be on display again in the hall.

The finest place to view other works by Saint-Gaudens, including numerous plaster casts for the Shaw/54th, is the Saint-Gaudens National Historic Site in Cornish, New Hampshire. Saint-Gaudens's elegant country estate is open from Memorial Day weekend through October 31; call (603) 675-2175 for more information.

THE ESSENTIALS

ADDRESS: Boston Common, at Beacon and Park streets, Boston.

TELEPHONE: Boston African American National Historic Site, (617) 742-5415.

VISITOR INFORMATION: Memorial accessible to the public at all times. Free Black Heritage Trail tours available year-round, though schedules vary with season; call Boston African American National Historic Site for information. Monument is wheelchair accessible from Beacon Street.

35 The Black Heritage Trail

THOUGH IT'S still not as well known as the Freedom Trail, the Black Heritage Trail—a ninety-minute, 1.6-mile trek through nineteenth-century Boston—is one of the most extraordinary walking tours in town. Its treasures bring to life tales of secret tunnels, runaway slaves, fiery abolitionist orators, and military massacres. The trail evokes stories of early desegregation battles in Boston's public schools, the successes of former slaves, and the best gambling hoax on Beacon Hill, and includes the largest concentration of pre–Civil War black historic sites in the United States.

Moreover, it's the only U.S. trail that commemorates the development of a free African-American community with extant historic buildings—as opposed to small bronze markers reminding visitors what *used* to stand on this site.

The first aspect of the Black Heritage Trail to both confound and delight visitors often is its location. Since Boston's African-American community has been associated with areas like Roxbury, the South End, and Mattapan in recent decades, to some it's surprising to find the Black Heritage Trail meandering around Beacon Hill. But the fact is, Boston was home to one of the three largest communities of free blacks in the United States from the late eighteenth to the late nineteenth century; and during that period the north slope of Beacon Hill was an African-American neighborhood of major national significance.

Enslaved black Africans first arrived in Boston in 1638, only eight years after the founding of the town. As the century moved on, and as more and more blacks gained their freedom, a community of free blacks began to form in the North End. Prince Hall, founder of the African Lodge of Masons, was one such North Ender. He's buried in that neighborhood's Copp's Hill Burying Ground.

The American Revolution was a turning point in the emancipation process in Massachusetts. Individual blacks—such as poet Phillis Wheatley, Bunker Hill hero Peter Salem, and Crispus Attucks, a victim of the Boston Massacre—gained recognition in that period, and slavery was outlawed by the Commonwealth in 1783.

As Boston's free black community increased, it outgrew the North End neighborhood, and many black families began to move to the West End and the north slope of Beacon Hill. Throughout the nineteenth century, this Beacon Hill area grew into a tight-knit community where the battles of the day were played out: struggles to establish equal education, fight American slavery, and create independent supportive institutions by and for blacks.

★　★　★

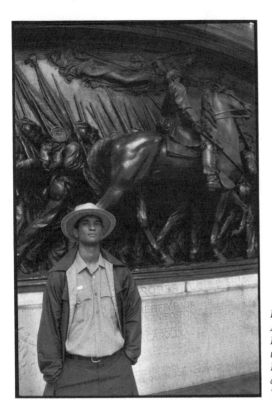

Rangers from the Boston African American National Historic Site guide visitors through fourteen Beacon Hill landmarks that comprise the Black Heritage Trail.

Soon after Howard and Sue Bailey Thurman moved to Boston in 1953, they became interested in the area's rich African-American heritage. Howard Thurman became the first black chaplain at Boston University, and in that role provided inspiration for the young Martin Luther King, Jr. Sue Bailey Thurman helped found the American Museum of Negro History and the Negro Freedom Trails of Boston, forerunners of today's Museum of Afro American History and the Black Heritage Trail. The latter organizations were spurred on by the events of 1963—the centennial of the Emancipation Proclamation and the year of the great March on Washington.

According to local black historian and longtime state representative Byron Rushing, "After meeting with a group of friends, doing research and developing the idea, Sue and her daughter, Anne Chiarenza, published a poster-sized map. It was called the 'Negro Freedom *Trails* of Boston'— not *trail*—because it included sites related to African-Americans on Beacon Hill, in Cambridge, in Roxbury . . . I remember it even included Symphony Hall, because of Roland Hayes, the famous American tenor. You couldn't walk it . . . unless you were a hiker!"

Meanwhile, J. Marcus Mitchell and his wife Gaunzetta—who had moved to Boston in 1947—had a similar plan. Marcus Mitchell had helped to create an artists' group called the Boston Negro Artists Association. In trying to formulate ways to celebrate the Emancipation Proclamation's centennial, Mitchell organized history and art exhibits, and set up another trail that followed black art and history in Boston.

Around 1964, the Mitchells and Mrs. Thurman met. Within a relatively short time, Sue Bailey Thurman's first dream became reality. The American Museum of Negro History opened, with the Charles Street Meeting House as its home and Marcus Mitchell as curator and director. At the time, the meetinghouse was owned by the Unitarian Universalist Association. With assistance from historians at the Boston Athenaeum, the Society for the Preservation of New England Antiquities, and the Beacon Hill Civic Association, more research was done into historic African-American sites, especially in the dense Beacon Hill area.

The second dream—developing the black version of Boston's Freedom Trail—followed naturally, and the Mitchells' concept of the trail, geographically and chronologically more focused than Thurman's, began to predominate. Because the area's history spoke volumes about abolitionism, black families, African-American neighborhoods, the struggle for freedom, political developments, and education, Beacon Hill became the center.

The last major change for the trail in the late 1960s was its name. The word *Negro* had fallen out of favor, both within the black community and without, so the museum became the Museum of Afro American History, and the walking tour was called the Black Heritage Trail.

The Mitchells typed up the first trail guide in 1968. It was a small booklet that concentrated on Beacon Hill, but also looped into the North End. On May 9 of that year, Marcus Mitchell led a crowd of some four hundred people on the trek. The Black Heritage Trail, in something akin to its modern incarnation, had been officially established.

Meanwhile, Henry Hampton, executive producer of the documentary *Eyes on the Prize* and honorary chair of the Museum of Afro American History, discovered that the old African Meeting House—which had been used as a synagogue on Beacon Hill since the turn of the century—was coming up for sale. Knowing Representative Byron Rushing's reputation as an ace fund-raiser, Hampton asked him to join the cause.

Thanks to the success of those fund-raising efforts, the African Meeting House—the oldest standing black church building in America and the core of the black Beacon Hill community—was purchased in 1972 by the Museum of Afro American History. In 1974, it became a National Landmark. The structure was renovated, and opened to the public in 1987.

These events had major effects on the Black Heritage Trail. The fact that the African Meeting House—the trail's major site, and the only trail structure owned by the museum—was a National Landmark gave the tour added prestige. That, in turn, helped attract people involved in Boston's U.S. Bicentennial celebrations, as well as the National Park Service.

As part of the nation's 1976 Bicentennial, the city funded a new Black Heritage Trail pamphlet. Written by Rushing, it was geographically broader than today's trail. Among the non–Beacon Hill sites included were the Copp's Hill Burying Ground in the North End, and the Emancipation Group statue in Park Square. Clearly, the trail still needed fine-tuning.

When yet another version of the trail was hammered out over the next four years—thanks in part to new information culled from intense research and archaeological digs—Rushing and the museum's board finally agreed on two criteria for inclusion. First, the trail would not commemorate buildings that were no longer standing. Second, the trail would include, in Rushing's words, "no 'Phillis Wheatley slept here' history. The site had to be more connected to the black community than that. That criterion eliminated the Old South Meeting House, where Phillis was once a member."

In 1980, the historic credentials of the trail were further enhanced when an act of Congress made these Beacon Hill stops the Boston African American National Historic Site. A new brochure was developed. And by 1982 the museum and the National Park Service had begun a cooperative partnership that endures to this day.

The Boston African American National Historic Site is unusual, as national parks go. There are no valleys, no fields, no mountains. Moreover, the land is not owned by the federal government: eleven sites on the trail are privately owned, two are retained by the city, and one belongs to the Museum of Afro American History.

Still, the Black Heritage Trail is an eye-opening and quite literally breathtaking trek that generally takes visitors less than two hours to travel, either alone or accompanied by a Park Service guide. One word of caution and conscience: please respect the privately owned sites by restraining your impulses to look, or get invited, inside; except for the Smith School and the African Meeting House, interior visits are not allowed.

The first stop on the trail, the **Shaw/54th Regiment Memorial,** is also its newest structure. Sculpted by Augustus Saint-Gaudens over a fourteen-year period, the compelling bas relief—considered by many to be Boston's finest piece of public art—was dedicated in 1897. It commemorates the Bostonian Colonel Robert Gould Shaw, and the volunteer, all-black 54th Regiment, many of whom were killed in their 1863 attack on Fort Wagner, South Carolina. (Their heroic Civil War tale was loosely depicted in the 1989 film *Glory*.)

George Middleton also led an all-black company of soldiers, "the Bucks of America." Middleton was an African-American jockey and horse-breaker, and the war was the American Revolution. **The George Middleton House,** at 5–7 Pinckney Street, dates from 1797, and is the oldest remaining house on Beacon Hill built by an African-American.

Although the inside of the old **Phillips School** has been renovated into pricey condos, the exterior still bears the clear carving "1824," the year this Boston schoolhouse was built. Until 1855, the Phillips, located on the corner of Anderson and Pinckney streets, was a white-only school; when educational segregation was declared illegal in 1855, it became one of the city's first integrated schools.

At 86 Pinckney is the **John J. Smith House.** Smith was a hairdresser-barber whose shop was frequently visited by black abolitionist activists, fugitive slaves, and the illustrious Charles Sumner during the turbulent antebellum period. After the Civil War, Smith was elected to the Massachusetts House of Representatives.

The Charles Street Meeting House, at Mount Vernon and Charles streets, played a vital role in the development of Boston's African-American culture. In 1835, white abolitionist Timothy Gilbert filled his front-row pew there with black Baptist friends, causing an uproar in the white establishment and leading to the founding of Tremont Temple Baptist Church, the first integrated church in America. From 1876 until 1939, the meetinghouse was home to the large black congregation of the Charles Street A.M.E. Church.

At 66 Phillips Street is the popular **Lewis and Harriet Hayden House.** Born into slavery, Lewis Hayden escaped on the Underground Railroad, resettled in Boston, and became a fervent abolitionist. The Haydens used their home as a fugitive slave station, and claimed to keep kegs of explosive gunpowder in their basement to protect those fugitives. They hosted antislavery celebrities like Harriet Beecher Stowe, John Brown, and Harriet Tubman. The house has been beautifully preserved and maintained, especially by present owners John and Mary Gier.

The stories about **Coburn's Gaming House,** at the corner of Phillips and Irving streets, are almost as wild as those about the Haydens'. Some are probably even true. Coburn, a clothing dealer by vocation, hired Boston architect Asher Benjamin to design his house in 1843. Shortly thereafter, he adapted part of this structure into a private gambling center for wealthy white men. The handsome (illegal) profits were invested in black culture—including Coburn's pocket, his church, and according to some accounts, abolitionist causes.

The centerpiece of the Black Heritage Trail, and the only building on the trail owned by a black organization, is the **African Meeting House,** at 8 Smith Court. The stately yet simple brick structure was built by free black laborers in 1806, and used as an African-American church, meetinghouse, school, community center, lecture hall, and center for antislavery activities. Speakers there included a who's who of abolitionism, from William Lloyd Garrison and Frederick Douglass to Angelina Grimké and Maria Miller Stewart. Today it's an active center for cultural events, with changing museum exhibits on the ground floor.

A stone's throw from the Meeting House are five **Smith Court** residences, which are considered typical of the homes of black Bostonians in the nineteenth century. Number 10 was built for black chimney sweep Joseph Scarlett in 1853. The enterprising Scarlett owned many pieces of real estate, including Numbers 7 and 7A. The double house at Number 3 was purchased by James Scott, a black clothing dealer, and rented for five years to William Nell, America's first published black historian.

The final stop on the trail, at Smith Court and Joy Street, is headquarters for the **Museum of Afro American History** and the **Boston African American National Historic Site.** Opened in 1835 as the **Abiel Smith School,** it was Boston's first public school built exclusively for black children. When public school segregation was outlawed in 1855, the Smith School was closed. It later served as a city storage area and as a post for several veterans' groups, including black veterans of the Civil War.

Over some thirty years of its existence, the Black Heritage Trail has clearly changed for the better. Moreover, members of the Park Service and museum staffs are planning further improvements and refinements, including "Phase II" renovations of the African Meeting House, the Smith School, and the adjoining courtyard. New cooperative educational programs are in the works, along with efforts to increase public awareness of the site. Meanwhile, the vibrant African Meeting House has been kept in continual cultural and community use.

In the eyes of Ken Heidelberg, site manager of the Boston African American National Historic Site, the greatest joys of the trail are still in visitors' reactions. "I hear it again and again," he reports. "Things like, I didn't know that! Why isn't that in the history books? You mean *all* of that *happened?*"

THE ESSENTIALS

ADDRESS: Trail begins at Shaw/54th Memorial, on Beacon Street near the intersection with Park Street, and extends across north slope of Beacon Hill, Boston. Headquarters at 46 Joy Street, Boston.

TELEPHONE: Boston African American National Historic Site, (617) 742-5415; Museum of Afro American History, (617) 742-1854.

VISITOR INFORMATION: African Meeting House open 10:00 A.M.–4:00 P.M. daily. Free; donations encouraged. Free ranger-guided Black Heritage Trail tours leave daily at 10:00 A.M., noon, and 2:00 P.M. Memorial Day through Labor Day, Monday through Friday only in winter; call in advance to confirm times or arrange group tours. Free self-guided tour brochures available through National Park Service office, (617) 742-5415. Trail extremely difficult to navigate by wheelchair due to slope, bumpy sidewalks, and erratic curb cuts on Beacon Hill; ground floor and restrooms at African Meeting House wheelchair accessible (plans are under way to make the meetinghouse sanctuary accessible); Abiel Smith School currently not wheelchair accessible; call about access plan in progress.

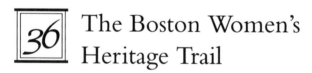

The Boston Women's Heritage Trail

IN SOME ways, the Boston Women's Heritage Trail is a lot like its older cousins, the Freedom Trail and the Black Heritage Trail. All three are downtown walking tours that lead visitors past venerable old Boston sites, educating and entertaining guests with colorful stories about the city's rich history. All three evoke Boston-based heroes—dead ones, for the most part. Like the Freedom Trail, the Boston Women's Heritage Trail—which made its debut in May of 1990—takes visitors to the Paul Revere House, the Granary Burying Ground, the Old South Meeting House, and Faneuil

Hall. Like the Black Heritage Trail, it includes sites on Beacon Hill, such as the African Meeting House and the Lewis and Harriet Hayden House, both nineteenth-century centers for abolitionist activity.

If all the Boston Women's Heritage Trail did was highlight some of the sites of its kindred treks, it would still be an important educational tool. But the scope and goals of the city's newest historic tour—which includes four different neighborhood walks and forty-six separate sites—are far grander and far more focused than that. One glance at the opening lines of the trail's self-guiding guidebook—an essential tool, since the trail is not yet guided by National Park rangers nor marked by a painted line—explains it all: "Women's lives and achievements have enriched the history of Boston for almost four centuries, yet the significance of their stories is often over-looked."

The result as experienced on the trail itself is twofold. When visitors pass sites they recognize from other tours, the tales they encounter have a decidedly different twist. At the Revere House, for example, people learn about Rachel Revere, who held the family and business together while her husband embroiled himself in politics and industry. The Granary Burying Ground stop focuses on Ben Franklin's mother and Boston's storytelling "Mother Goose," rather than on John Hancock, Sam Adams, and the men slain in the Boston Massacre. The Old South is heralded as the church of once-enslaved poet Phillis Wheatley, not the rallying place of raucous

The statue of free-thinking Anne Hutchinson and her daughter outside the State House is one of the few public memorials to famous women in Boston.

Boston Tea Party—goers. Faneuil Hall, "the Cradle of Liberty," becomes the place where an Omaha named Suzette LaFlesche spoke out against America's cruel "Indian" reservation system in 1879—and where the majestic statue of Samuel Adams is curiously missing a credit for its sculptor, Anne Whitney.

But the Boston Women's Heritage Trail offers far more than just a new perspective on familiar old places. More than half of the historic landmarks on the trail are not covered in most downtown walking tours at all. These range from the Telephone Exchange on Harrison Avenue, where eight thousand female employees waged a successful strike in 1919, to the one-time Byron Street offices of the Women's International League for Peace and Freedom, whose members included activist Florence Luscomb and Emily Greene Balch, the second woman to earn the Nobel Peace Prize.

"In that way, we borrowed more from the Black Heritage Trail than the Freedom Trail," explains Meg Campbell, who originated the women's trail idea in 1988. Although the accomplishments of wealthy white Boston men have been documented everywhere, the contributions of African-Americans, Asian Americans, Hispanics, Native Americans, and women from a variety of socioeconomic backgrounds have often gone unrecognized. "The idea of this trail," finishes Campbell, "is to make some of those people visible."

The idea of creating a trail to commemorate women's accomplishments in Boston first occurred to Campbell in the mid-1980s. At the time, she was a senior research analyst at the State House, and her children were attending Boston public schools. Campbell's concern began when she noticed children touring the State House; she became acutely aware of the paucity of positive female images available to children in and around the building. Inside, she saw only one woman represented—in a statue of an anonymous nurse comforting a wounded soldier. Outside were the only public sculptures of women in the entire city—Anne Hutchinson and Mary Dyer, two seventeenth-century women who were respectively banished and hanged for their outspoken and "unorthodox" views on faith. "There were no images of women of power in the seat of power in Massachusetts," observed Campbell. "So I wondered, What is the message here for children?"

In February of 1988, Campbell went to work for District A superintendent Diana Lam as a Boston Public School writing specialist. School administrator Isabel Mendes had already been encouraging the idea of doing something special in the schools for Women's History Month, celebrated in March every year. The group agreed to do something different and new, perhaps even pursue a grant. But the clincher came when Campbell announced, "I have this idea I've kind of been saving, but let's all do it. In the spirit of community." The Boston Women's Heritage Trail was semi-officially born.

Other visions of a women's history trail had been proposed before. In 1984, for instance, author Mary Maynard and her daughter Mary-Lou included a "Women's Freedom Trail" in their book, the useful and whimsical *Hassle-Free Boston: A Manual for Women*. As far back as 1978, Maynard had written about stops on such a trail in her columns for *Equal Times,* the now-defunct women's newspaper. But the trail we know and walk today was a product of the Boston Public School Department. Building a walking tour that visitors could see and students could travel, utilizing statues, markers, and other public art to commemorate historic women with Boston connections, was part of a broader plan to incorporate the contributions of women of all classes, races, careers, and historic periods into the public school curriculum. In a way, developing that part of the curriculum—especially for the very formative grades four through eight—was the "inside" goal; the trail was more a vehicle or catalyst than an end in itself.

With the help of a grant from the U.S. Department of Education, Boston students and teachers helped research and identify the accomplishments of local women, voted for their "favorite" historical figures, participated in related activities, and, in short, helped create the Boston Women's Heritage Trail. In July, 1989, educator Patricia C. Morris was hired as project director. Under her watchful eye, methodology and goals began to change and evolve. Though the grant specified that six elementary and middle schools would find and identify twelve women, and make twelve plaques in their honor, the numbers and interest grew. In the end, according to Morris, some seventeen schools, forty-two teachers and approximately a thousand children were involved, representing every neighborhood in Boston. Women and men from local schools, colleges, historic sites, arts organizations, museums, the National Park Service, and the city of Boston also contributed to the effort.

"Resident historian" Polly Kaufman—a theoretically retired Boston educator who was simultaneously teaching at the University of Massachusetts and writing her most recent women's history book—was hired to write the trail booklet. As Kaufman listened to and absorbed all the information given her by various sources, a major problem emerged: many more women's names were uncovered than ever imagined. Moreover, the researchers discovered that many of the accomplishments of women were done by groups—"ladies" clubs, unions, societies, and other organizations. The result was a nomination list of 123 women, many with organizational affiliations. Participating Boston students were then asked to vote for their 10 favorite women. Though many chose women from their own neighborhoods, the highest number of votes went to poet Phillis Wheatley.

The first version of the trail guide was published for the Women's Heritage Trail's grand opening on May 30, 1990. It highlighted twenty accomplished women—from Amy Beach (1867–1944), the first American woman to write a symphony, to Muriel Snowden (1916–1988), cofounder of Roxbury's Freedom House, and a major force behind interracial understanding and cooperation in Boston. Fifty-nine institutions founded by or for women were also listed. The gala May events included a parade of more than two hundred students and teachers, who marched with banners, cheers, and the occasional period costume, from City Hall to the State House.

The second, current and expanded edition of the guidebook features seventy-one women and fifteen related organizations. It has stops at forty-six sites, refers to multitudes of others, and deals with four full centuries of female life in Boston. In the latter respect, the Women's Heritage Trail is much more ambitious than its kindred walking tours: the Freedom Trail includes sixteen stops, all of which are tied to the American Revolution and the early national period; the Black Heritage Trail has fourteen sites, neatly and logically focused on the Beacon Hill community of the nine-teenth century.

Fortunately, the lengthy Boston Women's Heritage Trail is divided into four easier walks; each features roughly a dozen sites and a central theme, and can be covered in ninety minutes or less. When guided walking tours are given—primarily during Women's History Month and the summer tourist season—most of the guides limit their walks to select downtown stops, much as is done on "short form" Freedom Trail tours.

The Downtown Walk, with fourteen sites, illustrates "The Search for Equal Rights." It includes more Freedom and Black Heritage Trail sites than any of the other loops—all considered, of course, from a female perspective. Women who spoke out against slavery, for women's suffrage, for Native American rights, and for rights for the mentally ill are all included, featuring some familiar names like Anne Hutchinson, Phillis Wheatley, Dorothea Dix, and Elizabeth Foster Vergoose (Boston's "Mother Goose").

The North End Walk presents "A Diversity of Cultures." It spans ten sites and tells of the variety of ethnic groups that have lived in Boston's oldest neighborhood. It ranges from Rachel Walker Revere and the Revo-lutionary period to various Irish, Jewish, and Italian women and their civic groups, which emerged with the influx of nineteenth- and twentieth-century immigrants. Honorees include Pauline Agassiz Shaw, founder of America's first trade school; internationally known nineteenth-century actress Charlotte Cushman; and Clementina Poto Langone, who continu-ally aided twentieth-century Italian immigrants and the unemployed.

The South Cove/Chinatown Walk is arguably the most interesting, if only because it includes so many sites rarely visited by most Bostonians. Twelve stops tell of "Action for Economic and Social Justice," and include tales of educational reform, women's unions, women in a Catholic reli-gious community, telephone operators, and garment workers. Two favor-ite spots on this walk are actually empty ones: the site of the old Denison House on Tyler Street, where Amelia Earhart did social work in the late 1920s; and the corner of Beach and Tyler streets, where Phillis Wheatley first landed from a slave ship in 1761, debarking on a long-gone wharf. Another stop, at 15 West Street, shows where Elizabeth Peabody, "the grandmother of the American kindergarten," once ran her bookshop, a hotbed of nineteenth-century Transcendentalist and feminist thought. Yet another site showcases a four-story mural, called *Unity and Community,* honoring the work of Asian American women.

The Beacon Hill Walk features "Writers, Artists, and Activists" and ten different sites. Its highlights include the studio of sculptor Anne Whitney, the last Boston home of Louisa May Alcott, and the Under-ground Railroad site through which Ellen Craft escaped from slavery. Many of these sites focus on women's efforts throughout the nineteenth and twentieth centuries to bring peace to the world and freedom to its diverse peoples: on Byron Street is the old headquarters of the Massachusetts Women's International League for Peace and Freedom; the African Meeting House, off Joy Street, was a center for abolitionist and feminist thinkers like Maria Stewart; and Julia Ward Howe, whose many accomplishments included initiating the idea of Mother's Day as a day to demonstrate for peace, once lived on Chestnut Street.

Unlike the Freedom and Black Heritage trails, the Boston Women's Heritage Trail includes the former locations of buildings that have since been destroyed; many of its sites are empty lots or simple markers that tell what once was there. And though this women's trail, like the other tours, focuses on deceased heroes, the women who molded Boston's newest historic walking tour made one notable exception: Rose Kennedy's birthplace was included on the North End trail; the Kennedy matriarch, after all, had reached her one hundredth birthday in 1990, the year the trail made its debut.

Since the trail was founded, two separate entities have evolved from the original project. The board-led corporation known as the Boston Women's Heritage Trail focuses on developing school curricula, presenting slide shows on Boston women's history and distributing the trail guide and related materials. The National Women's Heritage Foundation is headed by Patricia Morris, who directed the trail project during its first, formative two years. Morris trains college and high school students to conduct guided walking and trolley tours; she also leads feminist workshops, offers dramatic presentations, and gives lectures, along with other qualified colleagues.

The official trail organizations have sparked interest in Boston women's history—and other women's history tours. Mary Smoyer, executive secretary of the Boston Women's Heritage Trail, has independently developed a women's history trail and brochure on the Boston neighborhood of Jamaica Plain, available by calling (617) 522-2872. The National Park Service regularly offers women's history tours of Freedom Trail sites as well as other special activities and programs related to women in Boston history; call the Boston National Historical Park's downtown or Charlestown headquarters for more information, at (617) 242-5688 or (617) 242-5692. The city of Boston's park rangers conduct a "Women's Herstory Walk" on the Boston Common and Granary Burying Grounds (telephone [617] 635-7383), while independent tour groups are incorporating women's stories in their tours as well. One of the best is Boston by Foot's "Great Women of Boston" walking tour, offered each year as a special tribute to Mother's Day as well as by special arrangement (telephone [617] 367-2345).

All of this activity furthers the goals of the Boston Women's Heritage Trail project. "Women have always been half the population—and always done at least half of the work," explains Patricia Morris. "But that fact has been undermined in our textbooks, our school curriculum, our public art. The issue in women's history, and the impetus behind the trail, is that we've lost the women and need to rediscover them."

ADDRESS: Trail includes sites in four Boston neighborhoods: Downtown, Beacon Hill, the North End, and South Cove/Chinatown.

TELEPHONE: Guidebooks and general information available from Boston Women's Heritage Trail, (617) 522-2872; related slide shows and lectures, (617) 646-4769. Books, guided walking tours, trolley tours, and other special events available through National Women's Heritage Foundation, (617) 731-5597.

VISITOR INFORMATION: Self-guided tour possible anytime; guidebooks available via mail (see above), at Boston National Park Service headquarters, 15 State Street, and in many downtown bookstores. Guided tours available by appointment for a moderate fee; call (617) 731-5597. Much of tour, which passes exteriors of sites, is fairly wheelchair accessible via curb cuts and sidewalks; some minor rerouting needed; Beacon Hill segment is very difficult for wheelchairs due to hills and bumpy sidewalks; Faneuil Hall Marketplace area also has bumpy surfaces.

37 Hanover Street

HANOVER STREET is best known today as the heart of Boston's Italian North End—home to dozens of quality Italian restaurants, interesting and unusual shops, and joyous summer street festivals. What's less immediately apparent to the casual visitor is the rich history that predates this neighborhood's most recent identity. For Hanover is not only the heart of the Italian North End—it's also the heart of Boston's oldest neighborhood.

The North End began as a center for maritime commerce and colonial housing in the seventeenth century, home to many middle- and upper-class residents of English descent who attended Puritan meetinghouses or Anglican churches. After the departure of a multitude of wealthy Tories following the American Revolution, the area became a center for craftspeople, tradespeople, and various shipping and mercantile enterprises. Then, throughout the nineteenth century, the North End welcomed a variety of foreign-born settlers, including large numbers of Irish Catholics, Eastern European Jews, and Italian Catholics. It was not until the early twentieth century that Italian-Americans became the dominant North End group.

Hanover Street itself is one of Boston's oldest public roads. As such, its buildings have included Revolution-era churches, colonial taverns, late Victorian casinos, and seedy sailors' delights. Among the street's most famous historic residents have been the Reverend Cotton Mather, Ben-

A hired horse and carriage take visitors through historic Hanover Street, toward St. Stephen's Church, in the North End.

jamin Franklin, colonial patriot Dr. Joseph Warren, and merchant Eben D. Jordan, founder of the local department store Jordan Marsh. (Jordan's first small dry goods store, begun when he was nineteen, once stood at 168 Hanover.) The road also boasts one of Boston's most infamous ghosts—poor Peter Rugg, whose spectral horse and carriage keep mysteriously passing by his Hanover Street home, from whence he and they disappeared in the 1770s.

Exactly when Hanover Street was laid out is not certain. What is clear is that from the earliest days of Boston's settlement—certainly from the 1630s or 1640s—it led up from the sea, bisected the North End, and terminated at what eventually became known as Tremont Street. During colonial times, Hanover was interrupted by a creek that ran from Boston's Town Cove to Mill Pond—an area outlined today by Blackstone Street. (A short bridge enabled colonists to cross the creek and continue on Hanover toward Tremont). During the 1950s and 1960s, that southwestern section of Hanover was again interrupted first by the construction of the highway known as the Central Artery, then by the building of Government Center, which simultaneously obliterated its old terminus at Scollay Square on Tremont Street. Though many people assume that Hanover now ends at

Mother Anna's Restaurant and the Artery, a small, inconspicuous sector remains on the other side of the highway, passing near Haymarket and the Union Oyster House.

Twentieth-century construction was not the only activity to change the face of Hanover Street, of course. Many of its oldest buildings were lost either to fires—the worst being in 1676, 1679, 1690, 1692, 1775, and 1835—or to a road-widening project after the Civil War.

One of Hanover Street's earliest epithets was "the Way to the Winnisimet [Chelsea] Ferry." The ferry did indeed land at the foot of Hanover, on the site where USS *Constitution* was completed in 1797, and a U.S. Coast Guard base is located today. In 1708, when all of Boston's byways were given official names, modern Hanover was given three separate designations: from the ferry to Bennett Street it was called North Street (not to be confused with the North Street now found in the North End), from Bennett to Blackstone it was Middle Street, and from there to "the Sign of the Orange Tree," a colonial tavern that boasted Boston's first hackney coach stand, it was Hanover. In 1824, all three sections were united as Hanover, after the British royal family.

Retaining the name Hanover was an unusual act for 1824. In the years following the Revolution, many Boston streets were renamed in honor of the new Commonwealth and the new nation. King became State Street; Queen became Court; and Cornhill was renamed for General George Washington. Still, Hanover wasn't alone in the North End. The names of a variety of other nearby roads—including Fleet Street, Sun Court, and Prince Street—hark back to Old England and the monarchy to this day.

Throughout the seventeenth and eighteenth centuries, the North End was a favored residence of Boston's elite English settlers, as well as hardworking tradespeople. The much-despised British Governor Sir Edmund Andros (1637–1714) and the much-beloved patriot Dr. Joseph Warren (1741–1775) both had homes on the section of Hanover near present-day Government Center. The reverends Increase and Cotton Mather, pastors of the Old North Meeting House on North Square and outspoken religious leaders, also lived on Hanover, near Bennett Street. (The Old North Meeting House, known as "the church of the Mathers," was pulled down for firewood during the Revolution; it's often confused with the Old North Church of Paul Revere fame, which still stands on Salem Street.) At Union and Hanover, not far from the current home of the Bell in Hand Tavern, was the Blue Ball, where Josiah Franklin resided and dipped candles for a living. As might be expected, his son Ben was a frequent visitor.

Hanover Street was as well known for its churches as for its numerous taverns. Its most famous church was built in 1712, when the Old North Meeting House on North Square was becoming overcrowded. "Seventeen substantial mechanics" founded the New North Meeting House, at 401 Hanover Street. Built in 1714 and enlarged in 1730, the New North was redesigned by architect Charles Bulfinch between 1802 and 1804, making it the only Boston Bulfinch church still standing. The chandeliers inside are replicas of those in the new State House, which had also been designed by Bulfinch, only a few years before.

The church was originally Congregational, reflecting the area's Puritan roots. Though many guidebooks and a plaque outside state that Paul Revere and his family were among its members, there is no historic evidence to substantiate the claim; in 1804, however, a bell cast by Revere was hung in its belfry. In 1813, the church became Unitarian—as did many Congregational churches of the time—and remained so until 1849. Francis Parkman, father of the famous historian, was the minister during that period. By 1850, the North End was populated largely by Irish immigrants, who were followed by an influx of Portuguese and Italian settlers. The New North Meeting House eventually became a Roman Catholic house of worship, as St. Stephen's Church. Among that church's well-known members was Rose Fitzgerald Kennedy, who attended St. Stephen's as a child.

The church has undergone a variety of changes over the years. In 1870, the entire building was moved back twelve feet to accommodate the widening of Hanover Street. Two major fires occurred, in 1897 and 1929. By 1964, there was talk of tearing down the very worn old building. Fortunately, Richard Cardinal Cushing became involved, and helped raise funds to restore the historic structure to its original Bulfinch appearance. The Boston Society of Architects gave its Award for Historic Preservation to the cardinal in 1970, honoring the fine restoration work on this Hanover Street landmark.

While many of the North End's Irish Catholic citizens attended St. Stephen's, other immigrant groups adapted or constructed their own houses of worship as well. The growing Italian presence of the late nineteenth and early twentieth centuries was reflected in the church and "Peace Garden" at the corner of Hanover and Prince streets. Built in 1873, St. Leonard's was the first Italian Catholic church established in New England.

Meanwhile, across the street from St. Stephen's is the broad, tree-shaded Paul Revere Mall, created in 1933 as an urban renewal project. Built along the lines of a *prado*—a park where people congregate in a typical small Italian village—the mall had two purposes: one was to create space to reduce the risk of fire to nearby historic churches; a second was to design a welcome open place in an overly congested neighborhood. Today, the mall is a favorite resting place for mothers and fathers with baby carriages, playful kids, neighborhood seniors, and Freedom Trail hikers. The majestic equestrian statue of Paul Revere at its center was modeled by Cyrus Dallin in 1885, though not cast and put in place until 1940, when the project finally found financing through the George Robert White Fund. Earlier in this century, the mall was filled with old buildings, including a men's hotel called the Webster House. At that time, Hanover Street was still paved with stones and lined with streetcar tracks that stretched from the ferry landing to Scollay Square.

Clubs, casinos, pawn shops, and flop houses filled the Hanover Street section near Scollay Square up until the 1950s and early 1960s. Save for that long-gone sailors' district and the paved-over roads, longtime residents agree, Hanover has actually looked much the same throughout this century. "Years ago no one had bathtubs or toilets in their homes," explains Frank Gulla, who was born on Hanover Street in 1923, "and they packed more people into the living spaces. I do miss seeing the horse and wagons all loading down by Blackstone Street. Horse and wagons also delivered ice, oil, and coal. But most of the buildings haven't changed much—except that everything now is an Italian restaurant!"

In fact, more than thirty sit-down Italian restaurants can be found on Hanover Street today, arguably the largest number on any street in the city. These range from pastry and coffee shops like Mike's and the Modern to popular restaurants like the European, the Daily Catch, Caffe Paradiso, and Giacomo's. One of Hanover Street's newest eating establishments, the posh Paolo Restaurant, is attached to an entertainment complex called the Theater Lobby and Cabaret.

Like its restaurants, Hanover Street's summer festivals draw both locals and guests from around the world. The popular weekend galas are Roman Catholic religious festivals honoring various patron saints, like St. Jude, St. Agrippina, and St. Anthony. Organized by religious societies—descendants of villagers from towns holding devotion to particular patron saints—these outdoor *festas* usually take place from mid-June through the end of August and feature plentiful food, colorful lights, waving banners, and joyous processions.

In other ways Hanover Street is like any other busy Boston street. Though less than a half-mile in length, it boasts churches, banks, pharmacies, dry cleaners, and convenience stores. There are shops where you can purchase cookware, tobacco, cold cuts, insurance, musical instruments, shoes, booze and airline tickets. There are places to fix your teeth, curl your hair, straighten your back, and put out your fire. (There was once a place to embalm your dead as well, but Langone's Funeral Home, lodged for decades at 383 Hanover, is now gone. Undoubtedly, Langone's most famous customers were immigrants Nicola Sacco and Bartolomeo Vanzetti, apparent victims of the political unrest, red-baiting, and xenophobia that followed the First World War. After their electrocution on August 23, 1927, the pair were embalmed at Langone's, from whence a huge funeral cortege stretched down Hanover Street.)

Today, it's summer *festas* that are most likely to pack the roadway. Meanwhile, many of the old four- and five-story buildings that line the street combine businesses on the ground floor with residential apartments in the upper stories.

One result of this plethora of activity is important to visitors: there is nowhere—*nowhere*—to park. Fortunately, there are parking lots on nearby Atlantic Avenue, as well as (a short walk away) under the Central Artery and in Dock Square. Though no subways travel to the North End, the Haymarket T stop is not far away, located on the truncated sector of old Hanover Street. The experience of visiting Boston's oldest, and one of its most delightfully Old-World neighborhoods is well worth the walk.

THE ESSENTIALS

ADDRESS: North End, Boston.

TELEPHONE: None.

VISITOR INFORMATION: North End festivals are celebrated almost every weekend from June through August; for more information, contact the Mayor's Office of Business and Cultural Development at (617)

635-3911. Parts of the North End are on both the Freedom Trail and Boston Women's Heritage Trail tours (see chapters 10 and 36 for details). A variety of other tours periodically include the North End, or specifically focus on the area; among the best are those given from late spring through early fall by Boston by Foot (telephone [617] 367-2345) and the Historic Neighborhoods Foundation (telephone [617] 426-1885); moderate fees are charged for these tours.

The Old Quincy School

HIDDEN AWAY on a quiet road in the Chinatown neighborhood of Boston is an old brick building that's not really the kind of structure that would immediately catch your eye. The simple, stark exterior is faded red brick, punctuated by large, multipaned sash windows. Two old flagpoles protrude from the front, while a statue of Confucius stands guard near the glassed entranceway. Aside from the inscription "QUINCY SCHOOL 1847"—set high on the structure's facade and virtually illegible today—you'd never guess the old building was a landmark of Boston educational history. But indeed it is.

During its 129 years as a public grammar school, the Quincy School at 90 Tyler Street was an educational melting pot for generations of immigrants who moved into Boston's South Cove. Those immigrants included the Asian-Americans who have molded Chinatown's character over the past five decades, as well as the English, Irish, Italians, Syrians, Jews, Lebanese, Greeks, Russians, and other immigrants who preceded them.

Moreover, the Quincy School—named for Josiah Quincy, Boston's second mayor and one of three Josiah Quincys elected mayor of the Hub—was a pioneer in nineteenth-century education. Begun as "the Experiment" of educational innovators such as Horace Mann, the Quincy was hailed as America's first school with graded classrooms, and was the first to provide a separate seat for each student. Though its years as part of the Boston public school system ended in 1976, the building continues to educate today, as a home to Chinese-American community associations and their related cultural activities.

During colonial times, the neighborhoods that later surrounded the Quincy School—Chinatown and Bay Village, as well as the area now occupied by the Tufts–New England Medical Center—were generally under water. In their place was a section of Boston Harbor known as South Cove, an area of spacious tidewater flats filled with wharves and stillhouses.

Winding wooden staircases in Chinatown's Old Quincy School, where generations of immigrants were educated and assimilated.

By the early nineteenth century, however, landfill fever had begun to infect local developers. Railroads were rapidly becoming the transportation of choice, and new land was needed for tracks and terminals. The first encroachment of land into the South Cove occurred in 1804, when the Front Street Corporation filled in what's now Harrison Avenue. Then, in 1833, the South Cove Associates began a landfill project that all but obliterated the cove in six years. Gravel from the nearby communities of Dorchester and Roxbury was hauled in, and fifty-five acres of new land, plus three miles of new streets, emerged. Among the area's earliest landmarks was the United States Hotel, at Lincoln and Beach streets, which enjoyed brief renown as America's largest hotel. The rest of the area was consumed, to a large degree, by railroads.

Boston's Chinese community did not begin to take shape in the South Cove area until later in the nineteenth century. Some Chinese men and women had come to Boston earlier, in the wake of the American Revolution, or as a result of the China Trade; increased knowledge of America's new frontiers and opportunities was enticing to a hearty few. But it was the completion of the transcontinental railroad, in 1869, that led to the first major Chinese settlements in Boston. Initially attracted by work on the cross-country tracks, Chinese laborers moved east in search of employment once the railroads were complete. By 1875, the core of a Chinese community had been established in a huddle of tents on Ping On Alley.

The community was doomed to remain small, insular, and predominantly male for a time by the Chinese Exclusion Act of 1882, which barred Chinese immigrants from entering the United States.

Immediately following World War II, partly as a result of the repeal of the Chinese Exclusion Act in 1943, the Boston Chinese community began to grow, and to include more women and children. It was not until the 1960s, however, that the liberalization of immigration laws under President Kennedy finally enabled the development of the large Chinatown we know today to take place.

The unprecedented influx of immigrants from other foreign nations beginning in the mid-nineteenth century prompted a major change in Massachusetts public school systems. Due in part to that immigration, Boston's population grew from 43,000 to 178,000 between 1820 and 1860. Overcrowding and an unusually heterogeneous population were among the results.

Many members of Boston's elite reacted to the increased immigrant population with a sort of benevolent xenophobia. They feared that increasing numbers of immigrant children on the streets would lead to truancy, vagrancy, and a threat to public safety; if those newcomers could be safely ensconced in schools, they reasoned, everyone would be better off. Hence, Massachusetts enacted the nation's first state-wide compulsory school attendance law in 1852.

The Quincy School was erected on Tyler Street in 1848 to relieve overcrowding at two of Boston's other grammar schools, the Brimmer and the Winthrop. But under the guidance of educational innovators like Horace Mann, Samuel Gridley Howe, and George B. Emerson, the new Quincy School took a decidedly modern turn. First, it was agreed that the school, established on September 6, 1847, would be housed in a four-story building with twelve classrooms and a large assembly hall. That multi-unit plan was deemed more economical than creating a series of one-room schoolhouses, as was customary at the time (the average Boston schoolroom of 1833 was a nineteen-by-twenty-six-foot chamber, with one teacher and sixty-two students of varying ages and abilities). In fact, it cost $6,000 to operate the entire Quincy School during its first year. (Today, more than $7,500 per year is spent for a single Boston public school student.)

Secondly, since the building was large enough to accommodate six hundred students, the children were separated by age and attainment. Prussian model schools had shown that the "factory system" of education—in essence, using a division of labor, and pushing the "product" through a step-by-step, year-by-year assembly line—was highly efficient. And so it was.

The Quincy School's designers added other innovations as well. When the building was dedicated as a boys' grammar school on June 26, 1848, it became the first Boston schoolhouse with a separate room for each teacher and class. As mentioned above, it was the first to provide each pupil with his own desk; long common benches had been the rule prior to that time. It was the first school to end the cumbersome system of two equally ranked headmasters, and to replace it with a headmaster and sub-master. This meant more uniformity in schooling; teachers no longer had to cope with two masters' divergent ideas on books and curriculum. It also featured a larger proportion of female teachers than ever before employed in a public school for boys. By 1860, the new methods inaugurated by the Quincy had been copied by all of Boston's primary and grammar schools.

Under the leadership of headmaster John Dudley Philbrick (1818–1886)—who later became superintendent of the Boston Public Schools and a national authority on education—the Quincy School flourished. From 404 boys in 1847, its enrollment grew to 562 students in 1848 and 662 in 1849. Philbrick added many creative changes. The *Ohles Biographical Dictionary of American Educators* summarized the headmaster's special appeal in one telling phrase: "He drastically reduced punishment by whipping, and added drawing and music to the curriculum."

The nationalities represented in the student body—and in the surrounding South Cove neighborhood—changed dramatically over the years. According to the old Quincy School's enrollment books, during the first decades after 1847 the students were boys, primarily 8–14 years of age, with English and Irish surnames. Among the school's nineteenth-century graduates were movers and shakers from many of Boston's oldest, most respected families—names like William B. Peabody, Samuel B. Capen, Joseph A. Sprague, Henry Lyman Shaw, Granville B. Putnam, Edward C. Burrage, and William Lloyd Garrison, Jr.

By the last quarter of the century, however, growing numbers of Murphys and O'Briens were sharing classrooms with boys named Jacobs, Liebman, Abramoff, D'Amico, Pacino, Apostoles, Alexanian, Sarkisian, and Assad. By 1921, Boston had a population of close to 800,000 people. More than a third were foreign born, while another third had at least one parent who was foreign born.

During the day, this international array of neighborhood children attended the Quincy School. By night, their parents often went to the Quincy for evening classes designed for working adult immigrants. Adults in the 1920s studied books like *A Little Book for Immigrants in Boston,* which gave the following suggestions:

> *Learn English well. Use good words. Pronounce them clearly. Copy the language of your teacher and of educated people. . . . Teach your children to be neat, industrious and polite. Give your wife a nice dress and let her have some recreation outdoors. . . . Make friends with Americans. If some are rude and arrogant, do not mind them.*

The Quincy evolved from a boys' grammar school to a coed K-through-6 facility during the first quarter of the twentieth century; still, as late as the 1940s boys and girls had separate play areas. Where the wheelchair ramp now enters the glass front door of the building there was an old fire escape, plus a small playground where schoolboys enjoyed stickball, handball, and other games. Throughout the 1940s and 1950s, Syrians comprised one of the largest ethnic groups in the school. Meanwhile, there was a rapidly growing number of Chinese students studying alongside an international mix of Greeks, Italians, Jews, African-Americans, Russians, Lithuanians, Lebanese, and even some white Anglo-Saxon Protestants.

"All the teachers were Caucasian when I was a student there in the 1950s," recalls Richard Chen, executive director of the South Cove Y.M.C.A. "As children, we were taught not to trust the rest of the world. But the teachers there were different—they were loving, trusting and wonderful to the Chinese kids."

Today, the *new* Quincy School—opened two blocks away from the old building in 1976—includes bilingual classes, Asian-American teachers, and regular education in Chinese holidays and culture. In the early Cold War era, however, no one wanted to appear "un-American" by accommodating the needs of foreign-born students. Hence, no "non-American" cultural education was offered in the old Quincy School (or any of the other Boston public schools) and children were taught English the "old-fashioned" way—sink or swim. In one teacher's classes during 1947, for example, students read books like *The Three Bears* into a microphone; if the reader made a pronunciation mistake, fellow students raised their hands in "cooperative objection." The beloved Mary Dowd's first-grade classes at the old Quincy—which spanned the years from 1949 to 1976—effectively used repetition and pictures rather than mikes.

In spite, or perhaps because, of those methods, the Chinese students of the old Quincy School overcame language barriers and other obstacles. "Success stories happened all the time," remembers teacher Bill Muello. "Most of them went on to Boston Latin School, which required both passing an exam and getting written recommendations."

Despite its years of educational excellence, the old Quincy School building has faced the threat of demolition many times during its history. The first came on December 17, 1858, when a fire destroyed the "model" school. It was rebuilt a year later, and lasted until 1938, when the Great Hurricane of that year destroyed the school's fourth-floor auditorium and roof. The fourth floor was eliminated when the school was repaired, and the building survived as a three-story structure. Since the auditorium was gone, students did their physical exercises next to their desks, and assemblies were held in the downstairs hallway.

Though the building underwent a $64,000 renovation in 1939, a 1944 report to the Boston School Committee argued that the aging Quincy School should be closed. It didn't happen. In 1962 and 1965, the Sargent report on Boston schools and a similar Harvard study recommended immediate demolition of the famous, but decrepit, old school. Again, the school remained open.

In the late 1950s and early 1960s, the Quincy School's enrollment—as well as the housing stock in the surrounding neighborhood—was badly hurt by the building of the highway known as the Central Artery, followed by the construction of an entrance to the Massachusetts Turnpike. The expansion of the Tufts–New England Medical Center in the 1960s and 1970s only exacerbated the problem. In the meantime, the school's utility systems became obsolete, the bathrooms decayed, and the roof leaked. Still, the school's administration, teachers, and students carried on in academically superior style through June of 1976.

In that year, a new Quincy School complex was opened a short walk away, at 885 Washington Street. The massive, award-winning building is a modern, multi-ethnic, bilingual elementary school filled with computers, bright colors, wide-open classrooms, a rooftop playground, and achieving students. Meanwhile, Mayor Kevin White sold the old Quincy building to the Chinese Consolidated Benevolent Association, representing the Chinatown community, for a token price of one dollar.

Today, 90 Tyler Street is a bustling community center, housing the offices of the Chinese Consolidated Benevolent Association, the Asian American Civic Association, and *Sampan,* Greater Boston's only bilingual Chinese newspaper. By day and by night, dozens—sometimes hundreds—of Asian-Americans move in and out of the old Quincy School building. Many attend the C.C.B.A.'s Kwong Kow Chinese School, a vital link to Chinese culture and community. Others go to A.A.C.A. counseling sessions or classes on topics ranging from immigration and naturalization to office-skill training, business development, and English as a second language.

It's appropriate that the old Quincy School building is used by service organizations that educate and help immigrants and the community, and that an image of Confucius—the revered fifth-century teacher, sage, and moralist—welcomes them at the door. Because even in its declining years as a public school, the building at 90 Tyler Street was a safe home-away-from-home for generations of youngsters. That tradition continues, in a new and unexpected form, to this day.

THE ESSENTIALS

ADDRESS: 90 Tyler Street, Chinatown, Boston.

TELEPHONE: Chinese Consolidated Benevolent Association (617) 542-2574, (617) 542-2578; Asian American Civic Association (617) 426-9492.

VISITOR INFORMATION: Building open for business 9:00 A.M.–5:00 P.M., Monday through Friday; sometimes open on evenings and weekends for special classes and events. No tours. First floor and restroom wheelchair accessible via ramp; other areas inaccessible due to long staircases.

39 The Vilna Shul

LIKE SO many of Beacon Hill's oldest structures, the walls of the Vilna Shul have a story to tell. But this particular building is a bit different from all the other quaint red-brick homes nestled in the narrow back roads of historic

The Vilna Shul on Beacon Hill is a living tribute to, and a sole survivor of, the synagogues built by Eastern European Jewish immigrants who arrived in Boston near the turn of the twentieth century.

Beacon Hill. Its tales are not of Puritan preachers or Revolutionary War heroes, abolitionists or freed slaves, nor even of State House politicians or picketing protesters. Instead, the Vilna Shul, at 14–18 Phillips Street, is a lone survivor from an altogether different era of Boston history—the time when thousands of impoverished and persecuted Eastern European Jews immigrated to America.

Although Boston was founded in 1630, the city was without a significant, stable Jewish population until the 1840s. In many ways, that was by design. The city's founding Puritans revered the Hebrew language, history, and culture, and even welcomed an Italian Jew, Judah Monis, to Harvard College as a student and teacher of Hebrew and Old Testament studies in 1722. But they saw the actual practice of the Jewish faith as a threat to the purity, homogeneity, and success of their community. Indeed, religious dissenters of all sorts—including Quakers, Native Americans, Roman Catholics, and witches—were often deported, banished, forcibly converted, or hanged. The first Jew to appear in the recorded history of Boston came face to face with this philosophy. Solomon Franco, or Frankel, arrived in 1649, but didn't stay long. A legal dispute with Major General Edward Gibbons, to whom Franco had brought cargo, ended with orders for Franco to vacate twelve days later.

While most seventeenth- and eighteenth-century Jewish immigrants settled in other, less hostile parts of the United States, some did come to Boston. The first were Sephardic Jews from Spain and Portugal, who followed Spanish trade routes to the New World in the colonial period. In the 1840s, German Jews made up a second, significantly larger wave. German Jews built Boston's first synagogue, Ohabei Shalom (Lovers of Peace) in the South End in 1851. They also benefited from vaguely liberalized laws in the Commonwealth; in 1821, Jews were granted full citizenship rights in Massachusetts. But though they could live here, they still encountered troubles when they *died* here; until 1840, when new laws superseded the old, bodies of deceased Jews had to be sent to Newport, Albany, or New York City for legal burial.

The third wave of Jewish immigration to Boston was by far the largest, and reflected a larger trend—so large, in fact, that America's Jewish population grew from 250,000 to 3.5 million between 1880 and 1920. Jews had lived in Eastern Europe since the twelfth century; by the seventeenth century, restrictions on their activities and periodic persecutions had grown significantly worse. In 1881, following the assassination of Tsar Alexander II of Russia, any remnants of freedom for Jews quickly evaporated. Alexander had actually been surprisingly liberal in his policies; his successors, however, loathed liberalism and reform, and began vigorous persecution of all minority nationalities, a policy called Russification. New laws fostered official Russian anti-Semitism, harsh legal restrictions, and pogroms—mass anti-Jewish riots and killings—in Russia, as well as in other parts of Eastern Europe.

Ships carrying nineteenth-century Jewish immigrants arrived in America at Castle Garden or Ellis Island in New York, and later on, at the Boston Immigration Building. If not poor before leaving the old country, the passengers were often impoverished by the costs of the trip. And though the established German Jews often headed charitable societies that offered benevolent aid, they were frequently hostile to the new immigrants. (Such has often been the case in American history: immigrants who were themselves once considered second-class citizens settle in and prosper, enabling them to treat subsequent generations of newcomers as second-class citizens.)

In many ways, the Eastern European Jews who arrived at the turn of the century had a more difficult transition than their predecessors. They were poorer. There were many more of them—representing entire families and sometimes whole towns. Finally, according to the American Jewish Historical Society study *On Common Ground: The Boston Jewish Experience, 1649–1980,* they were not well received by Boston's other residents. "They were lumped together as Russian, as Orthodox, as ignorant, as speakers of that 'ugly' language called Yiddish, as uncouth."

Some of the new Bostonians moved to the South End neighborhood, following in the footsteps of the German Jews who had lived there before departing for "finer" neighborhoods. Some moved to the North End (the former home of Irish immigrants), which became 80 percent Jewish and Italian by 1910. Most of the newly arriving Eastern European Jews, however, moved to the north slope of Beacon Hill and the adjoining West End (an area later obliterated by urban renewal). When the Vilna Shul was built in 1919—as a synagogue and community center for its poor, hard-working congregation—it was one of more than fifty neighborhood synagogues erected from scratch or adapted from other buildings to serve Boston's newest citizens. In later decades, as these immigrants departed the area, their synagogues disappeared one by one—sometimes demolished, sometimes abandoned, and sometimes converted to other uses. Few people still remember that the African Meeting House, the Charles Playhouse, and Boston University's Morse Auditorium were all once active synagogues.

Many of the new Jewish immigrants came from the city of Vilna. Vilna was located within or near Lithuania, Poland, or Russia, continually changing nationalities as border wars were resolved between those three countries. Despite the pogroms that plagued their city in the late nineteenth century, Vilna residents cherished their home as a center of Jewish intellectual, political, and cultural life—as "the citadel of culture" and "the Jerusalem of Lithuania."

Many of Vilna's Jews chose to come to Boston for a specific reason. "The streets of Boston reminded me of those in Vilna," wrote orator-preacher Zvi Hirsh Masliansky after his 1901 visit. "Large synagogues with truly Orthodox rabbis. Talmudic study groups. . . . [and] almost all the stores are closed on Saturdays." Mira Jedwabnik Van Doren, an artist and filmmaker born and raised in Vilna, confirms this assessment. "Most Vilna people that come to Boston say it reminds them of Vilna," she agrees. "In both cities, old and new coexist harmoniously. There's a pride and reverence in the life of the mind . . . the university, libraries, the pace. . . . A river runs through the city, and there is lots of greenery and parks. The crowded narrow streets and cobblestones were also similar."

Vilna immigrants, like most of the immigrant populations in the West End, were poor. Turn-of-the-century West End residents often came to Boston in the steerage sections of sailing vessels, where they were packed in like sardines. Once settled in Boston, they frequently lived in crowded tenement apartments, with no real baths or showers, no heat, no electricity, and no running water. Unheated toilets were found in a building's entry or hallway. Warmth was available only near heavy black stoves in the kitchen, stoves fueled by coal hauled up in buckets from the cellar. Children often shared a single bed, kept warm by a heated flatiron wrapped in a towel if they were lucky.

Both Edward Ross and Charles Smith were born in Eastern Europe in 1901, then immigrated to Boston. And both recall the West End's primitive methods of refrigeration: poorer folks would simply cool their food by placing it out on chilly window ledges, while more solvent families had an ice box. Ross and Smith fondly remember the West End's ice man, a one-armed black gentleman who carried treacherous-looking ice prongs, and wore a sheet of rubber on his back, on which he hauled huge blocks of ice into the tenements.

"They were hard days but fun," remembers Bill Cohen, who escaped the pogroms by moving to Boston. Many men and women earned just a dollar for a fifteen-hour workday, doing a variety of jobs including peddling, rolling pushcarts through the streets, tailoring, and butchering. Some did piecework at home, some toiled in large shops, and others worked smaller "mom-and-pop" groceries, bakeries, delicatessens, and the like. Anti-Semitism still reared its head, even in the Golden Land. Still, snide comments, backward glances, tugs on older men's beards, or job competition with other minorities was nothing when compared to Old World pogroms. Meanwhile, Jews took good care of one another. "If a person was in want," says Cohen, "the others would find some way to help him or her."

Part of that caring was channeled through the shul (*shul* is the Yiddish word for synagogue). In 1898, Vilna Jews living in the West End and the edge of Beacon Hill formed their own landsmanshaft, or religious group sharing common language, customs, and history. They prayed together in a rented, one-room, unheated apartment at the corner of Cotting Street and Lomasney Way. In 1903, the group was granted a state charter as a charitable corporation, the Vilner Congregation. They continued to worship in various apartments until able to purchase the Twelfth Baptist Church on Phillips Street. When the city bought that property in 1915 and converted it to the Phillips School, the Vilner Congregation saved its money while renting space at 27 Anderson Street.

Finally, in 1919, they purchased two tenement buildings at 14–18 Phillips Street, and hired Myer Feldman of Revere to demolish them. There they built the Vilna Shul, a lasting tribute to their heritage and a symbol of community pride. Throughout the construction process, neighbors offered services and contributed money toward the total cost of $20,150. Each time a holy Torah scroll was donated to or acquired by the Shul, festive parades would erupt along Phillips Street.

Boston architect Max Kalman designed the shul as an L-shaped red-brick synagogue, with two stories and a small basement below the entrance. The basic layout was probably inspired by the Touro Synagogue in Newport, the Worms Shul in Germany, and the Altneushul in Prague. The building is set back twelve feet from the street, with a front courtyard surrounded by black wrought-iron fencing. At the top of the arched entrance doors are fanlights, while above those doors soars a large round window depicting the Star of David in colored glass.

The architectural design aptly reflected the Vilna Jews' old life and new. The red-brick walls, wrought-iron fencing, and sixteen-over-sixteen double-hung windows are Beacon Hill Bostonian, echoing the simplicity of colonial meetinghouses. The religious symbols and interior design, on the other hand, reflect the congregation's East European heritage. The second floor main sanctuary, for example, is filled with long rows of hard wooden pews, divided—in typical Orthodox fashion—into separate men's and women's sections of 150 seats each. Glass chandeliers, a raised square wooden *bimah* (reader's platform), and a magnificent, hand-carved, dark wooden ark all add to the sanctuary's warmth and charm.

To this day, the fifteen-foot-tall, nine-foot-wide ark is the centerpiece of the Vilna Shul sanctuary. Possibly designed by local cabinetmaker Sam Katz, it is decorated with traditional religious symbols, many in gold bas-relief. Small replicas of the Ten Commandments tablets are flanked by lions of Judah. Two touching hands, with fingers parted to suggest the high priests' blessing, float below the symbolic eternal light and the Star of David. Above the light is a spread-winged gilded bald eagle—the symbol of American freedom.

The other most stunning architectural touches in the main sanctuary are three large skylights that seem to bring heaven to earth on sunny days. David Glater remembers attending services there for the High Holy Days during the shul's last active years, between 1968 and 1985. "As part of the Yom Kippur [Day of Atonement] service, there is a late afternoon prayer that essentially says, 'The gates of heaven are closing, get your prayers in now!' As the light gradually dimmed through the skylights at the Vilna Shul, you got the sense of gates closing. It was a remarkable feeling!"

In its heyday, the Vilna Shul, like dozens of other synagogues spread throughout the Boston community, was both a center for religious worship and study, and a place for immigrants to find social and cultural activities and mutual support. Following the Orthodox tradition, men were expected to attend services several times a day, while women came only on the Sabbath and the High Holy Days.

Because of the poverty of its East European membership, no full-time rabbi was ever hired at the Vilna Shul; a senior male congregant acted as daily leader, while visiting rabbis or cantors were hired to conduct important services. One unexpected advantage of the congregation's lack of monetary wealth was historic preservation: while wealthier shuls could constantly renovate to fit changing tastes and times, or could even move to more luxurious quarters, the Vilna Shul remained in its Phillips Street home virtually unchanged after 1919.

The building was kept in good repair through the 1970s, though the congregation itself declined. That decline was certainly no surprise. As far back as the 1920s, membership in Orthodox synagogues had suffered as Reform and Conservative movements gained in popularity. Also, as Jewish immigrants began to assimilate or gain financial stability, they moved from the South, North, and West ends of town to roomier streetcar suburbs. Any remaining West End populations were displaced by federally funded urban renewal projects in the 1960s—projects which replaced the old West End tenements with the dull strip of commercial spaces, public buildings, and sections of Massachusetts General Hospital found there today. For those and other reasons, by 1985 the Vilna Shul had just one member, Mendell Miller. Though many other Jews continued to attend services there, Miller was technically the president, caretaker, and last official congregant of the Vilna Shul.

In 1985, Miller petitioned the Massachusetts Supreme Judicial Court to have the Vilner Congregation dissolved, proposing to donate any proceeds from the sale of the building and land to Jewish charitable organizations. Miller initially tried to sell the land to a developer, who planned to raze the building and put a parking lot in its place. Because of soaring real estate prices, the sale was expected to raise more than a million dollars, and a number of local and overseas Jewish organizations and charities began competing for the anticipated windfall (in some cases their claims were based simply on their like status as Orthodox synagogues). Meanwhile, legal fees mounted as claims were evaluated, the shul's accounts with creditors settled, and other matters dealt with. Late in 1988, shortly before Miller died, the Supreme Judicial Court named a temporary receiver for the Vilner Congregation so that its assets would not be wasted.

By that time, falling real estate prices were puncturing the dream of a great financial gain, while a variety of neighbors and abutters organized to protect the last intact early-twentieth-century Jewish synagogue in Boston. They sought and won Boston Landmark status for the sanctuary in 1989. (The exterior was theoretically already protected, since the Vilna Shul was listed in the National Register of Historic Places as part of the Beacon Hill National Historic District.) In 1990, the organizers suffered a reversal of fortune when the Boston City Council overturned the designation previously approved by the Boston Landmarks Commission and Mayor Raymond L. Flynn (a landmarked interior, some worried, would limit the use and lower the value of the building).

Finally, with the support and counsel of Historic Boston Incorporated, and the formation of the nonprofit Vilna Center for Jewish Heritage in 1989, hope for preserving the Vilna Shul intact became a reality. Today, armed with a moving video about the shul's place in Boston Jewish history (a video narrated by Leonard Nimoy, who was born of Jewish immigrants in the West End), volunteers are actively seeking support. If all goes well and sufficient funding is found, the Vilna Shul will be purchased, restored, given an endowment, and molded into a Jewish cultural and heritage center for all of Boston within a few years.

Karen Arsenault, spokesperson for the Vilna Center for Jewish Heritage, explains her dreams for the building. "We're not saving the building to put a bell jar over it. We want it to be alive with the stories it evokes: the people, the culture, and the values they brought here." Adds Elinor Ross Woron, whose grandmother was a founding member of the synagogue on Phillips Street, "We need to preserve the heritage and keep the stories alive. The Vilna Shul is, and should be, a living tribute to our parents and grandparents who had the courage to come to this country."

THE ESSENTIALS

ADDRESS: 14–18 Phillips Street, Beacon Hill, Boston. Mailing address: Vilna Center for Jewish Heritage, Inc., 1 Financial Center, 40th floor, Boston, MA 02111.

TELEPHONE: None currently.

VISITOR INFORMATION: Shul currently closed to the public, except by appointment and for special events. Tours may be arranged by contacting the Vilna Center. No wheelchair access at present.

40 | The Peabody Museum Hall of the North American Indian

AMIDST THE on-campus complex known as the Harvard Museums of Cultural and Natural History is the largest, most meticulously documented ethnographic and archaeological collection of Native American objects in New England. The gallery in which these objects are displayed, however, is hardly a staid, static, old-fashioned museum that only academics could appreciate. Instead, the Peabody Museum Hall of the North American Indian is a modern, artfully arranged, beautifully lit gallery that's accessible to all—both physically and intellectually.

As visitors enter the hall's climate-controlled chamber, there is an immediate feeling of intimacy and involvement. Large paintings and photos, simply displayed handcrafts, and intricate dioramas engage the eye, as the sounds of native chants swell in the background. Visitors can push interactive buttons in the orientation area, or wander a gently winding path through several color-coded areas representing ten different Native American cultural regions. For each region, bold copy tells of changing tribal lifeways over the past five centuries. Fascinating tales of kachinas, potlatches, the fur trade, and how horses came to the Plains are intermingled with displays of Navajo blankets, Sioux saddle bags, Apache cradles, Passamaquoddy canoe models, and towering Kwakiutl totem poles.

Equally important is that the Peabody Museum Hall of the North American Indian is not just an educational and entertaining center dealing with the American past. Originally founded in 1866, the Peabody is currently grappling with some of the modern-day political questions surrounding the treatment of Native Americans in North America. The underlying theme of the hall's main exhibit, for example, is "Continuity and Change"—an exploration of how indigenous cultures coevolved with the European presence after 1492, sometimes for better, generally for worse. It also describes how some American Indian nations survived to this day, despite all odds—the disease, enslavement, land theft, and systematic genocide brought on first by European settlers and later by the government of the United States.

Like anthropological museums across the country, the Peabody has been very involved in the issue of repatriation—the returning of sacred objects to existing tribes; some of those objects were presumably acquired through grave-robbing, theft, or less obvious forms of plunder. Most recently, the Peabody's staff has also begun to give back to Native Americans in other ways—through educational programs and special events that actively involve and support existing American Indian populations.

★　★　★

Detail from a Kwakiutl pole, one of more than 500 Native American objects beautifully displayed and interpreted in the renovated Peabody Museum Hall of the North American Indian.

Understanding the motivations behind those current efforts, of course, requires a clearer picture of the Native Americans in the United States and how they have been studied over time. When Christopher Columbus and other European explorers first visited "the New World," the Americas were already inhabited by a variety of peoples. In the area we call New England were an estimated seventy-five to ninety thousand people, largely settled in the coastal regions and river valleys. The Wampanoag, Nipmuck, and Massachuset lived on lands that would later be known as Massachusetts. Most spoke dialects of the Algonquin language, communicated their history through oral tradition, and spent considerable time hunting, fishing, and growing crops which included beans, squash, corn, and root vegetables.

By 1620, the first permanent English settlement in this region had been created at Plimoth Plantation, located on the coastal lands southeast of Boston. By 1630, the Shawmut peninsula—whose name some claim meant "living waters" in one Algonquin dialect—had been settled and renamed Boston. Only six years later Harvard College was established in Cambridge. And by 1646, "apostle" John Eliot and a small group of his Harvard colleagues had begun their mission to civilize, Christianize, and "save" the local "heathens."

From a modern perspective, Eliot's imposition of European culture and religion on the native peoples was misguided at best, imperialistic at worst. Yet it was arguably less horrendous than the actions of his peers; for between 1492 and 1650, some 90 percent of New England's indigenous population had been wiped out by Europeans, primarily through disease and violence. In the most atrocious cases, people were hanged on Boston Common, their villages were set aflame in the dead of night, their leaders' bodies were desecrated and displayed on poles, and white warriors offered rewards for the delivery of American Indian scalps.

During the following two centuries, white settlers, often with the help of the U.S. government, gradually took away the land, the lives, the rights, and the identities of countless Native Americans. Then, in the nineteenth century, a new branch of science called anthropology began both to increase understanding of America's native peoples and to impose another sort of loss upon them.

On October 5, 1865, Professor O. C. Marsh of Yale College was digging in an ancient shell mound near Newark, New Jersey. Elated at the potential of his discoveries, Marsh wrote to his uncle, George A. Peabody (1795–1869) of Danvers, Massachusetts, a noted entrepreneur, financier, and philanthropist. Marsh knew that Peabody intended to make substantial gifts to Harvard College and other institutions, and he encouraged his uncle to establish a museum at Harvard to acquire and preserve material related to "primitive man." Peabody responded with a $150,000 trust. And on October 9, 1866, Harvard's Peabody Museum made its debut as the first American museum devoted specifically to archaeology and ethnology. (While the former discipline involved studies of extinct populations— analyzing physical remains of cultures for which no written records could be found—the latter focused on the life, behavior, and material culture of still-extant populations.)

According to their letters, nineteenth-century Harvard administrators had hoped to use Peabody's donation for the school library, the Museum of Comparative Zoology, or the general college budget. Still, they knew that anthropology was becoming a hot topic in Europe, in part because of Darwin's controversial new theories of evolution and the origin of species. Harvard president James Walker acknowledged in 1866, "When a generous man, like Mr. Peabody, proposes a great gift, we should accept it on his own terms, and not on ours. . . . [Moreover, we] will have the best chance of securing those relics of our Indian tribes, which are now scattered in so many private collections."

The Peabody was initially a separate institution allied with Harvard. But in 1897, its trustees formally transferred the property to the President and Fellows of Harvard College. The association was appropriate, since the museum's collections grew side-by-side with the modern science (and the academic department) of anthropology at Harvard. From 1897 on, the museum was actively used to train students in archaeology, physical anthropology, and cultural anthropology. Boston-area art students, history students, teachers, and school children also regularly used the Peabody's collections for educational purposes.

Today, Harvard's Peabody Museum of Archaeology and Ethnology boasts an internationally known collection of about two million objects from around the world—a collection that occupies five major galleries plus a dozen storage areas. Though objects from Oceania, Central and South America, Africa, and Asia were eventually included, the Peabody's Native American relics have always been central to the collection. In their first annual report, curator Jeffries Wyman noted that "the collection consisted of crania and bones of North-American Indians, a few casts of Crania of other races, several kinds of stone implements, and a few articles of pottery—in all, about fifty specimens." The first specimen catalogued by the museum was "an Indian cranium from Chelsea, Massachusetts."

In 1866, the Peabody's collections were housed in a display case of the Museum of Comparative Anatomy, then located in Harvard's Boylston Hall. By 1876, those collections had so expanded that a permanent home was needed; so between 1876 and 1913, at a cost of $185,000, a five-story Victorian brick structure was constructed on Divinity Avenue. The Peabody remains in that Victorian building today, sharing its galleries with the Department of Anthropology, classrooms, labs, workshops, storage space, offices, and a stellar museum shop. The Peabody is also connected to the other Harvard museums of cultural and natural history—the Botanical, Comparative Zoology, and Mineralogical and Geological museums—which are housed in adjoining Victorian buildings at 24 Oxford Street. (See Chapter 19 for more information on these institutions.)

The original fifty items that comprised the Peabody's collections in 1866 were rapidly augmented by other archaeological and ethnographic finds. Some were outright purchases. Many were gifts from individuals. Many others were "inherited" from other institutions, who had surplus or duplicate specimens in their collections, or other fields of expertise. Among those who gave or sold artifacts to the museum were the Boston Athenaeum, the Boston Museum of Natural History (the precursor to today's Museum of Science), the Smithsonian Institution, the Massachusetts Historical Society, the American Antiquarian Society in Worcester, and other Harvard collections.

The stories behind the 550 or more individual items now displayed at the Hall of the North American Indian—or the 65,000 others kept in archival storage areas—are as diverse as the objects themselves. A certain Naskapi hat, for example, was originally "collected" by explorer and adventurer William B. Cabot. A sculpted wooden beaver was received during the signing of the 1795 Greenville Treaty between the U.S. government and the tribes of the Illinois Confederacy. A group of ethnological objects brought back by the Lewis and Clark expedition were once owned by Thomas Jefferson and displayed at Monticello.

Once individuals acquired these objects, they usually sold them to private collectors or various local, state, or federal repositories. The popular Charles Willson Peale Museum, founded in Philadelphia in 1785, was one such institution. When it closed in the middle of the nineteenth century, the Boston Museum purchased many of its precious objects. By the turn of the century, a number of those items were transferred to the Peabody, where they were used both for scientific study and public display.

Though they are not exhibited today, skeletal remains have always been a part of the Peabody research collections. As with other collection items, their sources varied widely. Some may have been deliberately pulled from battlefields, others accidentally dislodged by highway and construction workers. Their collectors ranged from simple grave-robbers to serious archaeologists. For the first group, such skeletons were macabre toys. For scientists, they were materials used to study the history of nutrition, disease, fertility, migration patterns, and other demographic concerns.

Peabody anthropologists often brought back specimens from archaeological and ethnological expeditions led by museum staff and related Harvard faculty, particularly between 1870 and 1930. Beginning with curator Jeffries Wyman, who served during the Peabody's first decade, field work and excavations at Indian burial mounds, shell heaps, caves, and village sites were led by scientists and educators like Frederic Putnam, Henry Gillman, Edwin Curtiss, Philip Phillips, and Stephen Williams. The Peabody also led efforts to protect archaeological sites through purchase or government action—resulting in the 1887 founding of Serpent Mound Park in Adams County, Ohio, and the passage of the Antiquities Act of 1906, which protected lands owned or controlled by the U.S. government from random excavation and appropriation of historic and prehistoric objects.

Another Harvard anthropologist, Alice C. Fletcher, gained renown for her ethnological studies among the Omaha (Nebraska) and Oglalla Sioux, the Winnebago, the Nez Perce, and the Ponca between 1882 and 1923. Though she was lauded by her peers, some of her acquisitions were deemed inappropriate by later generations. In 1989 and 1990, the Peabody returned many of the Omaha objects collected by Fletcher a century earlier, including a widely publicized sacred pole.

Well into the twentieth century, such scientific collecting was rarely seen as robbing Native Americans. Before easily portable still cameras, video, and film were widely available, collecting physical objects was the only practical way to study them. Furthermore, many researchers erroneously believed that American Indians were rapidly vanishing peoples whose artifacts and noble heritage should be saved for future generations. That intensive focus on collecting objects began to recede in the 1930s, as anthropology's interest in "material culture" gave way to study of other issues such as rituals and linguistics. The results of that trend are apparent in the Hall of the North American Indian today; most of the objects displayed are from decades and centuries gone by, while the lives of modern Native Americans are alluded to in photographs, descriptive plaques, and recordings.

Today's Hall of the North American Indian is the result of extensive rethinking and renovation that took place between 1981 and 1990. Before those fundamental changes, the hall followed the quaint Victorian decor of most museums designed and developed in the nineteenth century—and featured a display method affectionately known in the trade as "cram 'n' jam." Dozens of seemingly redundant artifacts were displayed in row upon row of wooden, glass-sided cases, unprotected from the sunlight that streamed in through the tall windows. Tiny typed or hand-written labels identified each ethnological item, sometimes giving no more information than the object's name and donor. "There were once six thousand objects on display here," remembers Catherine Linardos of the Peabody's Development Office. "So, if we had ten pairs of beaded moccasins, they were all exhibited. Every last pair."

To update the hall's exhibits and make other necessary renovations, then-director C. C. Lamberg-Karlovsky closed it down from 1981 to 1990. Since Harvard's museums have always been largely self-sustaining, funds for the major overhaul came from donations, grants, and the sale of several museum paintings. Meetings with staff and consultants—who included several Native Americans—resulted in the exhibit theme of "Continuity and Change" and the choice of appropriate artifacts to display from a collection of twenty-three thousand. Meanwhile, designer Richard Riccio created today's engaging, accessible gallery from an awkward old space.

While, and in some cases before, those renovations were taking place, the Native American and civil rights movements were calling on the museum to look anew at its collections. Certain items, especially those related to religious life, were deemed inappropriate for museums to display or own. Acting in response to individual tribal requests, as well as to federal legislation enacted in November 1990, the Peabody has begun the arduous task of creating inventories and summaries of their collections as a basis to study future claims. Some sacred objects, cultural patrimony, and human remains together with funerary objects may be returned to descendants of the tribes from which they were once taken. In addition, since the hall's reopening in April 1990, several exhibits have been altered in response to requests, advice, and information provided by visiting Native Americans.

Since the Peabody's collecting of objects essentially ended with the 1950s, one more challenge faces the museum staff: celebrating and educating visitors about the lives of modern-day American Indians and their tribes, while working to make the collections more accessible for anthropological teaching and research. Though they don't have the resources to replicate the contemporary Native American activities of Boston's Children's Museum—or its spectacular permanent exhibit "We're Still Here"—the Peabody has developed new outreach programs that don't necessarily rely on the display of objects. Native American students from Harvard's Graduate School of Education are helping to develop special elementary and middle school programs, while Native American children from the Boston area are participating in Peabody youth enrichment activities. Family events relating to modern Native American culture are being held, featuring visiting tribal dancers and other artists.

Meanwhile, the Peabody's Hall of the North American Indian remains the best place in New England to absorb five hundred years of Native American adaptation and survival. What better backdrop for dealing with contemporary concerns—concerns that ultimately reflect on and affect us all?

THE ESSENTIALS

ADDRESS: 11 Divinity Avenue, Cambridge.

TELEPHONE: (617) 495-2248; school groups, (617) 495-2341. Contact the Peabody Museum Association (617) 495-2269, for general activities, including lecture-luncheons, film series, and special events.

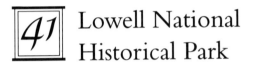

41 Lowell National Historical Park

MOST CITIES and their citizenries would be thrilled to have one period of glory, one stretch of national recognition, in their historic past. For the city of Lowell, however—located thirty miles northwest of Boston—glory has emerged twice in the past two centuries, thanks largely to good fortune, wise investments, communal efforts and long, hard work.

During its "golden years" in the nineteenth century, Lowell was a booming center of America's textile industry, renowned as the cradle of the American Industrial Revolution and home to a canal system considered a masterpiece of nineteenth-century engineering. In the late twentieth century, the city again came into the limelight—this time by hosting one of the first urban national parks in the country, and offering the nation's largest free folk festival.

Despite the years of stagnation and decline that separated these two periods, Lowell looks none the worse for the wear today: its downtown streets are filled with bright, renovated mills, turn-of-the-century trolleys, canal boats, art galleries, cobblestoned avenues, inviting parks and plazas, outdoor concerts, commemorative statues, free museums, friendly park rangers, and a wealth of multi-ethnic shops and restaurants. And locals are more than willing to boast of the city's famed sons and daughters—like actress Bette Davis, Beat writer Jack Kerouac, painter James McNeill Whistler (and his mom), the liberated mill girls, and comics Bob (Elliott) and Ray (Goulding), who began their radio career in Lowell, on WLLH-AM.

Historic "firsts" and "finests" do abound in downtown Lowell. Still, first-time visitors to the city and the Lowell National Historical Park are sometimes a bit confused, if only by the nomenclature. When people think of national parks, they often picture forests, wildflowers, picnic areas, and campsites—rather than buildings and sidewalks. But Lowell is an active city with an urban national park that commemorates and celebrates industrialization, labor, and ethnic diversity. That diversity is reflected in the annual Lowell Folk Festival, which runs the last weekend of every July and

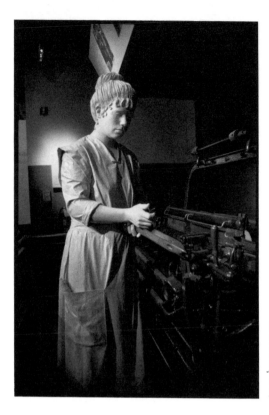

Stories and displays on the liberated "mill girls" of Lowell are among the fascinating exhibits at the new Boott Cotton Mills Museum.

features street parades, six outdoor stages, and traditional folk music, dance, crafts, and foods by a variety of cultural and community groups.

While that festival is a weekend affair, the revitalized "historic Lowell" is a year-round adventure, and includes a state park, a historic downtown district, and plenty of privately funded enterprises, all overlapping and supporting the National Park Service's work. In essence, the whole city of Lowell is like one of the constantly click-clacking looms in the Boott Cotton Mills Museum—a contemporary city-in-progress and a historic park-in-process, all rolled into one.

Long before there was a park, long before there was a city, long before there were mills and canals, there was the Merrimack River. The Native Americans who lived by the river for 14,000 years—chasing woolly mammoths and mastodons in the earliest days, and belligerently chased out by colonial settlers in the late 1600s—had named it Monumack, meaning sturgeon. The river's name remains, with spelling changes, to this day; native members of the Independent Pennacook Confederacy, for the most part, did not.

The white settlers who began farming in the valley near the junction of the Merrimack and Concord rivers in the seventeenth century eventually called the area Chelmsford Neck, then East Chelmsford. They found the broad waterway a wonderful power source for their few small mills, but a mixed blessing for commerce: the Pawtucket Falls, with their precipitous thirty-two-foot drop, proved a major hindrance to boat traffic. Eventually the problem was solved by digging the Pawtucket Canal—a falls-bypass project completed in 1796 by a group of shipbuilders and merchants from Newburyport, Massachusetts, called the Proprietors of Locks and Canals.

Fame and fortune did not come to the area until wealthy Boston merchant Francis Cabot Lowell decided to create a "mill city" on its peaceful pastures. Until the early 1800s, Lowell had made a healthy living from capital investments in transatlantic shipping, which included picking up furs in the Pacific Northwest and trading them for teas, silks, and porcelain from the Orient. The ascendance of Emperor Napoleon in France, however, and Napoleon's imperialist efforts to regulate the economy of the European continent while crippling Britain's export trade, endangered Lowell's profitable business; as a result of the fighting in Europe, France was sinking or seizing neutral American ships, while Britain sometimes pressed American seamen into its service, under the pretext that they had deserted from the Royal Navy. Rather than resort to war, President Thomas Jefferson instituted an embargo in 1807, forbidding U.S. vessels to sail to foreign ports. Understandably, Francis Cabot Lowell turned his attention to developing an industry that would minimize American dependence on European goods and overseas shipping.

Lowell had both a family and an ego to accommodate. Fortunately, the rich investor also had a plan and a remarkable memory. During an 1811 visit to the textile factories of England—where the Industrial Revolution was well underway—he literally memorized the complex mechanical elements of the power looms he observed there. With those images in mind, and with the aid of mechanical genius Paul Moody, Lowell returned to re-create the British power loom in America. Along with his colleagues, a group of businessmen-investors known as the Boston Associates, Lowell began planning a fully integrated textile manufacturing system—a system that could take raw cotton and turn it into finished fabric.

Though Lowell died in 1817, shortly after this bale-to-bolt system made a successful trial run in Waltham, Massachusetts, his vision lived on. In 1822, his partners began to build a textile mill city near the banks of the Merrimack River and Pawtucket Falls—together viewed as the finest source of water power in the area. They constructed machines and factory buildings, vastly expanded the existing canal system, recruited a unique new work force, housed these workers in factory boardinghouses, and changed the course of American economic and social history. In the process, they created America's first major planned industrial city. And to no one's surprise, they named it Lowell.

Today, a variety of exhibits and interpretive tours in Lowell National Historical Park (and Lowell Heritage State Park, whose offerings were significantly diminished after the massive state budget cuts of the early 1990s) tell the story of the city's origins and growth. A spectacular, eighteen-projector slide show at the visitor center in the refurbished Market Mills complex provides an overview and introduction to the Lowell story. Open intermittently, the nearby Queen Anne–style Mack

Building, marked by a mammoth red drive-pulley outside its entrance, houses two floors of displays about water power and mechanical wonders—from Native American canoes through the people and machines that carved Lowell's canals, harnessed its waters, and built or operated its mills and machines.

Several specialized interpretive historic tours are also regularly available. One of the park's most popular ranger-led excursions is the seasonal two-hour-fifteen-minute Mill and Canal Tour, which has a nominal admission charge. Visitors travel by trolley, foot, and canal boat through working canal locks into a partially recreated mill replete with whirring machinery, and to a canal sluice gate where costumed gatekeepers or their wives sometimes converse about their lives, work, and dreams as if they lived in the Lowell of the 1850s.

Throughout, well-informed rangers treat visitors to facts and anecdotes from Lowell's history. Some are tales about men at the top—like the arrogant, energetic, company agent Kirk Boott (1790–1837), a colorful prime mover in Lowell's first decades, who oversaw the construction and operation of Lowell's earliest canals and mills. Boott Mills was one of the ten original major textile corporations in Lowell—enduring from 1836 to 1956 and named to honor Boott, who was known as a heartless individual and hardworking business mastermind. Today the group of riverside buildings known as the Boott Mills Complex are the finest surviving examples of mill architecture in Lowell; they have recently been renovated in a multimillion-dollar public-private restoration project.

Boott Mill Number 6, built in 1873, houses the new Boott Cotton Mills Museum. Since opening in the summer of 1992, the fifteen-million-dollar industrial museum has become the centerpiece of Lowell National Historical Park. It includes an ambitious exhibit of eighty-eight working power looms, plus interactive exhibits and videos about the Industrial Revolution, labor history, and the rise, fall, and rebirth of the city of Lowell. Also in Boott Mill No. 6 is the Paul Tsongas Industrial History Center, named for the former U.S. senator and presidential candidate, plus a museum store, the New England Folklife Center, and the Lowell Historical Society. Nearby is the new Boarding House Park, with an outdoor concert stage that is actively used throughout the summer.

Though some of the tales told in these exhibits and tours are about men at the top, many others concern men at the bottom—like Hugh Cummiskey, who recruited and trekked hundreds of poor Irish immigrants up from Boston to dig the canals. Those immigrants cut through stone and swamp, using only small hand tools and deadly gunpowder, to create the more than five miles of canals in place today. Their backbreaking work formed what's now renowned as the second oldest canal system in the United States. Cummiskey and his colleagues are commemorated in a downtown fountain, *The Worker,* and their stories are told throughout the park, particularly in the Water Power exhibit. Meanwhile, a new fifteen-million-dollar loop of walkways, called the Canalway, leads from the National Park Service visitor center at Market Mills through the downtown area.

Some of the best nineteenth-century tales of Lowell, of course, are about neither men at the top nor men at the bottom. They are about women—

thousands of "female operatives," those legendary "mill girls," who were the core of Lowell's labor force for the mills' first decades. Social historians confirm that Lowell was not the first city to employ young Yankee farm women in its factories. Still, the Lowell experiment—and the corporate paternalism at its core—became world-famous and set the standard for dozens of other American cities that eventually emulated Lowell's pioneering processes in industrialization.

Modern women workers would hardly find the lives of Lowell's early mill girls enticing. Their lives were controlled by the company they worked for, and rigidly scheduled. They rose at 4:30 A.M., to the sound of a clanging bell, and reported to work by 5:00. They had a quick breakfast back at the mill boardinghouse at 7:00 A.M., then raced back to the humid, stuffy, noisy mill workrooms before 7:30. Their work days would often run twelve to thirteen hours, with breaks only for breakfast and dinner. At day's end, at 7:00 P.M., the young women would return to their boardinghouse dorm rooms—where they slept several to a small room and usually two or three to a bed—to eat supper, then perhaps attend a lecture or concert, before retiring by the 10:00 P.M. curfew bell. For their intensive labor, they were paid $1.00 to $1.50 per week—less than half of what their male counterparts were earning.

The mill girls got more than cash and exhaustion for their hard labors. Like the men who worked in the cotton mills, the women sometimes suffered deafness from the incessantly noisy looms, and respiratory illness from inhaling cotton dust. Unlike the men, the mill girls—and most women of the period—were expected to wear stiff corsets, which often caused impairment of their internal organs. Working amidst excessive heat and humidity was another job-related health risk, one considered relatively minor compared to a scalping or a lost limb—the dangers of working too close to the power looms.

Still, the social, economic, and cultural benefits for young farm women—at least during the 1820s and 1830s, before factory conditions began to deteriorate—often made life in Lowell worthwhile. It gave many young women financial independence, friendships, cultural experiences, and certain freedoms they never would have found at home. Most of them only worked in the mills for two or three years, saving enough money for a dowry. The greater the dowry, it seems, the greater chance a woman had of attracting a nonabusive husband.

Though the mills were never a good place to work, and were heavily romanticized over the decades, National Park Service ranger Liza Stearns explains that there *were* long-term benefits for the mill girls. "The exploitation of women in Lowell ironically led to their eventual empowerment. . . . There was lots of female bonding . . . women took care of women . . . and it aided the development of consciousness for women. The Lowell experience was also important to the later inclusion of working women in the women's movement of the nineteenth century."

The colorful two-floor mill-girl exhibit at Mogan Cultural Center—recreated in an actual Boott Mills boardinghouse—along with special tours with a women's history focus, are excellent sources of more information about these pioneering workers.

★   ★   ★

The mill girls of Lowell were the first of many groups of laborers to work in the mill system during its century of peak operation. Visiting the immigration exhibit at the Mogan Cultural Center, or simply reading the ethnic names on varied downtown restaurants, groceries, churches, and shops—from Irish, French-Canadian, Greek, Polish, and Portuguese to Hispanic and Southeast Asian—gives visitors an idea of the rich tapestry of humanity drawn there over the decades.

In many ways, artist Vassilios (Bill) Giavis's story is typical of the Lowell experience. His parents and other family members immigrated from Greece at the turn of the century, enticed by "unskilled" jobs in the mills. As their confidence and education grew, they branched out into private enterprise. In the Giavises' case, the result was a family grocery that opened in 1911. Young Bill once ran that store, finally closing it in 1984 to pursue his dream of becoming an artist.

Today, Giavis is back in the mills again; he's one of several artists working in the Brush Art Gallery and Studios, in the renovated Market Mills complex, across from the visitor center. Ninety percent of Giavis's artwork is about historic and modern Lowell—diners, churches, businesses, and buildings. The gallery is an artists' cooperative partly subsidized by the Lowell Historic Preservation Commission.

Like Bill Giavis, Arthur Morrissette is back in the Lowell mills again, too. But while Giavis has his studio there, Morrissette and his wife live in one of the 140 units in Market Mills set aside as apartments. Morrissette's parents emigrated from Quebec in the 1880s for the same reasons as their peers. "It was the draw of the mills. Money!" Morrissette admits. Arthur himself began mill work in the 1930s. He still remembers hard labor, nonstop eight-hour days, thirteen-dollar-a-week salaries, sweaty workrooms, tightly shut windows—and a brother-in-law who died at age fifty-three from lung problems caused by unhealthy mill conditions. "It was a hard life," he admits, "but those were our happiest days too. We paid our own way. And Lowell did give me my American Dream."

Dreams, of course, come and go. So, too, did the Lowell experiment. Eventually—after the Civil War, World War I, or the Great Depression, depending on whom you ask—the decline began. Competition from other cities, many of which had copied the Lowell industrial process, cut mill owners' profits, eventually driving salaries and working conditions down. Workers' unrest erupted into strikes. Some textile mills shut down. Others cut expenses by moving to the South.

As a result, "Spindle City" dwindled and almost died. For much of the twentieth century, in fact, Lowell was written off as a dreary has-been, a crumbling remnant of bygone days, full of boarded-up factories, empty row houses, high unemployment, and low morale.

What happened to bring about Lowell's rebirth is a book in itself. Perhaps the turning point came in the late 1950s and early 1960s, when the old Dutton Street boardinghouses were leveled—and part of the city's cultural heritage was swept away in the process. Perhaps it was in the late 1960s, when proposals to fill in Lowell's canals for parking lots were broached. In any event, the concept of creating a twentieth-century urban park from the decaying industrial city was originated by a local educator,

Dr. Patrick J. Mogan. The result was the creation of Lowell Heritage State Park in 1974, and the establishment of Lowell National Historical Park and the Lowell Historic Preservation Commission, both on June 5, 1978. Their goals are being achieved, year after year, through a new "Lowell process": the cooperative support of federal, state, city and private-sector resources. And save for the rigors of the recession, the city's economy and morale, as well as tourism, have been on the rise ever since.

THE ESSENTIALS

ADDRESS: National and State Park Visitor Center, Market Mills Court-yard, 246 Market Street, Lowell.

TELEPHONE: Visitor Center and National Historical Park offices, (508) 970-5000.

VISITOR INFORMATION: Visitor Center open 8:30 A.M.–5:00 P.M. daily. Free. Varied tours throughout the year; fees charged for selected offer-ings; reservations for tours suggested. Visitor Center, Boott Cotton Mills Museum, Mogan Cultural Center, Water Power exhibit, and restrooms all wheelchair accessible; tours require assistance; call for information.

PART VI

The Green, Green Grass
of Home:
Parks, Playgrounds,
and Open Spaces

HE CITY of Boston has long been known for its beautifully preserved historic structures, both secular and religious. Yet one of the true glories of wandering through its greater metropolitan area is discovering lands and open landscapes where few buildings exist at all.

There are dozens of such natural "escapes" in and around Boston—ranging from town and neighborhood commons to city parks, beaches, rivers, reservations, and other sanctuaries. Still, the fact that they remain intact and well-tended today was hardly the result of a natural process. To the contrary: lands have always been preserved in the Commonwealth of Massachusetts and the city of Boston with deliberate intent and vision. In the words of greenspace advocate Mark Primack, author of the *Greater Boston Park and Recreation Guide,* "The people of Boston and Massachusetts have much to be proud of: no metropolitan area in the United States has done more to protect its natural resources."

The name most commonly associated with the Boston Park System per se is that of internationally acclaimed landscape architect Frederick Law Olmsted, Sr. During the last two decades of the nineteenth century, Olmsted and his Brookline-based firm helped develop what is popularly known as the Emerald Necklace of parks for the city of Boston, while simultaneously inventing the field of landscape architecture in America. Since 1981, Olmsted's home and office have been open to the public as the Olmsted National Historic Site. It's a perfect place to begin exploring the Olmsted firm and understanding how they molded in-town landscapes from Back Bay's Fens, Charlesbank Park, and the Riverway to the Jamaica-way, the Arnold Arboretum, and Franklin Park.

Still, Greater Boston's parks and open spaces neither began nor ended with Frederick Law Olmsted. As early as 1634, only four years after the settlement of Boston by the Massachusetts Bay Colony, Puritan leaders set aside a forty-eight acre site in the center of town as a "commonage" for its citizens. In early colonial days, the concept of a public park for strolling, socializing, and recreation was unheard of; Boston Common was initially used for more practical pursuits, like grazing cows, training the militia, and hanging heretics.

During the nineteenth century, both Boston and the new nation grew and changed, in a sometimes frightening manner. Across America and New England, rolling farmlands were giving way to towns, while cities were rapidly becoming overcrowded centers of industry and commerce. Unprecedented numbers of immigrants arrived from the Old World, creating new labor forces and new problems of space. Boston proceeded to build on many of its last open lands, including the craggy pastures of Beacon Hill. When they ran out, the city created hundreds more in-town acres with the miracle of landfill.

Fortunately, many Bostonians acknowledged that urban congestion, pressures, and filth made public parks—as places for healthy escape and a breath of fresh air—essential to human survival. What became known as the parks movement of the nineteenth century was buttressed by other area events. In 1831, for example, scenic Mount Auburn Cemetery was founded in Cambridge, inspiring the development of garden cemeteries across the nation. In 1835, Concord philosopher Ralph Waldo Emerson published his *Nature,* expounding on the concept of nature as a thing to be nurtured and enjoyed.

Hence, as landfill was added to Boston's Back Bay, parks became an integral part of urban development. In 1837, a privately owned botanical garden was begun on the edge of Boston Common, and it soon evolved into today's Public Garden. As Commonwealth Avenue and its fine homes were built on landfilled marshes between 1857 and 1890, a long, tree-shaded walkway called Commonwealth Avenue Mall was laid out as well. As a result, when Olmsted began designing his string of city parks, he had the existing Common, Public Garden, and Mall—as well as an early incarnation of the Arnold Arboretum—to work with, and on.

Meanwhile, other parts of the metropolitan area developed public lands and recreational facilities as well, thanks largely to the pioneering work of landscape architect Charles Eliot, the son of Harvard president Charles W. Eliot, and the apprentice (and eventual partner) of Frederick Law Olmsted, Sr. Due in part to pressures from Eliot and his conservation-minded colleagues, the Metropolitan Park Commission was created in 1892. Al-most immediately, the commission began acquiring and developing parks and open spaces in and around Boston. By 1919, that group evolved into the Metropolitan District Commission (M.D.C.), which continues to this day to oversee and manage a host of parks and recreation sites, including those at the Blue Hills Reservation, Georges Island, and Castle Island.

Boston Common

IF YOU come to Boston, you really can't miss Boston Common. That's partly a matter of sheer mass: the sprawling public park is located at the hub of the bustling downtown area—near the shopping district, the theater district, and the State House. Down below the Common lies a cavernous public parking garage (closed for reconstruction until the fall of 1996) and the busy Park Street T stop. Above ground, visitors are frequently seen hopping onto tour buses, or beginning their walking tours of the Freedom Trail, the Black Heritage Trail, or the Emerald Necklace of Boston Parks.

All of this is meant to suggest that you not only *can't* miss Boston Common, but that you *shouldn't*. Boston Common, after all, is not just a busy thoroughfare. It's the oldest public green in America, and Boston's oldest, most actively used public area. And as such, it has several centuries of tales to tell.

In 1634, only four years after Boston was founded by English colonists, the Common was established as a cow pasture for the landholders of its first Puritan settlement. Since then, it's served as military training field, public punishment site, ball and game field, outdoor festival center, campground, swimming hole, performance stage, sledding hill, preaching pulpit, burying ground, balloon launching pad, public art gallery, deer park, rug-beating center, picnic ground, Victory Garden, recruiting office, lovers' lane, fast food stand, bucolic walkway, and haven for the homeless. You name it, it's been done there.

Unlike many other public and private parks, Boston Common's forty-eight acres have never been just a playground for the rich and famous. Today, these well-worn midtown lands reflect that democratic ideal more than ever. On any given day, you can find black and white, rich and poor, young and old wandering through—on foot, bike, skateboard, or wheelchair—sporting anything from three-piece suits to tattered cut-offs.

That's not to say that famous people haven't enjoyed the Common as well. Whitney Houston, Charles Lindbergh, Pope John Paul II, Martin Luther King, Jr., Mary Dyer, John Winthrop, Olivia Newton-John, George Washington, Willie Nelson, the Marquis de Lafayette, Franklin D. Roosevelt, and cast members of the television series "Cheers" have all held court there, drawing sizable crowds. Sometimes the occasions have been festive, like concerts, celebrations, and military parades. Sometimes they've been more somber: the day in 1979 when the Pope celebrated a Mass, the day in 1965 when Dr. King cried out for racial equality, or the day in 1660 when Mary Dyer was suspended there on a hangman's noose.

★   ★   ★

The Common's history began in the seventeenth century, when Boston itself—called Shawmut by the American Indians who first camped and cleared land there—was a pear-shaped peninsula, roughly half its present size. Native Americans had largely left the site by 1630, but Shawmut did have one white inhabitant that year: the reclusive Reverend William Blackstone.

When Blackstone (or Blaxton) heard that the British colonists who settled in nearby Charlestown were suffering from poor water, he allegedly invited them to share his peninsula and its cool, clear springs. John Winthrop and his Puritan followers accepted, officially moving their Massachusetts Bay Colony settlement there in 1630. They renamed the site Boston, after the English town in Lincolnshire that many had called home.

Interestingly, although the Puritans moved in search of cleaner water, they weren't planning to drink it straight. Experience in the Old Country had taught them that water-in-the-wild was generally unpotable. What they really needed was a plentiful supply for making beer, which both adults and children quaffed daily.

Meanwhile Reverend Blackstone, feeling cramped by his new neighbors, decided to move on. Though he sold Winthrop and company much of his land for a sum of thirty British pounds, the Puritans reimbursed two local sachems as well, just to be safe. The 1634 transaction is commemo-

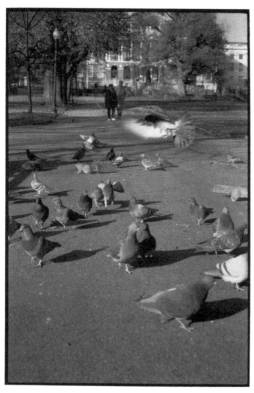

Pigeons still regularly flutter through Boston Common, though cows have been banned from grazing there since 1830.

rated in the Founders Memorial, erected in 1930 on the Beacon Street side of the Common, on the supposed site of an ancient spring.

According to Henry Lee, longtime president of the Friends of the Public Garden and Common, that Founders Memorial does have a few curious quirks. The memorial's representation of Blackstone, for example, bears a striking resemblance to James Michael Curley, Boston's mayor when the monument was erected. You may also note that the diminutive female figure behind Winthrop on the plaque looks like a girl, but is actually a woman—a symbolic suggestion, perhaps, of women's second-class status?

The roughly forty-eight-acre parcel bought from Blackstone, essentially the same irregular pentagon we know as Boston Common today, was intended as common land for prominent Puritan householders. As in England, the new Bostonians wanted a centrally located open green, or "commonage," to share as cow pasture, military training field, and public punishment site.

Contemporary accounts suggest that Boston's seventeenth-century Common had at least four hills, three ponds, one grand elm and a bathing beach. Though most of those hills were eventually leveled for landfill, vestiges of those early slopes can be seen on the upper Common's Liberty Mall, behind the stately Shaw/54th Regiment Memorial, and on Flagstaff Hill, where the Soldiers and Sailors Monument stands. Meanwhile, as the hills were leveled, the ponds and marshes were filled in, leaving only the shallow Frog Pond.

The Common's beach area began where Charles Street now divides the Common from the Public Garden. There, long before the Back Bay was filled and the Public Garden planted, Bostonians swam and boated during high tide, and clammed in the mudflats at low tide. There young Ben Franklin fished. And there, on the night of April 18, 1775, British soldiers hopped into their boats, as two lights flashed in the steeple of the Old North Church, warning colonial patriots of the enemy's departure "by sea" to Lexington and Concord (see chapters 4 and 5).

Before and during the American Revolution, the Common played host to both colonial and British troops. Colonial soldiers mustered on the Common in 1745 on their way to the French and Indian War, a war that provided military training later used against the British. Patriots celebrated the repeal of the Stamp Act on the Common, and hanged effigies there to protest the tax on tea. Under the boughs of the Common's Great Elm, the Sons of Liberty met and plotted revolutionary acts. And on the Common's open fields, General Washington reviewed his victorious troops.

The British, meanwhile, had used the Common for meetings, militia, and muster. From 1768 until their forced evacuation in 1776, in fact, British troops maintained a major encampment there. In 1775, 1,750 soldiers incensed the colonists, burned down the Common's trees and fencing for firewood and spite, and dug trenches that would pockmark the terrain for decades after. Despite the danger, young Boston boys refused to let the British encampment interfere with their favorite winter pastime— sledding across the Common.

If American freedom rang from Boston Common, so too did American intolerance. In the seventeenth century, crowds regularly assembled there to ogle wrong-doers confined in the stocks or hanged on trees like the Great Elm. Hanging trees were later replaced by gallows, first installed in

Throughout Boston's summer months in particular, the Common is often filled with ballgames, festivals, concerts, rallies, and other joyous events.

1769. "Witches," American Indians, deserters, pirates, and ordinary criminals met the noose on Common grounds. So did many who didn't fit the strict Puritan religious mold—like four people strung up for the crime of being Quakers. One such victim was Mary Dyer, whose statue stands on the lawn of the State House, watching over her own execution site.

But the Common's long history includes public amusements as well as political history. In the nineteenth century, the traditional Feast of Squantum featured proper Bostonians performing "Indian rites," while mounted cavaliers rode about in spurs and white boots. In 1848, an extravagant Water Festival was celebrated, with a flurry of bells, rockets, and leaping fountains heralding the opening of the city's public water system. Soapbox orators regularly gathered crowds at Brimstone Corner, on the junction of Tremont and Park, throughout the nineteenth century.

Today, over two hundred permits are issued each year for events on Boston's Common. Regular festivities include the popular holiday winter tree-lighting ceremonies—fifty-four trees are now illuminated throughout the winter holidays—and the annual arrival of the children's Christmas tree, a gift from St. John, New Brunswick. During Boston's First Night celebrations on New Year's Eve, the park is filled with outdoor art and working artists, including mammoth ice sculptures. The Halloween Parade is a fall family favorite, while the summer finds the Common a-flurry with free concerts, the annual Teddy Bear picnic, an Ice Cream Festival, the Gay Pride March, and other special events.

Though modern Bostonians think of the Common as a park lined with trees, crisscrossing pathways, malls, and monuments, that look really wasn't established until the early 1800s. The original Common probably had only a handful of trees, the most famous of which was the Great Elm. Some twenty-two feet around and seventy feet high in 1855, the tree sheltered or supported many activities during its long life. Among them were the aforementioned public hangings, revolutionary gatherings, and a Smoker's Circle of rebellious young nineteenth-century men that formed and met there after smoking was banned from public places. The Great Elm was irreparably damaged by an 1869 storm and blown down in February 1876. Today several paths converge on the marker that commemorates where the venerable tree is thought to have stood.

Like the nearby Commonwealth Avenue Mall, the nineteenth-century Boston Common eventually became a showplace of urban elms, especially the American and the English. And just as on the Mall, the Common's elms have suffered in recent decades, decimated by storms, pollutants from vehicle traffic, and Dutch elm disease. An 1891 history counted the Common's trees at 1,300, some 800 of which were elms. In 1977, there were a mere 822 trees left, 72 of which were dead. But today—thanks to increased city awareness and allocations, the Boston Parks and Recreation Department, and the volunteer Friends of the Public Garden and Common—a long period of deterioration is ending. Approximately 745 trees still stand, including 270 elms. Private tree "donations" are growing yearly, and in 1992 the Friends of the Public Garden and Common established a special fund to preserve the Common's mature trees.

On the Boylston Street side of the green sits the old Central Burying Ground, established in 1756 to relieve overcrowding in Boston's three other in-town graveyards. Overcrowding eventually became a problem in the new graveyard as well. In 1895, when excavations began under the Common for America's first subway, some 1,100 bodies were discovered beneath Boylston Street. They were soon reburied in a common grave in the northwest corner of the burial ground.

According to Ellen Lipsey, executive director of the city's Landmarks Commission, the remains of 300 Native Americans were discovered in relatively recent archaeological digs there, sharing a space that "officially" housed dead British and colonial soldiers, many killed at the Battle of Bunker Hill during the American Revolution. Those official graves are still marked by 487 headstones, most of which face east, the best angle for hearing the trumpet call on Judgment Day. The Burying Ground's most famous resident is painter Gilbert Stuart. Though Stuart is commemorated by a marker, no one is really sure of the whereabouts of his remains—a typical dilemma for older urban cemeteries, where stones were often rearranged with total disregard for who lay beneath.

As with any such active outdoor stage, both the scenes and scenery of the Common have changed over the centuries. Though its 5,520-foot perimeter has remained fairly constant, for example, its hills, ponds, and trees have diminished. Among other curious or significant changes that have occurred:

- Grazing cows, the first official residents of the Common, were gradually eliminated as Boston's population grew. In 1830, with the Common generally acknowledged as a public park and recreation ground, cows were banned altogether.
- The early Common had wooden fencing around the perimeter. In the 1820s and 1830s, decorative iron replaced the wood. Much of

that iron was taken for scrap metal in World War II, but since it was cast rather than wrought, it remained unused. Remnants of the original iron fence can still be seen along Beacon Street.

- In 1640, Boston's freemen voted that no one could ever build a "house" on the Common. The promise was rarely kept. Over the centuries structures have included an almshouse, a workhouse, and a house for the insane and criminal. Today there are three mausoleum-like subway kiosks, four box-shaped parking garage entrances, a park ranger's house and a visitors' center.

The Common's collection of public art now includes sixteen statues, plaques, and memorials fabricated from granite, bronze, stone, slate, and even cast aluminum, commemorating everything from the first football club in the United States to the founder of the local Filene's department store.

- The finest work of art in the park is sculptor Augustus Saint-Gaudens's memorial to Colonel Robert Gould Shaw and the all-black volunteer 54th Regiment, many of whom died in the attack on Fort Wagner in Charleston Harbor during the Civil War. First installed in 1897, the memorial has recently been refurbished. (See Chapter 34.)
- The most popular sculpture may well be the 1888 Boston Massacre Memorial, on Tremont Street near Boylston, nicknamed the "Crispus Attucks Monument" for the African-American who was the first to die in the 1770 event. The hand of one of the massacre victims, which protrudes from a bronze bas relief, has a constant shine due to passersby's "good luck" rubbings. (He's also lost a finger to the well-wishers.) Though popular mythology says the hand belongs to Attucks, the latter's body is actually depicted lying on the ground below.
- The most controversial piece of public art is certainly the ominous *Partisans* statue, near MacArthur Mall on the Charles Street side of the Common. Hyperactive kids must love sculptor Andrzej Pitynski's somber depiction of five mounted Polish freedom fighters, since they try to climb it constantly, occasionally toppling off portions of the sculpture. The related controversy is twofold: the statue's connection to Boston history is obscure at best, and it was originally slated to stand on the Common for only one month in 1983. That statue stands on the section of the Common known as the Parade Ground, incidentally—which will be closed through late 1996 due to the garage reconstruction below.

Despite the wealth of history connected to Boston Common, the park is hardly a worn-out has-been. The city's Parks and Recreation Department is continuing to raise funds for major capital improvements, which have already included new lights, improved litter collection and maintenance, more visible city rangers, and construction of a new visitors' center. The Friends of the Public Garden and Common have continually sponsored vital projects as well, from donating trees and saving statues to monitoring nearby high-rise development.

Such care and concern is well justified. Since 1972, this granddaddy of American public greens has been listed in the National Register of Historic Places. Moreover, Boston's 1822 city charter prohibits the sale of Boston Common except by vote of its citizens. Since no one is foolish enough to vote away those precious forty-eight acres, it's clear that the Common is there to stay.

THE ESSENTIALS

ADDRESS: Bounded by Beacon, Charles, Boylston, Tremont, and Park streets, Boston.

TELEPHONE: Boston Park Rangers, (617) 635-7383; Boston Common Ranger Station, (617) 635-7389; Boston Parks and Recreation Department, (617) 635-4505; Friends of the Public Garden and Common, (617) 227-8955.

VISITOR INFORMATION: Open twenty-four hours a day, 365 days per year. Free. Call city ranger station for information on free ranger-guided tours. Maps, brochures, and general tourist information available at Boston Common Visitor Information Center, on Tremont Street side of Common; open Monday through Saturday, 8:30 A.M. to 5:00 P.M., Sundays 9:00 A.M. to 5:00 P.M.; closed Christmas Day. Paths throughout Common are wheelchair accessible; Beacon Street side more difficult to enter, due to several entrances with stairs and steeper slopes near the State House corner; new visitors' center will have wheelchair-accessible restrooms.

43 The Public Garden

IT'S ONLY half the size and less than half the age of its neighbor, the venerable Boston Common. Yet the Public Garden, neatly bound by black iron fencing along Arlington, Beacon, Charles, and Boylston streets, is an acknowledged gem with a personality all its own—a twenty-four-acre oasis of trees, flowers, public art, and paddling Swan Boats in the middle of downtown Boston.

Though it's renowned worldwide as the first public botanical garden in the United States, life has never been easy for the Public Garden. First, there have been the enduring misnomers: no, it's not the Public *Gardens*, nor the Boston Garden, where the Celtics and the circus have historically held forth. Next have come the mishaps—a series of false starts, fierce controversies, and financial difficulties that have threatened the existence of the garden since its inception in the early nineteenth century.

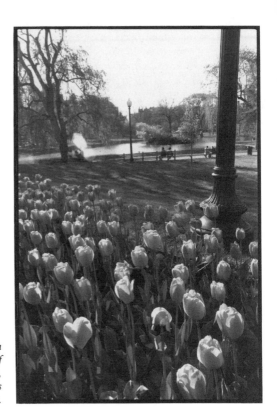

The Public Garden is a
twenty-four-acre oasis of
flowers, trees, public art,
and paddling Swan Boats
in downtown Boston.

The Public Garden, as it turns out, is a survivor—a survivor of foul-smelling ropewalk buildings, ill-conceived dams, and inadequate planning in the nineteenth century, and of vandalism, hurricanes, and shrinking public funds in the twentieth. But for the grace of one Horace Gray, moreover, Boston's magnificent Public Garden might never have existed at all. To understand all that, we'll have to go back even before Gray's time.

In the beginning, there was water. During high tide, that meant colonial Bostonians could swim, fish, or skate on the area we now know as the Public Garden. At low tide, those same flats became soggy marshland, and a fine spot for digging clams or shooting snipe. Sometimes it was called Round Marsh, while at other times it was simply known as the desolate shoreline on the western edge of the Common.

The grandest historic event to occur on Round Marsh in the eighteenth century took place on April 18, 1775. In the dark of that night, some seven hundred British troops embarked in barges and boats "from the foot of the Common" to cross over to Cambridge. From there they made a sunrise sweep into Lexington and then to Concord, initiating the first major battle of the American Revolution. The famous signal "one if by land, two if by sea" was made that night; thanks to two lanterns briefly lit in the steeple of the Old North Church, the colonists were warned of the British route across the flooding tides of the Charles River (see chapters 4 and 5).

During those marshy days, the summit of Fox Hill, near the Charles Street entrance of the Garden, was the only segment of the future Public Garden not inundated by the river during high tide. In 1794, the city of Boston gave Fox Hill and the rest of this wasteland to rope manufacturers whose businesses had been burned out by fires in the old South End. Fires periodically broke out there as well, but the ropewalks endured. Then, in 1821, Uriah Cotting's corporation built a dam across the adjoining Back Bay. Though the dam provided water power for mills and factories, it also created stagnation and stench—and became a favorite refuse dump. Looked at from any direction or perspective, the acreage that would someday become the Public Garden was, to date, a mess.

In 1824, the city decided to repurchase the site for $55,000—land that they had given away only thirty years before—and then tried to sell it. Vended in small segments, the lots would presumably have been used for residential construction. The sale was stopped, however, by a citizens' vote to fill in the marsh and maintain it as public property.

Landfill was added here and there over the next decade, but nothing of note occurred until 1837. In that year, seventeen Bostonians led by wealthy iron manufacturer and horticulturalist Horace Gray leased the marshland under the name the Proprietors of the Botanic Garden in Boston. Using funds from private donors, they began reclaiming the mudflats and planting on the site. The early flora included tulips, roses, camellias, and Boston's first poinsettia. But when financing went awry in 1852, Horace Gray and his colleagues were forced to return the site to the city.

Again, the city tried to sell the area, and again the public voted to hold onto their seminal downtown garden. They also voted to ban all buildings on the site, save those "expedient for horticultural purposes." In 1859, the city finally succumbed to the public will and set up a competition for a design of the city's Public Garden. George F. Meacham, a young Boston architect, won with his English-style garden design and was awarded $100 for his efforts. The Public Garden as we know it had begun.

For many visitors, the first attraction of the Public Garden is clearly its flowers and trees. Depending on the time of year, the fifty-seven flower beds may be showcasing laughing clusters of pansies, regiments of tulips, or burgeoning circles of brand-new roses—not to mention begonias, lantana standards, and various tropicals. Their ranks include fifteen thousand summer "bedding plants"—plants of the same species massed together to achieve colorful and artistic effects. The flowers, like those in public parks throughout the Hub, are grown in the city greenhouses at Franklin Park. They are maintained by the Boston Parks and Recreation Department, and planted twice a year, in spring and summer.

The Public Garden's trees are some of its best-loved plants. Among local favorites are the huge Japanese pagoda tree near the Beacon and Arlington street corner, of a species revered as the "scholar's tree" in the Far East; the looming metasequoia near the entrance at Beacon and Charles, now strong and beautiful though only thirty years ago it was believed to be near death; and, near the "Ether" Monument, the unique ginkgo with its fan-shaped leaves, one of a species that evolved some 150 million years ago. The garden is home to more than 750 trees and shrubs in all, including about 125 varieties of trees.

Beloved, too, are the twenty weeping willows that surround the Lagoon. The Lagoon itself was completed in the summer of 1861, as part of architect Meacham's original design. This three-acre artificial pond, which averages three to four feet in depth, is drained and refilled twice a year. Contrary to popular legend, the bridge spanning the Lagoon is neither "the world's smallest suspension bridge" nor a replica of the Brooklyn Bridge. It looks like a suspension bridge, but that is a matter of deceptive design. And though it does slightly resemble its big Brooklyn cousin, Boston built the Lagoon bridge in 1869, while Brooklyn's opened in 1883.

Since 1877, the public has been able to enjoy the Lagoon through peaceful, fifteen-minute Swan Boat cruises. The unique Swan Boats were the invention of Robert Paget, a nineteenth-century English immigrant and shipbuilder, who ran the first boat-for-hire concession on the Lagoon. In 1877, Paget scrapped his original fleet of rowboats and replaced them with foot-pedaled boats topped by man-made swans. He was inspired by the popularity of bicycles and by Richard Wagner's opera *Lohengrin,* in which a knight of the Grail crosses a river in a swan-drawn boat to defend his lady's innocence.

The Swan Boat experience has changed only slightly over the years. The five-cent fare of 1877 had grown to $1.45 by 1993, the boats in today's fleet are bigger than their predecessors, and the old copper swans have gradually been replaced by fiberglass facsimiles. Still, owner Paul Paget sees a continuity in mood from the days when his grandfather founded the Swan Boat business. "It's almost like a fantasy land," he muses, noting the boats' and Lagoon's enduring charm and ageless appeal.

Paul Paget's earliest memories, dating back to when his father, John Paget, was chief proprietor, include the day child star Shirley Temple requested a ride.

"She was staying at the Ritz, and had a cold for three or four days. When she finally came over to ride the boats, she had a police detail with her— since twenty-five thousand people were out there watching. The police were worried that the public's affection for her might lead them to jump into the pond to greet her!" Thankfully, no such disaster occurred. Other celebrity Swan Boat riders over the years have included Will Rogers, Gary Cooper, Bette Davis, Lucille Ball, Maurice Chevalier, Xavier Cugat, Theodore Bikel, Barbara Walters, Howard Cosell, Sid Caesar, Lynn Redgrave, Princess Grace of Monaco, President John F. and Jacqueline Kennedy, President Calvin Coolidge, and Ted Danson.

Paul Paget remembers another Swan Boat rider, affectionately known as Sally Mallard. Sally was a mother duck who, in the late 1950s began laying eggs under the back seat of the Number 3 Swan Boat (the boats are numbered 1 through 6). Her cache of eggs increased daily, much to the delight of the fascinated local press corps, who closely followed the event. By roughly 6:00 P.M. of the last day, Paget recalls, thirteen ducklings were hatched. Sally picked them up one by one and plunked them in the pond. They swam just fine.

Sally and two of her offspring returned to the Public Garden the following year, but disappeared soon after. Mother Duck was immortalized, though, when the Number 3 Swan Boat was renamed "Sally."

Immortalized ducks have also recently been added to the Public Garden's statuary—which constitutes another major attraction for visitors. Until the duckling statues arrived in 1987 (details below), the most famous figure was probably sculptor Thomas Ball's gargantuan equestrian version of General George Washington, which greets visitors at the Arlington Street entrance. The oldest is the popular "Ether" Monument, one of the few non-bronze memorials in the Garden. Emerging from a brick basin, the granite monument begins in a cube base, segues into decorative Venetian arches and columns, and is topped by a humanitarian figure administering aid to an ailing nude. It was erected in 1868 to commemorate the first successful use of anesthesia at Massachusetts General Hospital. Since a dispute arose as to just *which* doctor had first employed ether in surgery, the figure on top was made a generic Good Samaritan, and the monument dedicated to the discovery of ether itself.

Near these two famous sculptures are statues of a host of other Boston-related luminaries, cast primarily in bronze. Among them are abolitionist orators Charles Sumner and Wendell Phillips, Civil War hero Thomas Cass, Unitarian preacher William Ellery Channing, and Polish-American Revolutionary War hero Tadeusz Kosciuszko.

While all of the statues in the park represent men, the sculptures in the Public Garden's four circular fountains were all made by Boston women. Nevertheless, sexism certainly affected some art-related decisions in the nineteenth century, according to Henry Lee, president of the Friends of the Public Garden and Common. In a blind competition for the Charles Sumner statue, held shortly after Sumner's death in 1874, the work of Mrs. Anne Whitney was chosen; but when the judges discovered the artist was female they reneged and named the top male competitor, Thomas Ball, the winner instead. Mrs. Whitney's version of Sumner was eventually installed on the traffic island across from the Cambridge Common in Harvard Square.

The newest statue commissioned for the Public Garden depicts a female, but not exactly a woman. Newton artist Nancy Schon's bronze sculpture *Mrs. Mallard and Her Eight Ducklings* was installed in 1987 to commemorate the 150th anniversary of the Public Garden. The sculpture is based on a children's classic, Robert McCloskey's 1941 *Make Way for Ducklings*. The book has been reprinted time and time again over the past half-century, and helped familiarize thousands of children with the Public Garden. On any given day you can see several of them hugging, kissing, or riding the kid-sized duck statues—which serves to keep the bronze beautifully polished. The negative side to the sculpture's popularity is that duck-nappings have occurred several times since its installation.

Throughout the Public Garden's history, cooperative efforts of the public and private sector have been the key to its survival. And survival has generally meant protection from both natural forces and human activity. In recent decades, natural disasters here have ranged from hurricanes ripping through trees and fencing—as did the Great Hurricane of 1938 and Gloria in 1985—to Dutch elm disease, which has diminished the once large elm population in a much quieter manner.

Meanwhile, man-made disasters—including insidious city pollution—have taken their toll as well. As far back as 1897, for instance, the building of America's first subway system took precious land from the Public Garden; fortunately, the old subway entrance near the Arlington-Boylston corner was finally plugged up in 1941. In recent decades, a coalition of Public Garden lovers fought to keep the Park Plaza building project, on the Boylston side of the Garden, a reasonable size; they were well aware that ill-considered development along the Garden's borders could create chilly, shaded corners and unduly high winds.

Today, members of the Friends of the Public Garden and Common—a volunteer group which began organizing in 1971 in response to the Public Garden's decay—regularly step in to raise money and oversee projects that limited public funds cannot support. The Friends have recruited sponsors to help purchase and plant new young trees, replacing older ones that have died of age, disease, or exposure to the elements. Some of those older trees, of course, have succumbed to overzealous visitors, who thoughtlessly tromp across roots or pick off branches. The Friends' Horticultural Planning Committee also works to keep identifying labels, with English and Latin names, both on the trees and out of reach of vandals.

Meanwhile, the Friends have collaborated with the city's Art Commission as well, on an ambitious project to return all the statuary to its original beauty. Thanks in part to Boston citizens who participate in the city's Adopt-a-Statue program, many of the once-green bronze statues are now brown—meaning that the patina caused by decades of oxidation has been removed. Color is not the only way to tell if a statue has been renovated, however, according to Henry Lee. Some cleaning methods deliberately leave the look of patina behind, on the premise that such coloration is often part of the artist's long-term design.

The flagpole along the Charles Street border also represents a model of city, volunteer, and business cooperation. At the base of the flagpole is a memorial to architect Marvin Goody, a prominent Bostonian who was a director of the Friends, chair of the Boston Art Commission, and an important contributor to the Public Garden. The memorial and the "pods" around the flagpole were designed by Goody's wife, architect Joan Goody. The flagpole itself predates the 1868 "Ether" statue; the Friends designed the surrounding paths and pavement in the 1970s, and the city provided the money to build them. Mr. and Mrs. Roger Saunders of the nearby Park Plaza Hotel donated the flag in 1986, in addition to funds for flagpole painting and lighting (protocol demands that the flag be illuminated, since it is never lowered).

Assuming the city, volunteers, and local businesses continue their support, Boston's beloved Public Garden should survive—and indeed prosper—for decades to come.

THE ESSENTIALS

ADDRESS: Bounded by Arlington, Beacon, Charles, and Boylston streets, Boston.

TELEPHONE: Boston Park Rangers, (617) 635-7383; Swan Boat information, (617) 522-1966; Boston Parks and Recreation Department, (617) 635-4505; Friends of the Public Garden and Common, (617) 227-8955; City Adopt-a-Statue Program, (617) 635-3245.

VISITOR INFORMATION: Open twenty-four hours a day, year round, free. Swan Boat rides open between Patriots' Day weekend (mid-April) through the third Sunday in September, weather permitting; Swan Boat hours 10:00 A.M.–4:00 P.M. daily from Patriots' Day weekend through June 19; 10:00 A.M.–5:00 P.M. daily from June 20 to Labor Day; small fee. Call city Park Rangers for information on special Public Garden tours. No bicycling, skateboarding, autos, dogs without leashes, or game playing on grass; no filming without a permit; no loitering after 10:00 P.M. Public Garden is wheelchair accessible throughout, with minor re-routing required due to steps near bridge area.

The Commonwealth Avenue Mall

THE PEARLY Gates may have Saint Peter, but the Commonwealth Avenue Mall—a thirty-two-acre promenade of shady elms, heroic statues, comfortable benches, and trod-but-true grass stretching from the Public Garden to Kenmore Square—has Stella Trafford. For the past two decades, the Back Bay resident and Mississippi native has chaired the neighborhood-based Commonwealth Avenue Mall Committee. In practical terms, that means that Trafford is the acknowledged Guardian of the Mall, the firm-but-friendly "Tree Lady" who watches out for the well-being of this public park as if it were her own backyard.

Trafford—along with friends, the Neighborhood Association of the Back Bay, the city's Parks and Recreation Department, Art Commission, and Landmarks Commission—has helped preserve and replenish one of Boston's great urban treasures, an in-town park, walkway, and historic site that dates back to just before the Civil War.

Though most Northeasterners are aware of this tree-lined path down Commonwealth Avenue, surprisingly few know it by name. "Mall," after all, has come to mean an indoor, air-conditioned shopping plaza. In the nineteenth and early twentieth centuries, however, when Back Bay was the preferred domain of Boston's rich and famous, the word meant a shaded walk or public promenade, an elegant enclave exclusively for pedestrians.

As malls went, the Commonwealth Avenue version was unprecedented in the United States. It resembled the spacious French boulevards of Napoleon III more than an American avenue. And though the Mall is somewhat less splendid today—pollution, vandalism, dogs, storms, rambunctious students, limited funds, Dutch elm disease, and changing Back Bay demographics have all taken their toll—it remains a vital link in Boston's famed Emerald Necklace of parks, joining the Public Garden and Common with the Frederick Law Olmsted–designed parks in the Fens and beyond.

Besides, with gentle warriors like Trafford on its side, it's getting better all the time.

The story of the Commonwealth Avenue Mall begins in 1857, when trains and steam shovels began hauling gravel in a mammoth landfill project that eventually transformed the soggy Back Bay into terra firma. Before that time, Boston was a curious, pear-shaped peninsula, and today's Back Bay was exactly what its name suggests—the mudflat backside of Boston, which flooded twice daily when Atlantic tides swelled the lower reaches of the adjacent Charles River.

That was all well and good until 1821, when the Roxbury and Boston Mill Company built a poorly engineered dam across the bay. Though designed to harness the tides to generate power for city industry, the dam was a financial failure. Even worse, added to the criss-cross of railroad tracks laid nearby, it clogged up the bay's natural cleansing mechanism. By

The statue of Samuel Eliot Morison perched on a twenty-ton granite rock is the newest and most popular monument lining the Commonwealth Avenue Mall.

mid-century, the Boston City Council admitted that the Back Bay basin was "nothing less than a cesspool." Sewage and waste from surrounding areas accumulated, and the stench was appalling.

Though the state legislature ordered the Back Bay to be filled in 1852, the process was not begun for another five years. According to historian Walter Muir Whitehill, contractors Norman Munson and George Goss agreed to fill in the filthy expanse of marsh in return for parcels of the newly formed land. Since Boston's in-town hills had already been leveled—leaving no local landfill—the developers sent their thirty-five-car trains back and forth to Needham to haul in fresh gravel. Day and night the cars and crews ran, each averaging one round trip an hour and depositing its load into the basin in only ten minutes, thanks to the newly invented steam shovel. By 1871, the Commonwealth Avenue area was filled from Arlington to Exeter Street in some sections, and as far as Gloucester Street in others; and by 1890 the Back Bay landfill was complete.

The eminent architect, wit, and bon-vivant Arthur Gilman won a competition to improve and design the new lands in the 1850s. At that time, French architectural designs, gardens, and mansard roofs were all the rage in Boston's upper echelons. (The French influence held sway in the world of fashion as well, manifesting itself among wealthy Bostonians in the form of French phrases, Napoleon III mustaches, tall Second Empire coiffures, and crinolines.) Hence the design for Back Bay, and for the hundred-foot-wide promenade that bisected Commonwealth Avenue, was in the French Second Empire grid-pattern style. Along with architect George Snell and landscape gardeners Robert Copeland and Horace W. S. Cleveland, Gilman proceeded to make the avenue the axial street of Back Bay. (Though landscape architect Frederick Law Olmsted is commonly associated with the Commonwealth Avenue Mall, his firm only helped design the last section, from the statue of Leif Eriksson at Charles Gate East to Kenmore Square.) Elegant brownstone houses eventually rose on both sides of the street, tastefully and legally restricted in their height and distance from the roadway.

The plan called for the Mall itself to be flat, long, and symmetrical, with grass on each side, a walking path down the center, and four rows of elms—two on the left and two on the right, in decidedly soldierly ranks. Despite a few changes over the next century—new benches, new statues, fences, and gates, and overpasses and underpasses to accommodate busy intersections such as Massachusetts Avenue—this pattern prevailed.

Unfortunately, the graceful, seemingly sturdy elms did not. Those majestic, towering trees were logical choices for the Mall—to create shady, scenic archways down its center path. The trees planted were slender American elms, soaring and wineglass shaped, and heftier, lower-branching English elms. But the rigors of city life—including car exhaust, heavy foot traffic, and vandalism—gravely tested their endurance. Of the 182 elms planted between Arlington and Dartmouth streets during the Civil War, only 85 of them survived until 1909. Dutch elm disease—which first arrived in Boston from Europe around 1930—dealt the trees an additional, often fatal blow. In 1968 alone, 90 of the 413 living trees on the Mall died of the disease. In 1969, alarmed Back Bay neighborhood residents mobilized and began vigorously spraying the trees; as a result, only one elm died that year. Since then, the pace of elm loss has dropped significantly, though some annual attrition continues.

It's no coincidence that 1969 was also Stella Trafford's first year as chair of the Neighborhood Association of Back Bay's Commonwealth Avenue Mall Committee (the association itself dated back to 1955). From 1969 on, Trafford and her Back Bay neighbors and colleagues continually monitored incipient tree disease. One of their innovative fund-raising programs allows private donors to memorialize or celebrate a loved one with a new Back Bay tree. As a result, to the remaining handful of century-old elms have been added leafy, disease-resistant Japanese zelkovas (cousins of the American elm), along with sweet gum, green ash, maple, Chinese scholar, and other strong, young hardwoods. All in all, a pretty and practical complement to the last great stand of urban elm trees in the Northeast.

Though trees are a primary attraction of the Commonwealth Avenue Mall, its monuments are clearly another. The seven statues located between Arlington and Charles Gate are all of men, save for two allegorical females guarding the Mayor Collins bust; however, women artists created fully one-half of the sculptures. Anne Whitney molded Leif Eriksson; Penelope Jencks created Samuel Eliot Morison; Yvette Compagnion sculpted Argentine president Domingo Sarmiento; and Theo Alice Kitson shared credit for the bust of Boston mayor Patrick Andrew Collins with her husband.

The men immortalized on the Mall are an unlikely urban league of heroes. Most were not born in Boston, some never lived there, and one may have never even set foot within the city limits. It's no wonder, then, that the selections ignited protests beginning in 1865, the year the first statue was installed. Curious citizens have pondered such questions as, Why was that brilliant sculptor Rimmer allowed to put his mediocre Hamilton on the Mall? What does Leif Eriksson have to do with Boston? Why is an ominous Argentinian blocking the path? Why is Samuel Eliot Morison wearing shoes instead of sneakers? Why can't we fit Gandhi's statue there?

All of which goes to prove that though the statues have frequently been controversial, they've never been boring.

Walking west from the Public Garden, we first find Dr. William Rimmer's vision of a flamboyant, stubborn Alexander Hamilton (1757–1804), staring out at the equestrian statue of General Washington in the Public Garden. The Hamilton monument—both the Mall's and America's first granite statue—depicts the man who won stateside fame as a Revolutionary War soldier, a signer of the Constitution, the first secretary of the treasury, and the face on the U.S. $10 bill. Born in the British West Indies, Hamilton is also remembered as the victim of a pistol duel with Aaron Burr.

On the block between Berkeley and Clarendon streets is John Glover (1732–1797), a Marblehead, Massachusetts, fisherman and Revolutionary War general. Glover's "marine" regiment manned the boats at Washington's famous crossing of the Delaware River in 1776. The bronze statue by Martin Milmore was installed in 1875.

Another local hero memorialized on the Mall is beloved Boston mayor Patrick Andrew Collins (1844–1905), whose elevated bust is flanked by two mythic females: Erin, who represents Collins's Irish birthplace; and Columbia, the symbol of Collins's adopted home. Collins served the citizens of Boston as mayor, member of the Massachusetts state legislature and of the U.S. Congress, and counsel general—all that after years as a miner, upholsterer, and Harvard law student. While some of the other statues were the gifts of philanthropists, the Collins bust was a gift from the people, paid for by funds collected within six days after his death. The Collins memorial was moved to this site in 1968 from its original 1908 Charles Gate location near Kenmore Square.

Abolitionist William Lloyd Garrison (1805–1879) is the subject of the Mall's first seated statue, located between Dartmouth and Exeter streets. A celebrated orator and activist, and editor of the antislavery newspaper *The Liberator,* Garrison was once dragged through Boston's streets by an angry lynch mob, and saved from an impromptu hanging by Mayor Theodore Lyman, Jr. By 1886, Garrison's liberal views were somewhat more acceptable, and Olin Levi Warner's superb bronze statue of him was added to Back Bay.

The most recent monument on the Mall, of U.S. Navy Admiral Samuel Eliot Morison (1887–1976), was added to the Exeter-Fairfield block in 1982. While Garrison sits on a chair, symbolically adorned with inkpot and papers, Morison's figure is perched on a twenty-ton granite rock, which was hand picked and hauled in from Rhode Island. Morison's list of accomplishments is impressive and long: a Boston native and lifelong lover of New England, he was a sailor, a maritime historian, a Harvard professor, the author of forty-eight books, and a Pulitzer Prize winner. His modern statue is probably the most popular to date. It's the most natural, the most lavishly landscaped, and the first to be lighted at night. (The spotlights are mounted on opposite Commonwealth Avenue rooftops, to minimize shadows.)

If Morison's is the most inviting statue, the figure of Domingo Sarmiento (1811–1868), on the Gloucester to Hereford section of the Mall, is often called the most intimidating. The memorial to the Argentinian president, journalist, and diplomat, known in his country as the father of Argentinian public education, was offered to Boston in 1913. It was accepted as a free gift sixty years later. Depicted as a stocky, determined, rather brutish figure, Sarmiento was a dedicated disciple of celebrated Massachusetts educator Horace Mann.

Meanwhile, two blocks further down stands that romantic Viking Leif Eriksson, staring off toward the fly balls of Fenway Park and the traffic jams of Kenmore Square. The picturesque statue was purchased by Boston chemist, manufacturer, and philanthropist Evan N. Horseford in 1887. Horseford believed "Lucky Leif" had landed in Cambridge in the year 1000, making him the true European discoverer of America. Needless to say, not everyone in Boston shared this belief, which may explain why an earlier plan to place Anne Whitney's statue of Eriksson in downtown Boston's Post Office Square never came to fruition.

By 1993, incidentally, discussions were underway to finally add a women's memorial to the Mall, presumably on the Fairfield to Gloucester block. Representatives of City Hall, the Boston Women's Commission, the

Neighborhood Association of the Back Bay, the Boston Women's Heritage Trail, and other interested parties have not agreed on the woman to be so memorialized as of mid-1993, though Abigail Adams is a leading contender.

The statues and trees of Commonwealth Avenue Mall can only be appreciated on foot. Automobiles have always been banned from the park; today only a select few individuals—Parks Department workers and Stella Trafford among them—can legally drive there.

In 1906, an effort was made to eliminate automobiles from Commonwealth Avenue itself: eight worried horse-and-buggy drivers signed a petition claiming cars "traveled at such high rates of speed that there was grave danger to life and limb."

The battle of the buggies was lost, and modern traffic rushes by, faster than ever, on either side. But the Commonwealth Avenue Mall remains an oasis for amblers and ramblers—and a pleasant reminder of an earlier, slower time.

THE ESSENTIALS

ADDRESS: Center of Commonwealth Avenue, from Arlington Street intersection to Kenmore Square, Boston.

TELEPHONE: Boston Parks and Recreation Department, (617) 635-4505; volunteer maintenance and tree donations, Stella Trafford, Neighborhood Association of the Back Bay, Commonwealth Avenue Mall Committee, (617) 267-6837.

VISITOR INFORMATION: Open twenty-four hours a day, 365 days a year. Free guided walks of Commonwealth Avenue Mall included in Boston Park Rangers tours of the Emerald Necklace and of Back Bay architecture, (617) 635-7383. Special tours may also be arranged through the Neighborhood Association of the Back Bay, (617) 247-3961. Passive recreation only; dog refuse must be scooped, or owners will be subject to fines. Completely wheelchair accessible via long center path and curb cuts.

The Arnold Arboretum

THE SPRINGTIME view in Jamaica Plain's sprawling Arnold Arboretum is one of the more spectacular sights in town. As you wander down the 265-acre garden's main street, a winding paved path called Meadow Road, you can marvel at the glorious, colorful, and aromatic eruptions of azaleas, lilacs, honeysuckles, redbuds, dogwoods, and a host of other plants. And though May and June are prime blooming-and-viewing months for many trees, bushes, and vines, there's something fascinating happening on and around these rolling hillsides, ponds, meadows, and footpaths every month of the year.

Despite its well-known wealth of sensory splendor, the Arnold Arboretum is more than a beautiful parkland. An arboretum (from the root *arbor,* meaning "tree") is a specialized form of botanical garden. This one in particular has always been a place for scientific research and education, under the sponsorship of Harvard University. Founded in 1872, it was the first arboretum in the United States intended for both university and public use. Moreover, it's clear that putting diverse people and plants together— thereby aiding our understanding and appreciation of things botanical— has always been its central goal.

Case in point is the Arnold Arboretum's living plant collection of more than 6,500 varieties and forms. For aesthetic reasons, the plants have been laid out with an eye for colorful sightlines and magnificent views. For educational purposes, however, they've also been arranged by evolutionary classification and grouped by their botanical families. American, Chinese,

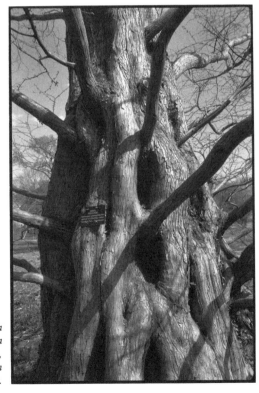

The Arnold Arboretum is a 265-acre parkland, with a living, and neatly labeled, plant collection of more than 6,500 varieties and forms.

and Japanese maples, for example, are planted near one another, allowing researchers to make comparisons not made by nature. In addition, some 175,000 dried and mounted plants from around the world, which make up what might aptly be called the "dead" collection, are stored and studied in the herbarium in Jamaica Plain.

(Contrary to popular belief, an herbarium is not an herb garden. Instead, it's a place where plants are pressed, dried, identified, stored and studied. Though the dried plant specimens—carefully mounted with linen tape on archival sheets of rag board—are stacked and stored in air-tight cases, hungry insects are still a major threat. The Jamaica Plain herbarium, by the way, stores only cultivated plants. A larger, companion herbarium at Harvard University in Cambridge, which houses more than a million other specimens, contains wild plants native to New England.)

As you explore the Arboretum, you may notice that much of its flora comes from specific sections of Asia, Europe, and North America, rather than from places like Australia, Africa, and Antarctica. The reason is that most of the Arboretum's plant life, though international in origin, is from the North Temperate Zone. "The Arboretum is situated in eastern North America," explains horticultural taxonomist Dr. Stephen Spongberg, "so climatically, we are able to grow here what is natural to this climate."

Virtually all the plants at the Arboretum—with the specially treated bonsai collection an obvious exception—have to endure the traumas of New England weather on their own. Trees and other plants are neither covered nor brought inside during intense snows, rains, or winds. (Calamities do happen; the infamous hurricane of 1938, for example, reportedly destroyed some 1,500 trees.)

Although the inclusion of so many Asian plants seems contradictory at first, "some basic climatic patterns of eastern North America recur on the other side of the world . . . in Eastern Asia," says Spongberg. "The two regions are almost mirror images of each other." Which explains why those Japanese, Chinese, and American maples can happily coexist on the gently rolling hillsides of Jamaica Plain.

More than a century ago, a variety of famous and not-so-famous men and women helped to conceive, build, and develop the Arnold Arboretum we know today. You can locate their names in local history books. Even better, however, is finding them commemorated in the names of buildings, hills, and trails, or on the labels attached to plants. Here's a quick "who's who" in Arboretum history:

The Arboretum began with James Arnold, a wealthy New Bedford whaler, land speculator, and Quaker pacifist. Arnold himself supported abolition societies and helped fugitive slaves in the pre–Civil War era, while his wife was beloved for her extensive charity work. James Arnold was a horticulturalist as well—a pastime affordable to few but the rich in nineteenth-century America. His New Bedford gardens were internationally renowned.

When Arnold died in 1842, his will allocated some $150,000 for "horticultural improvements." George B. Emerson, a trustee of Arnold's will, joined his colleagues in eventually deciding to invest this money in the

Arboretum project. Among Emerson's supporters in developing that project was Harvard professor Asa Gray, director of the seven-acre Harvard Botanical Garden in Cambridge. (That garden was torn down to make way for a housing development during the era of the Second World War.)

For the new arboretum, Gray and Emerson sought a broad stretch of land that would enable trees as well as smaller plants to be grown. Among the sites they initially considered was the open turf by the Charles River where Harvard Stadium now stands. Though it was eventually rejected as too expensive and too flat, Cambridge resident and poet Henry Wadsworth Longfellow continued to push for the Charles River site. Small wonder: it would have given him a marvelous (then unobstructed) view from his Brattle Street home, directly across the Charles.

Gray and Emerson eventually settled on land that had been donated to Harvard in 1843 by Benjamin Bussey, a wealthy gentleman farmer who pursued what his peers called "scientific farming" in the early 1800s. Bussey was famous within the community for a variety of reasons: he owned a fancy yellow coach, fought in the American Revolution, and donated bells to several area churches. He was also one of the first subscribers to Mount Auburn Cemetery in Cambridge, America's first garden cemetery, though he was never buried there.

The Bussey lands were a superior place for an arboretum. They had native woodland, ecological diversity, and a fascinating topological contour. Charles Sprague Sargent, a distant cousin of the famed portrait artist John Singer Sargent, became the Arnold Arboretum's first director in 1872. Sargent was already the director of the existing Harvard Botanical Garden and a horticulture professor at the Bussey Institution, Harvard's agricultural school, when he accepted the new position. (The Bussey Institution, incidentally, officially closed its doors in 1936.)

As director, Sargent worked with Frederick Law Olmsted—"the father of American landscape architecture"—in an effort to include the Bussey lands in plans for the city's famous Emerald Necklace of Boston parks. Olmsted was enthusiastic about helping to design an arboretum in Boston, particularly since he was unable to include one in his well-known New York City project, Central Park.

The plan worked. In 1882, Harvard turned over the land bequeathed to them in the Bussey will to the city of Boston. Arnold Arboretum officially became part of the city's new park system, Olmsted became part of the design team, and the Arboretum eventually became known as the flagship of Olmsted's Emerald Necklace.

Though the city held the deed, which it continues to hold to this day, it leased the land back to Harvard for a thousand years, charging a rent of a dollar per year. In practice, the city of Boston is financially responsible for walkways, walls, and security. Harvard pays for most of what happens inside the Arboretum's gates, including faculty and staff salaries. For other operating expenses and programs, the Arboretum depends on its own relatively small endowment income, plus gifts and grants.

In part because Sargent was involved in the first U.S. forest census, he initially concentrated on cultivating North American trees in the Arboretum. Soon, however, he began to exchange seeds and plants with gardens and nurseries around the world, and mounted horticultural expeditions to faraway lands. Emissaries eventually brought back specimens of everything from the cedars of Lebanon to the pines of Rome. One of the most legendary of these plant explorers was Ernest (Chinese) Wilson, who traveled throughout China, Japan, Korea, and Taiwan in the early 1900s. Wilson, whose name appears on many Arboretum plants, successfully introduced more than 1,500 trees and shrubs to the Arboretum that were previously not cultivated in the West.

As noted before, much within the Arboretum—buildings, hills, trails, and plants—was named for people like Wilson, Bussey, Gray, and Sargent, who were directly involved in Arboretum history. Other hills, paths, and fields bear the names of old area families, or were simply labeled according to the plants or collections nearby—as with Hemlock Hill, Meadow Road, and Oak Path.

Just about everything at the Arboretum has a name or label, in fact, including the plants. Identifying plaques include each plant's common name, scientific name, native land, and a number, which is an index to that plant's history. Botanical Latin, the scientific language for identifying plants, can make even the most familiar stuff sound exotic: *Davidia involucrata*, *Ulmus americana*, and *Syringa vulgaris* are more commonly known as the Chinese dove tree, the American elm, and the common lilac, respectively.

If you want to find out more about any of your favorite plants inside the Arboretum or out, the Hunnewell Visitor Center is a marvelous resource. Pamphlets, regular classes, lectures, and walks providing information on special plant-related topics are all available there, while a free brochure chronicling all these activities is printed each spring and fall. Furthermore, the library inside the center contains some 33,000 books, journals, pamphlets, and the like, plus 5,000 photos and 8,000 slides. (The library has limited public access, and is open by appointment only.)

Arboretum volunteers and guides can supply information about the cultivated inhabitants, as well as the "spontaneous flora"—grasses, ferns, and wildflowers that spring up on their own. They can show you how the silver maple got its name, or play "New England Smell 'n' Tell" by teaching you how to scratch, sniff, and identify sassafras and other plants. Be sure to ask about the "Amphibian Overture" that occurs near the Arboretum's three ponds, when a variety of frogs and toads trill, plunk, and peep at night or on overcast days. Arboretum tours, by the way, are now available from three different groups featuring three different perspectives: trained volunteer docents sponsored by the Arboretum, National Park Service rangers, and park rangers from the city of Boston.

There are obviously plenty of sights, stories, sounds, and smells that shouldn't be missed at the Arnold Arboretum. Perhaps the greatest single event, however, is the annual Lilac Sunday celebration in May—when thousands of guests arrive to revel in over 400 kinds of fragrant, multi-colored lilacs reaching their peak bloom along Meadow Road. On that day, lilac-lovers can also picnic—a recreation not usually permitted at the

Arboretum—and enjoy live entertainment. Local citizens began celebrating Lilac Sunday during World War I. They traditionally dressed up in their Sunday finest, then drove their horse-drawn buggies past the gloriously fragrant and vividly hued collection.

A curious footnote to the Lilac Sunday story is that the lilac—the traditional harbinger of spring, so much a part of New England's heritage that it's the state flower of New Hampshire—is not native to New England, nor even to America. The shrub is actually Middle Eastern in origin, though it transplants easily. Lilacs were brought first to Europe, then to the New World by colonists.

By the way, you may notice that the Arboretum's lilacs are located near both forsythia bushes and ash trees. The reason? Though to the lay observer they don't look alike, all three are members of the olive family. So, of course, are olive trees, but the latter are not hardy enough to survive this climate.

On Lilac Sunday and any other time of the year, the Arboretum is a favorite setting for shutterbugs. If you plan to bring your camera, you may appreciate a few tips from expert local photographer, volunteer guide, and unofficial Arboretum poet laureate Al Bussewitz:

- Early morning or late afternoon light is always the best for optimum color; midday overhead light washes color out.
- Use the Arboretum ponds as reflective backdrops for pictures; drop a pebble into the water to create a spiraling ripple. Breezes on the water give an Impressionistic feel.
- The ultimate tree to perch your loved ones on for photo sessions is the cork tree on Meadow Road. You won't be the first to photograph this beloved, broad "Climbing Tree," also known as *Phellodendron amurense*. The surface of its lower branch has been smoothed by the affection bestowed on it by hundreds of other people over the years.

THE ESSENTIALS

ADDRESS: The Arborway, Jamaica Plain, Boston. Main gates and Hunnewell Visitor Center one hundred yards south of rotary at the junction of Routes 1 and 203.

TELEPHONE: (617) 524-1718.

VISITOR INFORMATION: Open dawn to dusk, 365 days a year. Free. Guided tours are available on a seasonal schedule; call for information. No picnicking, except on Lilac Sunday; no bicycling or skating, or pets without leashes; cars allowed only for handicapped or elderly persons. Paved paths and Hunnewell Visitor Center are wheelchair accessible; accessible restrooms inside Visitor Center.

Franklin Park

WHAT CONSTITUTES Boston's best-kept secret is a matter of conjecture. But Boston's *biggest* secret is unquestionably the beautiful, vibrant, green and rolling five-hundred-acre stretch of urban flora, fauna, and festivities known as Franklin Park.

Franklin Park? Not long ago, the grand old parkland that straddles the neighborhoods of Jamaica Plain, Dorchester, and Roxbury was known as a home for abandoned cars, trash, and overgrown foliage; folks tended to mumble about its dilapidated old zoo and unusable golf course, or its high crime rate. But thanks to renewed public interest, increased funding, hard work—and an ample dose of pride and patience—the park once renowned as the finest green space in Frederick Law Olmsted's Emerald Necklace is in the midst of a renaissance.

As a result, the dumping is long gone. The abandoned cars have disappeared. The crime rate is extremely low. The overgrowth has been tastefully cleared, the lawns regularly mowed, and the park spaces—from tot lots to playing fields, and from the golf course to Scarborough Pond—generally refurbished and rehabilitated.

Most important is the revitalized sense of pride felt throughout this city treasure, evidenced by joggers, picnickers, maintenance crews, and city park rangers alike. And they're not the only ones by far. Every year, thousands of visitors flock to Franklin Park for the annual Kite Festival, while thousands more come from around the nation for Caribbean Carnival, celebrated on the last Saturday in August. Meanwhile, the eighteen-hole par 70 public golf course officially reopened in August 1989 with $1.35 million in renovations, while a fabulous $26-million walk-in exhibit, the domed African Tropical Forest, made its debut at the Franklin Park Zoo in September 1989.

"Franklin Park is a surprise!" exclaims longtime park advocate Richard Heath. "It's like a blind date . . . 'Why did I dread this?!' Whether you're a disillusioned resident of public housing or a newly married yuppie from the South End, the park has something to say to you."

It's called Roxbury puddingstone because that's a bit what it looks like—rounded plums floating in pudding. More importantly, it's Franklin Park's most curious natural feature, manifested in massive outcroppings, or ledges, throughout the park.

Nineteenth-century Boston poet Oliver Wendell Holmes offered his own magical, mythic explanation of how this distinctive mottled rock came to be: rude young giants from the northerly town of Everett,

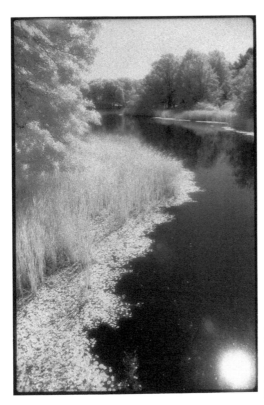

Franklin Park was considered the largest and most beautiful gem in Frederick Law Olmsted's Emerald Necklace of Boston parks.

Massachusetts, had hurled lumps of pudding at some equally rude young giants from Roxbury; since none of these insolent youths cleaned up the resulting mess, the land was left spattered with hardening clods of puddingstone.

Geologists, of course, explain Franklin Park's unusual rock motif in a slightly different way. The whole Boston basin, including the park, was once part of a drifting chain of volcanic islands that presumably formed near where Africa is today. Over a 900-million-year period, this archipelago drifted away from Africa, eventually crashing into and fusing with the North American continent. The massive collision left Himalayan-sized mountains in its wake.

About 600 million years ago, ancient streams began flowing from the foothills of these majestic mountain ranges, crisscrossing the Boston basin and leaving masses of sediment behind. That sediment eventually formed into "Roxbury conglomerate," popularly known as Roxbury puddingstone. In more recent times—a mere 10,000 years ago—the Wisconsin Glacier chiseled and eroded some parts of the area that became Franklin Park, leaving deposits of rock and sediment in others.

Today, giant dislocated puddingstone boulders, or "glacial erratics," are strewn throughout the park. In the Wilderness section, boulders range up to fifteen feet in diameter. Puddingstone also features prominently in some of the park's man-made structures, including the Ninety-nine Steps, the elegant Ellicott Arch, and numerous shelters, arches, walls, stairs, gates, and fountains.

By the time landscape architect Frederick Law Olmsted and his stepson John began designing Franklin Park for the Boston Park Commission in 1884, the land had evolved into rocky pastures, dotted with about a dozen small farms, each with its own farmhouse, barn, and outbuildings. Many of these early landowners' names live on in the park today.

Joseph Ellicott's big white house, for example, stood near what we know as the Williams Street entrance at Ellicott Arch. Williams Street itself was named after Jeremiah Williams, who once owned the park's elevated center—with its splendid terraces and scenic view of surrounding meadows and the distant Blue Hills. Williams's hill became known as Schoolmaster Hill to honor yet another illustrious resident, Ralph Waldo Emerson, who lived nearby as a schoolteacher from 1823 to 1825.

Other names reflect even earlier times. The Nazingdale section of today's golf course was named for the English hometown of many of Roxbury's first European settlers. John Scarborough was one of those seventeenth-century settlers and the original owner of most of this area. He, too, was immortalized here, both in Scarborough Hill and the seven-acre, man-made Scarborough Pond. That pond, spanned by two graceful granite bridges, has become a favorite fishing, picnicking, and walking spot for all ages.

By the time Olmsted began designing Franklin Park, he had relatively little missionary work to do. The parks movement of the late 1860s and the 1870s had already attuned many Americans to the importance of urban wilderness (see Chapter 47). Most enlightened folks agreed that urban growth posed hazards to human health and sanity, and that large, natural "country parks" were an important solution. Moreover, Olmsted's work on New York's Central Park had proved a smashing success.

Olmsted was reportedly a charming, quiet fellow with a bit of a limp and a lot of ideas. He came to landscape architecture with a wealth of prior work experiences, ranging from ship's hand, farmer, and engineer, to newspaper correspondent and head of the precursor to the Red Cross. Working alongside Boston's new Parks Commission and Mayor Hugh O'Brien, Olmsted proceeded to design and develop what became known as the Emerald Necklace of Boston Parks. The final gem in the necklace, the 527-acre West Roxbury Park, was considered his design masterpiece—comparable in excellence to his two famous New York creations, Central Park in Manhattan and Prospect Park in Brooklyn.

As planning began, the city opted to alter the park's name from West Roxbury Park to Franklin Park in hopes that money left to the city by Ben Franklin a century earlier would be used to finance construction. The funds, alas, were directed elsewhere, though the name remained.

Unlike finely sculpted, symmetrical, "fussy" parks like the Public Garden, Franklin Park was meant to be pastoral, natural, and simple, creating the illusion of the rural New England countryside. To attain this effect, Olmsted employed "design by subtraction." He removed structures, walls, and other elements to reveal the land's native beauty, then used natural elements—like plantings and the plentiful puddingstone—to mold new functional forms.

Olmsted's favorite area was the gentle valley that rolled through the park's center. This section, comprising two-thirds of the entire site, was called the Country Park. It was intended for "passive recreation"—of the strolling and picnicking rather than the football and Frisbee variety—as was the adjoining hundred-acre Wilderness. Home to more than wildlife, the Country Park was originally kept tidy by a flock of nibbling sheep. Peacocks also ran about, but were later removed when neighbors complained about their shrieking.

Olmsted died in 1903, so he never lived to see his beloved, psyche-soothing Country Park evolve from a passive to an active center. The Ellicottdale portion of the Country Park erupted in forty lawn-tennis courts—which have dwindled to two courts today—while most of the meadow gave way to a sprawling golf course.

Golfers had actually been puttering and putting in Olmsted's sculpted rolling valley as early as 1896, though golfing wasn't officially permitted until 1915. In 1922 the eighteen-hole William J. Devine Golf Course was completed—making it the country's second oldest municipal golf course—and by 1926, some 55,000 golfers were teeing off there annually. Longtime Franklin Park Coalition member Murray Cooper remembers learning to play golf there as a child and hearing neighbors brag about how legendary U.S. Open champion Bobby Jones used to practice on the formidable eighth hole.

Though Olmsted didn't plan it for his Country Park, he did realize that Victorian Bostonians wanted to engage in more than just passive recreation. Hence the famed landscape architect added an "Ante-Park" to his original design, including a children's recreation area called the Playstead. Teams of mules were brought in to level the land and to remove thousands of rocks. Once new turf had been planted and facilities added, Boston's first playground was ready for its gala opening, on June 12, 1889. Today the Playstead is still filled with youngsters, who use its ballfields, the rustic Overlook, and the ungainly, large White Stadium, which was added in 1949 and renovated in 1990.

Olmsted's original plan called for the Greeting, intended as a formal park entrance and posh promenade. The latter never came to pass, however. Instead, former Olmsted apprentice Arthur Shurcliff was hired in 1910 to design a zoo for the undeveloped space.

Over the next two decades, the zoo emerged: first with dens for cougar and bear, and an enclosure for elk; then with the elephant house, whose most famous residents—a gaily lumbering trio known as Waddy, Molly, and Tony—are still fondly remembered by some Bostonians. The zoo's decorative touches included fluted granite columns, added to the entrance in 1917, and sculptor Daniel Chester French's statues of Commerce and Industry, placed at the far end of the zoo in 1929.

Though the Franklin Park Zoo suffered a long period of decline, beginning with the Great Depression and lasting through the 1960s, it has enjoyed new life and popularity since the mid-1970s. The completion and grand opening of the African Tropical Forest in 1989, with its cast of Western Lowland gorillas stealing the show much like the elephants of yore, has added prestige and allure to both the zoo itself and to Franklin Park as a whole.

Franklin Park remained a Boston showplace throughout the early part of the twentieth century. People flocked to it on foot, in trolley cars, on horseback, and in posh horse-drawn carriages on sunny Sunday afternoons. Kids reveled in the marvelous Refectory building and the toboggan slides on Schoolmaster Hill. By 1925 park officials were even letting motor cars tour about.

The heyday of the park—and the zoo within it—was the 1930s. Certainly by the end of World War II a steady decline had set in. The reasons were many—including lack of funds, limited city input, official apathy, the onslaught of the automobile, competing interests, demographic shifts in area neighborhoods, Boston's racism, changes in tax laws (the infamous Proposition 2½), and changes in the "vision" for the park's future. Controversies erupted, for example, when open park lands were used for the construction of White Stadium in 1949, and for Shattuck Hospital in 1954.

By the 1960s and 1970s, the park's condition was downright dirty and dismal. And then reform efforts began to take shape, led by longtime Roxbury cultural activist Elma Lewis. Lewis created the Franklin Park Advisory Committee, corralled friends and supporters into cleanup projects, and began a decade of summer cultural events with her legendary Playhouse in the Park—a stage that welcomed both local talent and internationally known performers like Duke Ellington and Arthur Fiedler and the Boston Pops.

The Franklin Park Advisory Committee was a prototype for the Franklin Park Coalition, which emerged in 1975 with Richard Heath initially at the helm. For more than a decade the four-hundred-member volunteer coalition was a primary—and occasionally lone—force in helping to improve, maintain, promote, and police the park. In the mid-1980s, Boston's Parks and Recreation Department joined with the coalition, consultants, a community-based task force, and the state Department of Environmental Management to bring new life, massive funding, and people back to Franklin Park, in part under the auspices of the Olmsted Historic Landscape Preservation Program.

The progress to date has been stunning. If sensitive, sensible management schemes can be worked out—and if the public will come, believe, and participate in growing numbers—the Franklin Park renaissance might just come to full bloom.

THE ESSENTIALS

ADDRESS: Bounded by Forest Hills Street, Walnut Avenue, Seaver Street, Blue Hill Avenue, American Legion Highway, and Morton Street, in the Jamaica Plain, Roxbury, and Dorchester neighborhoods of Boston.

TELEPHONE: Boston Park Rangers, (617) 635-7383; Boston Parks and Recreation Department program information, (617) 635-4505; Commonwealth Zoological Corporation, (617) 442-2002; Franklin Park Golf Course, (617) 265-4084.

VISITOR INFORMATION: Park open dawn to dusk, 365 days a year. Free. Various zoo facilities open at different hours, beginning at 9:00 A.M., year-round; zoo closed Thanksgiving, Christmas, and New Year's Day; moderate zoo admission fee. Free tours and programs available through Boston Parks and Recreation Department; call for times and details. Wheelchair access difficult in Wilderness section with its many steps; no access in Humboldt tot lot; most other sites wheelchair accessible via paved paths or roads; zoo fully accessible, including restrooms.

The Frederick Law Olmsted National Historic Site

WITH ITS stockade fence, stately foliage, and quiet unobtrusiveness, the Olmsted National Historic Site could easily pass for just another charming old Brookline homestead. But in fact, this pretty plot called Fairsted has been the center of a quiet little storm for over a century now—a storm that changed the face of parks and public lands throughout Boston and across North America.

Fairsted began as the home and office of Frederick Law Olmsted, "the father of American landscape architecture," in 1883. Between 1857 and 1950, Olmsted, his sons, and his successors participated in some five thousand landscaping projects, spanning forty-five states and Canada. Their most famous works—including New York's Central Park, Boston's Emerald Necklace, and the Capitol Grounds in Washington, D.C.— became world-renowned landmarks and prototypes in the development of the American public park.

Today, as many as eight thousand visitors come to the Olmsted National Historic Site annually to tour the beautifully maintained grounds and restored office spaces, or to do research in the archives. What these visitors discover is a decidedly low-key, but vibrant center. While some park rangers are giving detailed tours, others are processing numerous research requests; and as the Olmsted archival team is working on the preservation and inventory of their collections, the horticultural staff is tackling projects like landscape preservation, hi-tech computer mapping systems, and experimental trellises. Various new outreach and training programs are blossoming every day—including collaborative workshops with the Arnold Arboretum, technical assistance to other national parks throughout the northeast, innovative school curricula, and a winter lecture series.

In sum, the Olmsted site balances a dual existence as a living museum and a working archive of American landscape architecture.

The man who initially inspired all this activity, the legendary Frederick Law Olmsted (1822–1903), has been heralded not only as the father of American landscape architecture, but as the father of urban planning and of the American public park as well. His early efforts to preserve Niagara Falls

The sturdy old "Olmsted elm" still stands outside the famed landscape architect's former home and office, now a national park site.

and Yosemite have even led some to give him a somewhat paternal status for the National Park System and the conservation movement. He was also the father of two men—his son, Frederick junior, and stepson, John Charles—who actually executed most of the work that bears the Olmsted name. As the Olmsted Brothers, they brought the firm to its height of influence and activity in the 1920s and 1930s, three decades after their father's death.

Still, Frederick Olmsted, Sr., was the source—a fascinating figure who was in many ways as interesting as his designs. The elder Olmsted was born in Connecticut, the son of an upper-class merchant. His mother died when he was three years old. His brother John died when Frederick was thirty-five. Rejected by at least one true love, Elizabeth Baldwin, Olmsted remained a bachelor until he was thirty-seven, when he married Mary Cleveland Perkins Olmsted, the wife of his deceased brother.

As a child Olmsted was sickly. As an adult he suffered from an artistic temperament, perfectionism, and "workaholism," which were manifested in occasional depression, anxiety, exhaustion, and in apoplectic-like attacks that included hysterical blindness. He was also known for his limp, which he acquired in an 1860 carriage accident in Central Park.

Olmsted was never graduated from any grammar or high school, and his college studies at Yale lasted just a few months. Instead, his real education came from a series of travels and careers, including work as an engineer's apprentice, counter clerk, sailor, scientific farmer, journalist, publisher, and adventurer. During the Civil War, for example, he set up hospitals in the field, working with the U.S. Sanitary Commission, the precursor to the American Red Cross.

Olmsted himself called his early years "vagabondish and somewhat poetical." Whether one sees them as charmingly eclectic or merely haphazard, the result was positive. Olmsted was transformed into a Renaissance man.

Throughout his travels, Olmsted nurtured an appreciation of the land that would later serve him well. Since childhood he had loved the natural landscape of New England, with its woodlands and meadows. As an adult, he worked occasionally as a farmer and wrote articles on the Southern agricultural economy. In travels abroad, he observed English and other European parks, and was impressed by their growing importance for modern societies.

Perhaps most significant was that as Olmsted matured, so did nineteenth-century America—changing from a land of rolling rural farmlands to overcrowded industrialized cities. He had not yet found his calling, but the scene had been perfectly set.

In 1857, at the age of thirty-five, Olmsted stumbled into a career that would both define his life and change the urban landscape of America for decades to come. He was appointed the first superintendent of Central Park in New York City, a project that put all his experiences, skills, observations, neuroses, and energies to practical use.

Collaborating with architect Calvert Vaux, Olmsted designed and engineered a plan that eventually changed 840 acres of Manhattan swamps, rocks, pigsties, and slaughterhouses into a remarkable, varied, world-renowned public park. Despite the frustrations of battling big-city politics throughout their tumultuous fourteen-year tenure there, Olmsted and Vaux essentially "invented" the American pleasure park in New York and the profession of landscape architecture in America.

During the next two decades Olmsted's reputation grew. His major projects included Brooklyn's Prospect Park, Chicago's Riverside Park, Mount Royal Park in Montreal, and the Capitol Grounds in Washington, D.C. By the time the nascent Boston Park Commission hired him to design a new "Back Bay Park" in 1878, his concepts of the function and fashion of public parks were well-formed.

The ideal city park, as Olmsted viewed it, offered a fresh-air escape from urban pressures, creating a place where body and soul could be replenished. Olmsted despised the exotic, sculpted European gardens that were monopolized by aristocrats—and off-limits to ordinary people. His ruggedly naturalistic parks were meant to reflect America's democratic ideal; they would provide moral uplift, mental calm, and a unifying experience for both rich *and* poor.

According to C. Sue Rigney, chief of visitor services at the Olmsted site, "In Boston, and in Central Park too, Olmsted was working to transform uninhabited, dead spaces into desirable ones. But he was just as concerned with improving the mental, spiritual, and physical health of people by providing these parks. Olmsted wanted to function as a social reformer. He believed in 'democracy in dirt'—creating public parks that were accessible to all classes of people. And that really sets him apart."

Olmsted based his designs on eighteenth-century English landscape gardens, mixing elements of the pastoral and picturesque schools into his own unique vision. His landscapes grew out of respect for "the genius of the place," the site's natural topography. He considered proper sanitation and drainage crucial, and subordinated detail to the overall design. In an Olmsted park, the visitor encounters "passages of scenery"—distinct environmental vignettes—as well as liberal use of plantings and a sense of spaciousness. Conscious separation is made between areas done in different styles or those used for different purposes. The elm tree became Olmsted's personal signature on his landscapes; perhaps not coincidentally, the name Olmsted translates from Old English as "the place of the elm."

All of Olmsted's design concepts are in evidence in Boston's Emerald Necklace, especially Franklin Park—and on the Fairsted grounds.

In 1883, Olmsted became a Boston-area resident, moving his home and offices from Manhattan to Brookline. Precisely why he relocated is a matter of conjecture. Olmsted was, of course, a New Englander by birth, and his disenchantment with New York bureaucrats may have contributed to his decision. Certainly his work on a linear park system for Boston—begun back in 1878—was an enticement, as was the fact that the town of Brookline was home to one of his dearest friends, the architect H. H. Richardson. Brookline was also Olmsted's vision of a perfect suburb—beautiful, quiet, bucolic, and easily accessible to Boston by the trolley or by the road that eventually became Route 9. Although many of these factors may have played a role, some say that Olmsted's desire to relocate was based on a single event: awakening at Richardson's Brookline house one snowy morning to find the streets freshly, and impressively, plowed.

Whatever the reasons, Olmsted's move into the 1810 farmhouse once owned by the Clark sisters, Sarah and Susannah, was permanent. Over the decades, Olmsted and his two sons molded the property's buildings and grounds into distinctive "Olmstedian" forms. The barn was moved and used as a model shop. A glass-windowed conservatory was created to allow all-weather access to the outdoors. The original house was periodically enlarged, creating a hodgepodge of rooms and half-staircases, a curvilinear design of thirty-six connecting chambers.

Ranger-guided tours through Fairsted (every Friday through Sunday) give visitors a glimpse of several Olmsted rooms, which look much as they did during the firm's halcyon days. While most of the chambers once used as Olmsted's home are currently filled with museum displays and National Park Service offices, the old work spaces are surprisingly intact. Particularly fascinating is the print processing room, where copies of huge design drawings were made by a primitive pre-Xerox photo process. The "upper planting department" is furnished with original tables, stools, and footrests, plus a framed plan for George Vanderbilt's Biltmore Estate in North Carolina—the last project the senior Olmsted worked on.

Outside, rangers guide guests through a small-scale sampler of typical Olmsted landscapes, featuring multiple changes of environment, or "passages of scenery." Looming below Olmsted senior's former bedroom and the firm's drafting rooms is the sunken, shady Hollow, filled with varied foliage tints, textures, and terraces. On the far side of the circular driveway is the picturesque Rock Garden, once a gloomy gravel pit.

The Rock Garden's path leads into the dense Woodland, which opens magnificently into the rolling green South Lawn. This lawn was cluttered with trees and a driveway when Olmsted bought the property; he left just a single tall elm at its center. Known as the Olmsted Elm, this carefully tended, 140-year-old tree has survived both the deadly Dutch elm disease and periodic hurricanes—including 1991's Hurricane Bob, whose death toll at Fairsted included a beautiful old red oak and a tulip poplar.

Since the Olmsted National Historic Site is an active research and outreach facility—and because of its unique collaborative ventures with the Arnold Arboretum—the destroyed trees will almost literally rise again. Staff horticulturists periodically take cuttings from historically significant plantings on the site, which they root and grow to replacement size in a new historic and native plants nursery. Hence when a parent plant dies, genetically identical offspring can replace it. With the aid of hi-tech equipment and ongoing experiments at the Olmsted site and the Arboretum, the National Park Service is learning to better understand, manage, and preserve culturally important landscapes of the past. The new Olmsted Center for Landscape Preservation, located at the Olmsted site, is now officially providing technical assistance and training to national parks throughout the northeastern states. Their collaborative projects include inspection and stabilization of hazardous trees, and identification, rejuvenation, and propagation of historic plants.

The house, grounds, and research facilities of the Frederick Law Olmsted National Historic Site were not always in such fine fettle as they appear today—having undergone both prosperous and lean periods since Olmsted's time. Frederick Law Olmsted himself died in 1903, after spending the last years of his life in McLean Asylum, a Boston-area psychiatric hospital for which, ironically, he had once submitted landscape plans. Though the senior Olmsted had supplied the enduring fame, it was his two sons, Frederick junior and John Charles, who brought in the bulk of the Olmsted work and wealth, in the 1920s and 1930s. The last Olmsted left the firm in 1950, and the firm itself—known as Olmsted Associates—departed the Fairsted grounds in 1979.

Between 1979 and 1980, the National Park Service bought the old house, grounds, and voluminous archives. The good news was that they had acquired a unique site—an artist's home, complete with original artwork, both on paper and on the grounds themselves. The bad news was that all of the above were in nightmarish condition.

By 1980, when the Park Service moved in, the house was severely damaged. Most of the original landscaping was lost or overgrown. The interior vault, where decades of precious drawings and documents were stored in rolls, was a downright disaster. "The vault had been unheated for more than ten years," explains Park Superintendent Rolf Diamant. "Environmental conditions were awful, because of the mold. You could not enter the vault without a face mask." When the initial dust had cleared, the prognosis was equally dismal: experts estimated it would take more than a century to conserve the Olmsted archives and make them accessible to researchers.

Thanks to years of hard work, substantially increased funding from Congress, and support from the National Park Service, those dark days are past. Today, research requests that once took six months or more to process can be dealt with in a month. Meanwhile, the expanded archival crew estimates that the initial inventory and preservation of the collections will take a decade, rather than a century, to complete.

In the vast Olmsted archives, collections manager Liz Banks and staff sift, flatten, preserve, and catalogue tens of thousands of rolled drawings and other documents. In their historic landscape architecture stash are some 140,000 drawings, 60,000 photographs, and 30,000 negatives—accessed by research requests which come in at the rate of 1,000 per year. Though the archives will not be completely research-ready for many years, their rescue from decay seemed unthinkable less than two decades back. "We are now gaining intellectual control!" grins Banks, acknowledging that total physical control is yet to come.

Since opening its doors to the public in 1981, the Olmsted site has attracted serious researchers and curious visitors alike. The work of the Olmsteds has always been of special interest to Massachusetts residents, since Olmsted's firm created 1,200 design projects in 150 Bay State communities between 1866 and 1950. Among the lesser known are parks in Lynn, Brockton, New Bedford, Fall River, Worcester, and Springfield; college and university campuses at the University of Massachusetts-Amherst, Mount Holyoke, Smith, Wellesley, and Harvard; community subdivisions in Brookline and Swampscott; the sites of the Massachusetts General Hospital in Boston, the Thomas Crane Library in Quincy, and Town Hall in Easton; Charlestown Playground; the Weld Estate in Dedham; the Tanglewood Estate in Lenox; Amherst Common; and World's End in Hingham.

The quietly dynamic site is much more than a stop for knowledgeable Bostonians. "Of the more than 350 national parks, this is one of the few in the system that talks about landscape architecture, land use, and planning," explains Diamant. "We like to think all parks have at least local constituencies. But this small site has a truly national audience as well."

THE ESSENTIALS

ADDRESS: 99 Warren Street, Brookline.
TELEPHONE: (617) 566-1689.
VISITOR INFORMATION: OPEN 10:00 A.M.–4:30 P.M., Friday–Sunday for ranger-guided tours; groups may arrange tours other days by appointment. Free. Grounds and house partly wheelchair accessible with assistance; house and garden have several single and multiple steps; ramps and accessible restrooms have recently been installed.

48 Castle Island

NO TROOPS ever stormed its parapets nor rushed its sturdy earthworks with bayonets. No frigates were blown asunder by its cannon, nor were fighter jets blasted down from its skies. No battles were lost, no wars won within the confines of its shores. Indeed, volunteer summer guides from the Castle Island Association (C.I.A.) proudly tell visitors that "no shot was ever fired in anger by American forces from this island." Still, as the oldest continuously fortified site in British North America, Castle Island played a long and vital role in American military history.

The name Castle Island itself may seem a bit confusing to those who first encounter the historic site today. Though once an island in Boston Harbor, the area has been connected to South Boston by a causeway since the 1920s. Moreover, the largest structure on the island is no castle in the flowery, Disneyesque sense of the word. Instead, Fort Independence is an imposing, low-slung, pentagonal, granite fortress built by Sylvanus Thayer, "the father of West Point," in the decades preceding the Civil War. Believed to be the eighth fort on this site, it's descended from a long line of harbor defense works built on the island since 1634.

Since those early colonial days, military activities on Castle Island have ranged from demagnetizing warships to confining prisoners of war, and from training of artillery and infantry to burying the dead. The fort was also garrisoned during every major war from 1634 through World War II. Meanwhile, the site has played host to such diverse luminaries as Franklin Delano Roosevelt, Paul Revere, and Edgar Allan Poe. It has also been the scene of countless freak accidents, including deathly bolts of lightning, accidental explosions, fatal duels, overturned boats, and a drowning caused by a "killer" whale.

Castle Island has even been used to improve the quality of everyday Boston life. Once the site for various hospitals and the state's first penitentiary, it's now an active, twenty-two-acre public park with more than a million visitors each year. Today, the park and fort are owned and operated by the state's Metropolitan District Commission (M.D.C.), in cooperation with the volunteer Castle Island Association.

Castle Island acquired its first fort in 1634, just four years after the founding of Boston. Although the Puritan settlement was well protected by the defense works on Fort Hill, not far from Rowes Wharf, the Massachusetts Bay colonists wanted a second layer of security—to stop pirates, plunderers, and other enemies as they entered Boston Harbor. As a result, Governor Thomas Dudley and his advisors agreed to build a front-line fort on Castle Island. The hilly isle was a drumlin, a remnant of the last glacier

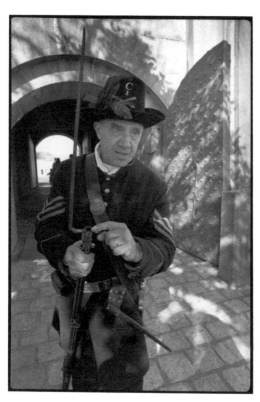

Volunteers from the Castle Island Association offer seasonal tours and special events to visitors of the oldest continuously fortified site in British North America.

to pass through these parts some twelve thousand years earlier. Its curious shape had inspired colonists to name it Castle Island, even before a single structure had been built on its shores.

That first "castle" was a rustic little building, consisting of two wooden platformed earthworks and a small dwelling. The masonry was fabricated from crushed oyster shells. Four forts, all presumably called "the Castle," were built on the island that century. Since military action was minimal, the island's death toll was small.

The most unusual demise was that of Commander Richard Davenport, felled by a lightning bolt one summer night in 1665. The late Edward Rowe Snow, preeminent chronicler of Harbor Islands history and lore, wrote of another, equally unlucky death: in 1688, one John Evered became tangled in his own fishing line, and was drowned by the whale snagged on the other end.

When the island's fifth fort was built, around 1700, it was named Castle William, after the new English monarch. This particular incarnation of the Castle became a British refuge during the early stages of the American Revolution. When the incendiary Stamp Tax was levied in 1765, the hated stamps were hidden out in the island fort for protection. British regulars also fled to Castle William in the turmoil following the Boston Massacre of 1770. In the wake of the battles at Lexington and Concord, British troops sent out three unsuccessful expeditions from Castle Island.

General George Washington, securely lodged on Dorchester Heights, finally proved too competent a warrior for the English enemy; late in March of 1776, the British were forced to abandon Castle Island and quit Boston altogether. This event is celebrated in Boston as Evacuation Day every year. Though the actual British evacuation date was March 20, the holiday is celebrated locally on March 17—which conveniently coincides with St. Patrick's Day.

Determined to have the last word when they departed, the British set fire to Castle Island and dumped its ammunition into the harbor. As an encore, they later blew up Boston Light in the outer harbor, the oldest lighthouse in the area. Undaunted, the resourceful patriots proceeded to build a sixth fort on the charred island. Among the construction supervisors were Richard Gridley, a renowned veteran of the Battle of Bunker Hill, and the ubiquitous Paul Revere.

By the end of the eighteenth century, this fort was renamed, replaced, and transferred from state to federal ownership. The U.S. government was designing the first of many systems of coastal defenses, which eventually stretched from Maine to New Orleans. Having already built Fort McHenry in Baltimore, Jean Foncin was sent to construct a larger version of McHenry on Castle Island. By 1801, the first Fort Independence was well underway.

The Fort Independence that rests on the island today is the second by that name, and the eighth defense work on the site. Designed by Braintree's Sylvanus Thayer, it was built between 1833 and 1851, at a cost of about $260,000. The new Fort Independence—with walls up to thirty feet high, and five and a half feet thick—was the most formidable fortress in the island's history. Its pentagon shape was like that of Foncin's previous structures, though Thayer replaced the old brick with Rockport and Quincy granite, doubling the earlier fort's height. The newly enlarged Fort Independence was still relatively small when compared to another in Boston Harbor, Fort Warren on Georges Island, which Thayer built during the same period.

"This is about one-sixth the size of Fort Warren," explains M.D.C. Harbor Region supervisor Don Fraser. "You could fit the entire thing in Fort Warren's parade ground!"

Though Fort Independence was garrisoned by the U.S. military during the Spanish-American and the two world wars, its heyday was the Civil War period. Ninety-six cannon were there at the fort's height, including a fifteen-inch Rodman which could lob a 300-pound shell or 450 pounds of solid shot more than three miles. More important to the fort's defense line was that using all ninety-six cannon, they could hurl 5,000 pounds of cannonballs at the enemy at any given time.

As it turned out, the cannon at Fort Independence did little more than fire practice balls at nearby Thompson Island. The cannon themselves were replaced over time, or sold for scrap during World War II. Of the seven cannons at the fort today, five were borrowed from places like Mount Hope Cemetery and USS *Constitution*. The two Rodmans are actually precise fiberglass replicas, commissioned by the Castle Island Association for some $20,000.

★   ★   ★

As both a military fort and the site of Massachusetts's first state prison, Castle Island has housed its share of prisoners over the years, including Native Americans, French sailors, and British soldiers—and a fellow named Stephen Burroughs. Burroughs, true to his name, ingeniously weaseled out of the state prison there, then published his memoirs in a 1798 best-selling book. Castle Island's most famous prisoner was probably Sir Edmund Andros, the tyrannical royal governor of the northern colonies, who was held in the Castle during Britain's "Glorious Revolution" of 1688–89. Meanwhile, across the Atlantic, British citizens were successfully overthrowing King James II in favor of the more democratic William of Orange.

Though the various incarnations of the fort have received the most attention over the centuries, they were far from Castle Island's only buildings. According to Bill Stokinger of the M.D.C., the island has had more than 120 structures over the years, including hospitals, barracks, officers' quarters, storehouses, powder magazines, and dungeons. Military graveyards were part of the island from the 1600s on. One such burying ground lay on the bluff behind where Sullivan's concession stand rests today. Both the British and Americans sculpted elaborate gardens on the grounds, echoed today in the well-kept flower beds maintained by the Castle Island Association.

New England's first marine hospital—a 1799 treatment center for sick sailors—was built on the island, as was an inoculation center for smallpox. In 1721, Dr. Zabdiel Boylston, supported by the Reverend Cotton Mather, introduced the controversial new medical practice of inoculation to Boston. Though initially dreaded and resisted, the inoculations were ultimately effective in curbing the disease. In later years, the island was occasionally used as a smallpox isolation hospital, as during Boston's deadly outbreak of 1764.

Today, the only buildings left besides Fort Independence are an M.D.C.–built restroom and a former U.S. Army Signal Corps facility, a remnant from the era of the world wars. The latter is utilized as a Castle Island Association meeting place and an M.D.C. field office. Meanwhile, the entrance to Castle Island has been guarded by Sullivan's, a popular local hangout and fast-food joint, since 1951. The current building, constructed in 1988, was designed to loosely resemble one of the three officers' quarters that stood nearby a century ago.

The site where Sullivan's now stands—as well as the whole parking lot and approaching causeway—was under water before 1916. Prior to that time, Castle Island really *was* an island.

In 1891, a wooden-pile bridge was built connecting South Boston to the island, in anticipation of extending Frederick Law Olmsted's Emerald Necklace of Boston Parks out to the harbor. That Castle Island bridge, along with the decommissioning of Fort Independence in 1879, heralded the beginning of the area as a popular and accessible Boston park. Hydraulic dredging, begun in 1916, created enough landfill to complete a concrete walkway to the island by 1928. By 1932, a roadway had been laid. Boston had expanded a popular picnic area, and given South Boston a new front yard.

Military personnel had long been memorialized on Castle Island, but once the roadway and circle were laid, prestigious local civilians began getting their due here as well. In 1933, a group of private donors—including Franklin Delano Roosevelt—contributed to the tallest monument on the island, a fifty-two-foot obelisk honoring Donald McKay, the famous nineteenth-century East Boston shipbuilder. Other names immortalized here reflect contemporary neighborhood heroes, as well as the area's Irish heritage. A lifelike bust and a tot playground are dedicated to firefighter Robert M. Greene, while the fishing pier is named for another fireman, John J. McCorkle. The Harry McDonough Sailing Center is not far from Father Timothy J. O'Connor Memorial Walk. The island's newest monument is South Boston's Korean War Memorial.

The Metropolitan District Commission acquired the island and fort from the federal government in 1962—in totally dilapidated condition. Five million dollars' worth of renovations since that time has accomplished a great deal: the grounds have been improved and landscaped; the fort has been made relatively safe and sound; and several interior rooms have been restored to their nineteenth-century appearance.

Today, Castle Island attractions include a summer sailing program, a beach on Pleasure Bay, a fishing pier, a tot playground, picnic areas, rambling walkways, well-kept gardens, and free parking. The volunteer Castle Island Association, formed in 1977, has continually worked side-by-side with the M.D.C. Its members have given fort tours to summer visitors, outfitted the fort interior with dozens of historic and contemporary flags, and helped to organize special events, including a gala annual pre-Halloween bash.

Halloween is an appropriate time to visit the site, incidentally, since the most enduring legend about Castle Island is that it inspired Poe's classic tale, "The Cask of Amontillado." According to historian-storyteller Edward Rowe Snow, a duel took place on the island on Christmas Day, 1817, between young Robert Massie and the fort bully, Lieutenant Gustavus Drane (called Captain Green in Snow's stories). When the other soldiers learned of Massie's cruel death, they were enraged. They got Drane drunk, hauled him into the fort's dungeon, chained him down, and sealed up the vault. Edgar Allan Poe enlisted in the 1st Regiment United States Artillery at Castle Island ten years later, heard the tale . . . and the rest is literary history.

In 1905, workers digging in the area allegedly uncovered a skeleton wearing the remnants of an old military uniform—a piece of evidence that seemed to support the story. But the finding was never supported by subsequent research. Moreover, Drane didn't die until 1846, twenty-nine years after his alleged entombment, and there were no interior chambers or subterranean dungeons in the fort on the island at that time.

Still, on Castle Island truth has often been stranger than fiction—and other archaeological digs have spawned stories of their own. When a Brown University archaeological team collected artifacts on the island during the mid-1970s, another skeleton was found. The workers first called it Casper the Friendly Ghost, but later analysis by the Smithsonian Institute showed that the bones were actually the partly charred remains of not one, but *two* individuals. Since one was a young male and the other an old female, they were affectionately dubbed Harold and Maude, after the cult film which starred Ruth Gordon in a tale of May–December romance.

Who Castle Island's Harold and Maude were, when they arrived, and why they were there, are all still mysteries—or, better yet, a tangled web waiting to be unraveled by the right storyteller.

THE ESSENTIALS

ADDRESS: End of William J. Day Boulevard, on Boston Harbor, South Boston.

TELEPHONE: Metropolitan District Commission Harbor Region Headquarters, (617) 727-5290.

VISITOR INFORMATION: Island open twenty-four hours a day, 365 days a year. Free. Free tours of fort interior given by members of the Castle Island Association on weekends and Monday holiday afternoons from Memorial Day to Labor Day, and on Sunday afternoons from Memorial Day to Columbus Day. Restrooms generally open from Memorial Day through Columbus Day. Island, fort, and most facilities wheelchair accessible via flat or gently sloping walkways; upper sections of the fort interior require steep ramp for access; restrooms accessible.

49 Georges Island

WHEN BOSTON temperatures hit their warm summer highs, some people seek relief in a cool drink and a canopied outdoor cafe. What fewer folks realize, however, is that a real escape from the sizzling city is only a short boat ride away. Seven miles east of downtown Boston lies a thirty-acre park called Georges Island, one of the seven islands scattered throughout Boston Harbor that comprise Boston Harbor Islands State Park. For the nominal cost of a boat ticket, Georges Island offers visitors fresh sea breezes, chirping birds, lapping surf, summer sun for tanning, picnic tables, shade trees, and open space for light recreation, plus regularly scheduled nature and history walks and talks.

Once on the island, visitors will also discover the unique role Georges Island has played in Boston history. One very visible reminder of that role is the site's magnificent "white elephant"—a sprawling Civil War–era fort that dominates the island, and which guests can explore at will. A second

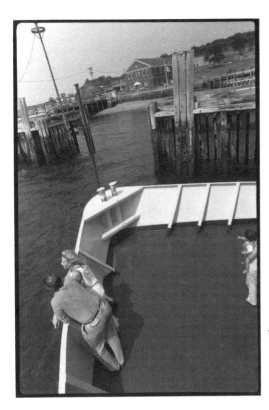

From late spring to early fall, regular boat service takes visitors to Georges Island, part of Boston Harbor Islands State Park and home to a fascinating Civil War fortress.

reminder of days gone by is harder to see and impossible to verify: one of Boston's best-known ghosts, the mysterious Lady in Black, is said to stalk the island to this day.

Georges Island, like the other thirty-three islands found throughout Boston's harbor today, was originally formed by glaciers. Native Americans had canoed in the harbor and camped on many of these islands for several thousand years before white settlers arrived in Boston, but no evidence of any permanent native settlements on Georges has been found. Presumably, they came only during the summer months and set up temporary campsites, digging clams and catching fish. James Pemberton of nearby Hull is acknowledged as the island's first white settler. Pemberton claimed the island in 1622 and began farming there in 1628. Farming and grazing remained major uses of Pemberton's Island under subsequent owners for almost two centuries.

In 1710, the island was renamed in honor of a prominent, civic-minded Boston merchant and town official, Captain John George; it is assumed that he once owned the island as well. *George's*—meaning "of or belonging to George"—is theoretically the correct spelling of the name, though "Georges" is used today.

Throughout the colonial period, and especially during the American Revolution, both the young nation and the prosperous city of Boston were aware of the need for seacoast defense from external enemies. Events of the War of 1812—especially the burning of Washington, D.C., by the British army—confirmed that notion, and resulted in the establishment or improvement of a series of forts along the East Coast, including Fort Adams in Newport, Rhode Island, and Fort Independence on Castle Island in Boston Harbor. In pursuing these seacoast defense plans, the U.S. government bought Georges Island in 1825. Several years later, they selected Lieutenant Colonel Sylvanus Thayer of Braintree, the illustrious "father of West Point," to oversee construction of a fort.

A seawall had already been completed on Georges Island in 1832. From 1833 to 1857 Thayer supervised the massive fort project, which included hauling huge, hand-hewn granite stones from Quincy quarries, then transporting them to the island on special sailing ships. The name chosen, Fort Warren, commemorated Joseph Warren, a highly respected colonial doctor, patriot, and Revolutionary War general who had been killed at the Battle of Bunker Hill. Although the commemorative block over the sallyport (main entrance) gate reads, "Fort Warren, 1850," the date is not entirely accurate. Much of the fort's structure was completed by 1850, but the interior finish work and gun platforms were not. When the first battalions of Union soldiers arrived for training on Georges Island in 1861, in fact, the fort was still unfinished.

Thayer's design for Fort Warren was very French, very seventeenth-century, very practical and at the same time, very romantic. It has a lovely drawbridge that doesn't draw, and a winding moat that was never filled with water. It also has a multitude of ingenious ways to thwart attacking enemies—from heavy bolt-studded oak doors, to portcullises (sliding iron grates that can quickly close off entrances), to devilishly well-positioned light cannon embrasures designed to fend off intruding infantry. Other particularly fascinating features are the fort's dungeon-like casemates (fortified firing positions), burrowing tunnels, large fireplaces, and self-supporting arches.

All the good design and defense work by Thayer and his crew was never tested; Fort Warren was never attacked. When the Civil War began in 1861, several units of the Massachusetts Volunteer Infantry were stationed there for military training—often using the central parade ground to practice cannon maneuvers, equipment maintenance, and marching techniques. Fort Warren's most important role during that war, however, was as a prison; some 1,200 Confederate soldiers and sympathizers were housed there in all. Unlike the infamous Confederate prison in Andersonville, Georgia, Fort Warren was renowned as a humane, well-kept jail—a credit to the fort's well-respected commander, Colonel Justin Dimick. Among its well-known inmates were Confederate ambassadors James M. Mason and John Slidell, and, at the war's conclusion, Alexander Hamilton Stephens, vice-president of the Confederacy.

All kinds of legends, tall tales, and real historic events are intertwined in Georges Island's rich past—so inextricably, in some cases, that it's hard to tell fact from fiction. Among those stories, however, two stand out: one concerns the origins of the Civil War-era song "John Brown's Body"; the second relates to the island's resident ghost.

The John Brown was a zealous abolitionist, best known for the raid he led on the village of Harper's Ferry, Virginia, in 1859. When Brown and a tiny army of black and white men tried to incite a slave rebellion there, the federal government captured and hanged him, thereby assuring Brown the status of hero. Meanwhile, two years later, the 12th Massachusetts Infantry arrived for military training at Fort Warren in Boston Harbor. As one story goes, one of these Union soldiers was also named John Brown, which inspired some comrades to joke, "You can't be John Brown, 'cause he lies a-moulderin' in the grave"; as an extension of that comment—part of which ended up in one of the song's verses—ordinary soldiers supposedly created the lyrics to "John Brown's Body" while they busily cleaned up rubble in the uncompleted fort.

According to M.D.C. archivist and military historian Al Schroeder, however, "Boston Brahmins" among the troops wrote the song, in the evening, after work was done. Whatever the lyrics' source, the tune the soldiers used was that of an old camp song, "Say, Brothers, Will You Meet Us," and most important was the final product, "John Brown's Body," which quickly became the Union's favorite marching song as the Fort Warren–trained troops marched south.

How did "John Brown's Body" inspire a patriotic hymn? Though abolitionist and poet Julia Ward Howe lived in Boston, she first heard the Massachusetts regiments singing "John Brown's Body" on a trip to Washington. Howe was so smitten by the catchy music that she had her carriage chase after the soldiers. Then, of course, she borrowed the tune, the chorus, and an image or two for her new anthem, "The Battle Hymn of the Republic."

The second Civil War tale centered on Georges Island concerns the site's haunting presence, affectionately known as the Lady in Black. According to legend, a young woman named Melanie missed her new husband, a Confederate soldier imprisoned at Fort Warren. Disguised in a Union soldier's uniform, Melanie had friends transport her in a rowboat from Hull to the island. Once there, she hid, prowled about, and finally located husband Samuel by whistling their favorite song outside the fort's windows, or musket loops. In some versions of the tale, their goal was simply to spring Samuel; others claim the couple meant to incite a rebellion in the fort's prison.

Unfortunately, the escape plan literally backfired. Melanie's antique gun exploded, killing her husband instead of the oncoming guards. Tried and convicted of treason, Melanie was allowed one last request before her hanging. She asked to die in women's clothing. Since there were no women or women's garments on the island at the time, they gave her a dark mourning shroud, which was wrapped around her.

Many versions of the story, incidentally, identify Melanie and Samuel's last name as Lanier. A Samuel Lanier was indeed imprisoned at Fort Warren, which lent credence to the tale for decades. According to M.D.C. spokespersons, however, Samuel Lanier died of kidney failure while imprisoned on the island, and the Lanier name has been deleted from modern tellings out of respect for the real—as opposed to the *surreal*—dead.

Although historical documentation for the Lady in Black's life is scant, records of her alleged afterlife are not. If you believe the stories, her hauntings have been many. Many journals of soldiers stationed at Fort Warren through the World War II period, for example, have included frightening passages about a spectral presence: taps on the shoulder, or icy fingers around a soldier's neck; fresh female-size footprints appearing in the snow, with no body attached; and phone messages taken by a female voice, though no women were on the island.

After the Civil War, the technology of warfare evolved swiftly and the granite walls of Fort Warren became vulnerable to new weapons. The fort and its munitions were overhauled and updated for every foreign naval threat—including the Spanish-American War and both world wars. Thanks to these upgrades, Fort Warren remained a vital link in America's seacoast defense system until after World War II.

The most interesting additions, around the turn of the century, were the so-called disappearing guns—including twelve-inch artillery with ranges of eight to nine miles. (In an age before computers, hitting a moving target eight miles away was quite a feat.) The disappearing guns recoiled down into their concrete emplacements after firing, thus protecting the loading crews from returning volleys. Whenever the fort's two twelve-inch guns were fired during practice—and practice is all they did, since battle never came to Boston Harbor—Quincy residents assumed an earthquake had struck.

Despite its impressive armaments, the military personnel stationed on Georges Island during the twentieth century spent more time laying mines than firing guns. None of the guns remain to be seen; they'd become scrap metal by 1944, while other military artifacts were lost to vandals. The only cannon on the fort's parade ground—a three-inch (model 1903) field piece from the Spanish-American War era—is not originally from Fort Warren.

Georges Island was a spotless, impeccably kept military installation for decades. Following World War II, however, the military abandoned it, retiring Fort Warren as a fort in 1951. For a time both the land and the structure were sorely neglected. In 1958, a private company tried to acquire the island for a hazardous waste dump site—an act that finally incited Bostonians to action. Led by the late storyteller-historian Edward Rowe Snow—whose books on the Harbor Islands are the classics of the genre—a citizens group halted the sale and the dumpsters. Instead, the site was turned over to Boston's Metropolitan District Commission and the park eventually co-run by the M.D.C. and the Department of Environmental Management. Today, the island's many activities are overseen by the M.D.C., with resident managers and interpreters providing educational programs and special events. Special trips, exhibits, cleanups, and other activities related to Georges and other islands are also regularly sponsored by the nonprofit volunteer group the Friends of the Boston Harbor Islands. Ambitious renovation projects for the fort and island are in process as well.

★   ★   ★

Since the military past of Georges Island included a series of levelings, clearings, and defoliations, the plant and animal life that survives there today must be hardy indeed. Resident plants include plenty of wild edibles—so many that an entire nature walk is devoted to this interesting topic. Nonpoisonous staghorn sumac, beach roses, wild apples, maple trees, and even a scarlet pimpernel are also found on the island. The wealth of birds that stop at Georges Island is one of its greatest attractions. Barn swallows are the most frequent visitors, though pheasants, snowy owls, and most migratory birds have also been sighted.

The most populous mammal on Georges Island is the Norway rat, or "ship rat," an unpopular reflection of the island's military past. Muskrats have also been seen, and Al Schroeder remembers a big black "attack rabbit" who once roamed the island as well. Another famous rabbit was a white domestic bunny named Warren, who was fatally buzzed by a snowy owl in the winter of 1987. Warren was buried at sea; land burial was prohibited since Georges is a National Historic Site.

A fascinating footnote to Fort Warren's past is its connection to Baltimore socialite Bessie Wallis Warfield Simpson (1895–1986). In the 1990s, of course, tongues wagged around the world about the scandalous marital mistakes of various members of the British royal family. In 1936, similar gossip surrounded Mrs. Simpson, the American divorcee who won the heart of the heir to the English throne, Edward VIII. Many remember that Edward abdicated to marry Bessie and that they became known as the Duke and Duchess of Windsor, but fewer recall that Bessie was named for two Confederate sympathizers who were imprisoned at Fort Warren. Henry M. Warfield and S. Teakle Wallis met while incarcerated at Fort Warren during the Civil War. Warfield became so attached to his friend Wallis that he named his son, and hence his granddaughter Bessie, after his former cellmate.

THE ESSENTIALS

ADDRESS: Boston Harbor, seven miles east of downtown Boston.

TELEPHONE: Metropolitan District Commission, Harbor Region, (617) 727-5359; Bay State Cruise Company, (617) 723-7800; Friends of the Boston Harbor Islands, (617) 523-8386 and (617) 740-4290.

VISITOR INFORMATION: Island open 10:00 A.M. until dusk, May–September; exact dates vary yearly. Admission and tours free. Accessible by private boat or forty-five-minute Bay State Cruise boats, which run late spring through early fall. Bay State Cruise charges moderate round-trip fare; earliest boats leave Long Wharf at 10:00 A.M.; call for exact schedules. Free, regularly scheduled water taxis from Georges to other Harbor Islands, July Fourth weekend through Labor Day. Hour-long tours of Fort Warren take place 11:15 A.M. and 2:15 P.M. weekdays; 11:15 A.M., 2:15 P.M., and 3:15 P.M. weekends and holidays. Self-guided tours and nature walks available any time. Fishing permitted; no swimming, camping, or alcohol. Most boats and island paths wheelchair accessible with some assistance; wheelchair-accessible restrooms in administrative building.

Blue Hills Reservation

FINDING A vast expanse of nearly unadulterated nature amid the concrete jungle of urban development is a rarity. But the Blue Hills Reservation, with more than 6,500 acres of near-wilderness, is only nine miles—or an easy twenty-minute drive—from the center of bustling Boston. Spanning portions of Quincy, Milton, Canton, Randolph, and Braintree, it's the largest reservation in Greater Boston's Metropolitan Parks System. Moreover, Blue Hills' treasures include thirty-six holes, twenty-two hills, fifteen National Historic Sites, three national environmental study areas, and one of the oldest weather observatories in the United States.

The thirty-six holes are found at the Reservation's Ponkapoag Golf Course, a well-worn championship green during fair weather and a good novice ski-touring spot when the snows arrive. The twenty-two hills—including Great Blue Hill, the highest and most popular peak in the metropolitan area—attract local hikers, mountain climbers, and nature lovers.

The fifteen National Historic Sites tell the fascinating tales of inventors, explorers, farmers, quarriers, and Native Americans who once lived there. Meanwhile, three natural environmental study areas include the first bog boardwalk in the United States, built in 1949 and reconstructed in the 1980s. As for the weather, the observatory atop Great Blue Hill, now a National Historic Landmark, has been a post for professional and amateur weather-watchers since 1885.

In its century of existence, Blue Hills Reservation has become many things to many people: a place to hike, swim, boat, fish, ski, picnic, ice skate, rock climb, snow shoe, birdwatch, mountain bike, camp, ride horses, or orienteer. Some folks go there to play tennis, golf, or softball, while others see it as the ultimate outdoor schoolroom, a place to study nature and natural history.

There's a lot more "in them thar' hills" than recreation, as a glimpse into the area's past will quickly reveal. Carved by glaciers, the land is part of the highest coastal range on the eastern seaboard of the United States. Though calling the hills blue may seem illogical to those wandering through their vast greenery today, it wasn't to the folks who named them. Early European explorers who sailed along the coast three or four hundred years ago saw a bluish hue on the slopes when they viewed them from a distance.

More than ten thousand years before those Europeans arrived, Native Americans had camped and farmed in the Blue Hills. They even quarried there, seeking a brown volcanic rock known as Braintree hornfels, which

Among the treasures at Blue Hills Reservation are twenty-two hills, several national historic sites, a golf course, and the popular swimming area at Houghton Pond.

they crafted into tools, spearheads, and arrowheads. According to ethno-archaeologist Dr. George Horner, these natives were known as the Massa-chuseuks and the site they lived in as Massachusetts. This latter Indian word, translated by Horner as "the place of the great hills," is generally accepted as the origin of the state's name.

Native American words also live on in the Blue Hills Reservation. The Ponkapoag, whose name means "the place of the great or red spring," were among the "praying Indians" Christianized by the English; their name graces a pond, a bog, the golf course, and an archaeological site. The sachem Chickatawbut, who died of smallpox in 1633, is immortalized in the names of a hill, a road, and the environmental education center on today's Blue Hills Reservation. And Neponset, the name of the river reservation linked to Blue Hills by the Skyline Footpath, means "a place to have a summer vacation," according to Horner. "The natives had different sites for spring, summer, and winter villages. They also visited the Harbor Islands. We think Calf Island was probably a special ritual island for them." Houghton's Pond bears the name of the white settler family that farmed nearby for seven generations, but the site's Native American name was Wissahissic, translated as "beautiful still water" (most modern histories still mispronounce that original name as "Hoosic-whisick," which, in the Algonquin Indian dialects spoken there, means absolutely nothing.)

The Native American population diminished quickly once white colonists began settling and farming in the Blue Hills region. Diseases brought by the Europeans—including what is presumed to have been a virulent strain of chicken pox—were partly responsible for their untimely demise: while Europeans had built up immunities to many of these maladies, the natives had not.

These white seventeenth-century settlers and their descendants—whose names are still used for sites like Houghton's Pond and the historic Redman Farmhouse—introduced orchards and honeybees, built houses and barns, logged hillsides for lumber and grazing, and cleared fields for crops. The open fields were divided by the distinctive stone walls still found throughout Blue Hills today. Only after the fields were sold or donated for public parkland, in 1892, did the forests begin to grow back again in abundance.

Many of the paths first walked by Native Americans became the trails and roads the early Europeans used for their farm carts. A large number of these thoroughfares, large and small, are still used today. Archaeological evidence suggests that Sawcut Notch Trail, for example, may be some eight thousand years old.

The natural phenomenon that really put the Blue Hills area "on the map" in terms of history was its granite. Though Native Americans had quarried there for thousands of years, it was not until the early nineteenth century that granite quarrying in the Blue Hills, especially in the Quincy section, became a major, world-renowned industry. It was near today's reservation that Gridley Bryant created the first commercial railroad in 1826—a horse-drawn apparatus that hauled granite from inland quarries to the water. Among the famous Boston structures constructed with Quincy granite were the Bunker Hill Monument, Quincy Market, King's Chapel, Fort Warren on Georges Island, and the Charles Street Jail.

Though some of the land containing these historic quarries has been purchased for preservation within the Blue Hills Reservation, much more remains in private hands. Encroaching developers could well build over these significant historic and recreational sites. Dave Hodgdon, founder and executive director of the Friends of the Blue Hills and curator of the reservation's Quarry Museum, is among those fighting a long campaign to acquire the remaining Quincy quarries—from ancient Native American sites to the famous Swingles Quarry, which closed in the mid-1960s. The quarries may someday serve as interpretive and recreational areas, and make up part of a green-belt buffer for the current reservation.

In many ways, the efforts of Hodgdon and other concerned environmentalists to preserve and protect the Blue Hills from development and destruction resemble those of young Charles Eliot over a century ago. Eliot, son of Harvard president Charles W. Eliot, was a landscape architect who worked with Frederick Law Olmsted, first as an employee and later as a full partner. Though Olmsted has garnered most of the fame—partly due to his association with Boston's Emerald Necklace of parks—it was Eliot who was the true "father" of the Blue Hills Reservation. Eliot was a major force behind the creation of the Metropolitan Park Commission, which evolved into the Metropolitan District Commission in 1919. (Among the M.D.C.'s modern duties are overseeing a vast array of public parks, recreation areas, and other open spaces in the metropolitan Boston area, as well as organizing programs and special events on those sites.) Eliot also helped create the Blue Hills Reservation itself, one of the first acquisitions of the Metropolitan Park System in 1893. The Eliot Footbridge near the summit of Great Blue Hill was erected in his honor in 1902, seven years after Eliot's death from cerebral meningitis at age thirty-seven.

There were well-thought-out reasons for Eliot's energetic crusades. "For crowded populations to live in health and happiness," he wrote, "they must have space for air, for light, for exercise, for rest, and for the enjoyment of that peaceful beauty of nature which, because it is the opposite of the noisy ugliness of the town, is so refreshing to the tired souls of townspeople."

The Civilian Conservation Corps, one of the Roosevelt administration's unemployment programs developed during the Depression, also played a major role in shaping the Blue Hills Reservation. C.C.C. workers built, repaired, and improved many of the facilities, roads, footpaths, and trails still used today, when they worked and camped on the reservation from 1933 to 1937. Historical film clips from the C.C.C. days are shown each year on Blue Hills Day, celebrated in September.

The treasures of the Blue Hills today include flora, fauna, and natural phenomena—from red foxes to rattlesnakes, dogwoods to orchids, and cedar swamps to Ice Age bogs. All are accessible to the public through a well-numbered trail system that crisscrosses the reservation in intersecting loops. There are close to five hundred miles of trails and paths in all.

To begin any serious study of the nature, culture, and history of the Blue Hills, start at the Trailside Museum, run by the Massachusetts Audubon Society for the M.D.C., or at the Quarry Museum, operated by the nonprofit Friends of the Blue Hills. At both museums you can get maps, orientation, and advice. One word to the wise: wear sturdy shoes, not sandals, for any hike.

The most popular hike is up Great Blue Hill, which offers a stunning view from the top, at 635 feet above sea level. Chickatawbut Overlook gives another magnificent aerial perspective. The best birdwatching is in Fowl Meadow. Try the walk through Ponkapoag Bog, if you want to see what this area probably looked like right after the Ice Age.

You may encounter some unusual wildlife along the way. For example, Blue Hills Reservation is the only place in eastern Massachusetts where copperheads and rattlesnakes live. (You'll probably never see one, except in the reservation's museum displays, since they try to avoid contact with humans.) You may also encounter huge turkey vultures flying overhead; don't mistake them for pterodactyls, as some stunned motorists have done.

Among the historic sites on the reservation is the turreted stone weather observatory, known as one of the birthplaces of modern meteorology. The curious building, declared a National Historic Landmark in 1990, was the brainchild of Abbott Lawrence Rotch, an MIT graduate who pioneered weather experiments there beginning in 1885. The station once made weather forecasts for the area and wired these reports to daily Boston newspapers for publication. Today, daily temperatures are still collected, making the Blue Hill Observatory the site with the longest continuous record of comparative temperatures in the United States. Its observations are no longer used for daily weather predictions, but for studying climate trends.

As part of his landmark work in defining upper atmospheric flows, meteorologist Rotch conducted endless experiments there with kites and balloons. The kites were flown on expensive piano wire—the lightest, strongest cord available at the time—and sometimes caused disaster. One famous incident, explains observatory expert Dr. Bill Minsinger, occurred when a kite wire accidentally wrapped around the axle of a New York– New Haven railroad engine, bringing the train to a halt. The scientists lost some six miles of wire in that mishap. In another unfortunate incident, a cow accidentally ate a downed weather balloon and its instruments, then died.

The old observatory is open to the public, with tours by appointment. Another attraction is the historic Quarry Museum, which opened in the summer of 1991. This museum includes displays on the geology and archaeology of the area dating back to Native American days. Visitors can also see a replica of a Granite Railway car, learn to rock climb on a twenty-foot climbing wall, and see tools and photographs from quarry history.

Clearly, there are many tantalizing tales linked to the long history of the Blue Hills. One favorite bit of trivia involves radio transmissions: atop Great Blue Hill is the antenna that transmits the signal for WGBH-FM, a Boston public radio station, whose call letters stand for Great Blue Hill— not God Bless Harvard, as some folks like to believe.

THE ESSENTIALS

ADDRESS: Metropolitan District Commission, Blue Hills Reservation Headquarters, 695 Hillside Street, Milton. Quarry Museum, Mullin Avenue, West Quincy.

TELEPHONE: Reservation Headquarters, (617) 698-1802; Trailside Museum, (617) 333-0690; Chickatawbut Hill Education Center, (617) 696-0920; Friends of the Blue Hills and Quarry Museum, recorded information on activities and directions, (617) 326-0079. Quarry Museum, (617) 786-9942.

VISITOR INFORMATION: Reservation open 8:00 A.M.–dusk, 365 days per year. Free. Trailside Museum open 10:00 A.M.–5:00 P.M., Wednesday–Sunday; small admission fee. Quarry Museum open 10:00 A.M.–3:00 P.M., Thursday–Sunday; donations encouraged. Interpretive programs, hikes, lectures, and events sponsored by Metropolitan District Commission, Massachusetts Audubon Society, Friends of the Blue Hills, and other affiliated groups. Trailside Museum and its restrooms are wheelchair accessible; rest of reservation is difficult, due to natural surfaces, steps, and slopes; wheelchair accessibility plans currently in process.

Index

Page numbers in boldface refer to the primary discussion of sites.